WORKSHOP MANUAL

FOR

BONNEVILLE 750
(T140V & T140E)

AND

TIGER 750
(TR7V)

UNIT CONSTRUCTION TWINS

FROM ENGINE No. KH 17124 (UP TO AND INCLUDING 1978 MODELS)

TRIUMPH MOTORCYCLES (MERIDEN) LTD.

MERIDEN WORKS · ALLESLEY · COVENTRY CV5 9AU · ENGLAND

TELEPHONE: (0676) 22331/6   TELEX: "TRUSTY" GB 311762
                               TELEGRAMS: "TRUSTY" GB COVENTRY

IMPORTANT NOTE

Any modifications to any Triumph motorcycle made by you or to be made by you in the future shall be held by our company to have been modified at your own risk and responsibility and without either the explicit or implied consent of Triumph Motorcycles Ltd. or Triumph Motorcycle America Inc. We will assume no liability, obligation or responsibility for any defective or modified parts or for the modified motorcycle itself, or for any claims, demands or legal action for property damage or personal injuries which may result from the modification of any Triumph motorcycle.

INTRODUCTION

Welcome to the world of digital publishing ~ the book you now hold in your hand was printed using the latest state of the art digital technology. The advent of print-on-demand has forever changed the publishing process, never has information been so accessible and it is our hope that this book serves your informational needs for years to come. If this is your first exposure to digital publishing, we hope that you are pleased with the results. Many more titles of interest to the classic automobile and motorcycle enthusiast, collector and restorer are available via our website at www.VelocePress.com. We hope that you find this title as interesting as we do.

NOTE FROM THE PUBLISHER

The information presented is true and complete to the best of our knowledge. All recommendations are made without any guarantees on the part of the author or the publisher, who also disclaim all liability incurred with the use of this information.

TRADEMARKS

We recognize that some words, model names and designations, for example, mentioned herein are the property of the trademark holder. We use them for identification purposes only. This is not an official publication.

INFORMATION ON THE USE OF THIS PUBLICATION

This manual is an invaluable resource for those interested in performing their own maintenance. However, in today's information age we are constantly subject to changes in common practice, new technology, availability of improved materials and increased awareness of chemical toxicity. As such, it is advised that the user consult with an experienced professional prior to undertaking any procedure described herein. While every care has been taken to ensure correctness of information, it is obviously not possible to guarantee complete freedom from errors or omissions or to accept liability arising from such errors or omissions. Therefore, any individual that uses the information contained within, or elects to perform or participate in do-it-yourself repairs or modifications acknowledges that there is a risk factor involved and that the publisher or its associates cannot be held responsible for personal injury or property damage resulting from the use of the information or the outcome of such procedures.

WARNING!

One final word of advice, this publication is intended to be used as a reference guide, and when in doubt the reader should consult with a qualified technician.

INTRODUCTION

THIS manual has been compiled and prepared to provide the necessary service information for workshop, fitter, technical staff and individual owner, wishing to carry out basic maintenance and repair work on the TRIUMPH 750 twin cylinder models.

GENERAL DATA for all models within the above range is provided in ready reference form, and a separate section covering Service Tools is fully illustrated at the end of this manual.

The manual is divided into sections dealing with major assemblies, throughout the machine, each section sub-divided into sequence order corresponding to normal operations of strip down, examination and rebuilding procedure.

NOTE: All references to the L.H. or R.H. side of the machine relate to a rider sitting astride the machine and facing forwards.

ENGINE AND FRAME NUMBERS

Note: The engine number is located on the left side of the engine, immediately below the cylinder barrel flange. The number is stamped onto a raised pad.

The first letter indicates the month of manufacture as follows:—

- A January
- B February
- C March
- D April
- E May
- G June
- H July
- J August
- K September
- N October
- P November
- X December

The second letter indicates the season year of manufacture as follows:—

- C 1969
- D 1970
- E 1971
- G 1972
- H 1973
- J 1974
- K 1975
- N 1976
- P 1977
- X 1978
- A 1979
- B 1980

The third Section is a numerical block of five figures which commence with engine number 00100.
The fourth Section indicates the model.

Example

Month	Year	Number	Model
N	C	00100	T140V

The frame number is stamped on the L.H. front frame down tube near the steering head lug.
The engine number is stamped on the L.H. crankcase half immediately below the cylinder barrel flange.
Both the Engine and Frame No. coincide.

GUARANTEE

Please refer to your local dealer or distributor where required for the latest terms of guarantee.

FACTORY SERVICE ARRANGEMENTS

UNITED KINGDOM ONLY

CORRESPONDENCE

Technical Advice and Guarantee Claims

Communications dealing with any of these subjects should be addressed to the **TECHNICAL/WARRANTY DEPT.**

> **In all communications the full engine number complete with all prefix letters and figures should be stated. This number will be found on the L.H. side of the crankcase just below the cylinder flange.**

TECHNICAL ADVICE

It will be appreciated how very difficult it is to diagnose trouble by correspondence and this is made impossible in many cases because the information sent to us is so scanty. Every possible point which may have some bearing on the matter should be stated so that we can send a useful and detailed reply.

REPLACEMENT PARTS

Replacement parts are no longer supplied direct from the factory to the individual owner. They should be obtained from the nearest local Triumph dealer.

There is a World-Wide network of stockists, a list of which is available from the factory on request.

CONTENTS

	SECTION
GENERAL DATA	GD
ROUTINE MAINTENANCE	RM
LUBRICATION SYSTEM	A
ENGINE	B
TRANSMISSION	C
GEARBOX	D
FRAME & ATTACHMENT DETAILS	E
BRAKES, WHEELS & TYRES	F
TELESCOPIC FORK	G
ELECTRICAL SYSTEM	H
SERVICE TOOLS	J
CONVERSION CHARTS	CT

T140V BONNEVILLE 750 (U.S.A VERSION)

T140V BONNEVILLE 750 (HOME & GENERAL EXPORT)

TR7V TIGER 750 (HOME & GENERAL EXPORT)

TR7V TIGER 750 (U.S.A VERSION)

GENERAL DATA

T140E Bonneville 750
T140V Bonneville 750
TR7V Tiger 750

Note: Throughout this Section, read for **All** Models unless otherwise detailed as a particuar Model.

GENERAL DATA

Read for T140V unless otherwise stated.

LUBRICATION SYSTEM

OIL PUMP
- Body material ... Brass
- Bore diameter: Feed ... ·40675/·40625 in. (10·33/10·317 mm.)
- Scavenge ... ·4877/·4872 in. (12·388/12·375 mm.)
- Plunger diameter: Feed ... ·40615/·40585 in. (10·315/10·307 mm.)
- Scavenge ... ·4872/·4869 in. (12·375/12·377 mm.)
- Valve spring length ... $\frac{1}{2}$ in. (12·70 mm.)
- Ball diameter ... $\frac{7}{32}$ in. (5·556 mm.)
- Aluminium crosshead width ... ·497/·498 in. (12·624/12·649 mm.)
- Working clearance in plunger heads ... ·0015/·0045 in. (·038/·124 mm.)

OIL PRESSURE RELEASE VALVE
- Piston diameter ... ·5605/65610 in. (14·237/14·249 mm.)
- Working clearance ... ·001/·002 in. (·0254/·0508 mm.)
- Pressure release operates ... 60 lb./sq. in. (4·22 kg./sq. cm.)
- Spring length ... 1⅜ ins. (35 mm.)
- Load at $1^{3}/_{16}$ in. ... 8 lbs. (3·6 kg.)
- Rate ... 42·3 lb./in.^{2} (3 kg./cm.^{2})
- No. of coils ... 13

OIL PRESSURE
- Normal running ... 65/80 lb./sq. in. (4·57/5·62 kg./sq. cm.)
- Idling ... 20/25 lb./sq. in. (1·406/1·76 kg./sq. cm.)

OIL PRESSURE SWITCH
- Operating pressure ... 3/5 lb./sq. in. (·2/0·35 kg./sq. cm.)

ENGINE

BASIC DETAILS
- Bore and stroke ... 76 × 82 mm. (2·992 in. × 3·228 in.)
- Cubic capacity ... 747 cc. (45 cu. in.)
- Compression ratio ... 7·9:1

CRANKSHAFT
- Crankshaft Type ... Forged two throw crank with bolt-on flywheel. Located by the timing side main bearing
- Main bearing (drive side) size and type ... $2\frac{13}{16} \times 1\frac{1}{8} \times \frac{13}{16}$ in. Single lipped roller bearing (71·5 × 28·6 × 20·6 mm.)
- Main bearing, (timing side) size and type ... 72 mm. × 30 mm. × 19 mm. Ball race.
- Main bearing journal diameter (timing side) ... 1·1812/1·1808 (30/29·99 mm.)
- Main bearing journal dia (Drive side) ... 1·1247(1·1250 (28·576(28·575 mm.)
- Main bearing journal dia. ... 1·1247/1·1250 in. (28·567/28·575 mm.)
- Main bearing housing dia. ... 2·8095/2·8110 in. (71·361/71·399 mm.)
- Big end journal dia. ... 1·6235/1·6240 in. (41·237/41·25 mm.)
- Min. regrind dia. ... 1·6035/1·6040 in. (40·73/40·742 mm.)
- Crankshaft end float ... ·003/·017 in. (·0762/·432 mm.)

CONNECTING RODS
- Length (centres) ... 6·001/5·999 in (152·4254/152·3746 mm.)
- Big end bearings—type ... Steel backed white metal
- Bearing side clearance ... ·012/·016 in. (·305/·406 mm.)
- Bearing diametral clearance ... ·0005/·0020 in. (·0127/·0508 mm.)

GENERAL DATA—(contd)

CYLINDER BLOCK
- Material ... Cast iron
- Bore size ... See Engine Section
- Maximum oversize ... +·020 in. (·508 mm.)
- Tappet guide block housing diameter ... ·9990/·9985 in. (25·37/25·362 mm.)

VALVES
- Stem diameter: Inlet ... ·3095/·3100 in. (7·86/7·874 mm.)
- Exhaust ... ·3090/·3095 in. (7·849/7·861 mm.)
- Head diameter: Inlet ... 1·592/1·596 in. (40·437/40·538 mm.)
- Exhaust ... 1·434/1·440 in. (36·388 mm/36·576 mm.)

VALVE GUIDES
- Material ... Aluminium—Bronze
- Bore diameter (Inlet and exhaust) ... ·3127/·3137 in. (7·943/7·958 mm.)
- Outside diameter (Inlet and exhaust) ... ·5005/·5010 in. (12·713/12·725 mm.)
- Length: Inlet ... $1\frac{31}{32}$ in. (50 mm.)
- Exhaust ... $2\frac{11}{64}$ in. (55·2 mm.)

VALVE SPRINGS (RED SPOT INNER) (GREEN SPOT OUTER)

	Outer	Inner
Free length (when new)	$1\frac{5}{8}$ in. (41·3 mm.)	$1\frac{17}{32}$ in. (38·9 mm.)
Total number of coils	$5\frac{1}{2}$	$7\frac{1}{4}$

VALVE TIMING
- Checked at nil tappet clearance. Valve lift ... Inlet opens 0·190 ins. (4·85 mm.) at T.D.C.
- Exhaust closes 0·130 ins. (3·27 mm.) at T.D.C.

ROCKERS
- Material ... High tensile steel forging
- Bore diameter ... ·5002/·5012 in. (12·705/12·731 mm.)
- Rocker spindle diameter ... ·4990/·4995 in. (12·675/12·687 mm.)
- Tappet clearance (cold): Inlet ... ·008 in. (0·203 mm.)
- Exhaust ... ·006 in. (0·15 mm.)

CAMSHAFTS
- Journal diameter: Left ... ·8100/·8105 in. (20·564/20·577 mm.)
- Right ... ·8730/·8735 in. (22·174/22·187 mm.)
- Diametral clearance: Left ... ·0010/·0025 in. (·0254/·0635 mm.)
- Right ... ·0005/·0020 in. (·0127/·0508 mm.)
- End float ... ·013/·020 in. (·331/·508 mm.)

TAPPETS
- Material ... High tensile steel body—Stellite tip
- Tip radius ... ·75 in. (19·1 mm.) inlet, and 1·125 in. (28·56 mm.) Exhaust
- Tappet diameter ... ·3110/·3115 in. (7·9/7·913 mm.)
- Clearance in guide block ... ·0005/·0015 in. (·0127/·267 mm.)

GENERAL DATA—(contd)

TAPPET GUIDE BLOCK
Diameter of bores	·3120/·3125 in. (7·925/7·938 mm.)
Outside diameter	1·0000/·9995 in. (25·4/25·387 mm.)
Interference fit in cylinder block	·0005/·0015 in. (·0127/·267 mm.)

CAMSHAFT BEARING BUSHES
Material	High density sintered bronze
Bore diameter (fitted): Left	·8125/·8135 in. (20·648/20·663 mm.)
Right	·874/·875 in. (22·1/22·1 mm.)
Outside diameter: Left	1·0010/1·0015 in. (25·425/25·438 mm.)
Right	1·126/1·127 in. (28·601/28·628 mm.)
Length: Left inlet	1·104/1·114 in. (28·042/28·296 mm.)
Left exhaust	·932/·942 in. (23·637/23·927 mm.)
Right inlet and exhaust	1·010/1·020 in. (25·025/25·508 mm.)
Interference fit in crankcase: Left	·001/·002 in. (·025/·051 mm.)
Right	·0010/·0025 in. (·025/·064 mm.)

TIMING GEARS
Inlet and exhaust camshaft pinions:	
No. of teeth	50
Interference fit on camshaft	·000/·001 in. (·0254 mm.)
Intermediate timing gear:	
No. of teeth	47
Bore diameter	·5618/·5625 in. (14·27/14·288 mm.)
Intermediate timing gear bush:	
Material	Phosphor bronze
Outside diameter	·5635/·5640 in. (14·313/14·326 mm.)
Bore diameter	·4990/·4995 in. (12·675/12·687 mm.)
Length	·6775/·6825 in. (17·209/17·336 mm.)
Working clearance on spindle	·0005/·0015 in. (·0127/·267 mm.)
Intermediate wheel spindle:	
Diameter	·4980/·4985 in. (12·649/12·662 mm.)
Interference fit in crankcase	·0005/·0015 in. (·0127/·267 mm.)
Crankshaft pinion:	
No. of teeth	25
Fit on crankshaft	+·0003/−·0005 in. (·0076/·0127 mm.)

IGNITION TIMING
Crankshaft position (B.T.D.C.)	
Fully advanced	38
Piston position (B.T.D.C.)	
Fully advanced	·415 in. (10·4 mm.)
Advance range:	
Contact breaker	12°
Crankshaft	24°

CONTACT BREAKER
Gap setting	·014–·016 in. (·35–·40 mm.)
Fully advanced at	2,000 r.p.m.

SPARKING PLUG
Type	Champion N3 (or equivalent)
Gap setting	·025 in. (·635 mm.)
Thread size	14 mm. × ¾ in. reach

PISTONS
Material	Aluminium Alloy – diecasting
Clearance: Top of skirt	See Engine Section
Bottom of skirt	
Gudgeon pin hole dia.	·7502/·7504 in. (19·011/19·162 mm.)

GD

GENERAL DATA—(contd)

PISTON RINGS
Compression rings (tapered):
- Width ... ·121/·113 in. (3·073/2·896 mm.)
- Thickness ... ·0625/·0165 in. (1·589/1·563 mm.)
- Fitted gap ... ·008/0·13 in. (·203/·330 mm.)
- Clearance in groove ... ·0035/·0015 in. (·089/·038 mm.)

Oil control ring:
- Thickness ... ·125 in. (3·18 mm.)
- Width ... ·121 in. (3·073 mm.)
- Fitted gap ... ·010/·040 in. (·254/1·016 mm.)
- Clearance groove ... ·0015/·0025 in. (·038/·0635 mm.)

FUEL SYSTEM

	Twin Carburettors	Single Carburettors
Amal type Mk I	L930/92 R930/93	R930/94
Main jet	190	270
Needle jet size	·106	·106
Needle type	STD	STD
Needle position	1	2
Throttle valve: Cutaway	3	3½
Carburetter nominal bore size	30mm.	30mm.
Air cleaner type	Surgical gauze and metal gauze	Surgical gauze and metal gauze

T140E Models:
- Amal type Mk II ... R2930/1 L2930/2
- Main jet ... 200
- Needle jet ... ·105 (2928/030)
- Needle type ... 2C3
- Needle position ... 2
- Throttle valve cutaway ... 3
- Starter jet ... 50

TRANSMISSION

CLUTCH DETAILS
- Type ... Multiplate with integral shock absorber
- No. of plates: Driving (bonded) ... 6
- Driven (plain) ... 6

Pressure springs:
- Number ... 3
- Free length ... 1·75 in. (43·5 mm.)
- No. of working coils ... 7½
- Spring rate ... 169 lbs. ins.
- Approximate fitted load ... 83 lbs. (37·65 kg.)

Bearing rollers:
- Number ... 20
- Diameter ... ·2495/·2500 in. (6·337/6·35 mm.)
- Length ... ·231/·236 in. (5·831/5·958 mm.)
- Clutch hub bearing diameter ... 1·3733/1·3743 in. (33·882/34·907 mm.)
- Clutch sprocket bore diameter ... 1·8745/1·8755 in. (47·612/47·638 mm.)
- Thrust washer thickness ... ·052/·054 in. (1·312/1·372 mm.)
- Engine sprocket teeth ... 29
- Clutch sprocket teeth ... 58
- Chain details ... Triplex endless—$\frac{3}{8}$ in. pitch × 84 links

CLUTCH OPERATING MECHANISM
Conical spring:
- Number of working coils ... 2
- Free length ... $\frac{13}{32}$ in. (10·3 mm.)
- Diameter of balls ... $\frac{3}{8}$ in. (9·525 mm.)

Clutch operating rod:
- Diameter of rod ... $\frac{7}{32}$ in. (5·6 mm.)
- Length of rod ... 11·822/11·812 in. (300·279/300·025 mm.)

GD5

GD GENERAL DATA

GENERAL DATA—(contd)

KICKSTART OPERATING MECHANISM
- Bush bore diameter ... ·751/·752 in. (19·085/19·11 mm.)
- Spindle working clearance in bush ... ·003/·005 in. (·076/·127 mm.)
- Ratchet spring free length ... ½ in. (12·7 mm.)

GEARCHANGE MECHANISM
- Plungers:
  - Outer diameter ... ·4315/·4320 in. (10·92/10·937 mm.)
  - Working clearance in bore ... ·0005/·0015 in. (·0127/·038 mm.)
- Plunger springs:
  - No. of working coils ... 12
  - Free length ... 1¼ in. (31·75 mm.)
- Outer quadrant bush bore diameter ... ·6245/·6255 in. (15·86/15·888 mm.)
  - Clearance on shaft ... ·0007/·0032 in. (·0178/·081 mm.)
- Inner quadrant bush bore diameter ... ·7505/·7510 in. (19·063/19·075 mm.)
  - Clearance on shaft ... ·0005/·0025 in. (·0127/·064 mm.)
- Gearchange shaft bushes: (After engine no. HN62501)
- Timing side Inner bush bore diameter ... ·7505/·7510 (19·063/19·075 mm.)
- Timing side Outer bush bore diameter ... ·752/·7525 (19·1/19·11 mm.)
  - Quadrant return springs ... 9½
  - Free length ... 1¾ in. (44·5 mm.)

GEARBOX (5 SPEED)

RATIOS
- Internal ratios:
  - 5th (Top) ... 1·00 : 1
  - 4th ... 1·19 : 1
  - 3rd ... 1·40 : 1
  - 2nd ... 1·837 : 1
  - 1st (Bottom) ... 2·585 : 1
- Overall ratios:
  - 5th (Top) ... 4·70
  - 4th ... 5·59
  - 3rd ... 6·58
  - 2nd ... 8·63
  - 1st (Bottom) ... 12·25
- Engine R.P.M. @ 10 M.P.H. in 5th (Top) gear ... 627
- Gearbox sprocket teeth ... 20

GEAR DETAILS
- Mainshaft high gear:
  - Bearing, type ... Needle roller (torrington B1314)
  - Bearing length ... ·875/·865 in. (22·23/21·97 mm.)

GEARBOX SHAFTS
- Mainshaft:
  - Left end diameter ... ·8103/·8098 in. (20·58/20·57 mm.)
  - Right end diameter ... ·7494/·7498 in. (19·044/19·054 mm.)
  - Length ... 11·23 in. (285·2 mm.)
- Layshaft:
  - Left end diameter ... ·6875/·6870 in. (17·46/17·404 mm.)
  - Right end diameter ... ·6875/·6870 in. (17·46/17·404 mm.)
  - Length ... 6·47 in. (164·33 mm.)

BEARINGS
- Mainshaft bearing (left) ... 1½ × 2½ × ⅝ in. Roller bearing (38·1 × 63·5 × 15·9 mm.)
- Mainshaft bearing (right) ... ¾ × 1⅞ × 9/16 in. Ball Journal (19 × 47·5 × 14·3 mm.)
- Layshaft bearing (left) ... 11/16 × ⅞ × ¾ in. Needle roller (17·5 × 22·23 × 19 mm.)
- Layshaft bearing (right) ... 11/16 × ⅞ × ¾ in. Needle roller (17·5 × 22·23 × 19 mm.)
- Layshaft 1st gear bush:
  - Bore diameter ... ·800/·795 in. (20·32/20·203 mm.)
  - Shaft diameter ... ·8075/·8070 in. (20·511/20·498 mm.)
- Layshaft 2nd gear bush:
  - Bore diameter ... ·800/·795 in. (20·32/20·203 mm.)
  - Shaft diameter ... ·8075/·8070 in. (20·511/20·498 mm.)

GENERAL DATA—(contd)

FRAME AND ATTACHMENT DETAILS

HEAD BEARINGS
Type	Timken Taper Roller Bearing
Bore size	·7508/·7500 in. (19·08/19·06 mm.)
Outer diameter	1·7820/1·7810 in. (45·27/45·24 mm.)

SWINGING FORK
Bush type	Pre-sized phosphor bronze
Bush bore, diameter	1 in. nominal (25·4 mm.)
Sleeve diameter	·9984/·9972 in. (25·35/25·32 mm.)
Distance between fork ends	8·018 in. (203·653 mm.)

REAR SUSPENSION
Type	Swinging fork controlled by gas-filled telescopic coil spring damper units
Spring details:	
Fitted length	7·84 in. (199·2 mm.) at mid position
Free length	9·5 in. (241·3 mm.)
Spring note	100 lbs/in.

REAR SUSPENSION (EARLY MODELS)
Type	Swingin fork controlled by combined coil spring hydraulic damper units
Spring details:	
Fitted length	8 in. (203·2 mm.) at mid position
Free length	9·5 in. (241·3 mm.)
Spring rate	88 lbs./in.
Mean coil diameter	1·98 in. (50·29 mm.)

WHEELS, BRAKES AND TYRES

WHEELS
Rim size: Front	WM2-19
Rear	WM3-18
Spoke details: Front: Spoke (Inner) R.H. & L.H.	20 off 10 SWG 7·75 in. (mean length) 96° head
Spoke (outer) R.H. & L.H.	20 off 10 SWG 7·85 in. (mean length) 80° head
Rear: Left side (outer)	10 off 9 SWG 5·8 in. (mean length) 10° head
Left side (inner)	10 off 9 SWG 5·7 in. (mean length) 102° head
Right side	20 off 9 SWG 7·2 in. (mean length) 135° head

REAR WHEEL DRIVE
Rear wheel spocket (teeth)	47 teeth
Chain details: No. of links	106 links
Pitch	⅝ in. (15·875 mm.)
Width	⅜ in. (9·525 mm.)
Speedometer drive gearbox ratio	1·25/1
Speedometer cable length (outer)	66 in. (1676·4 mm.)
Speedometer cable length (inner)	67·63 in. (minimum) (1717·7 mm.)

GD GENERAL DATA

GENERAL DATA—(contd)

BRAKES

Front and rear:
- Type ... Hydraulically operated disc.
- Disc diameter ... 10in. (254mm.)
- Friction pads type ... DON 230 FGDO8K
- Lining thickness ... ·25in. (6·35mm.)

Rear: (Prior to engine no. HN62501)
- Type ... Internal expanding single leading shoe
- Lining thickness ... ·187/·197in. (4·75/5mm.)
- Drum diameter ... 7in. (+0·002in.) 177·8mm. (−0·0508mm.)

TYRES

- Size: Front ... 4·10 × 19 (104 × 484·6mm.)
- Rear ... 4·10 × 18 (104 × 457·2mm.)
- Tyre pressures: Front (4·10 × 19) ... 28lbs./in.^{2} (1·90kg/cm^2)
- Rear (4·10 × 18) ... 32lbs./in.^{2} (2·25kg/cm^2)

- Size: Front ... 3·25 × 19in. (82·5 × 484·6mm.)
- Rear ... 4·00 × 18in. (101·6 · 457·2mm.)
- Tyre pressure: Front (3·25 × 19) ... 24lbs./in.^{2} (1·685kg/cm^2)
- Rear (4·00 × 18) ... 24lbs./in.^{2} (1·685kg/cm^2)

FRONT FORKS

TELESCOPIC FORK

- Type ... Telescopic (hydraulic damping)
- Spring details: Free length (when new) ... 19·1in. (485mm.)
- Compressed length ... 11·4in. (289·5mm.)
- No. of coils ... 68
- Wire diameter ... ·168ins. (4·26mm.)
- Stanchion diameter: (Bottom) ... 1·3610/1·3605in. (33·04/33·03mm.)
- Outer member bore diameter ... 1·365/1·363in. (33·15/33·1mm.)

ELECTRICAL SYSTEM

ELECTRICAL EQUIPMENT

- Battery type ... 12 volt-8 amperes/hour
- Rectifier type ... Lucas 2DS 506
- Alternator type ... Lucas RM21
- Horn type ... Lucas 6H
- Zener diode type ... Lucas 2D715
- Ignition coil type ... Lucas 17M12
- Ignition switch type ... Lucas S45
- Handlebar switch type ... Lucas 169SA
- Flasher unit type ... Lucas 8FL
- Contact breaker type ... Lucas 6CA
- Condenser ... Lucas 54420128

BULBS

	No.	Type
Headlight	Lucas 410	45/40W pre-focus
Parking light	Lucas 989	6W M.cc
Stop and tail light	Lucas 380	5/21W
Hi-beam, ignition and direction indicator warning light	Lucas 281	2W (WL.15)
Speedometer, Tachometer	Lucas 504	3W MES
Direction indicators	Lucas 382	21W
Fuse rating (Amperes)		35

GENERAL DATA—(contd)

GENERAL

CAPACITIES
Fuel tank	Small: 2·8 imp. galls. (3·4 U.S. galls.) Large: 4·10 imp. galls.
Oil tank	4 pints (4·8 U.S. pints, 2·27 litres)
Gearbox	⅞ pint (500 c.c)
Primary chaincase (initial fill only)	⅜ pint (150 c.c.)
Telescopic fork legs	⅓ pint (190 c.c.)

BASIC DIMENSIONS
Wheel base	56 in. (165 cm.)
Overall length	87·5 in. (222 cm.)
Overall width	33 in. (84 cm.) 27 in. (68·5 cm.) – U.K. & General export models
Seat height	31½ in. (80 cm.)

WEIGHTS
Unladen weight Dry	395 lbs. (179 kg.)

TORQUE WRENCH SETTING (DRY)
Flywheel bolts	33 lb. ft. (4·6 kg.m.)
Conn. rod bolts	22 lb. ft. (3·9 kg.m.)
Crankcase junction bolts	13 lb. ft. (1·8 kg.m.)
Crankcase junction studs	20 lb. ft. (2·8 kg.m.)
Rocker box bolts—inner (5/16 in. dia.)	10 lb. ft. (1·38 kg.m.)
Cylinder head bolts—outer (⅜ in. dia.)	18 lb. ft. (2·49 kg.m.)
Cylinder head bolt—centre (5/16 in. dia.)	16 lb. ft. (2·07 kg.m.)
Cylinder head bolt—inner (⅜ in. dia.)	18 lb. ft. (2·49 kg.m.)
Rocker box nuts	5 lb. ft. (·7 kg.m.)
Rocker box bolts (¼ in. dia.)	5 lb. ft. (·7 kg.m.)
Rocker spindle domed nuts	22 lb. ft. (3·0 kg.m.)
Oil pump nuts	5 lb. ft. (·7 kg.m.)
Kickstart ratchet pinion nut	35 lb. ft. (2·5 kg.m.)
Clutch centre nut	70 lb. ft. (·7 kg.m.)
Rotor fixing nut	50 lb. ft. (3·5 kg.m.)
Stator fixing nuts	20 lb. ft. (2·8 kg.m.)
Primary cover domed nuts	10 lb. ft. (1·4 kg.m.)
Headlamp pivot bolts	10 lb. ft. (1·4 kg.m.)
Headrace sleeve nut pinch bolt	15 lb. ft. (2·1 kg.m.)
Stanchion pinch bolts	25 lb. ft. (3·5 kg.m.)
Front wheel spindle cap bolts	15 lb. ft. (3·5 kg.m.)
Rear brake drum to hub bolts (Prior to engine no. HN62501)	15 lb. ft. (2·1 kg.m.)
Brake cam spindle nuts (Prior to engine no. HN62501)	20 lb. ft. (2·8 kg.m.)
Zener diode fixing nut	1·5 lb. ft. (·21 kg.m.)
Fork cap nuts	15 lb. ft. (1·0 kg.m.)
Stanchion top nut	30 lb. ft. (2·1 kg.m.)
Brake disc retaining bolts (front and rear)	27 lb. ft. (1·9 kg.m.)
Gear box sprocket retaining nut	80 lb. ft. (5·6 kg.m.)

RM ROUTINE MAINTENANCE

Section Ref:

500 MILE FREE SERVICE
All items marked (•) are carried out during the 500 mile free service plus the additional three items:
Retorque the cylinder head nuts … B14
Check the cylinder barrel nuts … B19
Check the wheel spoke tension … F20

DAILY
- Check the oil reservoir level and return oil flow … A3
- Check the tyre pressures … "General Data", F25
- Check the operation of the tacho/speedo/horn and lights … H9, H14 & H15
- Check the operation of the front and rear brakes … F28

EVERY 1500 MILES (2400 kms)
- Change the engine oil and clean the filters … A3
- Grease the rear swinging fork pivots … A16
- Check the tyre pressures … "General Data", F25
- Adjust/check/lubricate the rear chain … A12, F24
- Check the front and rear brake reservoir levels … F2
- Check and adjust the primary chain … C2
- Adjust and lubricate all control cables … A17, A18
- Check the battery electrolyte level … H1
- Check all accessible nuts and bolts … F1
- Check rear brake pedal clearance … F1

EVERY 300 MILES (4800 kms)
- Check the contact breaker gap and lubricate … A9
- Adjust the tappets … B5
- Check the ignition timing … B28 & B29
- Check and adjust the spark plugs … H3
- Change the oil in the primary chaincase … A11
- Check the wheel bearings for play … F3
- Check the tyres for wear … F3
- Check the brake disc pads for wear … F3
- Check the rear brake shoes for wear (prior to frame no. HN62501) … F15
- Grease the rear brake pedal spindle … A19
- Clean the air filter element(s) … B6
- Clean the fuel filters … E1
- Check the clutch push rod adjustment … C1
- Check the gearbox oil level … A10
- Grease the rear brake cam spindle (prior to frame no. HN62501) … A16

EVERY 6000 MILES (9600 kms)
- Change the gearbox oil … A10
- Check and adjust the steering head races … G1
- Change the oil in the front fork legs … A15

EVERY 10000 MILES (16000 kms)
Check the metal brake pipes and rubber hoses for signs of deterioration or corrosion … F6

EVERY 15000 MILES (24000 kms)
Grease the steering head bearings … G2
Grease the wheel bearings … F12, F14, F17

EVERY 24000 MILES (38400 kms)
Drain and refill the front and rear hydraulic systems … F5

EVERY 40000 MILES (64000 kms)
Service or replace the FRONT brake master cylinder and front/rear brake calipers … F9, F8
Replace the REAR brake motor cylinder and front and rear metal pipes and brake hoses … F7, F6

SECTION A

	Section
TABLE OF RECOMMENDED LUBRICANTS	A1
ENGINE LUBRICATION SYSTEM	A2
CHANGING THE ENGINE OIL AND CLEANING THE OIL FILTERS	A3
OIL PRESSURE	A4
STRIPPING AND REASSEMBLING THE OIL PRESSURE RELEASE VALVE	A5
STRIPPING AND REASSEMBLING THE OIL PUMP	A6
REMOVING AND REPLACING THE OIL PIPE JUNCTION BLOCK	A7
REMOVING AND REPLACING THE ROCKER OIL FEED PIPE	A8
CONTACT BREAKER LUBRICATION	A9
GEARBOX LUBRICATION	A10
PRIMARY CHAINCASE LUBRICATION	A11
REAR CHAIN LUBRICATION AND MAINTENANCE	A12
GREASING THE STEERING HEAD RACES	A13
WHEEL BEARING LUBRICATION	A14
TELESCOPIC FORK LUBRICATION	A15
LUBRICATION NIPPLES	A16
LUBRICATING THE CONTROL CABLES	A17
SPEEDOMETER CABLE LUBRICATION	A18
REAR BRAKE PEDAL SPINDLE LUBRICATION	A19
CHECK PROCEDURE FOR WET SUMPING	A20

A
LUBRICATION SYSTEM

SECTION AI
RECOMMENDED LUBRICANTS (All Markets)

UNIT	MOBIL	CASTROL	B.P.	ESSO	SHELL	TEXACO
Engine and Primary Chaincase	Mobiloil Super	Castrol GTX or Castrol XL20/50	B.P. Super Visco-Static	Uniflo	Shell Super Motor Oil	Havoline Motor Oil 20W/50
Gearbox	Mobilube GX90	Castrol Hypoy	B.P. Gear Oil SAE 90 EP	Esso Gear Oil GX90/140	Shell Spirax 90 EP	Multigear Lubricant EP 90
Telescopic Fork	Mobil ATF 210	Castrol T.Q.F.	B.P. 'B' Autron	Esso Glide	Shell Donax T.7	Texomatic 'F'
Wheel Bearings, Swinging Fork and Steering Races	Mobilgrease MP or Mobilgrease Super	Castrol LM Grease	B.P. Energrease L2	Esso Multipurpose Grease H	Shell Retinax A	Marfak All Purpose
Easing Rusted Parts	Mobil Handy Oil	Castrol Penetrating Oil		esso Penetrating Oil	Shell Easing Oil	Graphited Penetrating Oil

The above lubricants are recommended for all operating temperatures above −18°C (0°F).
Approval is given to lubricants marketed by companies other than those listed above provided that they have similar multigrade characteristics and meet the A.P.S. Service M.S. performance level.

Also approved are:

	Engine and Primary Chaincase	Gearbox	Telescopic Fork	Swinging Fork and Steering Races	Easing Rusted Parts
DUCKHAM'S	Duckham's Q20/50	Duckham's Hypoid 90	Duckham's Q-Matic	Duckham's LB10 Grease	Duckham's Adpenol Penetrating Oil
FILTRATE	Filtrate Super 20W/50	Filtrate EP.90	Filtrate A.T. Fluid 'F'	Filtrate Super Lithium Grease	

LUBRICATION SYSTEM

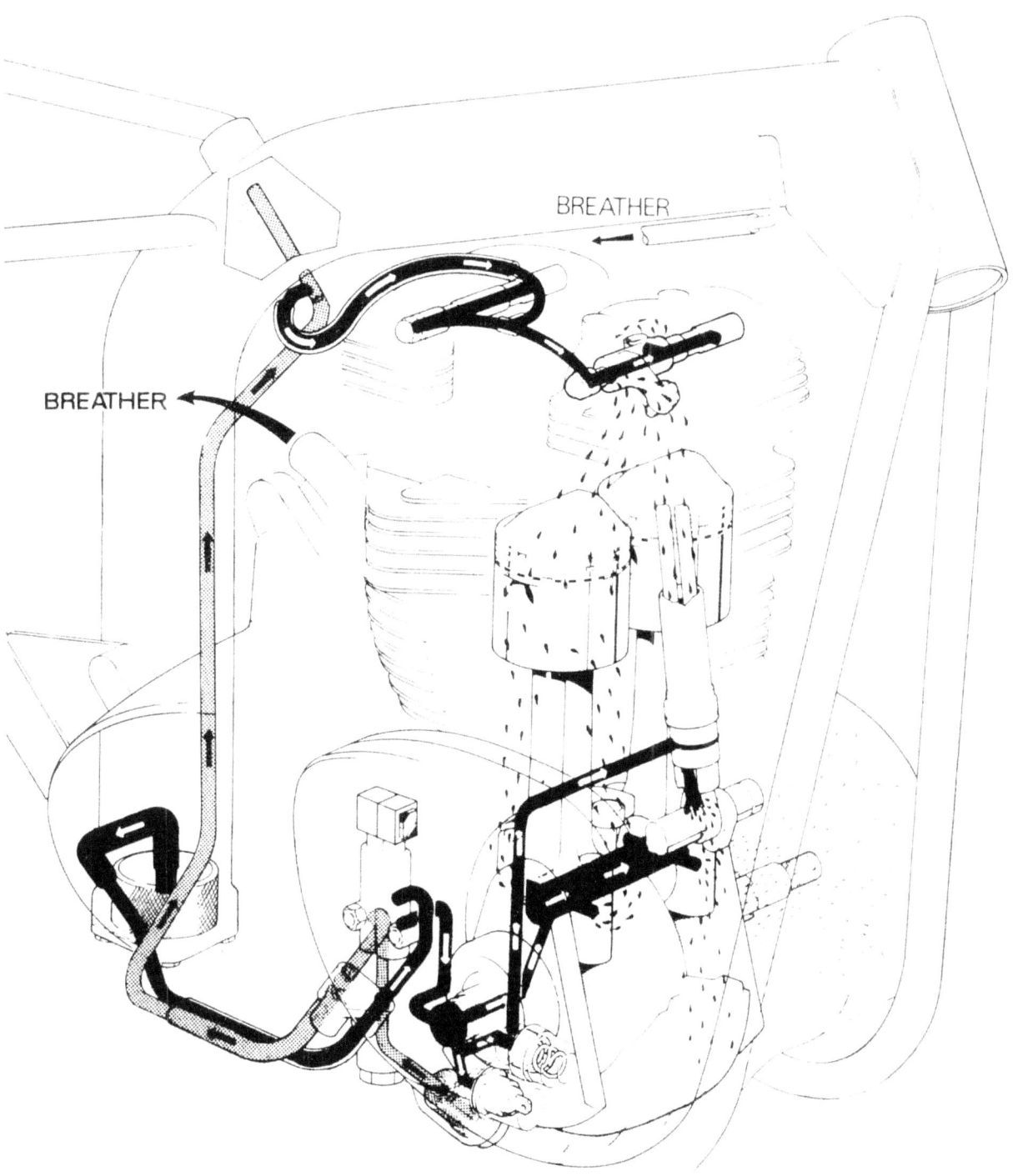

Fig. A1. Engine lubrication diagram

LUBRICATION SYSTEM

SECTION A2
ENGINE LUBRICATION SYSTEM

The engnie lubrication system is of the dry sump type. The oil is fed by gravity from the oil reservoir tank to the oil pump; the oil, under pressure from the oil pump, is forced through drillings to the crankshaft big ends, where it escapes, and lubricates the cylinder walls, ball journal main bearings and the other internal engine parts.

The oil pressure between the oil pump and crankshaft is controlled by the oil pressure release valve. After lubricating the engine, oil falls to the sump where it is scavenged through the sump filter, and returned to the oil reservoir by the action of the oil pump scavenge plunger. The oil pump has been designed so that the scavenge plunger has a greater capacity than the feed plunger; thus ensuring that the sump does not become flooded.

Oil is fed to the valve operating mechanism by means of the rocker oil feed pipe which is connected to the scavenge return pipe just below the oil reservoir. After travelling through the rocker spindles, the oil is fed into the rocker boxes after which it falls by gravity down the push rod cover tubes. The oil then passes through holes drilled in the tappet guide blocks and into the sump, where it is subsequently scavenged.

A positive oil feed is provided for the exhaust tappets. The lubricant is ported through drillways from the timing cover, and on through the crankcase and cylinder block base flange to an annular groove machined in the tappet guide block. Two oil holes are provided in the groove to mate with the oil holes in the tappets which provide a channel for the lubricant to the tappet and camshaft working faces. See Fig. A3 and Fig. A4. Current models use tappets ground to provide a timing effect for the lubricant.

SECTION A3
CHANGING THE ENGINE OIL AND CLEANING THE OIL FILTERS

It is advisable to drain the oil when the engine is warm as the oil will flow more readily. When changing the oil it is essential that the oil filters are thoroughly cleaned in paraffin (kerosene).

The hexagon-headed sump drain plug, which also houses the sump filter, is situated underneath the engine adjacent to the engine bottom mounting lug, as shown in Fig. A2, reference No. 4. Remove the plug and allow the oil to drain for approximately ten minutes. Clean the filter in paraffin (kerosene) and refit the plug but do not forget the joint washer.

The oil reservoir filter is contained in the bottom of the reservoir by means of a rectangular plate secured by four nuts. Remove the reservoir filler cap, place a drip tray underneath the base of the reservoir and remove the drain plug from the center of the base plate. Allow the oil to drain for approx. 10 mins. Remove the four nuts and withdraw the cover plate from its studs. Note that there are two gaskets, one above the filter base flange and the other below. Clean the filter thoroughly in kerosene (paraffin).

It is advisable to flush out the oil reservoir with a flushing oil, or, if this is not available, paraffin (kerosene) will do. However, if this is used ensure that all traces are removed from the inside of the oil reservoir prior to re-filling with oil. (For the correct grade of oil see Section A1).

When refitting the filter do not forget to replace the gaskets. Refit the drain plug.

The capacity of the reservoir is 4 imperial pints (4·8 U.S. pints, 2·27 litres). The level can be checked with the combined dipstick and filler cap.

Check that the oil is returning from the engine sump by starting the engine and removing the reservoir filler cap. Oil should be seen to be flowing from the pipe which protrudes into the filler neck tube.

LUBRICATION SYSTEM

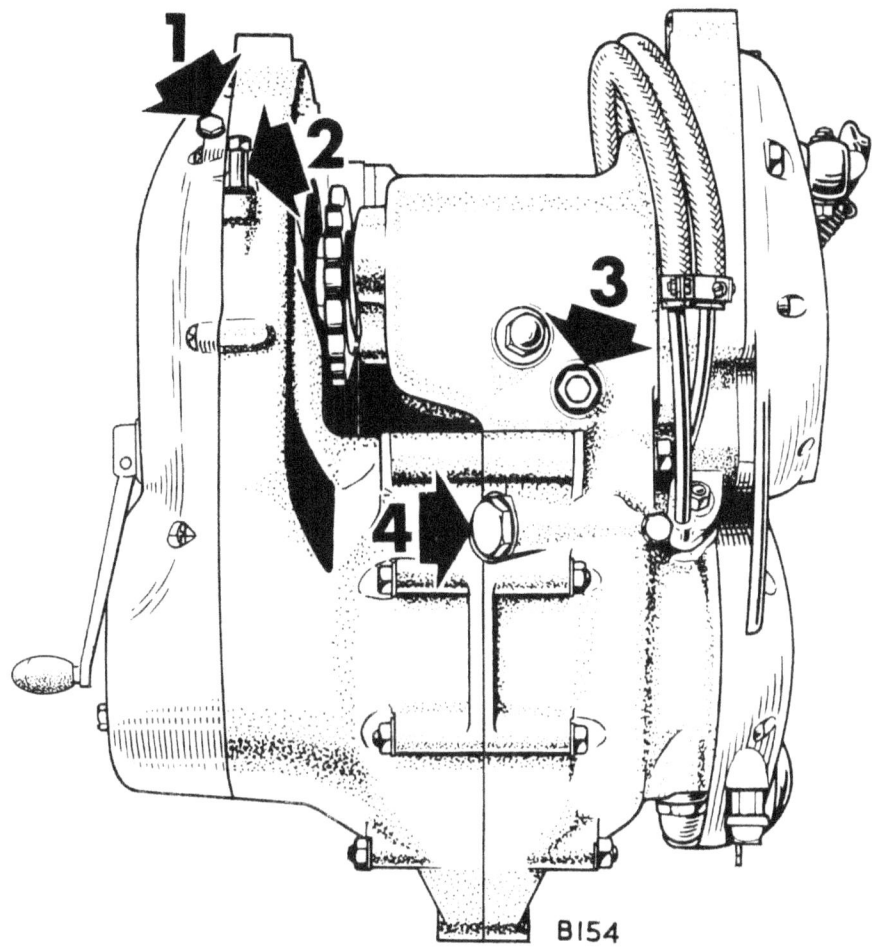

Fig. A2. Underside view of engine/gearbox unit

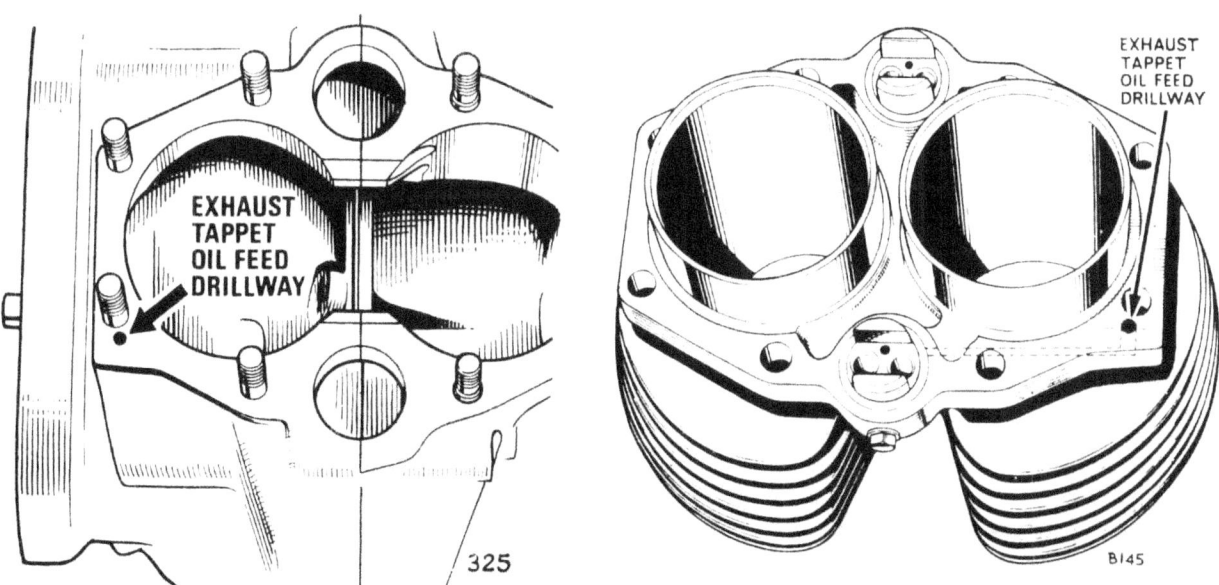

Fig. A3. Tappet oil feed drillway

Fig. A4. Tappet oil feed arrangement

SECTION A4

OIL PRESSURE

The oil pressure is controlled by means of the release valve situated at the front of the engine at the right side adjacent to the timing cover.

When the engine is stationary there will be nil oil pressure. When the engine is started from cold pressure may be as high as 80 lb./sq. in. reducing when hot to a normal running figure of 65/80 lb./sq. in. At a fast idle when hot pressure should be 20/25 lb./sq. in.

Pressure can only be checked with an oil gauge connected to an adaptor replacing the oil pressure switch on the front of the timing cover.

If satisfactory readings are not obtained, check the following:—

(1) That the oil pressure release valve is clean and that the piston has the correct working clearance in the valve body as detailed in "General Data".

(2) That the oil reservoir level is not below minimum and that the oil is being returned to the reservoir.

(3) That the sump filter and oil reservoir filter are clean and not blocked.

(4) That the oil pump is functioning properly and that there is a supply of oil to the pump. Refer to Sections A6 and A8 for checking the oil pump and oil pipes with junction block respectively.

(5) That the drillings in the timing cover are clean and that the drillings in the crankcase connecting the oil pipe junction block to the oil pump are clear.

(6) That the oil seal in the timing cover which fits over the crankshaft is not badly worn, thus resulting in the oil escaping to the sump.

(7) That the big ends are not badly worn. Should the big end bearings not have the correct working clearance, the oil will escape more readily, particularly when the oil is warm and is more fluid, thus giving a drop in pressure.

Extensive periods of slow running (such as in heavy traffic), or unnecessary use of the air control, can cause dilution in the oil reservoir, and an overall drop in lubricating pressure due to the lower viscosity of the diluted oil.

Most lubrication and oil pressure troubles can be avoided by regular attention to the recommended oil changes.

SECTION A5

STRIPPING AND REASSEMBLING THE OIL PRESSURE RELEASE VALVE

The oil pressure release valve is very reliable and should require no maintenance other than cleaning. It is situated at the front of the engine on the right side, adjacent to the timing cover.

Oil pressure is governed by the single spring situated within the release valve body. When the spring is removed it can be checked for compressive strength by measuring the length. Compare this figure with that given in "GENERAL DATA".

To remove the complete oil pressure release valve unit from the crankcase, unscrew the hexagonal nut adjacent to the crankcase surface. When removed

LUBRICATION SYSTEM

the cap can then be unscrewed from the body thus releasing the piston which should be withdrawn.

Thoroughly clean all parts in paraffin (kerosene) and inspect for wear. The piston should be checked for possible scoring and the valve body filter for possible blockage or damage. To reassemble the release valve unit offer the piston into the valve body and screw on the valve cap using a suitable loctite thread sealant and a new fibre washer. Similarly, when screwing the release valve unit into the crankcase, fit a new fibre washer between the release valve body and the crankcase. See Fig. A5.

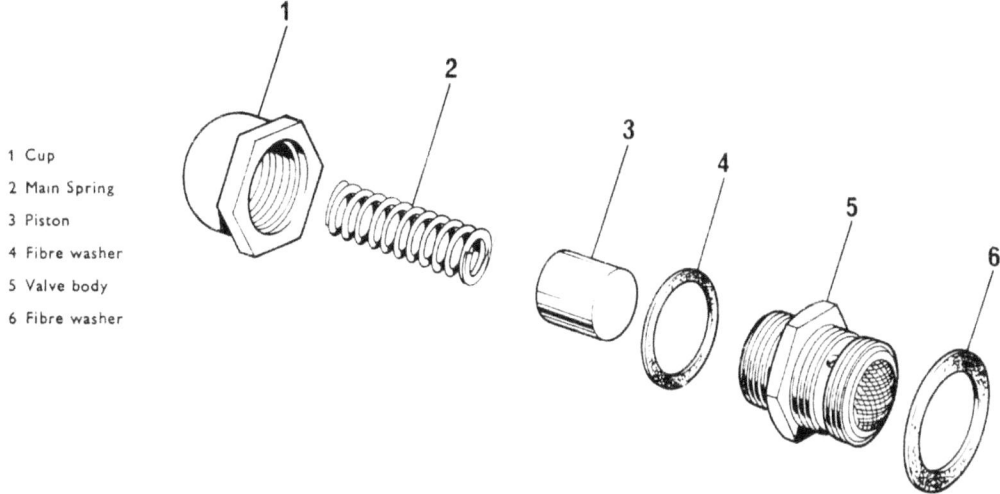

1 Cup
2 Main Spring
3 Piston
4 Fibre washer
5 Valve body
6 Fibre washer

Fig. A5. Oil pressure release valve

To dismantle, remove the complete valve and cap and seperate the cap from the valve body. The spring and piston can then be removed for cleaning and examination.

On reassembly, note that the open end of the piston faces towards the spring and cap.

SECTION A6

STRIPPING AND REASSEMBLING THE OIL PUMP

The oil pump is situated inside the timing cover and is driven by an eccentric peg on the nut fitted to the end of the inlet camshaft. The only part likely to show wear after considerable mileage is the oil pump drive block slider, which should be replaced to maintain full oil pumping efficiency. The plungers and pump body being constantly immersed in oil, wear is negligible.

For removal of the timing cover see Section B30.

The oil pump is held in its position by two conical nuts. When these are removed the oil pump can then be withdrawn from the mounting studs. The scavenge and feed plungers should be removed and the two square caps from the end of the oil pump unscrewed. This will release the springs and balls.

All parts should be thoroughly cleaned in paraffin (kerosene).

A LUBRICATION SYSTEM

The plungers should be inspected for scoring, and for wear by measuring their diameters and comparing them with those given in "GENERAL DATA". The springs should be checked for compressive strength by measuring their lengths. Compare the actual lengths with those given in "GENERAL DATA".

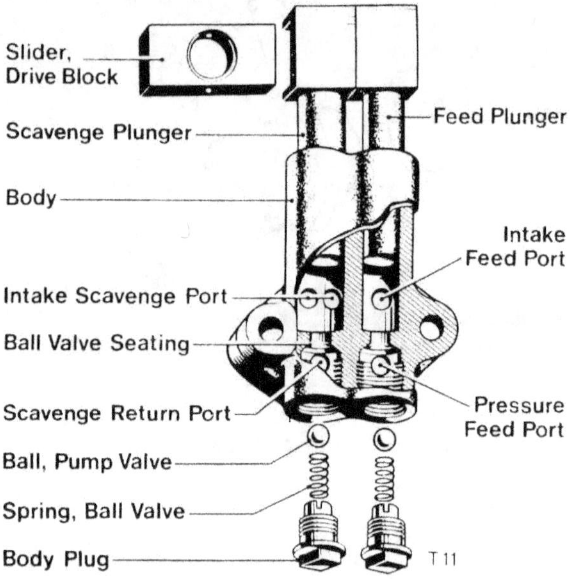

When reassembling the oil pump all parts should be well lubricated and the oil pump finally checked for efficiency by the following means:—

Place a small amount of oil in both bores (approximately 1 c.c.) and press the plungers until oil is forced through both outlet ports (these are the two holes nearest the square caps (see Fig. A6). Place the thumb over the intake ports (the holes nearest the plunger tops) and withdraw the plungers slightly. If the oil level falls in either outlet port then the ball valve is not seating properly and the square caps should be removed and the cleaning process repeated. The ball valve can be tapped lightly, but sharply to ensure an efficient and adequate seal.

The aluminium drive block slider which fits over the eccentric peg on the inlet camshaft nut should be checked for wear on both the bore and in the plunger cross-head.

When refitting the oil pump a new gasket should be used and always remember that the cones of the conical nut and washers fit into the countersunk holes in the oil pump body.

When replacing the timing cover care should be taken that the junction surfaces are cleaned prior to application of the fresh coat of jointing compound.

Fig. A6. Oil pump

SECTION A7

REMOVING AND REPLACING THE OIL PIPE JUNCTION BLOCK

Drain the oil from the gearbox by removing the oil drain plug situated underneath the gearbox as shown in Fig. A2, reference No. 3.

Remove the right-hand exhaust pipe, and the right footrest, then remove the gearbox outer cover as shown in Section D2.

Place a drip tray underneath the engine and remove the drain plug where fitted, or, alternatively, remove the nut securing the oil pipe junction block to the crankcase and allow the oil reservoir to drain for approximately ten minutes.

Disconnect the rubber pipes from the oil resevior, remove the junction block and thoroughly clean it in paraffin (kerosene).

Check the pipes for cuts and abrasions and that the rubber connections are a good tight fit on the junction block pipes. If there is any doubt about the reliability of the rubber connectors, they should be renewed.

Reassembly is the reversal of the above instructions but remember to fit a new gasket between the junction block and the crankcase.

LUBRICATION SYSTEM

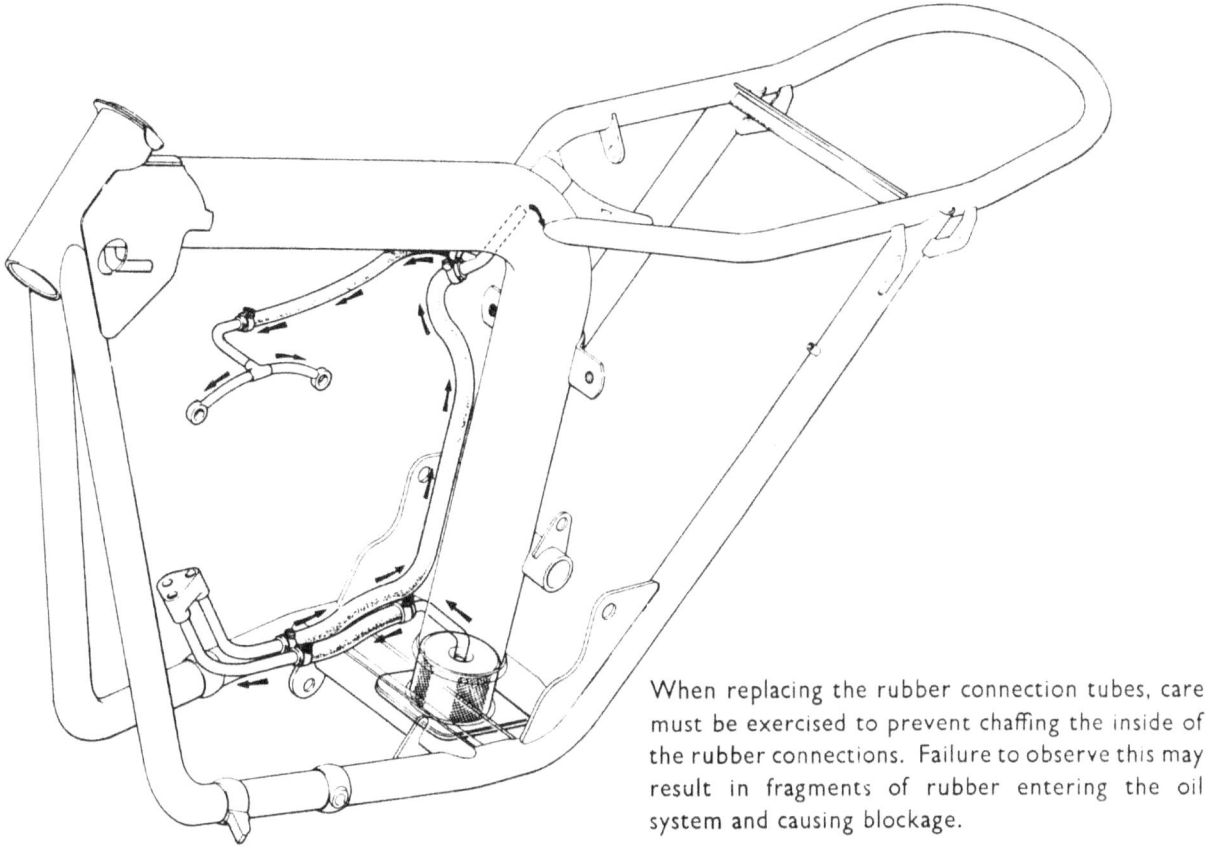

Fig. A7. Oil pipe securing clips

When replacing the rubber connection tubes, care must be exercised to prevent chaffing the inside of the rubber connections. Failure to observe this may result in fragments of rubber entering the oil system and causing blockage.

Replace the screwed clips and firmly clamp them in position.

SECTION A8

REMOVING AND REPLACING THE ROCKER OIL FEED PIPE

To disconnect the rocker oil feed pipe for removal, the two domed nuts should be removed from the ends of the rocker spindle, and the banjos withdrawn.

Disconnect the rocker oil feed pipe from the oil reservoir.

When removed, the rocker oil feed pipe should be thoroughly cleaned in paraffin (kerosene) and checked for blockage by sealing the first banjo with the thumb and first finger, whilst blowing through the other. Repeat this procedure for the other banjo.

When refitting the rocker oil feed pipe it is advisable to use new copper washers, but if the old ones are annealed they should give an effective oil seal. Annealing is achieved by heating to cherry red heat and quenching in water. Any scale that is formed on the washers should be removed prior to re-fitting them.

SECTION A9

CONTACT BREAKER LUBRICATION

The contact breaker is situated in the timing cover and it is imperative that no oil from the engine lubrication system gets into the contact breaker chamber. For this purpose there is an oil seal at the back of the contact breaker unit pressed into the timing cover. However slight lubrication of the auto advance unit spindles is necessary.

LUBRICATION SYSTEM

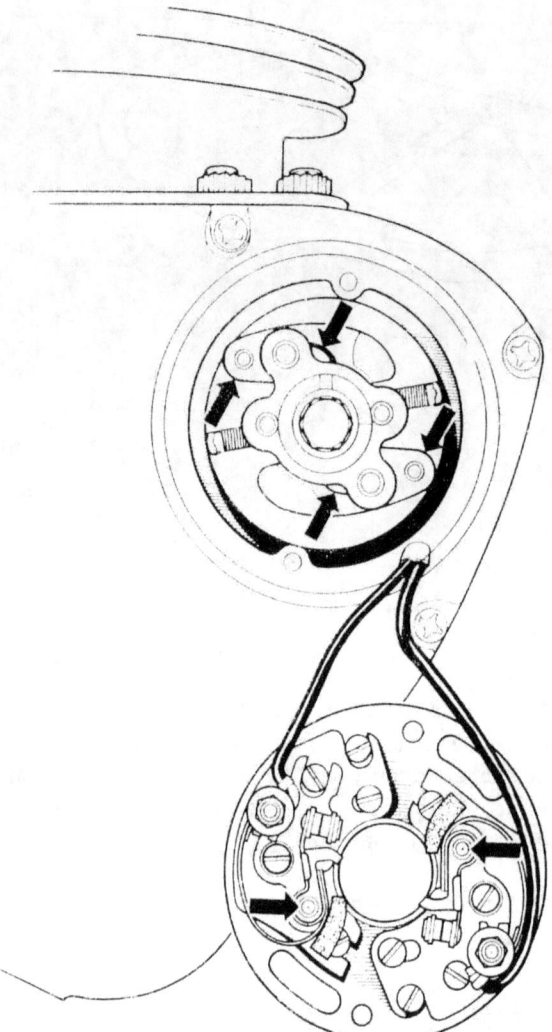

To lubricate the auto advance mechanism it is necessary to withdraw the mounting plate. Mark the C.B. plate and housing so that it can be subsequently replaced in exactly the same location, then unscrew the two hexagonal pillar bolts. When the mounting plate is removed, the mechanism should be lightly oiled (see arrows shown in Fig. A8) at the same interval that is given above for the cam wick. Do not allow more than one drop onto each pivot point, and wipe off any surplus.

Two drops of oil should be applied to the spindle which supports the cam to prevent corrosion and possible seizure.

Finally, replace the mounting plate and re-set the ignition timing. If the setting has been disturbed, the correct procedure for accurate ignition timing is given in Sections B27, B28 and B29.

The lubricating wicks adjacent to the contact breaker nylon heels are treated intially with Shell Retinax A grease and thereafter, 3 drops of clean engine oil should be added to the wicks at 3000 mile intervals.

Fig. A8. Contact breaker mechanism lubrication points 10CA

SECTION A10
GEARBOX LUBRICATION

The gearbox is lubricated by means of an oil bath. Oil is splash fed to all gearbox components including the enclosed gearchange and kickstarter mechanisms. The oil in the gearbox should be drained and the gearbox flushed out after the initial 500-mile (800km.) running-in period. Thereafter, the oil should be changed as stated in "Routine Maintenance".

The oil can be drained from the gearbox by means of the oil drain plug located underneath the gearbox (see Fig. A2, reference No. 3). It is best to drain the oil whilst the engine is warm as the oil will flow more readily.

The gearbox oil filler plug is situated on the outer cover. When replenishing the oil, the oil drain plug should be replaced omitting the smaller oil level plug which screws into it. Oil should be poured into the gearbox until it is seen to drip out through the oil level plug hole. (See Fig. A9). The correct level has then been obtained (see Section A1 for recommended oil).

LUBRICATION SYSTEM

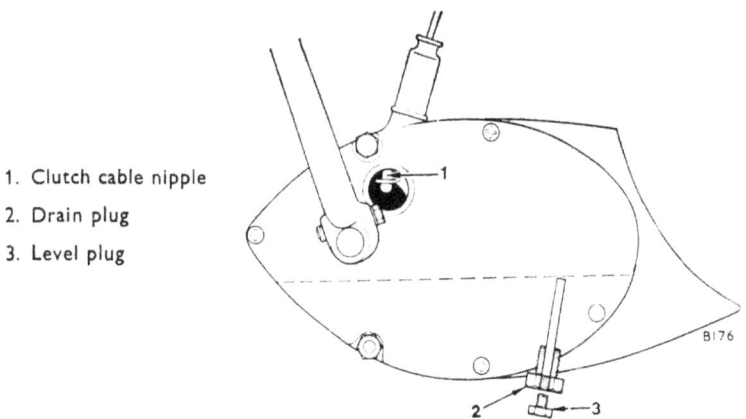

1. Clutch cable nipple
2. Drain plug
3. Level plug

Fig. A9. Gearbox drain and level plugs

SECTION A11

PRIMARY CHAINCASE LUBRICATION

The level of the oil in the primary chaincase is automatically maintained by the engine breathing system which operates through the drive side roller bearing. Three small holes drilled in the crankcase provide an inlet back into the crankcase when the oil reaches a predetermined level.

Oil should be added to the chaincase when the oil has been drained, or lost when using the chain tensioner. When 'priming' the chaincase with fresh oil use approximately ¼ pint of engine oil. (See Section A1).

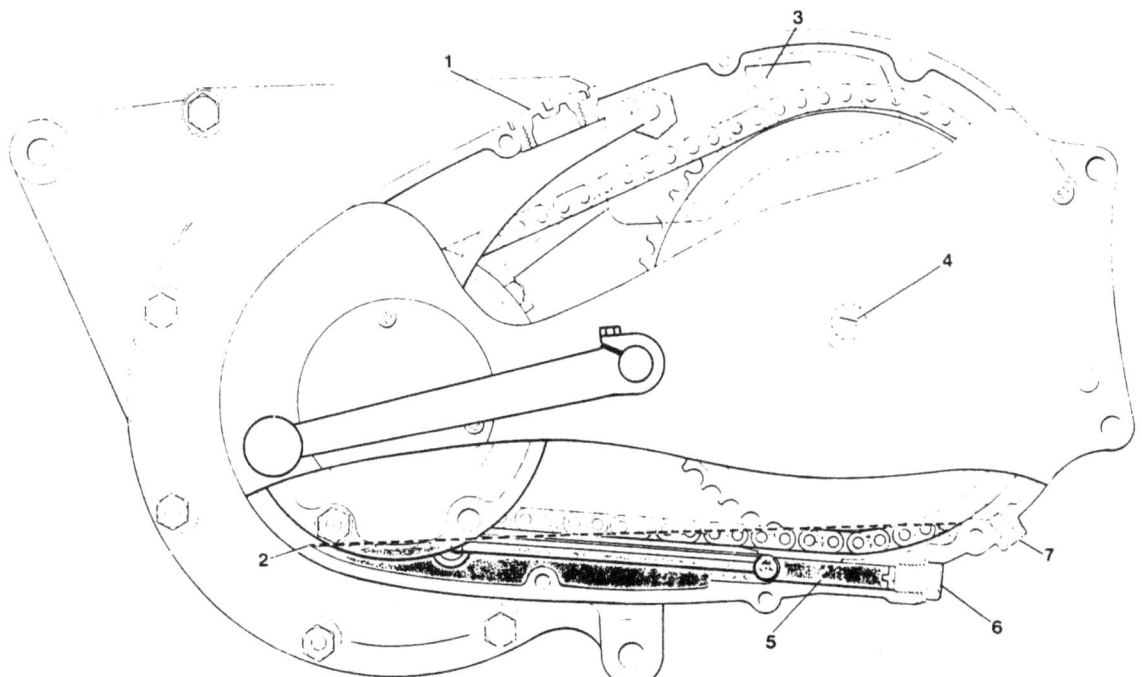

Fig. A10. Section through the primary chaincase

The oil drain plug is siutated in the bottom of the chaincase towards the rear of the machine. This plug also gives access to the chain tensioner.

Fresh oil can be added by removing the filler plug adjacent to the cylinder base flange or the clutch adjuster aperture in the centre of the outer cover.

The primary chain is lubricated by means of a collection chamber and oil feed pipe built into the primary chain housing. The oil feed pipe directs a continuous supply of oil at the point where the chain runs onto the engine sprocket. To check this for possible blockages it is necessary to remove the primary chaincase outer cover, and remove the front clip securing the oil feed pipe.

The oil ways can then be cleaned by a jet of compressed air from such as a cycle pump. When replacing the feed pipe clip ensure that the pipe is parallel to the top portion of the chain and firmly gripped by the clip.

SECTION A12
REAR CHAIN LUBRICATION AND MAINTENANCE

The rear chain should be periodically lubricated with an oil can or preferably with an oil soaked brush whenever signs of dryness occur. But as recommended in "Routine Maintenance" the chain should be removed and thoroughly cleaned and greased.

Disconnect the connecting link and remove the chain. If available, connect an old chain to the end of the chain being removed and draw it onto the gearbox sprocket until the chain to be cleaned is clear of the machine and can be disconnected.

Remove all deposits of road dust etc. by means of a wire brush. Clean thoroughly in paraffin or kerosene and allow to drain.

Inspect the chain for excessive wear of the rollers and pivot pins and check that the elongation does not exceed $1\frac{1}{2}\%$. To do this first scribe two marks on a flat table exactly $12\frac{1}{2}$ inches (31·75 cm.) apart, place the chain opposite the two marks. When the chain is compressed to its minimum free length the marks should coincide with two pivot pins 20 links apart. When the chain is stretched to its maximum free length, the extension should not exceed $\frac{1}{4}$ in. (6·25 mm.). If it is required to remove a faulty link, or shorten the chain, reference should be made to Section C12.

To lubricate use a proprietary chain lubricant.

The chain is now ready for refitting to the machine.

For chain adjustment refer to Section F.

NOTE: The connecting link retaining clip must be fitted with the nose-end facing in the direction of motion of the chain.

SECTION A13
GREASING THE STEERING HEAD RACES

The steering head bearings are packed with grease on assembly and require re-packing with the correct grade of grease at the interval stated in "Routine Maintenance". Removal and replacement of the bearings is comprehensively covered in the front fork section.

When the bearings are removed they should be cleaned in paraffin (kerosene), also, the races fitted to the frame head lug should be cleaned thoroughly by means of a paraffin (kerosene) soaked rag, then inspected for wear, cracking or pocketing.

LUBRICATION SYSTEM

SECTION A14
WHEEL BEARING LUBRICATION

NOTE: Later models are fitted with sealed bearings which do not require external lubrication. These can be recognised by the plastic covers fitted on each side of the ball races. (To inspect first remove the wheel and bearing retainers, see Section F).

EARLY MODELS

The wheel bearings are packed with grease on assembly but require re-packing with the correct grade of grease at the interval stated in "Routine Maintenance".

The bearings on both the front wheel and rear wheel should be removed, cleaned in paraffin (kerosene) and assembled with the hubs well packed with the correct grade of grease. For details concerning the grade of grease to be used (which is the same for both wheels), see Section A1.

To obviate further lubrication periods it would be advantageous to fit the later sealed type bearing at the first lubrication period of 15000 miles.

Removing and replacing the bearings for the front and rear wheels is comprehensively covered in Section F11 and F14.

SECTION A15
TELESCOPIC FORK LUBRICATION

The oil contained in the front fork has the dual purpose of lubricating the stanchion bearing surface and also acting as the suspension damping medium. Therefore it is imperative that the fork legs have an equal amount of oil in them and that it is the type as stated in Section A1.

Oil leakage at the junction between the stanchion and bottom fork leg is prevented by means of an oil seal. If there is excessive oil leakage at this junction it may be necessary to renew the oil seal (see Section G3), but before undertaking this work, the fork should be checked to ensure that there is the correct amount of oil in each of the fork legs.

The correct amount is 190 c.c.

Particular attention should be given to the oil change period.

To drain the oil from the fork legs remove the two small hexagonal drain plugs adjacent to the left and right ends of the front wheel spindle.

Oil can be expelled at a greater rate by compressing the fork two or three times.

To refill the fork legs, the fork hexagonal cap nuts and the stanchion top nuts must be unscrewed and withdrawn, and the correct amount of oil poured into each fork leg. This will necessitate removal of the handlebar.

On reassembly use a suitable jointing compound on the stanchion top nut threads. To obviate leakage.

SECTION A16

LUBRICATION NIPPLES

Both the rear brake operating camshaft (prior to engine no. HN62501) and the swinging fork pivot bearings should be lubricated by means of the lubrication nipples.

The rear brake camshaft has an integral lubrication nipple. Care should be taken that the surface of the nipple is not damaged. Slight distortion may be removed with a fine grade file.

The rear wheel brake cam and spindle bearing surfaces should be sparingly lubricated with the correct grade of grease (Section A1). This can be done by giving the lubrication nipple on the end of the camshaft one stroke from a grease gun. However, if the grease does not penetrate, the brake cam should be removed and cleaned thoroughly in paraffin (kerosene). The cam bearing surfaces should then be greased on reassembly.

SWINGING FORK PIVOT

The two nipples are situated at each end of the fork pivot. Give each nipple several strokes with a high pressure grease gun until grease is visible at the dirt excluders.

If the grease does not penetrate then the pivot must be removed to ensure adequate lubrication.

Removal of the swinging fork is detailed in section E20. When the fork is removed all parts should be thoroughly cleaned out in paraffin (kerosene) and allowed to drain.

Reassembly is a reversal of the above instructions. The space surrounding the distance tube should be carefully packed with the correct grade of grease, and the sleeves should be well greased on their bearing surfaces.

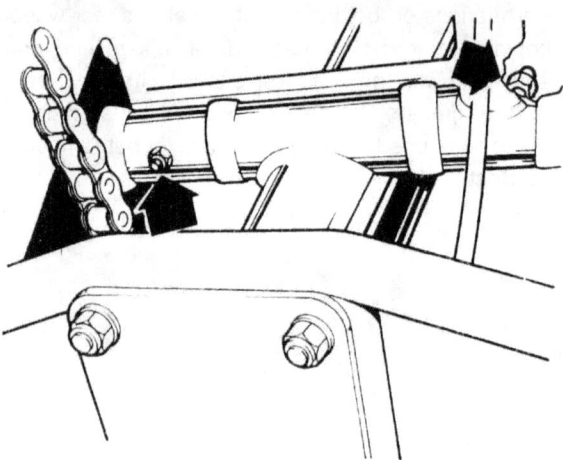

Fig. A11. Swinging fork pivot lubrication nipples

SECTION A17

LUBRICATING THE CONTROL CABLES

The control cables can be periodically lubricated at the exposed joints with a thin grade oil (see Section A1).

A more thorough method of lubrication is that of feeding oil into one end of the cable by means of a reservoir. For this the cable can be either disconnected at the handlebar end only, or completely removed.

The disconnected end of the cable should be threaded through a thin rubber stopper and the stopper pressed into a suitable narrow-necked can with a hole in its base. If the can is then inverted and the lubricating oil poured into it through the hole, the oil will trickle down between the outer and inner cables. It is best to leave the cable in this position overnight to ensure adequate lubrication.

LUBRICATION SYSTEM

SECTION A18

SPEEDOMETER AND TACHOMETER CABLE LUBRICATION

The speedometer and tachometer cables should be lubricated by means of grease (see Section A1 for correct grade).

It is not necessary completely to remove the cable, but only to diconnect if from the speedometer or tachometer and withdraw the inner cable. Unscrew the union nut at the base of the instrument, withdraw the inner cable and clean it in paraffin (kerosene). Smear the surface with grease, except for 6 in. (15 cm.) nearest to the instrument head.

The cable is now ready to be offered into the outer casing and excess grease wiped off. Care should be taken that both "squared" ends of the inner cables are located in their respective "square" drive housings before the union nut is tightened.

SECTION A19

BRAKE PEDAL SPINDLE LUBRICATION

No external grease nipple is provided, therefore the spindle must be removed and greased at the intervals stated in "Routine Maintenance".

See Section E6 for removing and servicing the brake pedal spindle.

Prior to engine no. HN62501

The brake pedal spindle is bolted to the left rear engine mounting plate. The spindle should be covered with a fresh supply of grease occasionally otherwise corrosion and inefficient operation may result.

To gain access to the spindle, slacken off the rear brake rod adjustment, unscrew the brake pedal retaining bolt and withdraw the pedal.

Remove any rust from the spindle with fine emery. Clean the bore of the pedal and smear the spindle with grease (see Section A1) prior to refitting.

SECTION A20
CHECK PROCEDURE FOR WET SUMPING

'Wet sumping' or a lack of scavenge is a condition which can occur due to a number of causes. The symptoms of this condition are:—

(1) Excessive oil emitting from crankcase breather tube and resulting high oil consumption.
(2) Smoking exhaust.

To verify that a wet-sumping condition exists, run the engine until it is thoroughly warm. Within five minutes after engine shutoff drain the sump. Measure the amount of oil that drains out. An amount of oil over 100 c.c. indicates a wet-sumping condition and corrective measures should be taken.

POSSIBLE CAUSES OF WET-SUMPING ARE

(1) Foreign material preventing ball valve from seating in the scavenge side of oil pump (most common cause).
(2) Poor check valve ball seat.
(3) Air leak in crankcase oil scavenge pipe.
(4) Air leak in oil pump to crankcase joint.
(5) Porous crankcase casting.
(6) Air leak at E9336 plug bottom of engine.
(7) Oil pressure release valve piston in full bypass position due to a stuck piston or broken or missing spring.
(8) Restriction in oil reservoir vent pipe.

SCAVENGE SUCTION TEST (for checking above causes numbers 1 to 6)

Obtain a vacuum gauge calibrated in inches of mercury. Attach a length of standard Triumph oil pipe to it and proceed as follows:

(1) Run engine until it is thoroughly warm.
(2) Remove the oil sump cap and screen.
(3) Connect hose from vacuum gauge to oil scavenge pipe.
(4) Run engine at a fast idle—gauge should read a vacuum of 18-26 inches of mercury.
(5) Stop engine and observe gauge. The needle should gradually—not immediately—drop to zero.

IF THE SCAVENGE SUCTION TEST IS SATISFACTORY

(1) Check oil pressure relief valve assembly and also check oil pressure.
(2) Check the return system from the pump to the oil reservoir and also the reservoir vent.

TO CHECK FOR A BLOCKED OR RESTRICTED OIL RETURN TO THE RESERVOIR

(1) On the oil reservoir using a hand brace or and $\frac{7}{64}''$ and $\frac{13}{64}''$ drill bits, run the drill bits into the return tube and rocker feed tube at the top of the reservoir to see that both tubes are free from internal burrs and restrictions that can occur at their welded joints.
(2) After doing the above, blow out the return oil line and the return tube in the oil reservoir with compressed air.

IF THE ABOVE TEST IS NOT SATISFACTORY

(1) Remove oil pump—clean thoroughly and see that ball seats are concentric and free from pits or grooves. Re-assemble pump, tighten check valve caps securely and re-install pump with a new gasket.

To check for crankcase scavenge tube leakage or case porosity, fill a **good** "pumper" type oil can with light oil and squirt through a folded rag into pickup tube. Back pressure could prevent pumping oil out of the can in a few pumps. If the oil can still be pumped with no evidence of substantial back pressure, obviously there is a leak in the the crankcase tube or crankcase scavenge oil passageways.

To be sure that the oil can is satisfactory for this test, fill it with light oil and block the outlet tube. After one or two pumps the can should "liquid lock". If the can can stil be pumped, the pump mechanism is suffering from excessive blow-by and the can will not suffice for this test.

SECTION B

ENGINE

DESCRIPTION	Section
REMOVING AND REPLACING THE ENGINE UNIT	B1
REMOVING AND REPLACING THE ROCKER BOXES	B2
INSPECTING THE PUSH RODS	B3
STRIPPING AND REASSEMBLING THE ROCKER BOXES	B4
ADJUSTING THE VALVE ROCKER CLEARANCES	B5
REMOVING AND REPLACING THE AIR CLEANER	B6
CONCENTRIC CARBURETTER—DESCRIPTION	B7
REMOVING AND REPLACING THE CARBURETTER	B8
STRIPPING AND REASSEMBLING THE CARBURETTER	B9
INSPECTING THE CARBURETTER COMPONENTS	B10
CARBURETTER ADJUSTMENTS	B11
TWIN CARBURETTER ARRANGEMENT	B12
REMOVING AND REPLACING THE EXHAUST SYSTEM	B13
REMOVING AND REFITTING THE CYLINDER HEAD ASSEMBLY	B14
REMOVING AND REPLACING THE VALVES	B15
RENEWING THE VALVE GUIDES	B16
DECARBONISING	B17
RE-SEATING THE VALVES	B18
REMOVING AND REPLACING THE CYLINDER BLOCK AND TAPPETS	B19
INSPECTING THE TAPPETS AND GUIDE BLOCKS	B20
RENEWING THE TAPPET GUIDE BLOCKS	B21
REMOVING AND REFITTING THE PISTONS	B22
REMOVING AND REPLACING THE PISTON RINGS	B23
INSPECTING THE PISTONS AND CYLINDER BORES	B24
TABLE OF SUITABLE REBORE SIZES	B25
REMOVING AND REPLACING THE CONTACT BREAKER	B26
IGNITION TIMING—INITIAL PROCEDURE	B27
IGNITION TIMING WHERE A STROBOSCOPE IS NOT AVAILABLE	B28
IGNITION TIMING BY STROBOSCOPE	B29
REMOVING AND REPLACING THE TIMING COVER	B30
REMOVING AND REPLACING THE OIL PUMP	B31
EXTRACTING AND REFITTING THE VALVE TIMING PINIONS	B32
VALVE TIMING	B33
DISMANTLING AND REASSEMBLING THE CRANKCASE ASSEMBLY	B34
SERVICING THE CRANKSHAFT ASSEMBLY	B35
REFITTING THE CONNECTING RODS	B36
INSPECTING THE CRANKCASE COMPONENTS	B37
RENEWING THE MAIN BEARINGS	B38
RENEWING THE CAMSHAFT BUSHES	B39
REMOVING AND REFITTING TACHOMETER DRIVE	B40

ENGINE

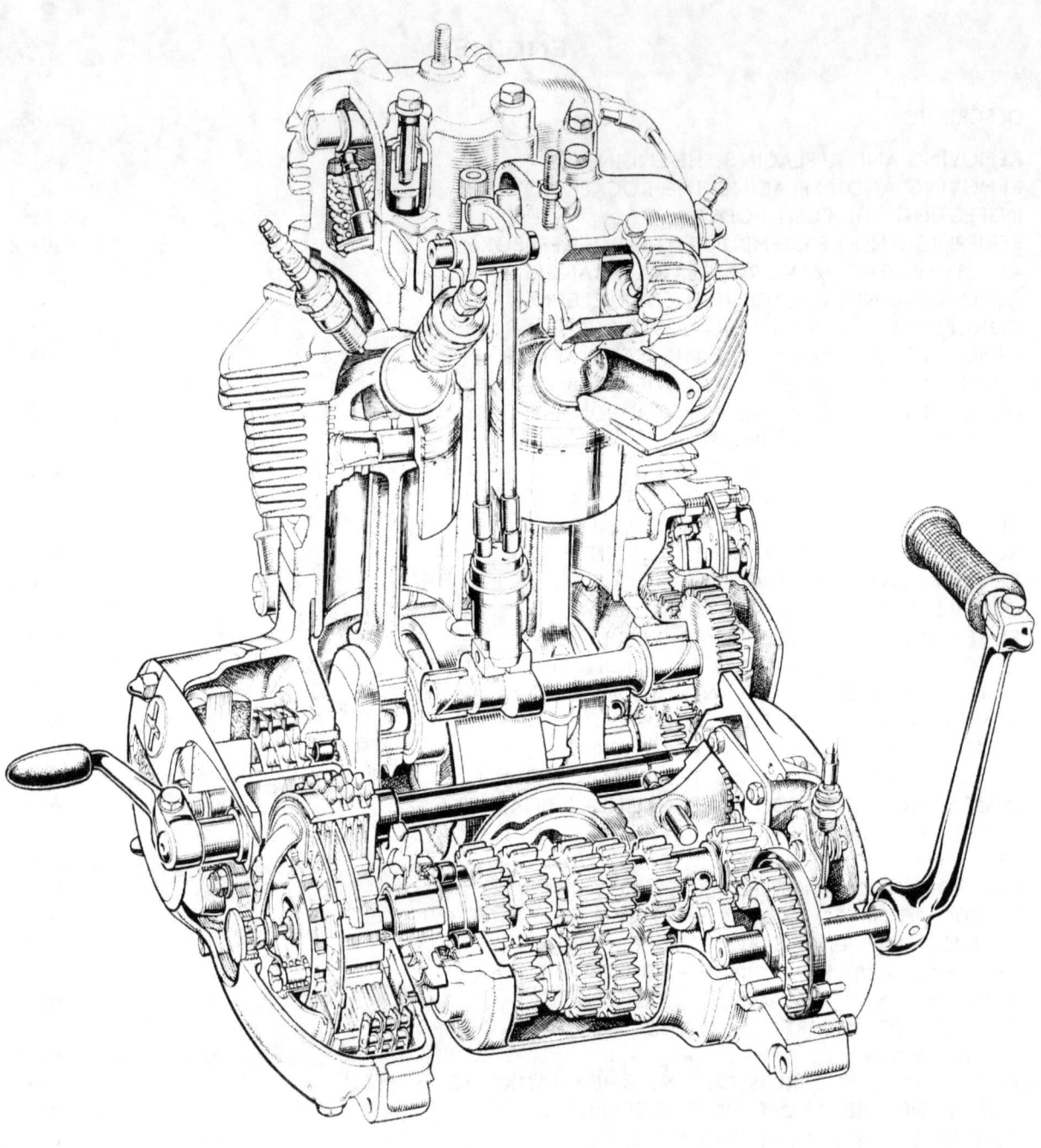

Fig. B1. Exploded view of 750c.c. engine gearbox unit

ENGINE B

DESCRIPTION

The engine is of unit construction having two aluminium alloy mating crankcase halves, the gearbox housing being an integral part of the right half-crankcase and the primary chain case an integral part of the left half-crankcase.

The aluminium alloy cylinder head has cast in Austenitic valve seat inserts, and houses the overhead valves, which are operated by rocker arms housed in detachable alloy rocker boxes. Four aluminium alloy push rods operate the rocker arms, which are each fitted with adjusters, accessible when the rocker box inspection caps are removed.

The aluminium alloy die cast pistons each have two compression rings and one oil scraper ring. The connecting rods are of H Section in RR56 Hiduminium alloy, with detachable caps, and incorporate steel-backed renewable "shell" bearings. Each of the connecting rod caps is machined from a steel stamping and held in position by means of two high tensile steel bolts, which are tightened to a pre-determined torque figure to give the correct working clearance of the bearings on the crankshaft journals.

The inlet and exhaust camshafts operate in sintered bronze bushes which are housed transversely in the upper part of the crankcase. The inlet and exhaust camshafts are driven by a train of timing gears from the right end of the crankshaft. The inlet camshaft also operates the oil pump whilst the exhaust camshaft drives the adjustable contact breaker, which is fitted with an automatic advance and retard unit, and the tachometer gearbox (when fitted).

The two-throw crankshaft has a detachable shrunk-on cast-iron flywheel which is held in position by three high tensile steel bolts, locked by the use of "TRIUMPH LOCTITE" sealant and tightened to a pre-determined torque figure.

The big end bearings are lubricated at pressure with oil which travels along drillings in the crankcase and crankshaft from the double plunger oil pump: oil pressure in the lubrication system is governed by means of the oil pressure release valve situated at the front of the engine, adjacent to the timing cover.

The cylinder barrel is made from a high-grade cast-iron and houses the press-fit tappet guide blocks.

Power from the engine is transmitted through the engine sprocket and primary chain to the shock absorbing clutch unit and five speed gearbox. Primary chain tensioner is governed by an adjustable rubber-pad chain tensioner which is immersed in the primary chain oil bath.

The electrical generator set consists of a rotor, which is fitted to the left end of the crankshaft, and an encapsulated six coil stator which is mounted on three pillar bolts inside the primary chain housing.

Carburation is by twin Amal carburetters with integral float chamber. The TR7 has only one such instrument.

SECTION B1

REMOVING AND REPLACING THE ENGINE UNIT

Ensure that the fuel taps are in the "OFF" position and disconnect the feed pipes. Remove the rubber grommet from the centre of the fuel tank and unscrew the sleeve nut below. The tank can now be pulled away from the frame. Note assembly of rubber sleeve and washers securing the tank. See Section E1.

Remove Exhaust system as described in Section B13.

Disconnect the oil pressure switch at the timing cover, the contact breaker leads and the alternator leads.

Detach the engine torque stay by removing the securing nut at each rocker box and removing the nut and bolt at the frame.

Disconnect the tachometer cable (where fitted) by unscrewing the union nut at the drive gearbox on the left side crankcase.

Detach the carburetter(s) see Section B8.

Drain the oil from the reservoir by removing the drain plug situated at the base of the main frame tube behind the gearbox. Allow to drain into a suitable receptacle for approximately 10 minutes. The oil feed pipe and return pipe should then be disconnected from the base of the reservoir and from below the oil filter neck respectively. Detach rocker feed pipe at the reservoir.

At this stage it is advisable to drain the oil from the gearbox and primary chaincase by removing the respective drain plugs. (See Section A3). The sump should also be drained; this is done by unscrewing the hexagon headed filter drain plug situated underneath the engine adjacent to the bottom engine mounting-lug. (See Fig. A2, No. 4).

Slacken off the clutch adjustment at the handlebar, withdraw the rubber sleeve from the clutch abutment at the gearbox and unscrew the abutment. Unscrew and remove the plug on the gearbox outer cover. Slip the bottom nipple of the clutch cable free of the operating arm and withdraw the cable.

Disconnect the engine breather tubes at the rear left crankcase by loosening the clips.

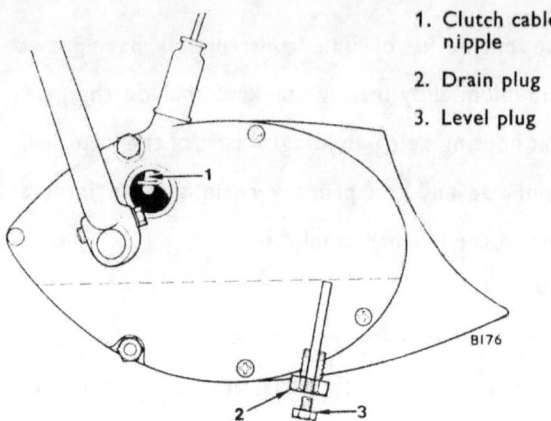

1. Clutch cable nipple
2. Drain plug
3. Level plug

Fig. B2. Clutch cable adjustment and gearbox drain plug

Remove the chainguard by removing the front retaining bolt and loosening the left side bottom rear suspension unit bolt. Withdraw the guard from the rear of the machine.

Remove the connecting link from the rear chain and withdraw the chain from the gearbox sprocket.

Remove the left and right side footrests. These are retained by bolts that screw into the footrest body.

Detach the two rear engine plates by removing the ten nuts and bolts.

Remove the bottom and front engine mounting studs. Note assembly of distance pieces on both these studs. The wider distance pieces fit on the right side of the machine in each case and the narrow ones on the opposite side.

It is now possible to remove the engine unit from the left side, but as the unit weighs approximately 135 lbs. (61 kg.) the use of a second operator or a small hoist is advised.

Replacement is the reversal of the above instructions. To ensure that the wiring harness is reconnected correctly refer to the appropriate wiring diagram in Section H19.

Do not forget to fit the distance pieces on the engine mounting studs.

For correct grade and quantity of lubricant for the engine, gearbox and chaincase, see Section A1.

SECTION B2

REMOVING AND REPLACING THE ROCKER BOXES

Disconnect the leads from the battery terminals and remove the fuel tank as detailed in Section E1.

Remove the torque stay by removing the nut at each rocker box and the bolt and nut at the frame.

Unscrew the two domed nuts from the rocker spindles and disconnect the rocker oil feed pipe. Care should be taken not to bend the pipe excessively as this may ultimately result in a fracture.

Remove the rocker inspection covers.

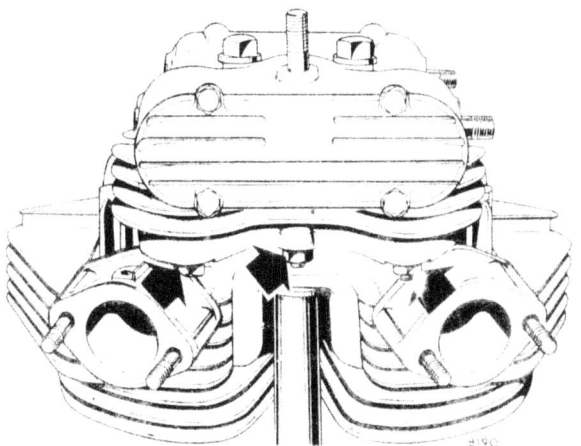

Fig. B3. Rocker box securing nuts

Unscrew three nuts from the studs fitted to the underside of the exhaust rocker box. Remove the outer exhaust rocker box securing bolts and unscrew the central hexagon retaining bolts. (Note that, at this stage the rocker box may rise slightly, due to a valve spring being compressed). The exhaust rocker box is now free to be removed. The procedure is the same for the inlet rocker box.

Care should be taken to collect the six plain washers which are fitted (one beneath each of the underside securing nuts), as they sometimes adhere to the cylinder head flanges and may be subsequently lost.

After completion of the rocker box removal operation, the push rods should be withdrawn and stored in the order of their removal so that they can be replaced in their original positions.

The junction surfaces of the rocker boxes and cylinder head should be cleaned for reassembly, by means of a soft metal scraper.

Replacement is a reversal of the above instructions.

When replacing the push rods place a small amount of grease into the bottom cup of each of the push rods, then locate the push rods, one at a time, by means of feeling the engagement of the tappet ball end and the push rod cup, and then testing the resistance to lifting caused by suction between the dome of the tappet and push rod cup. When the push rods are correctly located, remove the sparking plugs and turn the engine over until the INLET push rods are level and at the bottom of their stroke. The inlet rocker box should then be assembled. Repeat this procedure for the exhaust rocker box.

Before finally clamping the rocker boxes in position, check that the valves are being operated by turning the engine over slowly.

NOTE: It is important that the four central rocker box bolts are tightened to the correct torque setting. (See GENERAL DATA). The setting must be less than that of the cylinder head bolts which the rocker box bolts screw into.

Before fitting the rocker oil feed pipe the four copper washers which fit over the rocker spindle should be annealed by quenching in water from cherry red heat. Finally, remove any scale that may have formed. Annealing softens the copper thus restoring its original sealing qualities.

SECTION B3

INSPECTING THE PUSHRODS

When the pushrods have been removed, examine them for worn, chipped or loose end-cups; also check that the push rod is true by rolling it slowly on a truly flat surface (such as a piece of plate glass).

Bent pushrods are found to be the cause of excessive mechanical noise and loss of power and should be straightened if possible, or, preferably, renewed.

SECTION B4

STRIPPING AND REASSEMBLING THE ROCKER BOXES

Removal of the rocker spindles from the rocker boxes is best achieved by driving them out, using a soft metal drift. When the spindles are removed the rocker arms and washers can be withdrawn. All parts should be thoroughly cleaned in paraffin (kerosene) and the oil drillings in the spindles and rocker arms should be cleaned with a jet of compressed air.

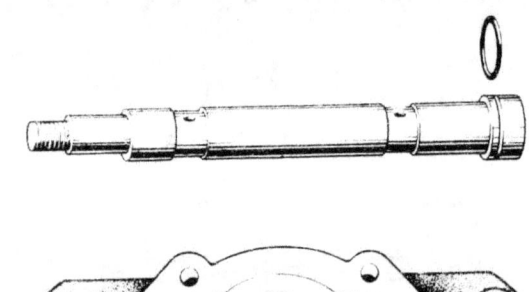

Remove the oil seals from the rocker spindles and renew them.

If it is required to renew the rocker ball pins, the old ones should be removed by means of a suitable drift.

To ensure an oil-tight seal between the rocker box and cylinder head, in cases where an oil leak cannot be cured by fitting new gaskets, the joint surface of the rocker box should be linished to remove any irregularities.

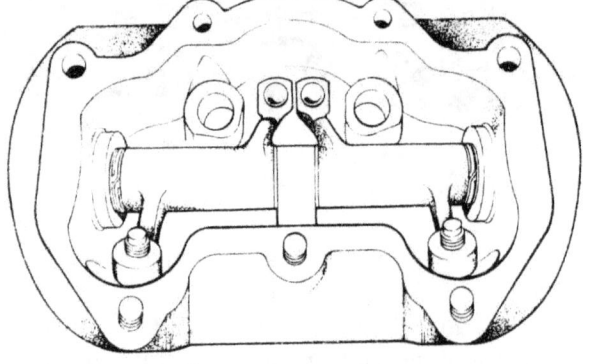

An effective linish can be achieved by first extracting the rocker box studs (two nuts locked together on the stud should facilitate an easy removal) then lightly rubbing the junction surface on a sheet of emery cloth mounted on a truly flat surface (such as a piece of plate glass).

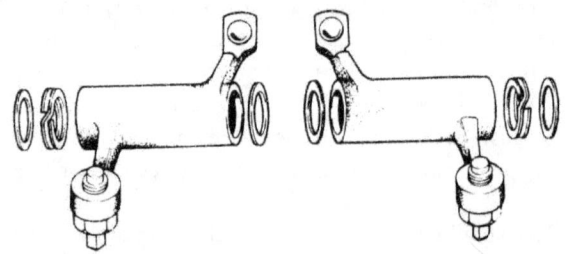

Fig. B4. Rocker box assembly

Assembly of the rocker spindles into the rocker boxes is assisted by the use of the oil seal compressor 61-7019.

The following method of assembly incorporates the use of a home made alignment bar, which can be made from a $\frac{7}{16}$ in. dia. bolt x 6 in. long by grinding a taper at one end.

Before reassembly note that the four plain washers on each rocker spindle are of differing size. The inside ones have a $\frac{1}{2}$ in. dia. hole and the outside ones have a $\frac{3}{8}$ in. dia. hole.

ENGINE

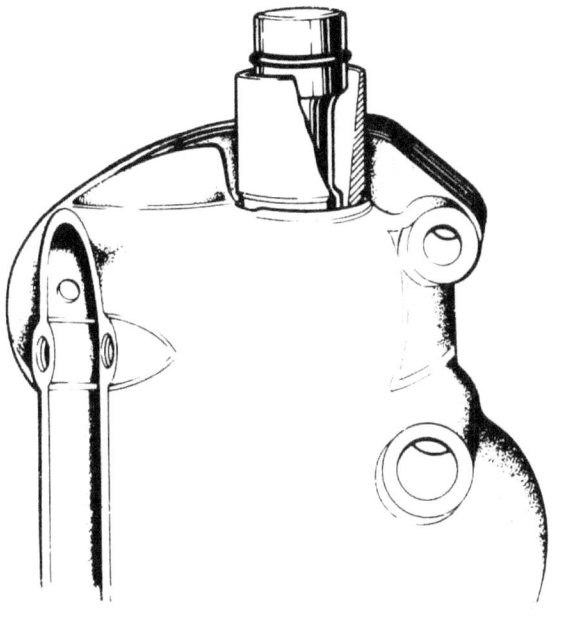

Smear two plain washers with grease and place them one either side of the centre bearing boss. Place the left rocker arm in position, bringing it into line with the alignment tool and slide a plain washer and a spring washer (in the order shown in Fig. B4) into position. Carefully repeat this procedure for the other rocker arm and spring washer and slide the last plain washer into position. Finally bring each rocker arm in turn into line with the alignment bar.

Lubricate the spindle with oil and slide it (complete with oil seal) through the compressor (61-7019) and as far as possible into the rocker box, finally tapping it home with a hammer and soft metal drift (see Fig. B5).

Fig. B5. Refitting the rocker spindle

SECTION B5
ADJUSTING THE VALVE ROCKER CLEARANCES

The valve rocker clearance should be checked and adjusted if necessary every 3,000 miles (4,800 Km.). The correct clearance, for the type of camshaft employed, ensures that a high valve operating efficiency is maintained and that the valves attain their maximum useful lives. The correct clearances are given in "General Data"

NOTE: Adjustments should only be made when the engine is COLD.

There are four adjusters on the rockers which are accessible after removing the inspection caps from the rocker boxes. A feeler gauge of the correct thickness can then be inserted. (See Fig. B6). The clearance must always be checked when the engine is cold. It will be easiest to find the correct point of the stroke to adjust the valve clearance if the machine is placed on the centre stand, top gear engaged and the sparking plugs removed. By revolving the rear wheel slowly the crankshaft will be turned and the valves can be positioned.

Inlet valves (towards the rear of the engine)

Turn the rear wheel until one of the inlet rockers moves downwards, thus opening the valve. When this valve is fully open the operating mechanism of the other inlet valve will be seated on the base of the cam and clearance can now be checked and adjusted if necessary. The clearance is 0.008 in. (0.203 mm.) and is correct when a feeler gauge of this thickness is a tight sliding fit between the valve tip and the adjuster. Tighten the locknut and re-check the clearance. Having adjusted one inlet valve, turn the rear wheel until the valve which you have adjusted is now fully open and repeat the procedure for the other inlet valve.

ENGINE

Exhaust valves

Having adjusted the inlet valves proceed to the exhaust valves which are situated at the front of the engine. Proceed in the same way as for the inlet valves and position one valve fully open whilst you check the clearance on the other. In this case the clearance is 0.006 in. (0.15 mm.).

Check that the inspection cover gaskets are in good condition and replace the covers making sure that they are tight.

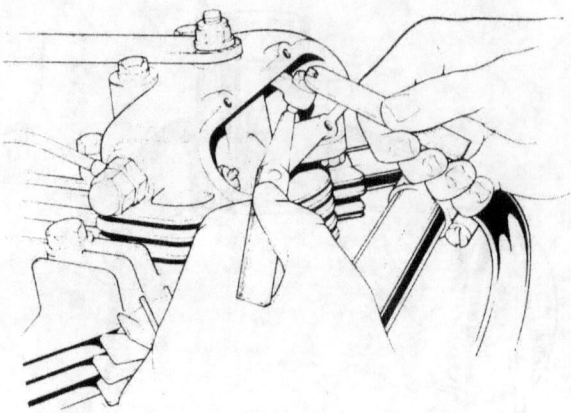

Fig. B6. Adjusting the valve rocker clearance

SECTION B6

REMOVING AND REPLACING THE AIR CLEANER(S)

The TR7 models have a similar air filter assembly to the T140 range except that it only has one aperture in the housing. Access is easily gained to the filter element by first removing the outer trim panels (disconnect the retaining springs) then removing the central fixing bolt and pulling the side cover away. The element can then be withdrawn.

The element is constructed from surgical gauze bound with metal gauze. They may be washed in gasoline and finally cleaned with a jet of compressed air.

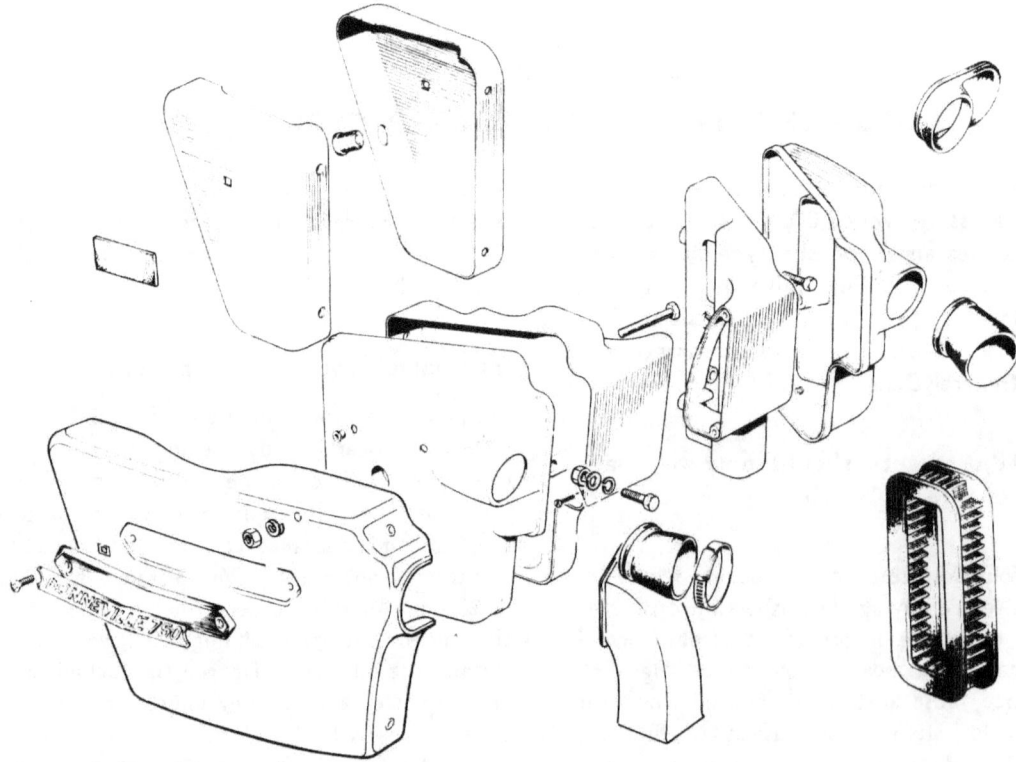

Fig. B7. Air cleaners (T140V shown)

ENGINE

AMAL Mk I
CONCENTRIC CARBURETTER TYPE 900
T140V AND TR7

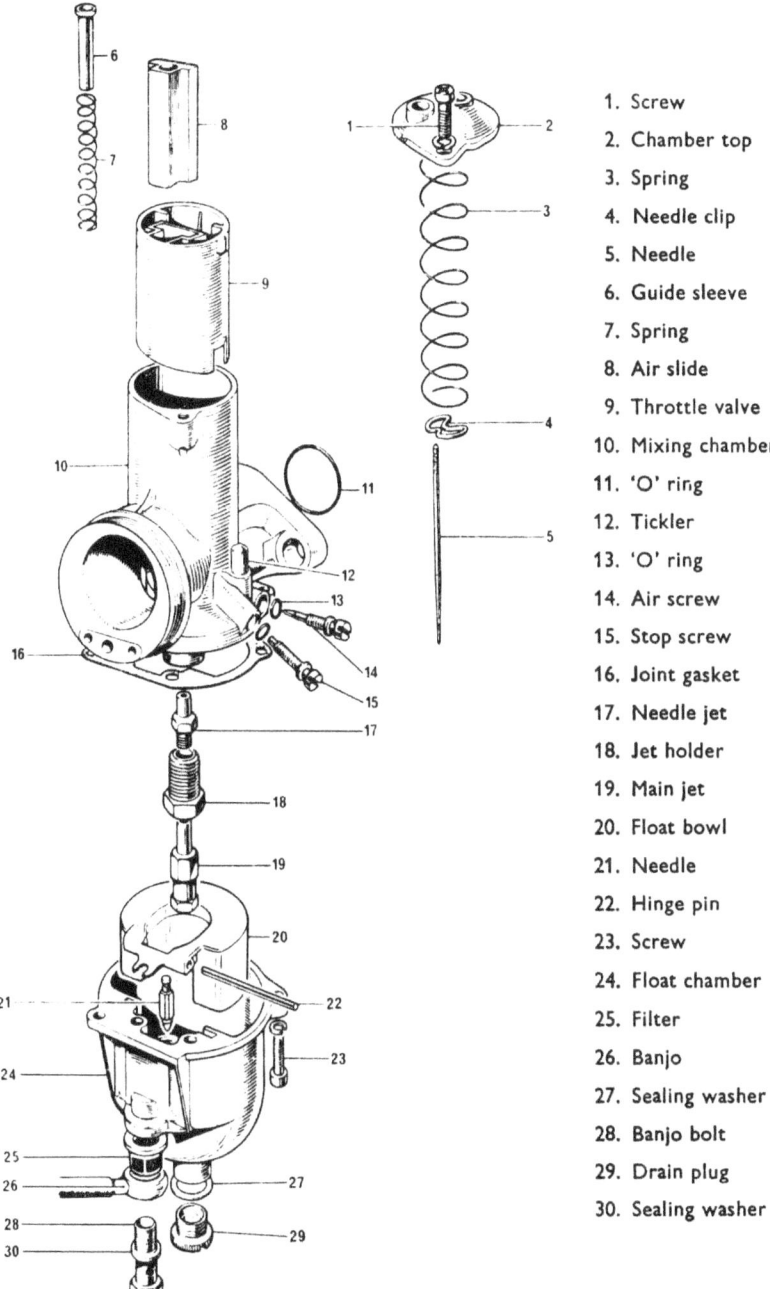

1. Screw
2. Chamber top
3. Spring
4. Needle clip
5. Needle
6. Guide sleeve
7. Spring
8. Air slide
9. Throttle valve
10. Mixing chamber
11. 'O' ring
12. Tickler
13. 'O' ring
14. Air screw
15. Stop screw
16. Joint gasket
17. Needle jet
18. Jet holder
19. Main jet
20. Float bowl
21. Needle
22. Hinge pin
23. Screw
24. Float chamber
25. Filter
26. Banjo
27. Sealing washer
28. Banjo bolt
29. Drain plug
30. Sealing washer

Fig. B8. Exploded view of Amal Mk I carburetter

ENGINE

AMAL MkII
CONCENTRIC CARBURETTER TYPE 2900 SERIES
T140E ONLY

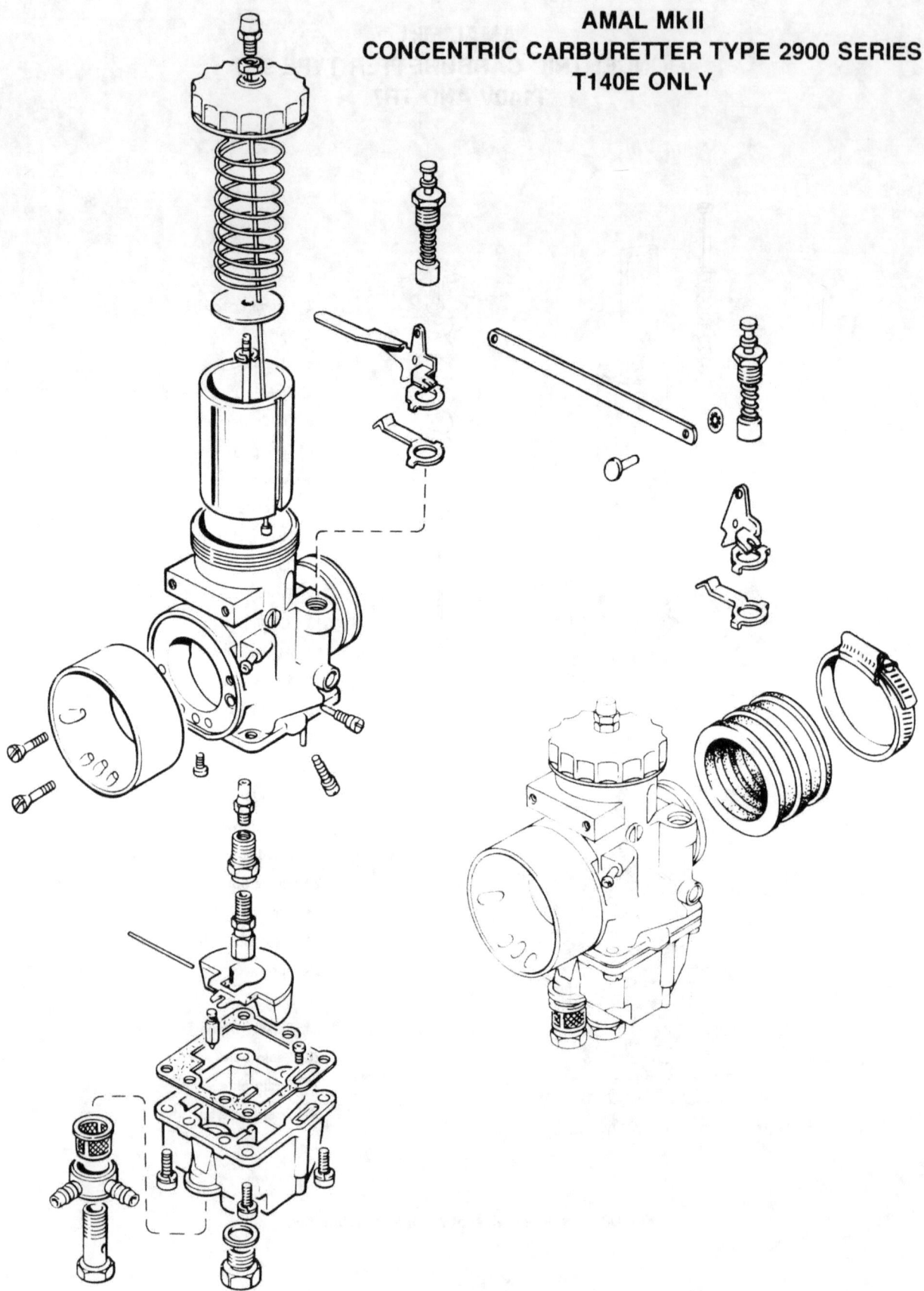

Fig. B9. Exploded view of Amal MkII carburetter

ENGINE B

SECTION B7

AMAL CONCENTRIC CARBURETTER

DESCRIPTION

All models are fitted with Amal concentric carburetters which are fully adjustable. Briefly, they operate in the following way:

When the engine is idling, mixture is supplied from the sealed pilot jet system, then as the throttle slide is raised, via the pilot by-pass. With the throttle just opening the mixture is controlled by the tapered needle working in the needle jet and finally by the size of the main jet. The pilot system is supplied by a pilot jet, permanently fitted into the carburetter body. The main jet does not feed direct into the mixing chamber but discharges through the needle jet into the primary air chamber and the fuel goes from there as a rich petrol-air mixture through the primary air choke into the main air choke.

This primary air choke has a compensating action in conjunction with bleed holes in the needle jet, which serves the double purpose of air-compensating the mixture from the needle jet, and allowing the fuel to provide a well, outside and around the needle jet, which is available for snap acceleration. The idling mixture is controlled by the pilot air screw which governs the amount of air that is allowed to mix with the fuel at tick-over speeds. The throttle stop screw is used to adjust the slide so that the throttle is kept open sufficiently to keep the engine running at a slow tick-over, when the twist-grip is closed.

On T140 machines the carburetters are left and right handed to allow for easy adjustment of the pilot air and throttle stop screws.

The carburetter(s) have a drain plug provided in the base of the float bowl. This plug is hollow and collects foreign matter that may be resent in the carburetter.

The Amal Mk II carburetter is designed to meet current U.S.A. emission regulations and is fitted to T140E models only.

SECTION B8

REMOVING AND REPLACING THE CARBURETTER

T140V AND TR7V MODELS ONLY

Due to the carburetter top securing screws being inaccessible with the petrol tank fitted (TR7V only) it will be necessary to dismount the carburetter before removing the top for any reason.

Remove the air cleaner outer covers as stated in Section B6. Ensure both taps are in the "Off" position and disconnect the fuel pipes at the taps beneath the rear of the tank. Unscrew the two carburetter flange securing nuts (self-locking) then carefully withdraw the carburetter from over its mounting studs at the same time disconnecting the rubber connectors from the air box. (Slacken the clip securing the single rubber connector – TR7V models). Lift off the cups and "O" rings.

As the carburetter is lowered, the top can be removed by taking out the two Phillips headed screws. Unless the top, slides etc. are to be removed from the cables they can be wrapped carefully in a piece of cloth until the carburetter is to be refitted.

When replacing the carburetter, great care should be taken to ensure that the slide does not become damaged as it is lowered into the mixture chamber. The peg at the top right of the slide locates in a corresponding groove in the carburetter body. Care must be taken when replacing the slide as the needle must be located in the needle jet, before the slide can be positioned in the mixing chamber. When the slide has been assembled satisfactorily, refit the mixing chamber top, two screws and lock washers.

Refit the carburetter over the locating studs followed by the rubber washers and cups.

Care should be taken not to overtighten the two carburetter securing nuts. Refitting continues as a reversal of the previous instructions.

ENGINE

T140E MODELS ONLY
Remove the petrol tank, see Section F.

Remove both side cover trim panels, see Section B6, then remove the L.H. and R.H. air filter covers by removing the central securing nut. Completely slacken off the L.H. cross brace securing bolt.

NOTE: All fasteners on T140E carburetters are METRIC sizes.

Disconnect the fuel feed pipe from the L.H. carburetter. Withdraw the retaining clip from the R.H. choke linkage and disconnect the linkage.

Slacken off the carburetter to cylinder head jubilee clips (4 off). Disconnect the crossbrace from the dowel on the L.H. carburetter using a screwdriver.

Withdraw the R.H. carburetter out to the R.H. side, disconnecting the cross brace for the L.H. carburetter at the same time.

NOTE: The mounting hole in the L.H. crossbrace is slotted to allow for removal without removing the securing bolt.

Withdraw the L.H. carburetter then unscrew the top caps and withdraw the throttle slides.

Refitment is the reverse of the above instructions.

SECTION B9

STRIPPING AND REASSEMBLING THE CARBURETTER

When the carburetter is removed, disconnect the slide assembly from the throttle cable. To do this pull back the return spring and remove the needle and needle clip. With the spring still retracted, push the cable through the slide and when the nipple is clear, across the figure of eight slot. The slide and return spring (and needle retaining disc – T140E) can now be removed.

T140V AND TR7V

To remove the air valve, push the valve guide tube and spring along with air cable until the cable nipple protrudes sufficiently out of its counterbore to be pushed out of the slot. The cable spring and guide can now be pulled clear of the valve.

T140E

To remove the cold start enrichment device unscrew the plunger assembly and remove the lever and bracket assemblies.

ALL MODELS

Unscrew the petrol pipe banjo connection and remove the banjo and nylon filter.

Unscrew four Phillips screws and remove the float bowl. The nylon float, spindle and triangular needle can now be withdrawn.

Remove the cold start jet – T140E models only.

Unscrew the jet holder which will allow the main jet to be removed.

Unscrew the air adjusting screw and throttle stop screw.

Thoroughly clean all parts in petrol (gasoline) several times and dry with compressed air, or a hand pump, to remove any particles of dirt. Any external deposits are best removed with the use of a light wire brush.

Reassemble in the reverse order, referring to Figs. B8 and B9 for guidance.

When refitting the float and needle valve, make certain that the recess on the valve is properly located in the "U" shaped slot in the float. Replace the float bowl sealing gasket, and if necessary, the two rubber "O" rings fitted to the adjusting screws.

When refitting the needle retaining disc on T140E carburetters only ensure the 'ear' on the disc faces downwards and locates against the lug inside the throttle valve casting. This prevents the throttle cable becoming twisted. See Fig. B10.

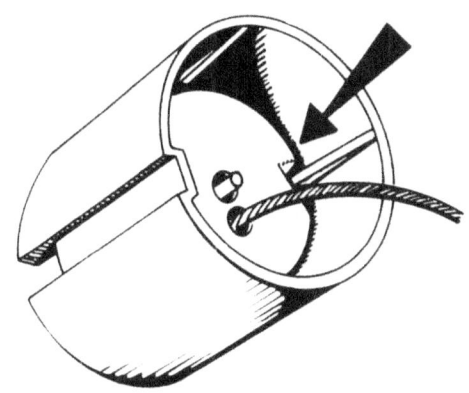

Fig. B10. T140E Needle retaining disc location

SECTION B10

INSPECTING THE CARBURETTER COMPONENTS

The only parts liable to show wear after considerable mileage are the throttle valve slide and mixing chamber (and the air slide – T140V and TR7V).

(1) Inspect the throttle valve slide for excessive scoring to the front area and check the extent of wear on the rear slide face. If wear is apparent the slide should be renewed. In this case, be sure to replace the slide with the correct degree of cutaway (see "General Data").

T140V AND TR7V ONLY

(2) Examine the air valve for excessive wear and check that it is not actually worn through at any part. Check the fit of the air valve in the body. Ensure that the air valve spring is serviceable by inspecting the coils for wear.

(3) Inspect the throttle return spring for efficiency and check that it has not lost compressive strength.

(4) Check the needle jet for wear or possible scoring and carefully examine the tapered end of the needle for similar signs. Check the correct needle is in use. The needle for petrol is marked above the top groove "000". The needle for alcohol is marked "Z".

(5) Check the float bowl joint surface for flatness and flatten if necessary on emery paper on a perfectly flat surface.

(6) Ensure that the float does not leak by shaking it to see if it contains any fuel. Do not attempt to repair a damaged float. A new one can be purchased for a small cost.

(7) Check the petrol filter, which fits into the petrol pipe banjo, for any possible damage to the mesh. Ensure that the filter has not parted from its supporting structure, thus enabling the petrol (gasoline) to by-pass it un-filtered.

(8) Concentric float carburetters have a pressed-in pilot jet which is not removable. If the jet becomes blocked the machine will be hard to start and will not run at low speeds. This can be cleared by blocking the low speed air passage at the bell end of the carburetter removing the pilot air screw and using a jet of air at this point.

(9) T140E carburetter only: Check the cold start enrichment plunger mesh filter for cleanliness.

SECTION B11

CARBURETTER ADJUSTMENTS

Throttle Stop Screw. This screw, which is situated on the right side of the carburetter (L.H. In case of the T140 left hand carburetter) sloping upwards and is fitted with a friction ring, should be set to open the throttle sufficiently to keep the engine running at a slow tick-over, when the twist-grip is closed.

Pilot Air Screw. To set the idling mixture, this screw, which is situated on the right side, is also fitted with a friction ring and should be screwed in to enrich the tick-over mixture or outwards to weaken it. As a guide to its approximate required position, screw it in fully, then unscrew it approximately $2\frac{1}{2}$ turns.

The screw controls the suction on the pilot jet by metering the amount of air which mixes with the petrol.

Needle and Needle Jet. Carburation is governed by the cut-away and needle jet in varying degrees from when the throttle is just open to when it is approximately $\frac{3}{4}$ full throttle. The needle jet orifice is governed by the position of the needle. The needle position should not be altered from its specified setting without specialist advice.

Throttle Valve Cutaway. The amount of cut-away to the bottom of the throttle valve slide is indicated by a number marked on the slide, e.g. $930/3\frac{1}{2}$ means throttle type 930 with number $3\frac{1}{2}$ cutaway; a larger number such as 4 means that the throttle valve slide has a slightly larger cutaway and consequently gives a weaker mixture during the period of throttle opening through which a cutaway is effective, i.e. from just open to approximately $\frac{1}{4}$ throttle. Similarly, 3 indicates a slightly smaller cutaway and a slightly stronger mixture.

Jet Sizes. The recommended jet sizes are given in "General Data". The main jet is operative from approximately $\frac{3}{4}$ to full throttle, this is when the needle jet or orifice ceases to have any reduction effect on the petrol flow.

ENGINE B

SECTION B12

TWIN CARBURETTER ARRANGEMENT

DESCRIPTION

Twin carburetters are fitted to T140 machines. There is a balance pipe fitted between the inlet manifolds to improve tickover.

THROTTLE CABLE

The single throttle cable from the twistgrip enters a junction box where it is fitted into a slide. The twin shorter carburetter cables are fitted to the other side of the junction box slide. Both the slide and junction box being made of plastic require no maintenance.

A similar cable arrangement is used for air slide operation. (T140V only).

SETTING TWIN CARBURETTERS

The twin carburreters fitted to the T140 may require synchronisation and a simple method is as follows: First adjust the cables from the juction box so that they have the minimum of free play.

Now start the motor and take off one plug lead and then adjust the pilot air screw and throttle stop screw in the OPPOSITE carburetter until the motor runs regularly. Replace the plug lead and repeat the process similarly for the other carburetter. With both plug leads replaced the tickover will be too fast and the stop screws should be lowered simultaneously until correct. It is most important the throttle slides lift simultaneously or the motor will run roughly, particularly when accelerating.

SECTION B13

REMOVING AND REPLACING THE EXHAUST SYSTEM

ALL T140 AND TR7 MODELS

To remove the complete exhaust system first slacken the balance tube clamps forward of the cylinder head. Remove the two cruciform headed screws from the front attachment brackets and slacken both silencer to exhaust pipe clips.

Now using a hide mallet tap both exhaust pipes away from the cylinder head so that they are removed together. This will allow the balance tube to be detached from between the pipes.

Remove the silencers from the machine by detaching the pillion footrests.

Replacement of the exhaust system is the reversal of the above instructions. Remember to assemble the exhaust pipes to the head together in one operation with the balance tube and clips in between their respective stubs. Finally tighten all nuts and bolts securely.

SECTION B14

REMOVING AND REFITTING THE CYLINDER HEAD ASSEMBLY

Proceed as detailed in Section B2 for removal of the rocker boxes and pushrods.

Remove the exhaust system as in Section B13.

Detach the carburetter(s) from the cylinder head, (see section B8), and place well clear of the cylinder head.

Unscrew the ten cylinder head bolts/nuts, a turn at a time, until the load has been released.

Remove the push rod cover tubes and note that it is essential to renew the rubber seals. Check for sharp edges on the corners of the top portion of the tappet guide blocks which could cut the new 'O' rings when reassembling. Use a file or emery cloth to smooth any such sharp edges.

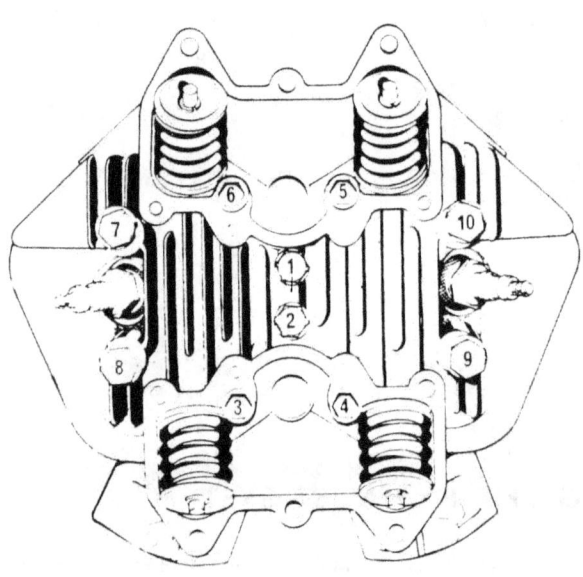

Fig. B11. Cylinder head bolt tightening sequence (T140V shown)

REFITTING THE CYLINDER HEAD

Ensure that the junction surfaces of the cylinder block, gasket and cylinder head are clean. Grease the gasket and place it in position. Coat the tappet guide blocks with heavy grease and locate the push rod cover tubes (complete with top and bottom oil seals). Relieve any roughness at the push rod tube counterbores in the head.

Lower the cylinder head into position over the push rod cover tubes and fit the cylinder head-bolts/ finger tight, also, fit the central nuts finger tight.

Tighten the ten cylinder head bolts/nuts in the order given in Fig. B11 and to the torque settings given in "General Data". Refit the rocker boxes as detailed in Section B2.

To facilitate torquing the inner head nuts (A) Fig. 12 use servicing tool 61/7010

NOTE: Always re-torque the cylinder head bolts nuts after the engine has thoroughly warmed up for the first time, i.e. Run the machine for approximately 5 miles then re-torque the cylinder head bolts/nuts.

Reassembly then continues in the reverse order to the removal instructions. To obtain the correct valve rocker clearance settings, reference should be made to Section B5.

ENGINE

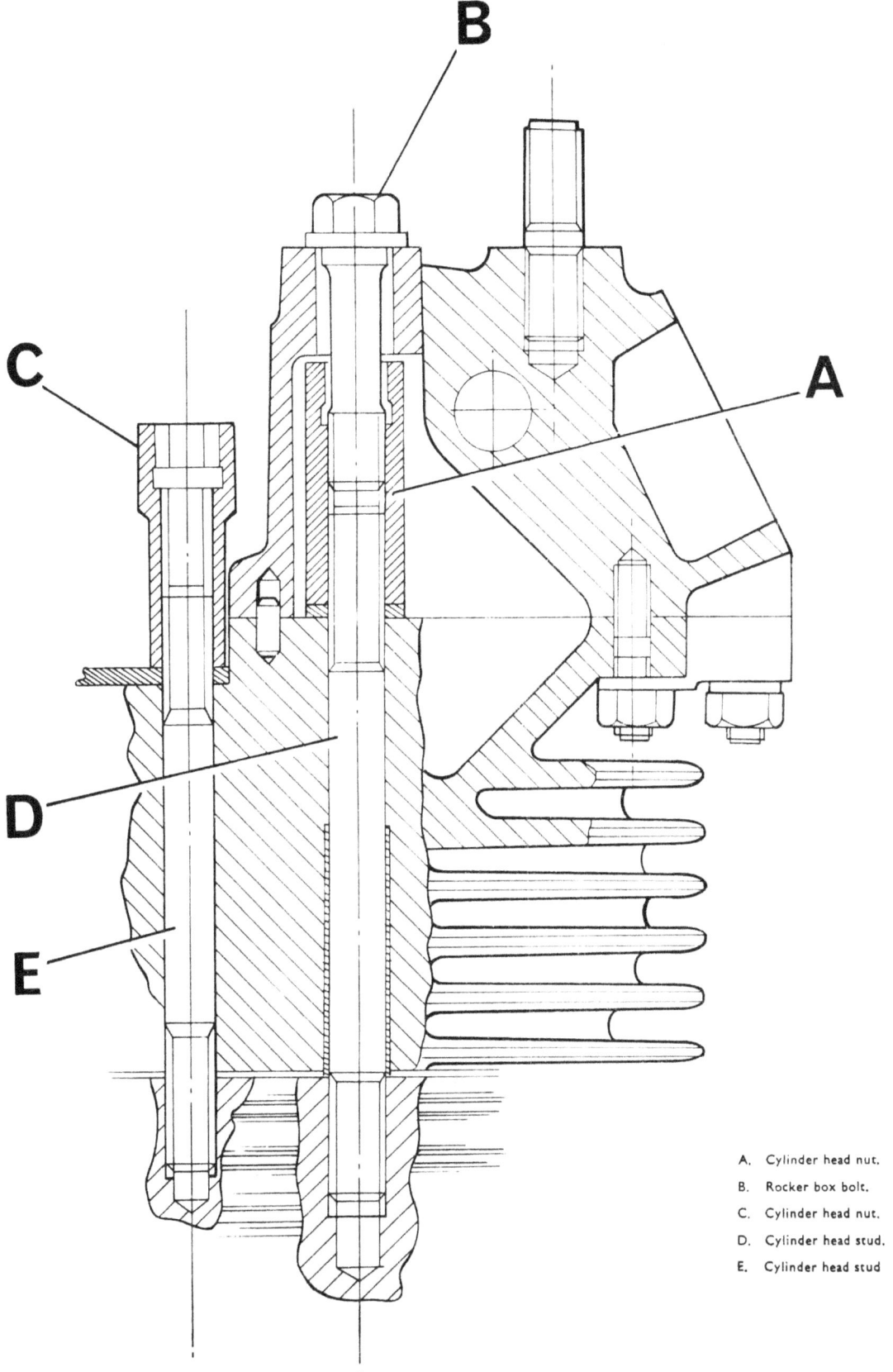

A. Cylinder head nut.
B. Rocker box bolt.
C. Cylinder head nut.
D. Cylinder head stud.
E. Cylinder head stud

Fig. B12. Showing assembly of cylinder head studs and nuts

SECTION B15

REMOVING AND REFITTING THE VALVES

Removal of the valves is facilitated by means of a "G" clamp type valve spring compressor. When the spring is compressed sufficiently, the split cotters can be removed with a narrow screwdriver, and the valve spring withdrawn when the compressor is released. As each valve is removed it should be marked so that it can be replaced in its original position.

NOTE: The inlet valves are marked "IN" and the exhaust valves "EX".

Fitting a new or reground valve necessitates seating by the grinding in process described in Section B18, but it does not necessitate recutting the cylinder head valve seat unless new valve guides have been fitted.

The valve springs should be inspected for fatigue and cracks, and checked for wear by comparing them with a new spring or the dimension given in "General Data".

All parts should be thoroughly cleaned in paraffin (kerosene) and allowed to drain before reassembling.

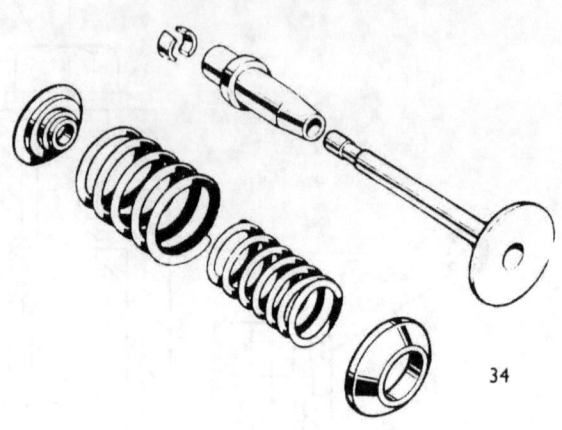

Fig. B13. Valve components

Assemble the inner and outer springs and top and bottom cups over the valve guide, then slide the valve into position lubricating the stem with a small amount of graphited oil.

Compress the springs and slide the two halves of the split cotter into the exposed groove in the valve stem.

SECTION B16

RENEWING THE VALVE GUIDES

The valve guides can be pressed or drive out using service tool 61-6013, with the cylinder head inverted on the bench. A suitable drift can be made by obtaining a 5in. length of ½in. diameter mild steel bar (EN8) and machining one end to ⁵⁄₁₆in. (8mm.) diameter for a length of 1in. (24.5mm.).

The same method may be employed to fit the new guide, although the use of a press is recommended. In either case lightly grease the valve guide to assist assembly. Ensure that the guide is pressed in until the shoulder is flush with the cylinder head.

Bronze valve guides are fitted, the shorter ones being used in the inlet position.

Where new valve guides have been fitted it is necessary to re-cut the valve seats in the cylinder head and grind in the valves (see Section B18).

ENGINE   B

SECTION B17
DECARBONISING

It is not normally advisable to remove the carbon deposits from the combustion chamber and exhaust ports until symptoms indicate that decarbonising is necessary.

Such symptoms as falling off in power, loss of compression, noisy operation and difficult starting are all indications that decarbonising may be necessary.

When the cylinder head is removed unscrew the sparking plugs and clean them in paraffin (kerosene), or preferably have them grit-blasted and checked. Before fitting the plugs, check that the gap setting is correct (see "General Data").

If special decarbonising equipment is not available then a blunt aluminium scraper or a piece of lead solder flattened at one end, should be used to remove the carbon deposits. Do not use a screwdriver or a steel implement of any kind on an aluminium surface.

When removing the deposits from the piston crown, a ring of carbon should be left round the periphery of the pistons to maintain the seal. Also the carbon ring round the top of the cylinder bore should not be disturbed. To facilitate this an old piston ring should be placed on top of the piston, level with the top surface of the cylinder block.

Remove the valves as shown in Section B15 then remove the carbon deposits from the valve stems, combustion chamber and ports of the cylinder head. Remove all traces of carbon dust by means of a jet of compressed air or the vigorous use of a tyre pump, then thoroughly clean the cylinder head and valves in paraffin (kerosene). Finally, check the valves for pitting. If necessary, the valves can be ground-in as shown in Section B18.

SECTION B18
RE-SEATING THE VALVES

Where the valve guides have been renewed or the condition of a valve seat is doubtful, it is advisable to re-cut the cylinder head valve seat then grind in the valve, using a fine grade grinding-in paste.

It is important that the cylinder head valve seat and the valve guide bore should be concentric. For the purpose of re-cutting the valve seats the following service tools are available.

61-7025 Valve seat cutter inlet and exhaust
61-7027 Blending cutter inlet and exhaust
61-7029 Arbour pilot and tommy bar

The valve seat cutting operation should be carried out with the greatest care, and only a minimum amount of metal should be removed.

After the seats have been re-cut, they should be blended to give an even seating of $\frac{3}{32}$ in. (2.4mm.).

Examine the face of the valve to see if it is pitted, scored or damaged. If necessary, the face can be reground, but excessive re-grinding is not advisable for this adversely affects the heat transference properties of the valve and will ultimately result in critical pocketing.

The stem of the valve should be inspected for wear or scuffing and if either is pronounced, the valve should be renewed.

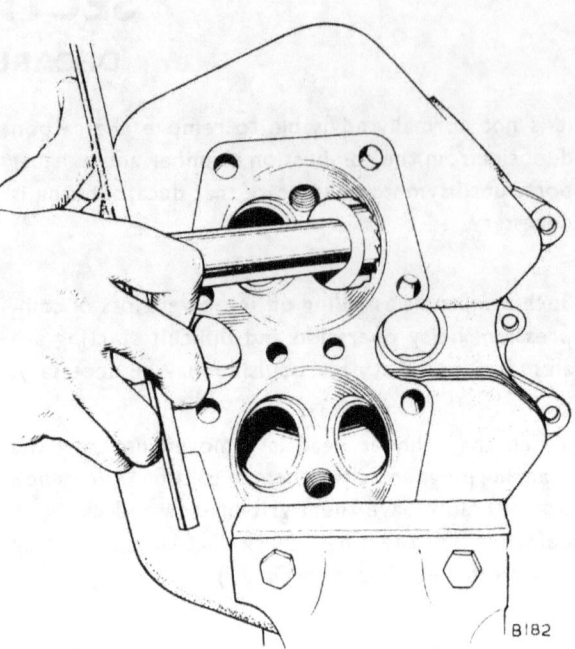

Fig. B15. Cutting a valve seat

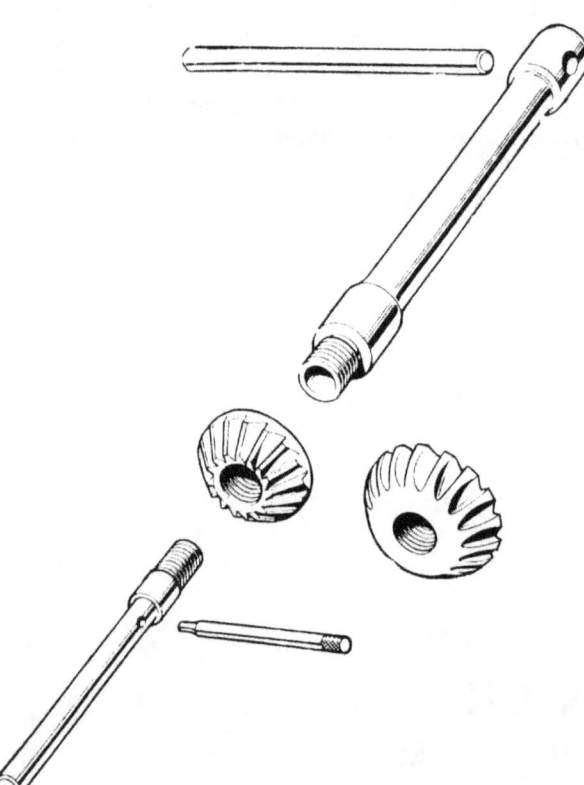

Fig. B14. Valve seating tools

To grind in the valve use a fine grade carborundum grinding paste. Place a small amount evenly on the valve seat and place the valve in its guide with a holding tool attached.

Use a semi-rotary motion, occasionally lifting the valve and turning it through 180°. Continue this process until a uniform seal results. Wash the parts in paraffin (kerosene) to remove the grinding paste. Apply a smear of "Engineer's" marking blue to the seat of the valve. Rotate the valve through one revolution and inspect both seats. Successful valve grinding will give an unbroken ring of blue on the valve seat.

Alternatively, assemble the springs and split cotters and pour a small amount of paraffin (kerosene) into the port. It should not penetrate the seating for at least 10 seconds if a good seal has been achieved.

Prior to reassembling the cylinder head, ensure that all traces of "Blue" or grinding paste are removed by thoroughly washing in paraffin (kerosene).

SECTION B19

REMOVING AND REPLACING THE CYLINDER BLOCK AND TAPPETS

Wedge a dis-used shock absorber rubber, or a suitable retainer between the inlet and exhaust tappets to prevent the tappets from falling through the tappet block into the crankcase when the cylinder block is removed. Turn the engine until the pistons are at T.D.C. then unscrew eight 12 point nuts from the base of the cylinder block and remove eight washers, carefully raise the block clear of the pistons.

Raise the block sufficiently to insert non-fluffy rag into the crankcase mouth. It is also advisable at this stage to fit four rubber protectors (e.g. gear change lever rubbers) over four cylinder base studs (see Fig. B16) to avoid any damage to the alloy connecting rods. Remove the cylinder base gasket and ensure that the two locating dowels are in their correct position in the crankcase.

Remove the tappets from the cylinder block storing them in the order of their removal, and thoroughly clean all parts in paraffin (kerosene). It is important that the tappets are replaced in their original positions; failure to observe this may result in subsequent excessive tappet and cam wear.

If it has been decided to fit new piston rings then the bores must be lightly honed as described in Section B24.

Lubricant is supplied under pressure direct to the exhaust tappet and camshaft working faces as described in Section A2.

When replacing the cylinder block ensure that the cylinder base gasket is not fitted in such a way that the oil feed hole incorporated in the crankcase and cylinder block is obscured, so preventing lubricant from reaching the tappets.

If for any reason the tappet guide block is removed, it should be refitted as described in Section B21, but the oil feed holes should be checked to ensure that they are not blocked by foreign matter.

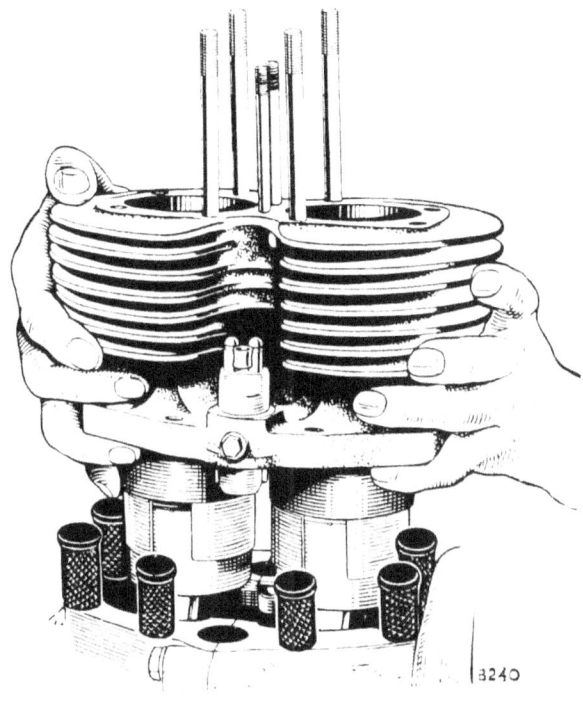

Fig. B16. Refitting the cylinder block

The correct method of assembly of the tappets is shown in Fig. B17. The machined cutaway faces (C) should be facing the outside of the tappet guide block, i.e. the tappets must not be fitted with the cutaways facing one another, otherwise the oil holes (B) drilled in the annular groove of the tappet block (A) will not be able to supply lubricant to the tappets.

Care should be taken to ensure that the cylinder block is correctly located over the two dowels in the left half-crankcase.

The tappets should be well lubricated prior to wedging them in their original positions in the tappet guide blocks. To facilitate an easy assembly of the cylinder block over the pistons, two collars, part number Z22, are required. The collars should be placed over the pistons to compress the piston rings, and withdrawn over the connecting rods when the pistons are sufficiently engaged in the block. Refit the eight cylinder base nuts.

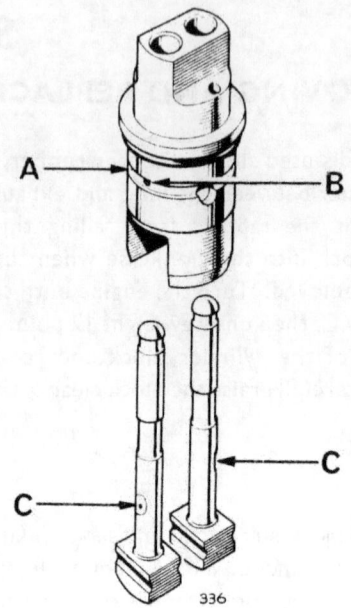

Fig. B17. Showing the correct method of assembly of the exhaust tappets

SECTION B20

INSPECTING THE TAPPETS AND GUIDE BLOCKS

The base of the tappet is fitted with a "Stellite" tip. This material has good wear resisting qualities but the centre of the tip may show signs of slight indentation. If the width of the indentation exceeds $\frac{3}{32}$ in. then the tappet should be renewed.

It is not necessary to remove the tappet guide blocks for inspection purposes; the extent of wear can be estimated by rocking the tappet whilst it is in position in the guide block. It should be a sliding fit with little or no sideways movement, (see "General Data" for working clearances).

Excessive play between the tappets and guide block may cause undesirable mechanical noise.

SECTION B21
RENEWING THE TAPPET GUIDE BLOCKS

Place the cylinder block in an inverted position on the bench. Remove the locking screw and drift out the guide block using service tool 61-6008, as shown in Fig. B18.

"O" ring oil seals are fitted between the tappet blocks and cylinder block. The seals must be replaced whenever oil leakage is noted at this point or whenever the tappet blocks are removed and refitted. Under no circumstances must the tappet guide blocks be interchanged. The exhaust tappets are pressure lubricated through the exhaust tappet guide block and the oilways must therefore be cleaned out carefully before assembly.

To fit the new guide block, first grease the outer surface to assist assembly, then align the location hole in the guide block and cylinder block base, and drive in the guide block using 61-6008, until the shoulder is flush with the flange.

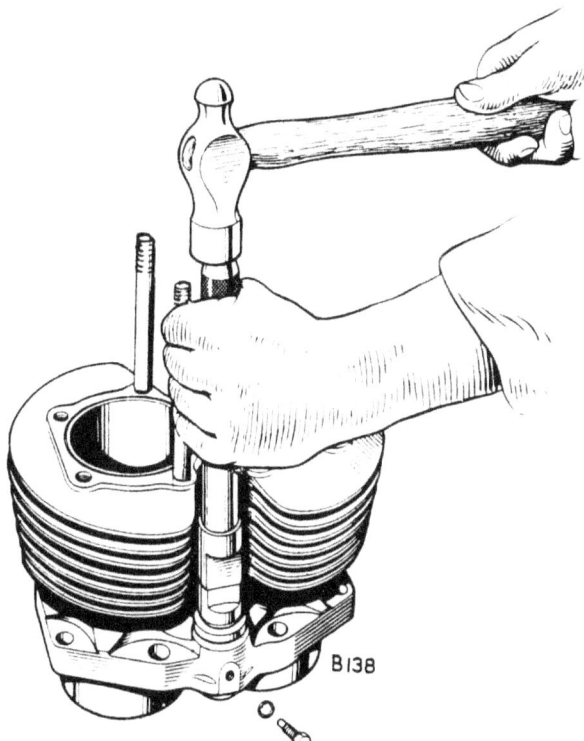

Fig. B18. Refitting a tappet guide block

SECTION B22
REMOVING AND REFITTING THE PISTONS

It is most important that the alloy connecting rods are not damaged by contact with the sharp crankcase edge. For this reason four gear lever rubbers should be placed over the four central cylinder base studs.

Remove the inner and outer circlips and press out the gudgeon pin. The pistons are then free to be removed.

When the pistons are removed they should be suitably scribed inside so that they can be refitted in their original positions. When refitting the pistons, first place the inner circlip in position to act as a stop, then press the gudgeon pin into position.

It is advisable to renew the four circlips; this can be done for negligible cost.

Finally, check that all the gudgeon pin retainer circlips are in position, and are correctly fitted. This is extremely important.

SECTION B23

REMOVING AND REPLACING THE PISTON RINGS

There should be little difficulty in removing piston rings, if the following procedure is adopted. Lift one end of the top piston ring out of the groove and insert a thin steel strip between the ring and piston. Move the strip round the piston, at the same time lifting the raised part of the ring upwards with slight pressure. The piston rings should always be lifted off and replaced over the top of the piston.

If the piston rings are to be refitted the carbon deposits on the inside surface of the rings must be removed and the carbon deposits in the piston ring grooves must also be removed.

When fitting new piston rings, the bores must be lightly honed with a fine-grade emery cloth so that the new piston rings can become bedded down properly. The honing should be carried out with an oscillatory motion up and down the bore until an even "criss-cross" pattern is achieved. The recommended grade of emery for this purpose is 300. Thoroughly wash the bores in paraffin (kerosene) and check that all traces of abrasives are removed.

Pistons and rings are available in ·010 and ·020 inches (·254 and ·508 mm.) oversizes. When fitting new rings the gap must be checked in the lowest part of the cylinder bore. The ring must lie square to the bore for checking purposes, and to ensure this, place the piston crown onto the ring and ease it down the bore. Check the gap with feeler gauges.

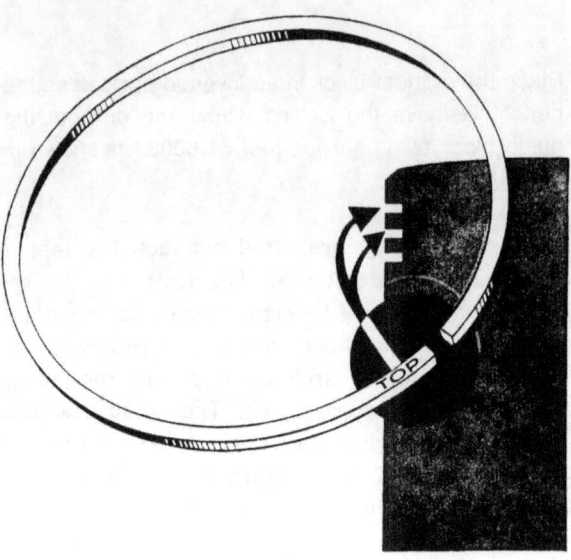

Fig. B19. Refitting a tapered piston ring

Piston rings, when new, should have the following gap clearances:

Compression ring gap: ·010" to ·014" (·25 to ·35 mm.)
Scraper ring gap: ·010" to ·014" (·25 to ·35 mm.)

Refitting the piston rings is straight forward, but check that the two compression rings are fitted the right way up.

The two taper compression rings are marked "TOP" to ensure correct assembly, and should be fitted with the "TOP" marking towards the cylinder head (see Fig. B19).

SECTION B24

INSPECTING THE PISTONS AND CYLINDER BORES

PISTONS
Check the thrust areas of the piston skirt for signs of seizure or scoring.
The piston skirt is of a special oval form and is designed to have limited working clearances within the bore.

Prior to inspection, ensure that both the cylinder bores and the pistons are clean and free from dirt, etc. Any deposits of burnt oil round the piston skirt can be removed by using a petrol (gasolene) soaked cloth.

ENGINE B

NOTE: The top lands of the piston have working clearance varying from ·016 in. to ·020 in. and thus allows the top piston ring to be viewed from above, and the piston to be rocked slightly. However, this is not critical, it is the skirt clearances that are all-important.

CYLINDER BORES

The maximum wear occurs within the top half-inch of the bore, whilst the portion below the piston ring working area remains relatively unworn. A badly worn block will have a lip at the thrust faces of each bore about ¼ in. from top face. Previous symptoms such as smoking exhaust, heavy oil consumption and noisy pistons when cold also indicate that a rebore may be necessary.

CYLINDER BORE AND PISTON GRADING

Pistons and cylinder blocks are graded to suit one another during manufacturing. The pistons are identified by a letter stamped on the piston crown and the barrels by the same letter on the top fin next to the appropriate bore (see Fig. B20). Two different identifications are in use i.e. (L) and (H). Each letter stands for LOW and HIGH grades respectively. The grades with their corresponding dimensions are shown below.

CYLINDER BLOCK AND PISTON GRADING

	LOW (L)	HIGH (H)
DIAMETER OF PISTON (ins)	2·9876/2·9871	2·9882/2·9877
DIAMETER OF PISTON (mm.)	75·885/75·872	75·900/75·888
BORE SIZE (ins.)	2·9918/2·9913	2·9924/2·9919
BORE SIZE (mm.)	75·992/75·979	76·007/75·994

SECTION B25

TABLE OF SUITABLE RE-BORE SIZES

Piston Marking in (mm)	+·010 (·254mm)	+·020 (·508mm)
Suitable bore sizes (ins)	3·0021/3·0010	3·0121/3·0110
Suitable bore sizes (mm)	76·2533/76·2254	76·5073/76·4794

ENGINE

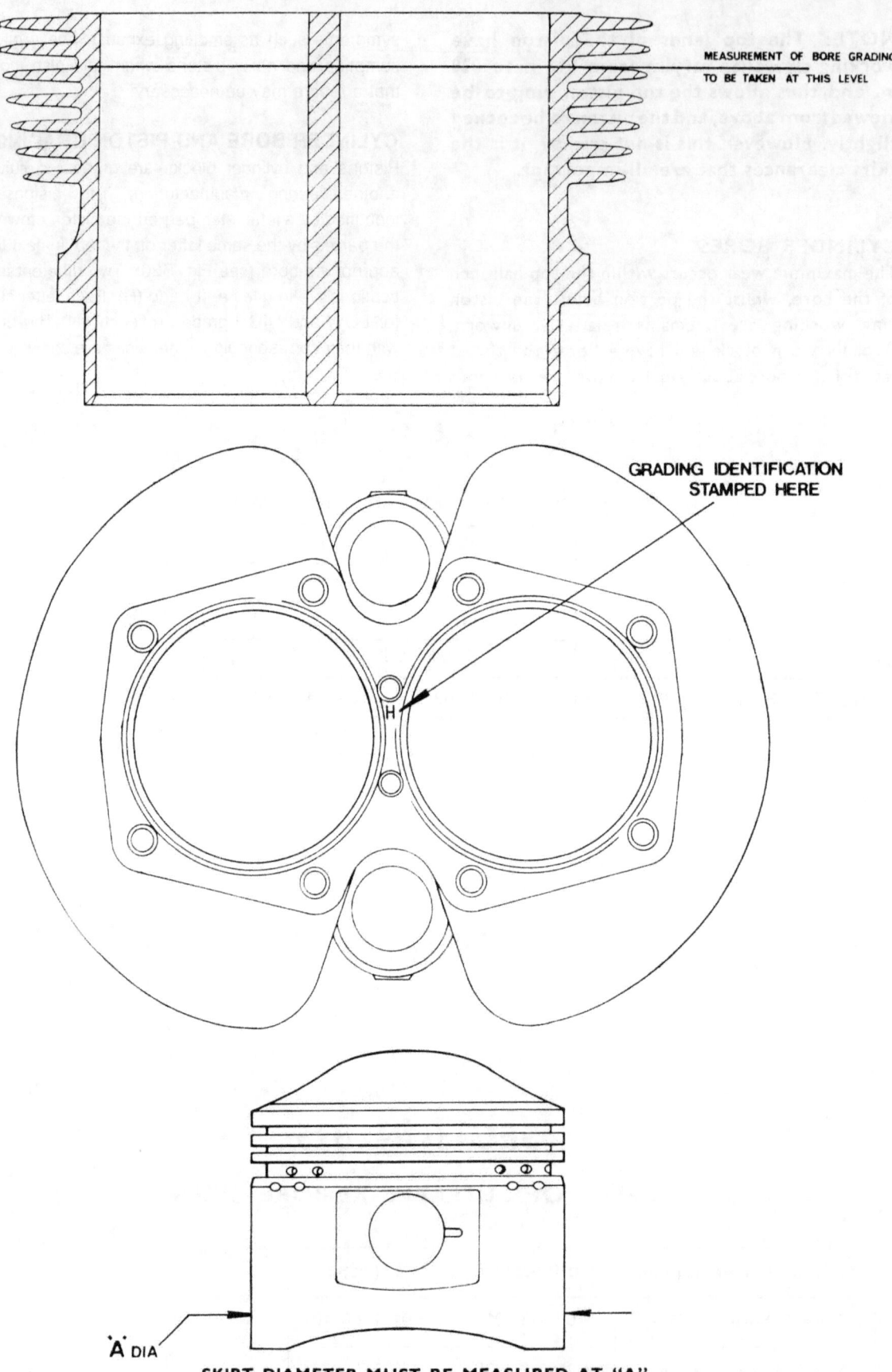

Fig. 20. Cylinder block and piston grading details.

ENGINE

SECTION B26

REMOVING AND REPLACING THE CONTACT BREAKER

The contact breaker mechanism is housed in the timing cover on the right of the engine and is driven by the exhaust camshaft. It consists of two sets of points (one per cylinder), two auxiliary backplates with cam adjustment and a fully automatic centrifugal type advance and retard mechanism. The working parts are protected by a circular cover and gasket. The engine oil is prevented from entering the contact breaker cavity by means of an oil seal fitted to the inner wall of the timing cover. The complete contact breaker unit can be removed from the timing cover with the aid of service tool 61-7023.

First, disconnect the leads from the battery terminals or remove the fuse from the holder adjacent to the battery, then remove the two screws and withdraw the outer cover and gasket. Remove the centre bolt and screw in service tool 61-7023 until the cam unit is released from its locking taper in the camshaft. Unscrew the tool and remove the cam unit.

To completely detach the contact breaker unit it will be necessary to disconnect the two leads from the ignition coils and remove the appropriate frame clips so that the leads can be withdrawn through the holes in the crankcase and timing cover.

It is advisable to make a note of the degree figure which is stamped on the back of the cam unit, as this indicates the advance range, which it is necessary to know for accurate static timing purposes.

Prior to replacing the cam unit it is advisable to add a small drop of lubricating oil to the pivot pins only, not the cam pivot. The cam unit slot should be located on the peg in the camshaft and the centre bolt screwed in and tightened.

IMPORTANT NOTE: "Run out" on the contact breaker cam or misalignment of the secondary backplate centre hole can result in contact between the cam and backplate. This can result in the auto advance remaining retarded or the spark retarding. To check for "run-out" check the point gap with the contact nylon heel aligned with the cam scribe mark for each set of points. Should there be a discrepancy greater than 0.003in. (0.076mm.) tap the outer edge of the cam with a brass drift with the cam securing bolt tight. In cases of misalignment of the secondary backplate hole, check the cam clearance in different positions and elongate the hole only where the backplate rubs the cam.

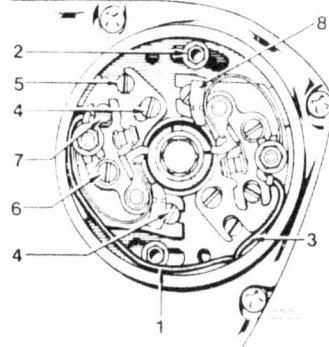

1. Black/yellow
2. Pillar bolt
3. Black/white
4. Secondary bracket screw
5. Eccentric screw
6. Contact locking screw
7. Contact eccentric adjusting screw
8. Lubricating pad

Fig. B21. Contact breaker

To adjust the contact breaker gaps, turn the motor with the starter pedal until the scribe mark on the cam aligns with the nylon heel of one set of points. Measure the point gap using a 0.015in. (0.38mm.) feeler gauge. If outside the limits, slacken the contact adjusting screw, adjust the gap by turning the eccentric screw, and re-tighten the adjusting screw.

Revolve the motor until the second set of points is lined up with the scribe line, and adjust as before.

NOTE: Setting the ignition timing is fully described in Sections B27 to B29.

SECTION B27

IGNITION TIMING — INITIAL PROCEDURE

Initial assembly of the contact breaker mechanism and auto advance unit prior to final timing of the engine:—

(1) Remove both sparking plugs and all four rocker box caps. Set the engine at T.D.C. with both valves closed in the right hand cylinder.

(2) Assemble the auto advance unit into the exhaust camshaft, locating on the camshaft peg where it is fitted.

(3) Assemble the C.B. plate taking care not to trap the C.B. leads, assembling the plate so that one set of C.B. points is located at 7 o'clock. Loosely assemble the hexagonal pillar bolts and flat washers.

(4) Lock the auto advance cam into the taper using the central fixing bolt. For static timing remove the bolt again, taking care not to release the taper of the cam. Temporarily fit another washer with a centre hole just large enough to fit over the cam bearing, thus allowing the washer to bear hard on the end of the cam. Rotate the cam carefully to its limit against the auto advance springs, holding in this position whilst the centre bolt is re-fitted and nipped up. The fully advanced position has then been located.

SECTION B28

STATIC TIMING WHERE NO STROBOSCOPE IS AVAILABLE

Rotate the engine until the nylon heel of the C.B. points aligns with the scribe marking on the cam. At this stage set both points gaps to 0·015in. (0·38mm.)

Locate the crankshaft at 38° B.T.D.C. using the timing body and plunger 61-2195 and 61-572 as shown.

It will be found easiest to start with the pistons at T.D.C. (checked through the sparking plug hole) and then, with both sparking plugs removed and second gear engaged, rotate the rear wheel backwards. As the crank is turned by this means, pressure on the timing plunger will locate it at 38° B.T.D.C. Remove the rocker caps to establish which cylinder is on the compression stroke (i.e. which cylinder has both valves closed). Note that the timing side cylinder is operated by the contact points with the black/yellow lead and the drive side with the black/white lead.

When it has been decided which cylinder is being timed, rotate the main contact breaker backplate in its slots until the particular contact points just open. This can be checked using a battery and light or by an 0·0015in. (0·038mm.) feeler gauge between the points.

Attention should now be turned to the other cylinder. Remove the timing plunger, turn the engine forwards through 360° (1 revolution) and relocate the timing plunger. The second set of points should now be adjusted as above but the main backplate must not be disturbed. Adjust only on the secondary backplate. Finally secure all screws, lubricate both sides of the cam with Shell Retinax A grease, replace the cover plate and the sparking plugs, finally engaging neutral gear.

ENGINE

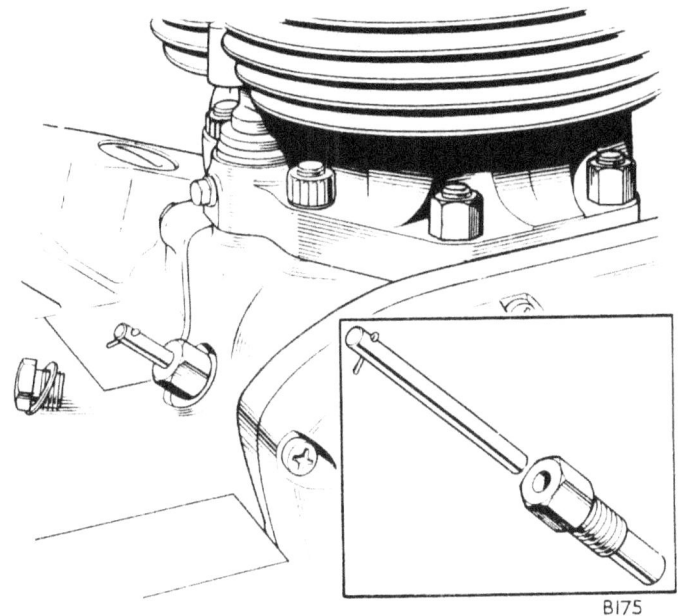

Fig. B22. Showing T.D.C. body and plunger in situ

SECTION B29
IGNITION TIMING BY STROBOSCOPE

Undertake the initial procedure as in Section B29.

Remove the inspection plate secured by three screws from the primary chaincase. As seen in Fig. B23 there is a marking on the outer face of the rotor which is to coincide with an ignition pointer on the primary chaincase to achieve the correct 38° ignition timing position.

NOTE: When using a stroboscope powered by a 12 volt battery as on external power source, do not use the machines own battery equipment. (A.C. pulses in the low tension machine wiring can trigger the stroboscope and give false readings).

Fig. B23. Rotor marking

(1) Connect the stroboscope to the right hand spark plug lead and start the engine. Read the strobo-light on the rotor marking in relation to the timing pointer with the engine-running at 2,000-R.P.M. or more.

Adjust the main backplate on its slots until the marks align whereupon the timing on the one cylinder is correct.

(2) Repeat for the L.H. plug and adjust the timing by slackening off the clamping screw on the auxilliary backplate and turning the eccentric screw (see Fig. B21) until again the markings align. Timing is then correct. Refit the primary chaincase inspection plate.

ENGINE

SECTION B30

REMOVING AND REPLACING THE TIMING COVER

Remove the contact breaker as described in Section B28.

Disconnect the oil switch lead at the spade terminal. Unscrew the eight recessed screws which serve to retain the timing cover and if necessary tap the cover on the front blanking plug with a hide mallet until the cover is free. When the cover is removed, the crankshaft and contact breaker oil seals should be inspected for wear and cracks and renewed if necessary. To remove the crankshaft oil seal, the retainer circlip must first be removed by means of long-nosed pliers or a narrow screwdriver.

Unscrew the hexagonal plug from the front edge of the cover and thoroughly clean all parts in paraffin (kerosene). Clean out the oil drillings with a jet of compressed air and replace the plug and copper washer.

The oil pressure switch in the front of the timing cover has a taper thread and requires no sealant on the threads, for competition use a blanking plug is available to take the place of the switch.

To replace the cover, first check that the oil seals are facing in the correct direction (see Fig. B24) and that the circlip is located correctly in its groove, then carefully clean the junction surfaces of the timing cover and crankcase and remove any traces of used jointing compound. Apply a fresh coat of a suitable proprietary jointing compound evenly over the timing cover junction surface. Screw the tapered adaptor pilot (service tool 61-7013) into the exhaust camshaft and smear it with oil to assist assembly. Check that both the location dowels are in their correct positions, slide the cover into position and screw in the eight recessed screws.

Finally, replace the contact breaker assembly and reset the ignition timing as shown in Sections B27 to B29.

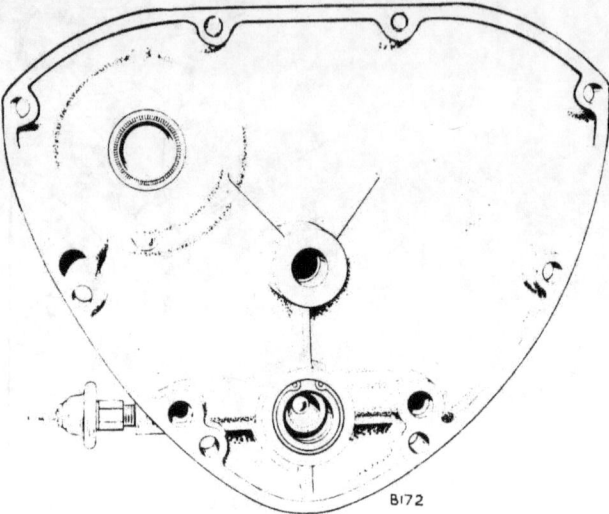

Fig. B24. Timing cover oil seal location

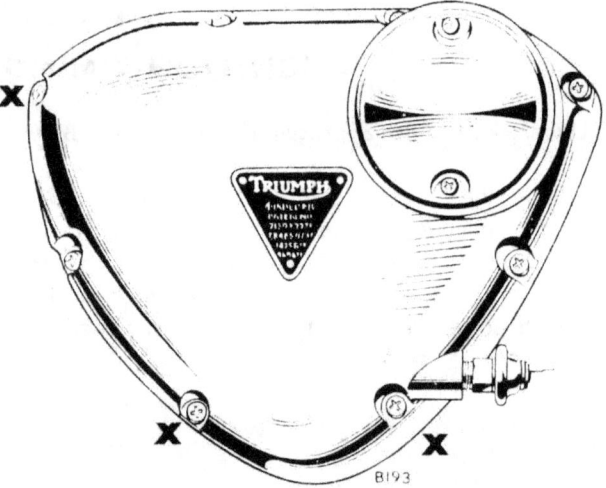

Fig: B25. Location of three long screws in timing cover

NOTE: The three longer screws should be fitted in the holes marked "X" in Fig. B24.

SECTION B31

REMOVING AND REPLACING THE OIL PUMP

To remove the oil pump, first remove the contact breaker mechanism, and the timing cover as described in Sections B26 and B30.

The oil pump is held in position by two conical nuts. When these are removed, the oil pump can be withdrawn from the mounting studs. The paper gasket should be renewed.

Full details concerning inspection, testing and rectification of the oil pump are given in Section A6.

When replacing the oil pump, care should be taken to ensure that the new gasket is fitted correctly and that the cones of the conical nuts and washers fit into the counter-sunk holes in the oil pump body.

ENGINE

SECTION B32

EXTRACTING AND REFITTING THE VALVE TIMING PINIONS

Before attempting to remove any of the valve timing gears it is necessary to release the load on the camshafts caused by compressed valve springs. This should be done by removing the rocker boxes as detailed in Section B2, or may be achieved by sufficiently slackening the valve clearance adjuster screws; however, this is not always advisable as it may result in a push rod becoming disengaged.

Remove the contact breaker as detailed in Section B26.

Remove the timing cover as described in Section B30 and the oil pump as shown in Section B31. Select 5th (top) gear, apply the rear brake and unscrew the nuts retaining the camshaft and crankshaft pinions, then withdraw the intermediate wheel.

NOTE: The camshaft pinion retainer nuts have **LEFT-HAND** threads. The crankshaft pinion retainer nut has a **RIGHT-HAND** thread.

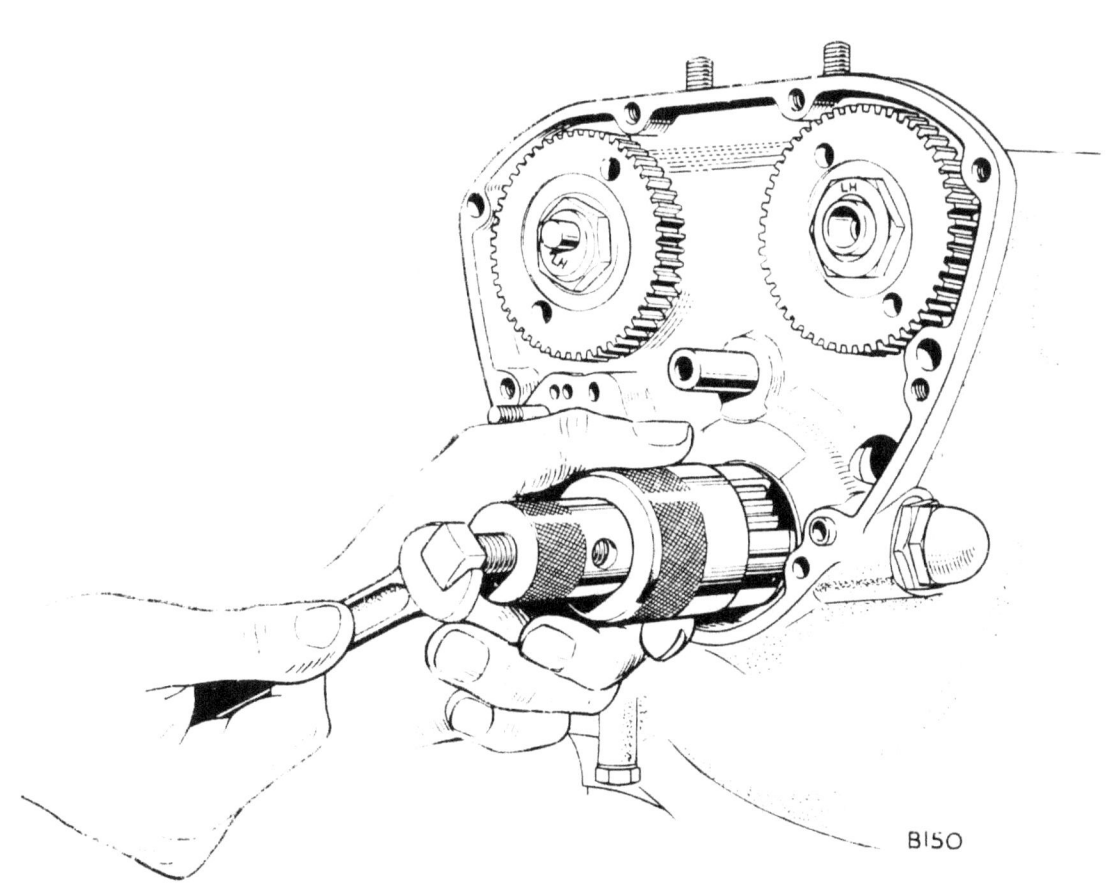

Fig. B26. Extracting the crankshaft pinion

CRANKSHAFT PINION

Removal of the crankshaft pinion is facilitated by service tool 61-6019, which consists of a protective cap and three claw extractor body, complete with extractor bolt.

To extract the pinion, first press the protection cap over the end of the crankshaft, then place the extractor over the pinion, locate the three claws behind the pinion and screw down the body to secure them. Using a tommy bar and spanner the crankshaft pinion can then be extracted (see Fig. B26). When this is achieved, the key and (clamping washer if fitted) should be removed and placed in safe-keeping.

When replacing the clamping washer ensure that the chamfered side is towards the crankshaft shoulder. Screw the guide onto the crakshaft. Smear the bore of the crankshaft pinion with grease to assist assembly and position it over the guide, so that the counter bore is outwards. Align the key and keyway and drive the pinion onto the crankshaft.

CAMSHAFT PINIONS

To extract both the inlet and exhaust camshaft pinions extractor Pr. No. 61-6132 should be used. To extract pinion screw the two outrigger bolts into the camwheel and screw in the central bolt; the pinion will then be withdrawn from the camshaft. See Fig. B28.

The location keys in each of the camshafts are a tight fit and may be left in position if it is not intended to subsequently remove the camshafts from the crankcase. When replacing the camwheels use a suitable hollow drift and lightly drive the camwheels onto the camshaft as far as possible. They will not drive fully home because of the camshaft float, but when the retaining nuts are replaced and tightened the camwheels will then seat into position.

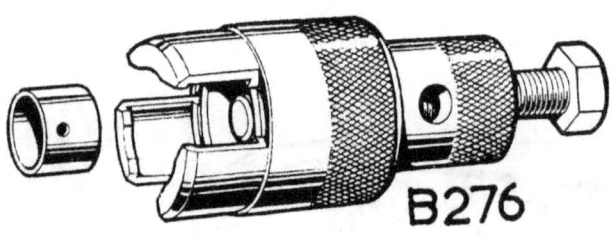

Fig. B27. Extractor tool 61-6019 showing protection cap which fits over crankshaft

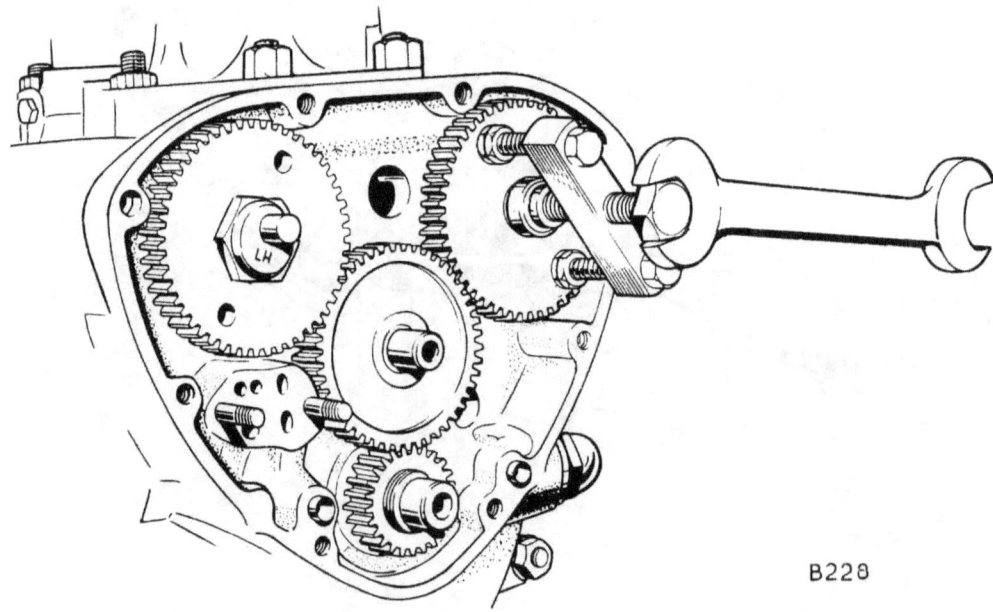

Fig. B28. Extracting the cam wheels

ENGINE B

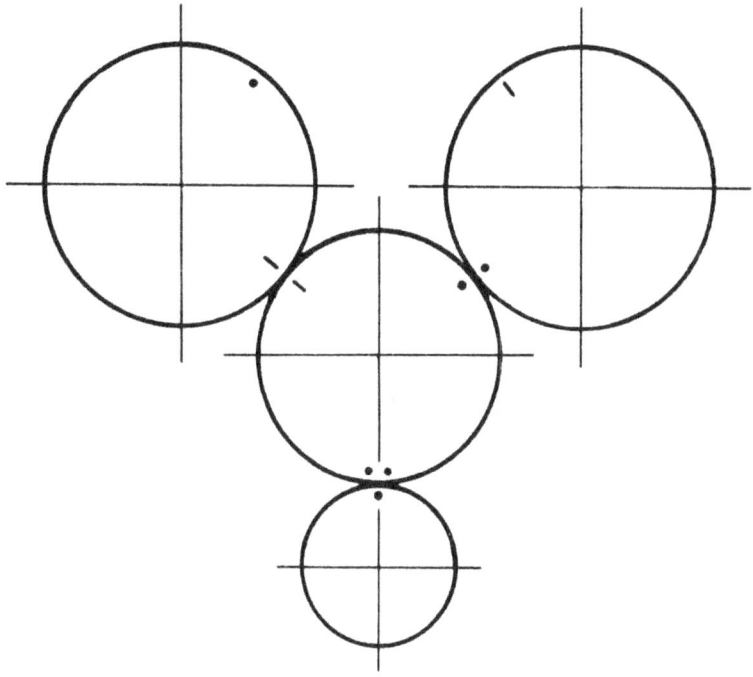

Fig. 29. Valve timing marks from ENG No. CX06001

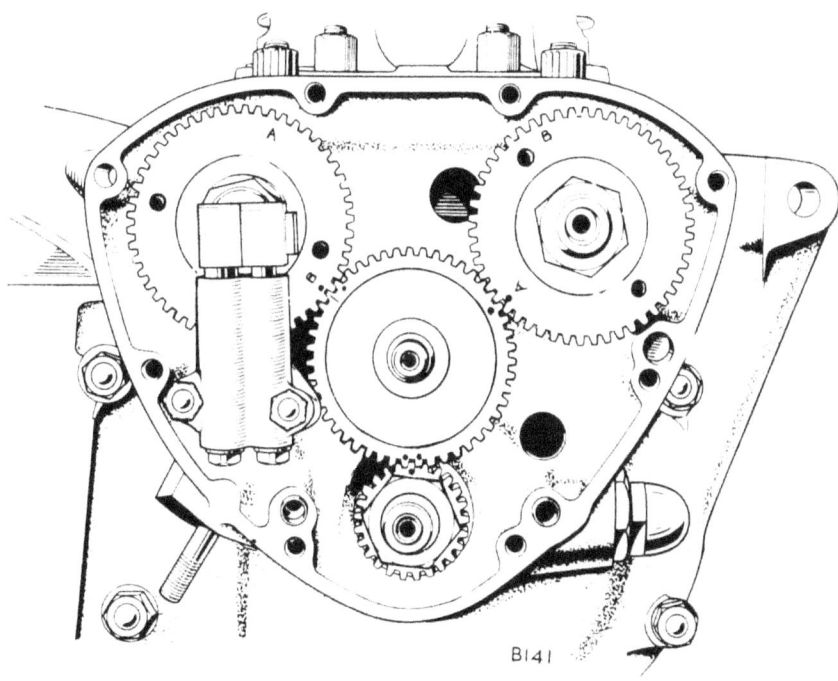

Fig. B30. Valve timing marks – EARLY MODELS ONLY

SECTION B33

VALVE TIMING

The valve timing is sufficiently accurate for machines which are to be used under normal conditions, when the intermediate wheel is assembled in the position shown in Fig. B29, (Fig. 30 refers to EARLY MODELS only), and the camshaft pinions are located by means of the keyway directly opposite the timing mark.

It should be noted that, due to the intermediate wheel having a prime number of teeth, the timing marks only coincide every 94th revolution, thus there is no cause for alarm if the timing marks will not readily re-align.

When checking the valve timing against the figures given in "General Data" for the particular model, it should be noted that these figures are relative to a valve rocker clearance of ·020 in. (·5 mm.) for checking only.

SECTION B34

DISMANTLING AND REASSEMBLING THE CRANKCASE ASSEMBLY

It is advisable to partially dismantle the engine unit whilst it is fixed to the motorcycle, then remove the remaining crankcase assembly and dismantle it on a work bench.

Proceed as described in Section B1 for removal of the engine unit, but leave the rear chain connected and the engine firmly mounted in the frame by means of the front and bottom engine mounting bolts. Remove the outer primary cover as shown underneath the engine (two snap connectors).

Unscrew three nuts securing the stator and withdraw it from over the mounting studs. Do not try to withdraw the leads at this stage.

Remove the pressure plate and clutch plates as detailed in Section C4. Select 5th gear and apply the rear brake, then unscrew the clutch hub securing nut and extract the clutch hub with the gearchange shaft as shown in Section C9. When the primary chain has been threaded over the stator the sleeve nut should be unscrewed and the stator leads withdrawn.

Remove the gearbox outer cover and dismantle the gearbox (see Section D) then remove the rocker boxes, cylinder head, block and pistons as shown in Sections B2, B14, B19 and B22 respectively, then disconnect the control cable(s) and remove the carburetter(s).

Remove the contact breaker, timing cover complete with oil switch and oil pump (Sections B28, B32 and B33) then extract the crankshaft pinion. If it is required to inspect or change the camshafts or bushes, the camshaft pinions should also be extracted.

Remove the front and bottom engine mounting studs, disconnect the rear chain and remove the crankcase assembly.

Remove the crankcase filter and oilway blanking plug located at the bottom of the crankcase in line with the oil pump, and catch any oil that may be present in the crankcase.

Grip the crankcase firmly in a vice by means of the bottom mounting lug and unscrew the three bolts from the left side which are situated at the cylinder barrel spigots and rear of the primary drive breather outlet. Then the remaining four studs and unscrew two nuts adjacent to the gearbox housing. The crankcase-halves may now be parted. If difficulty is encountered parting the crankcase halves it will be due to the front TOP (crankcase to frame) hollow dowel which is a press fit. Prior to splitting the crankcase drift the dowel out of position using a suitable bar (an old rocker shaft is ideal for this purpose). When the halves are apart, withdraw the crankshaft assembly and store it carefully.

Remove the timing side main bearing, See Section B38.

Thoroughly clean and degrease the crankcase paying particular attention to the oilways. DO NOT DAMAGE the scavenge pipe to crankcase joint.

ENGINE

REASSEMBLY

Prior to reassembly, the junction surfaces should be carefully scraped clean, giving special attention to the location spigot and dowels. Replace the oilway blanking plug located at the bottom of the R/H crankcase in line with the oil pump, and crankcase filter.

Mount the left half-crankcase on its side on two wooden blocks, or a bench with a hole in for crankshaft clearance, lubricate the main bearings and camshaft bushes. Assemble the crankshaft into position ensuring that it is right home in the bearing by giving it a sharp blow with a hide mallet.

Apply a fresh coat of jointing compound to the junction surface of the left half-crankcase then lubricate the main bearings and camshaft bushes in both halves of the crankcase. Position the con-rods centrally and lower the right half-crankcase into position over the crankshaft. When the halves are mated, check the crankshaft and camshafts for freedom of rotation. The crankshaft should revolve freely whilst the camshafts should offer little or no resistance to rotation by hand.

Refit the crankcase securing bolts and studs, and tighten them until they are just "pinched-up".

Check that the cylinder block junction surface of the crankcase is level.

If there is a slight step between the two halves, this should be corrected by tapping the front and rear of the crankcases as required, until a level surface is achieved. The crankcase securing bolts should then be tightened, a turn at a time, to the torque figures given in "General Data".

Reassembly then continues as a reversal of the dismantling instructions. Prior to refitting the cylinder block, pour approximately ¼ pint (0·14 litres) of oil into the crankcase.

SECTION B35
SERVICING THE CRANKSHAFT ASSEMBLY

Grip the crankshaft conveniently in a suitable vice and place rag over any sharp edges to avoid the connecting rods becoming damaged. Mark the connecting rods, caps and crankshaft so that they can be replaced in their original positions.

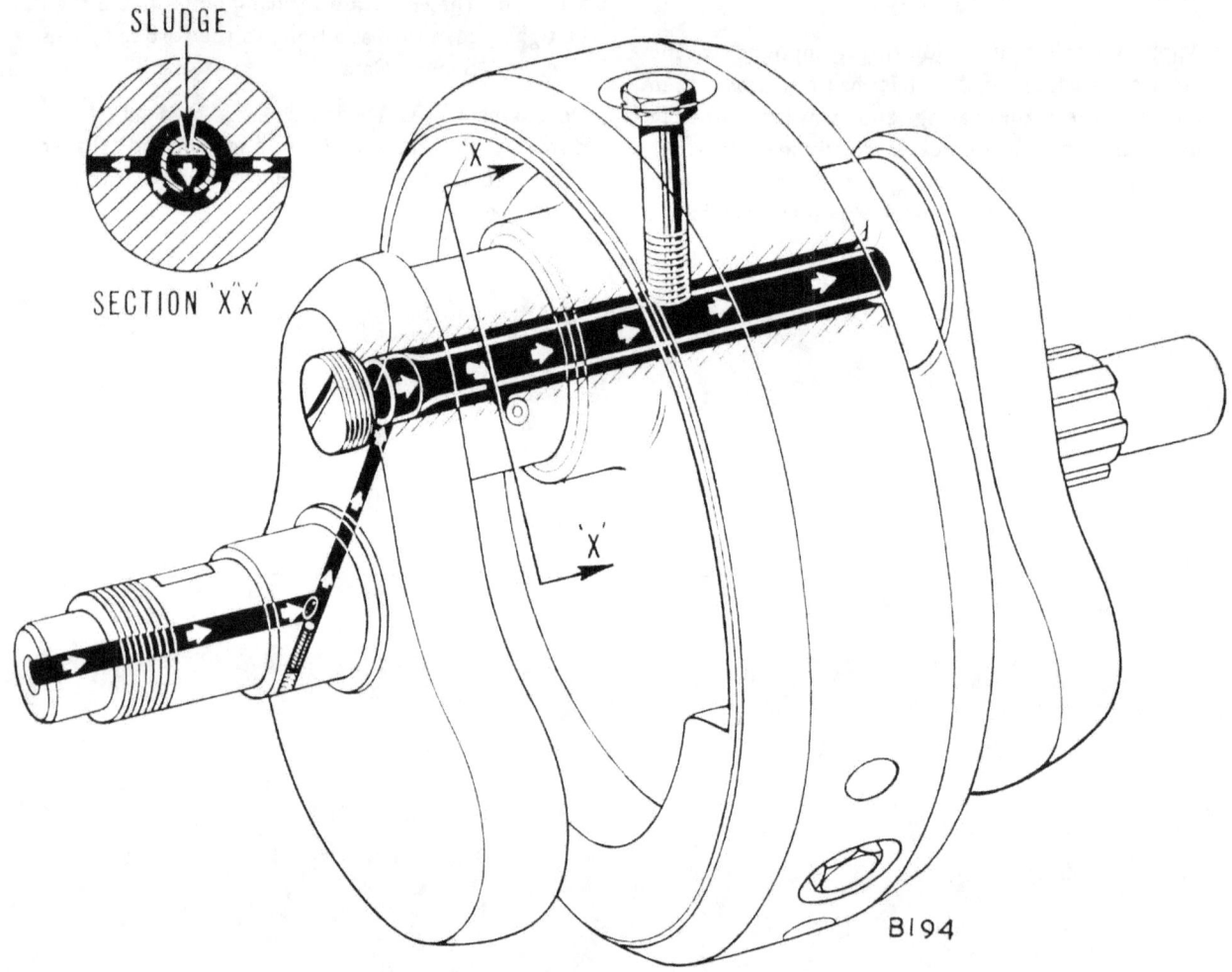

Fig. B31. Sectional view of crankshaft—showing oil tube

ENGINE

Unscrew the cap retainer nuts, a turn at a time to avoid distortion, then remove the caps and connecting rods. Refit the nuts to their respective bolts to ensure correct reassembly.

Using a large impact screwdriver, unscrew the oil tube retainer plug from the right end of the big-end journal. If difficulty is encountered, drill a ⅛in. (3mm.) dia. hole to ⅛in. (3mm.) depth in the crankshaft, to remove the centre punched indentation which locks the oil tube retainer plug in position.

Unscrew the flywheel bolt adjacent to the big-end journal, then withdraw the oil tube using a hooked rod located in the flywheel bolt location hole (see Fig. 31).

Thoroughly clean all parts in paraffin (kerosene) then clean the oil drillings using a jet of compressed air. Particular attention should be given to checking that each oil drilling is free from blockage.

SECTION B36
REFITTING THE CONNECTING RODS

First, ensure that the connecting rod and cap and both the front and rear of the bearing shells are scrupulously clean, then offer the shells to the rod and cap and locate the shell tabs into their respective slots. Smear the bearing surfaces with oil and refit the rod and cap to their original journals, ensuring that the tab location slots are adjacent (see Fig. B32).

Refit the bolts and screw on the nuts to the given torque figure.

Finally, force oil through the drilling at the right end of the crankshaft with a pressure oil can until it is expelled from both big-end bearings, thus indicating that the oil passages are free from blockage and full of oil.

NOTE: The connecting rod, cap and nut are centre punched on initial assembly so that the cap may be refitted correctly relative to the connecting rod.

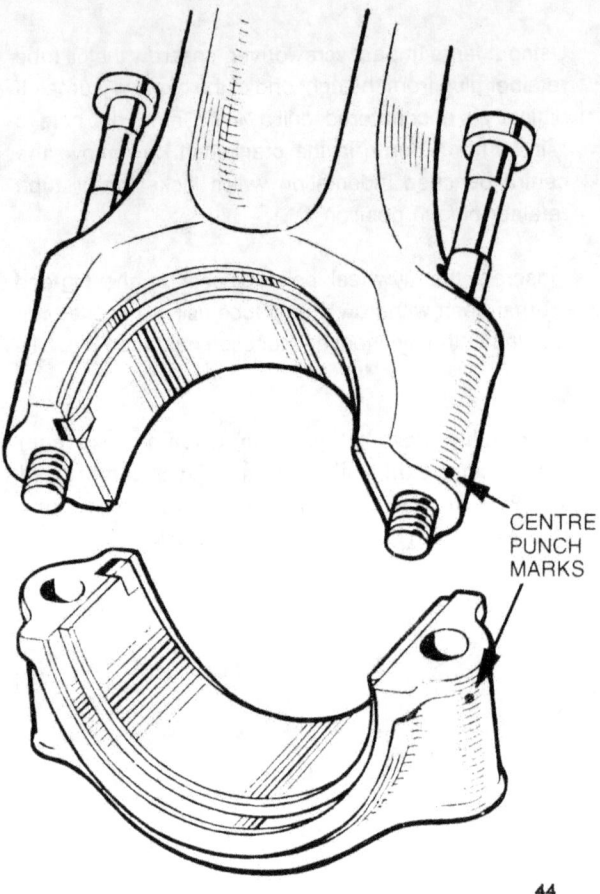

Fig. B32. Refitting the connecting rods

SECTION B37

INSPECTING THE CRANKCASE COMPONENTS

In preparation for inspection, thoroughly clean the crankcase-halves, main bearings, crankshaft and connecting rods, etc., in paraffin (kerosene) and allow them to drain. If there is an air pump accessible, then dry the components with a jet of compressed air and examine them as follows:—

(1) BIG-END BEARINGS

The extent of wear to the big-end journals can be determined by inspecting the bearing surfaces for scoring and by measuring the diameter of the journals. Light score marks can be reduced with smooth emery cloth but ensure that all parts are carefully washed after this operation.

Where a journal has been slightly scored the big-end shell bearings should be renewed. If the scoring and wear is extensive the big-end journals should be reground to a suitable size as given below.

NOTE: The replaceable white metal big-end bearings are pre-finished to give the correct diametral clearance. Under no circumstances should the bearings be scraped or the connecting rod and cap joint faces filed.

Shell bearing marking	Suitable crankshaft size	
	in.	mm.
Standard:—	1·6235 1·6240	41·237 41·250
Undersize:— —·010	1·6135 1·6140	40·983 40·996
—·020	1·6035 1·6040	40·729 40·742

Service re-ground crankshafts are available from your TRIUMPH dealer.

(2) MAIN BEARINGS

Clean the bearings thoroughly in paraffin (kerosene), then dry them with a jet of compressed air. Test the bearing for roughness by spinning. Check the centre race for side-play and inspect the balls and tracks for any signs of indentation and pocketing. Examine the main bearing diameters on the crankshaft for wear. The bearings should be a tight push fit on the crankshaft and a press fit in the crankcase. A loose fitting bearing would tend to cause crankcase "rumble". The correct diameters of the main bearing journals are given in "General Data".

(3) CAMSHAFTS AND BUSHES

The camshaft bushes normally show very little sign of wear until a considerable mileage has been covered. A rough check on the wear can be made by inserting the camshaft into the bearing and feeling the up and down movement. An exact check can be made by measuring the camshaft with a micrometer and measuring the camshaft bushes with calipers. The working clearance figures are given in "General Data". Wear on the cam form will be mainly centred on the opening flank of the cam and on the lobe of the cam. Particular attention should be given to these areas when examining the cam form for grooving. In a case where there is severe grooving the camshaft and tappet followers should be renewed.

A method of estimating the extent of wear on the cam form is that of measuring the over-all height of the cam and the base-circle diameter. The difference is the cam lift. If all other aspects of the camshaft are satisfactory and the wear on the cam form does not exceed 0·010in. (0·25mm.) then the camshaft may be used for further service.

(4) CRANKCASE FACES AND DOWELS

Ensure that the faces of the crankcases are not damaged in any way and that any dowels are in position, particularly the metering dowel on the timing cover face near the pressure release valve. The dowel is counter bored, incorporates a metering pin, and should be assembled with the larger bore outermost.

SECTION B38
RENEWING THE MAIN BEARINGS

To remove the timing side ball journal bearing heat the crankcase to approximately 100°C and drive the bearing inwards. A suitable drift can be made from a piece of 1¼in. (31mm.) diameter mild steel bar, about 6in. (150mm.) long by turning it to 1⅛in. (28·6mm.) diameter for ½in. (12mm.) at one end.

On the drive side roller bearing the inner portion will be withdrawn with the crankshaft. The outer spool however will still involve heating the crankcase and if it is very tight in the case will require the use of special tool 61-7017 which expands to grip the outer spool.

The roller and cap can be removed from the crankshaft using a suitable extractor.

To assemble the new bearings first ensure that the main bearing housing is clean, then heat the crankcase to approximately 100°C and drive in the bearing using a tubular drift onto the outer race. Ensure that the bearing enters its housing squarely. If possible, use a press. Suitable dimensions for the drift are 2¾in. (70mm.) outside diameter × 6in. (150mm.) long.

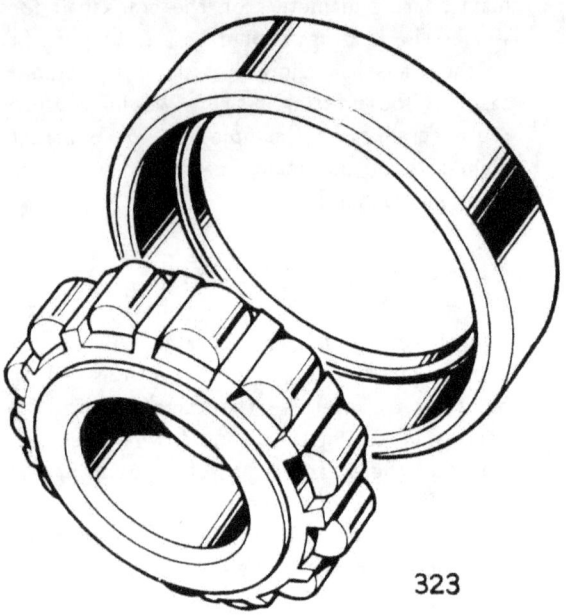

Fig. B33. Roller main bearing

ENGINE

SECTION B39
RENEWING CAMSHAFT BUSHES

To remove the camshaft bushes in the RIGHT half-crankcase heat the crankcase to 100°C and drive the bush out from the outside, using a suitable drift. While the crankcase is still hot, drive in the new bush, ensuring that the oil feed hole in the bush and the crankcase drilling are aligned. A suitable drift for this purpose can be made from a 6in. (150mm.) long piece of M.S. bar of 1⅛in. (28·6mm.) diameter, by machining a pilot on one end ⅞in. (22·2mm.) ×1in. (25mm.) long.

To remove the camshaft bush from the LEFT half-crankcase, a tap is necessary. An ideal size is ⅞ in. diameter x 9 Whit. When a good thread has been cut in the old bush, heat the crankcase (100°C.) and screw in a suitable bolt. Grip the bolt in a vice and drive the crankcase with a hide mallet until the bush is removed. Do not attempt to lever the bush out of position with the bolt, or the case may be damaged. If the tap is used in place of the bolt, care must be taken not to give too hard a knock to the crankcase or the brittle tap may break.

Retained behind the inlet camshaft bush is the breather valve porting disc, which is located by means of a peg. When renewing the bush ensure that the disc is located correctly on the peg.

The sintered bronze camshaft bushes are machined to size before pressing in, therefore only the smallest amount of metal will need to be removed when they are renewed. See "General Data" for reaming sizes and working clearances.

When reaming is completed, the crankcase must be thoroughly washed in paraffin (kerosene) and allowed to drain. Preferably, use a jet of compressed air to ensure that all swarf is removed.

SECTION B40
REMOVING AND REPLACING THE TACHOMETER DRIVE

Where the optional tachometer is fitted, there is a right angled drive gearbox as shown in Fig. B34. It is not necessary to part the crankcases to remove the drive gearbox. When the large slotted end cap is removed and the engine turned over quickly the drive gear should be ejected. If this is not so, the gear can be withdrawn with long-nosed pliers. The left-hand threaded centre bolt holding the drive gearbox to the crankcase will then be seen. A thin box spanner is needed to release this and the box will then come away from the crankcase. The driven gear housing is secured by a locking pin and is a relatively tight fit.

It will be noted that a spade in the back of the tachometer gearbox slots into a slotted plug which is permanently driven into the end of the exhaust camshaft.

The reassembly procedure for the drive gearbox is the reversal of the above.

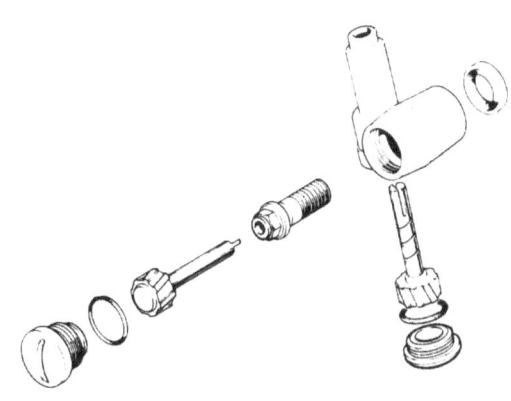

Fig. B34. Exploded view of tachometer gearbox

SECTION C

TRANSMISSION

DESCRIPTION	Section
ADJUSTING THE CLUTCH OPERATING MECHANISM	C1
ADJUSTING THE PRIMARY CHAIN TENSION	C2
REMOVING AND REPLACING THE PRIMARY COVER	C3
REMOVING AND REFITTING THE CLUTCH PLATES	C4
INSPECTING THE CLUTCH PLATES AND SPRINGS	C5
ADJUSTING THE CLUTCH PRESSURE PLATE	C6
RENEWING SHOCK ABSORBER RUBBERS	C7
REMOVING AND REPLACING THE STATOR AND ROTOR	C8
REMOVING AND REPLACING THE CLUTCH AND ENGINE SPROCKETS	C9
INSPECTION OF THE TRANSMISSION COMPONENTS	C10
CLUTCH AND ENGINE SPROCKET ALIGNMENT	C11
REAR CHAIN ALTERATIONS AND REPAIRS	C12

TRANSMISSION

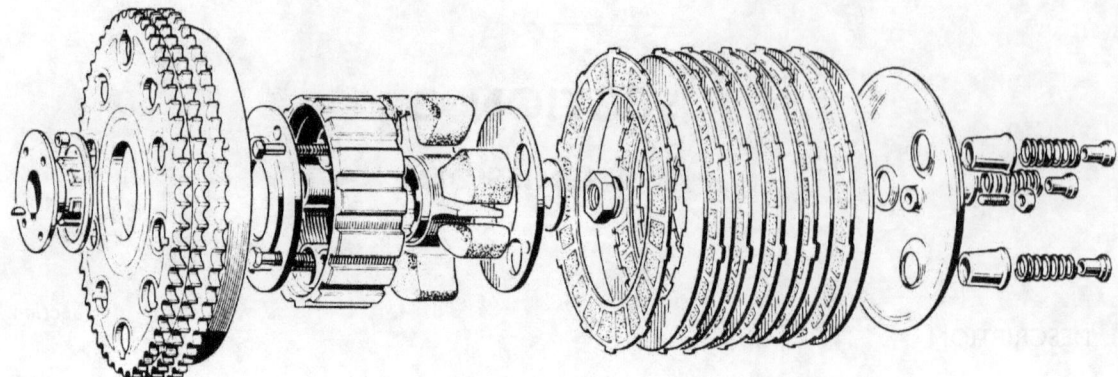

Fig. C1. General arrangement of clutch and shock absorber unit

DESCRIPTION

The clutch is of a multiplate type, using synthetic friction material on the bonded drive plates and incorporating a transmission shock absorber. The pressure on the clutch plates is maintained by three springs held in position by three slotted nuts.

The clutch is designed to operate in oil and it is essential that the oil level in the chaincase is maintained, otherwise the bonded segments of the driven clutch plates may burn and disintegrate under heavy loading. Always use the recommended grade of oil (see Section A1). If a heavier grade of oil is used the clutch plates will not readily separate when disengaged, which will cause a certain amount of difficulty when changing gear due to clutch drag.

The shock absorbing unit transmits the power from the clutch sprocket via the clutch plates to the gearbox mainshaft. Within the shock absorber unit the drive is transmitted through three large rubber pads to the three-armed spider which is splined to the clutch centre; this in turn is located to the gearbox mainshaft by means of a locking taper and key. In addition, there are three rubber rebound pads. The total effect of the rubber pads is to reduce the variations in engine torque at low speeds, providing an extremely smooth transmission of power to the gearbox.

SECTION C1

ADJUSTING THE CLUTCH OPERATING MECHANISM

The clutch, which is situated within the outer primary cover on the left of the machine, can be adjusted by means of the handlebar adjuster, pushrod adjuster and the pressure plate springs, the latter only being accessible for adjustment when the outer primary cover is removed. Section C4 fully describes adjusting the springs and pressure plate.

The clutch operating rod should have $\frac{1}{16}$ inches (1·5 mm.) clearance between the clutch operating mechanism and the pressure plate. To achieve this remove the inspection cap from the centre of the primary cover, then slacken the clutch cable handlebar adjustment right off.

Unscrew the hexagonal lock nut and screw in the slotted adjuster screw in the centre of the pressure plate until the pressure plate just begins to lift. Unscrew the adjuster one full turn and secure it in that position by re-tightening the lock-nut.

The clutch operating cable should then be re-adjusted, by means of the handlebar adjuster, until there is approximately $\frac{1}{8}$ inches (3 mm.) free movement in the cable.

TRANSMISSION

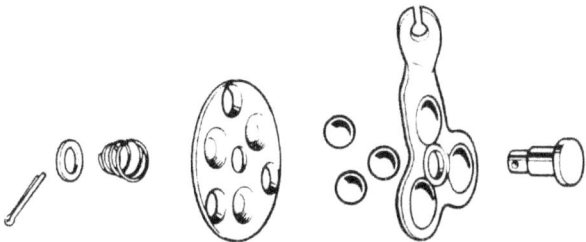

Fig. C2. Exploded view of clutch operating mechanism

If the clutch is dragging and normal adjustment of the operating rod and operating cable produces no improvement, it will be necessary to remove the outer primary cover and check the pressure plate for true running as shown in Section C6.

To maintain a smooth and easy clutch operation, particular attention should be given to the recommended primary chaincase oil change periods (see "Routine Maintenance") and clutch cable lubrication (see Section A17).

SECTION C2
ADJUSTING THE PRIMARY CHAIN TENSION

The primary chain is of the triplex type and is non-adjustable as the centres of the engine mainshaft and gearbox mainshaft are fixed. Provision for take-up of wear in the primary chain is made by means of a rubber faced tension slipper blade below the lower run of the chain. The free movement in the chain can be felt with the finger after removing the top inspection plug adjacent to the cylinder block, with the engine stopped, of course.

The correct chain adjustment is $\frac{3}{8}$ in. (9·5 mm.) free movement. To adjust the chain tension first place a drip tray underneath the chaincase and unscrew the hexagonal pillar bolt adjacent to the centre stand left hand lug.

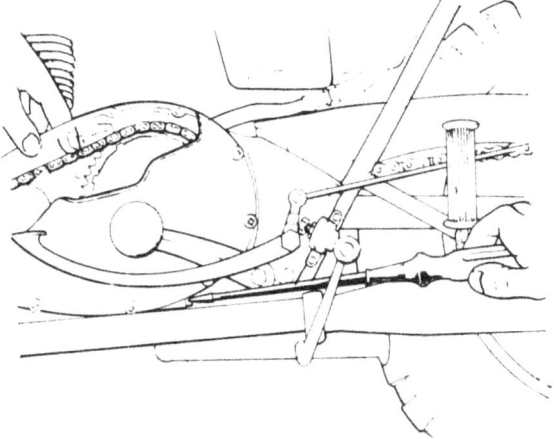

Fig. C3. Adjusting the chain tensioner

Insert the short screwdriver 61-7012 and adjust the tension as required.

When the adjustment is completed, check that the chaincase contans the recommended amount of oil (see Section A1).

SECTION C3
REMOVING AND REPLACING THE PRIMARY COVER

Slacken the left finned clip bolt, left silencer clip bolt and remove the nut and bolt securing the left exhaust pipe bracket forward of the engine. Remove the exhaust pipe as in Section B13.

For models with a right-hand gearchange slacken off the adjustment at the rear brake operating rod until the brake pedal is clear of the primary cover.

Unscrew the left footrest securing nut and withdraw the footrest.

Place a drip tray underneath the primary cover and remove the hexagonal pillar bolt adjacent to the centre stand lug and allow the oil to drain from the chaincase. It is not necessary to disturb the rotor cover plate.

Remove the two domed nuts and copper washers and unscrew eight recess screws from the periphery of the primary cover. Withdraw the cover and paper gasket.

Refitting the cover is the reversal of the above instructions but fit a new paper gasket and if necessary, replace the 'O' ring on the gearchange spindle. Take care when replacing the cover so as not to damage or displace the 'O' ring.

Finally, replace the drain plug and fibre washer and 'prime' the chaincase with approximately ¼ pint of fresh engine oil. (See Section A1).

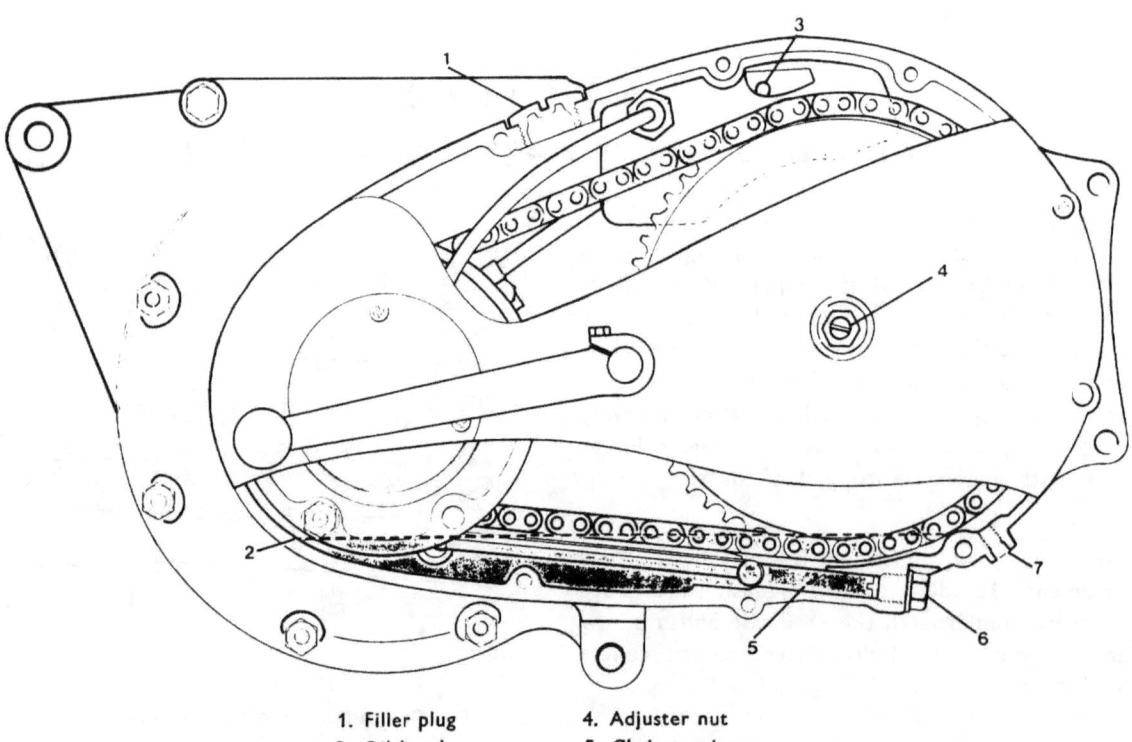

1. Filler plug
2. Oil level
3. Collection chamber
4. Adjuster nut
5. Chain tensioner
6. Drain plug
7. Level plug

Fig. C4. Section through primary chaincase

TRANSMISSION

SECTION C4
REMOVING AND REFITTING THE CLUTCH PLATES

Remove the outer primary cover as described in Section C3.

The three pressure plate springs are locked in position by means of location "pips" in the cups and on the drive adjuster nuts. To facilitate removal of the slotted adjuster nuts, insert a knife blade under the head of the nut whilst the nut is unscrewed (using a screwdriver of the type shown in Fig. C5). Withdraw the springs, cup and pressure plate assembly. Removal of the clutch plates is facilitated by means of two narrow hooked tools which can be made from a piece of $\frac{1}{32}$ in. dia. wire by bending to form a hook at one end. Thoroughly clean all parts in paraffin (kerosene) and inspect the clutch springs and plates for excessive wear (see section C5). When replacing the clutch plates remember that the bottom position is occupied by a bonded plate.

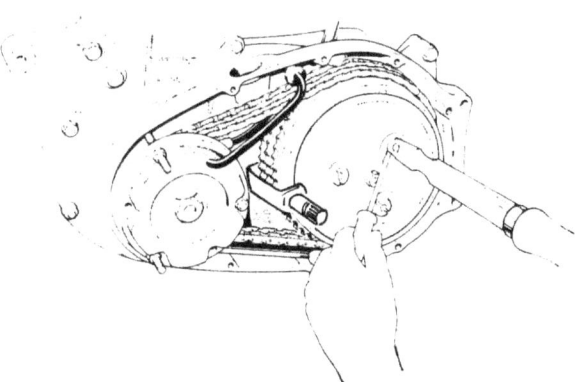

Fig. C5. Unscrewing the clutch spring nuts

Ensure that the cups are located correctly and assemble the springs and nuts, then adjust the pressure plate for true running as described below. Reassembly then continues as the reversal of the above instructions.

SECTION C5
INSPECTING THE CLUTCH PLATES AND SPRINGS

The bonded friction plates should be examined for excessive wear to the driving tags and the overall thickness of the clutch plates should be measured to determine the wear to the friction faces. If the reduction in thickness is more than ·030 in. (·75 mm.) when checked against a new plate the plate should be renewed. Check the fit of the driving tags in the clutch housing. The clearance should not be excessive.

Check the plain steel driven plates for flatness by placing the plates horizontally on a perfectly flat surface such as a thick piece of plate glass.

Original finish on the driven plates is a phosphoric acid etched surface and hence the plates need not be polished. Check the fit of the plate on the shock absorber housing. The radial clearance should not be excessive.

Inspect the clutch springs for compressive strength by measuring the length of the spring and comparing it with the dimensions given in "General Data". If a spring has shortened more than 0·1 in. (2·5 mm.) the complete set should be renewed. It is not advisable to renew just one or two springs as this may ultimately result in the pressure plate running unevenly.

SECTION C6
ADJUSTING THE CLUTCH PRESSURE PLATE

When the pressure plate is refitted or requires adjustment, the following procedure should be observed. With neutral selected, sit astride the machine, disengage the clutch, then depress the kickstart-pedal and observe the rotation of the pressure plate; it should revolve true relative to the clutch housing. If it does not do so, the three slotted nuts must be initially adjusted so the ends of the clutch pins are flush with the heads of the nuts. The nut is prevented from unscrewing by a "pip" on the underside and to unscrew a nut, a narrow screwdriver should be used to hold the spring away from the "pip" of the nut as shown in Fig. C5.

When the nuts are flush with the ends of the pins depress the kickstart again and mark the "high-spot" with chalk, then screw in the nearest nut(s) about half a turn and try again. Repeat this procedure until the plate rotates evenly without "wobbling".

SECTION C7
RENEWING SHOCK ABSORBER RUBBERS

When the primary cover and clutch plates are removed, access is gained to the shock absorber unit, which consists of a housing, paddle or spider, inner and outer cover plates and shock absorbing rubbers.

To remove the rubbers for inspection or renewal, first unscrew the three bolts which serve to retain the shock absorber plate and lever the plate free, using a suitable small lever.

The shock absorber rubbers can be prised out of position, using a sharp pointed tool, commencing by levering out the smaller rebound rubbers first.

When the three small rebound rubbers are removed the large drive rubbers will be free to be withdrawn.

If the rubbers show no signs of punctures or cracking, etc., they can be refitted, but remember that a slight puncture in the rubber can ultimately result in the rubber disintegrating.

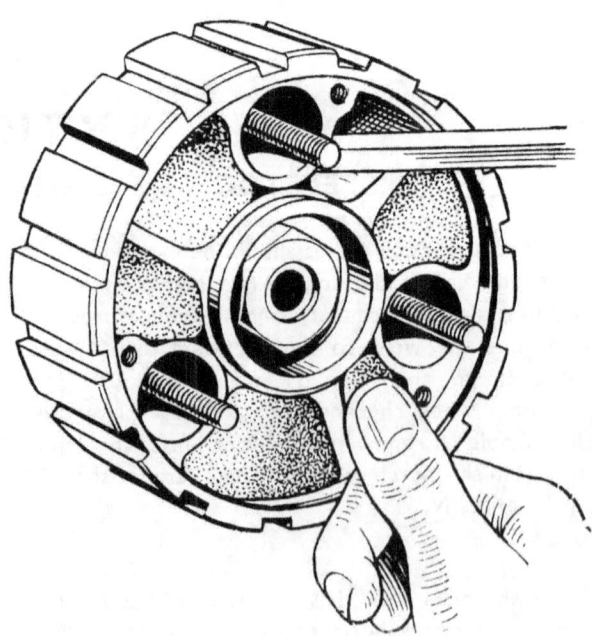

Fig. C6. Replacing the shock absorber rubbers

TRANSMISSION

To replace the shock absorber drive and rebound rubbers, first install all three of the larger drive rubbers in position as shown in Fig. C6. Follow through by inserting and replacing the smaller rebound rubbers. It may prove necessary to lever the shock absorber spider arms using a small tommy bar or similar to facilitate assembly, but this operation can be accomplished 'in situ' on the machine without the need for special tools or equipment, or necessity for removing the complete unit from the machine.

Although the rubbers are of an oil resistant type, it is not advisable to use oil or grease as an aid to reassembly as this may shorten the working life of the rubber.

Ensure that the three outer cover bolts are tight then 'peen' the protruding threads thereby preventing the bolts from unscrewing during service.

SECTION C8

REMOVING AND REPLACING THE STATOR AND ROTOR

First disconnect the stator leads at the top rear of the primary chaincase then, with the primary cover removed, unscrew the three stator retaining nuts and withdraw the stator from over the mounting studs and withdraw the lead from the sleeve nut. If any difficulty is encountered, unscrew the sleeve nut and the lead can then be withdrawn easily. To remove the rotor unbend the tab washer and unscrew the mainshaft nut using a box spanner and mallet, or, alternatively, select 5th (top) gear and apply the rear brake, then unscrew the nut.

Check the rotor carefully for signs of cracking or fatigue failure. Store the rotor within the stator to prevent metal particles adhering.

When replacing the rotor ensure that the key is located correctly, then tighten the nut to the torque figure given in "General Data".

When refitting the stator, ensure that the side of the stator with the leads connecting the coils together is outermost, then tighten the retaining nuts to the torque figure given in General Data Section. Insert the lead into the sleeve nut and connect the wires to those of the same colour code from the main harness at the frame saddle tube.

Check that the position of the lead is such that it cannot foul the chain.

Finally, rotate the crankshaft and ensure that the rotor does not foul the stator. It should be possible to insert a feeler gauge of at least 0·008 in. (0·2 mm.) thickness between each of the stator pole pieces and the rotor.

SECTION C9
REMOVING AND REPLACING THE CLUTCH AND ENGINE SPROCKETS

Remove the primary cover as shown in Section C3, then remove the pressure plate and clutch plates, as shown in Section C4. Insert the locking plate Z13 into the clutch housing and remove the stator and rotor as described in Section C8. Remove the rotor key and distance piece and slacken off the chain tensioner. Unscrew the clutch hub self locking nut then remove the plain washer.

As the primary chain is of the endless type, the clutch and engine sprockets have to be extracted simultaneously using extractor tool 61-7014 as shown in Fig. C8.

Screw the body of the clutch extractor into the clutch hub until the maximum depth of thread is engaged, then tighten the centre bolt until the hub is released. When this is achieved, assemble the engine sprocket extractor, No. 61-6014, and screw in the centre bolt and extract the engine sprocket.

Press out the hub from the shock absrber to release the sprocket, thrust washer, rollers and threaded pins.

Finally, remove the key from the gearbox mainshaft and check that the oil seal in the primary chain inner cover is a good fit over the high gear. To renew this oil seal the circular cover should be removed. When replacing the cover, use a new paper gasket and ensure that the oil seal is pressed in with the lip relative to the cover as shown in Fig. C9.

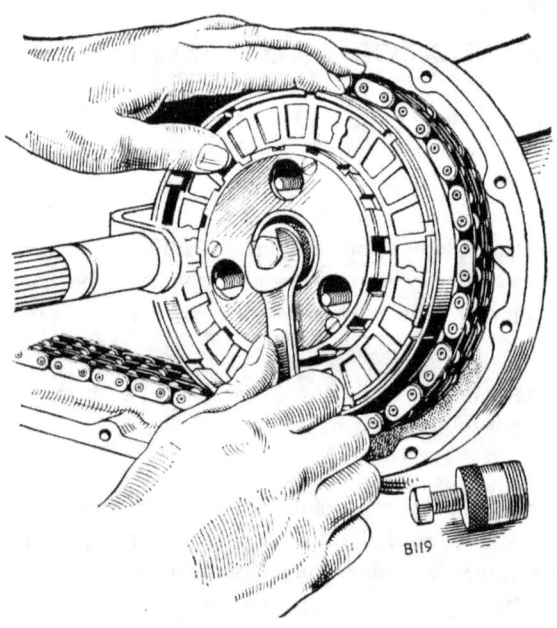

Fig. C8. Extracting the clutch centre, using extractor D662/3 and locking plate Z13

SECTION C10
INSPECTION OF THE TRANSMISSION COMPONENTS

(1) Inspect the primary chain for excessive wear of the rollers and pivot pins and check that the elongation does not exceed $1\frac{1}{2}\%$. To do this first scribe two marks on a flat surface exactly 12 in. (30·5 cm.) apart, then after degreasing or washing the chain in paraffin (kerosene), place the chain opposite the two marks. When the chain is compressed to its minimum free length the marks should coincide with the centres of two pivot pins 32 links apart. When the chain is stretched to its maximum free length the extension should not exceed $\frac{1}{4}$ in. (6·25 mm.).

Inspect the condition of the sprocket teeth for signs of hooking and pitting.

A very good method of indicating whether the chain is badly worn or not is to wrap it round the clutch sprocket and attempt to lift the chain from its seating at various points round the sprocket. Little or no lift indicates that both the sprocket and chain are in good condition.

(2) Check the fit between the shock absorber spider and the clutch hub splines. The spider should be a push fit onto the clutch hub and there should not be any radial movement.

Similarly check the fit of the engine sprocket splines onto the crankshaft. Again, there should not be any radial movement.

If either the spider or the engine sprocket are tight fitting on the clutch hub and crankshaft respectively, there is no cause for concern as such a fit is to the best advantage.

(3) Check the clutch hub roller bearing diameter, the rollers themselves and the bearing of the clutch sprocket for excessive wear and pitting etc. Measure the rollers, clutch hub and clutch sprocket bearing diameters and compare them with the dimensions given in "General Data".

If the diameters of the rollers are below the bottom limit, they should be renewed. When purchasing new rollers ensure that they are in accordance with the dimensions given in "General Data". In particular, check that the length is correct.

(4) Check that the shock absorber spider is a good working fit in the inner and outer retaining plates and that the arms of the spider have not caused excessive score marks on the inner faces of the retaining plates. A good idea is to check the working clearance by assembling the shock absorber unit without the rubbers.

(5) Inspect the clutch operating rod for bending, by rolling it on a flat surface such as a piece of plate glass. Check that the length of the rod is within the limits given in "General Data". This component should not be replaced with anything other than a genuine Triumph spare part. The ends of the rod are specially heat treated to give maximum wear resistance.

TRANSMISSION

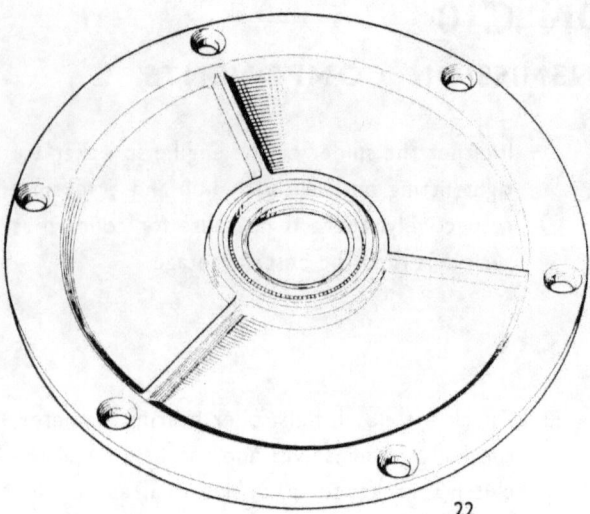

Fig. C9. Oil seal in gearbox sprocket detachable cover

When replacing the primary chain and sprockets, ensure that the taper ground boss of the engine sprocket is towards the crankshaft main bearing and the oil seal. With the gearbox mainshaft key carefully in position, locate the clutch hub onto the mainshaft taper and tap it slightly to lock it onto the taper.

Place the primary chain over the engine sprocket and drive the sprocket onto the crankshaft.

Offer the clutch locking tool Z13 into the clutch plate housing and then refit the plain washer, and clutch self-locking nut.

Engage fourth gear, apply the rear brake and tighten the clutch securing nut to the torque figure given in "General Data".

Do not forget to fit the distance piece between the engine sprocket and rotor and remember to refit the rectangular section rotor locating key. Reassembly then continues as a reversal of the above instructions. Finally, replenish the chaincase with the recommended grade of oil (see Section A1).

Note.—Alternatively, the clutch sprocket may be removed by prising out the twenty roller bearings and allowing the sprocket to move both outwards and forwards until it can be unmeshed from the primary chain. This alternative only applies if the shock absorber assembly can readily be detached from the hub to allow access to the rollers.

Thoroughly clean all parts in paraffin (kerosene) and inspect them for wear or fatigue as shown in Section C9.

Grease the clutch hub and fit the thrust washer and 20 of the correct rollers.

Do not use $\frac{1}{4}$ in. $\times$ $\frac{1}{4}$ in. bright ended rollers.

Place the sprocket in position and press on the shock absorber complete with the three threaded pins. If the splines are loose use Triumph "LOCTITE".

SECTION C11
CLUTCH AND ENGINE SPROCKET ALIGNMENT

It is important that the engine and gearbox sprockets are accurately in line, otherwise rapid wear of the primary chain and sprockets will occur. This will result in the chain rollers fracturing and the chain breaking. This would almost certainly cause irreparable damage to the crankcase.

Correct alignment of the sprockets is easily effected by the use of spacing shims removed or replaced from behind the engine sprocket. The alignment can be initally checked by placing a straight edge alongside both sprockets (e.g. a steel rule) after first removing the primary chain (See previous section). If any gap produced is in excess of 0·005" (0·127mm.) maximum tolerance, then the engine sprocket must be shimed accordingly. Place the appropriate shim between the engine sprocket and the spacer that sits up against the roller bearing.

Shims are avilable as follows:—

0.010" thick—Part Number 70-8038

0.030" thick—Part Number 71-2660

TRANSMISSION

SECTION C12
REAR CHAIN ALTERATIONS AND REPAIRS

If the chains have been correctly serviced, very few repairs will be necessary. Should the occasion arise to repair, lengthen or shorten a chain, a rivet extractor, as shown in Fig. C11, and a few spare parts will cover all requirements.

To SHORTEN a chain containing an EVEN NUMBER OF PITCHES remove the dark parts shown in (1) and replace by cranked double link and single connecting link (2).

To SHORTEN a chain containing an ODD NUMBER OF PITCHES remove the dark parts shown in (3) and replace by a single connecting link and inner link as (4).

To REPAIR a chain with a broken roller or inside link, remove the dark parts in (5) and replace by two single connecting links and one inner link as (6).

Fig. C10. Rear chain alterations

RIVET EXTRACTOR

The rivet extractor can be used on all motorcycle chains up to ¾ in. pitch, whether the chains are on or off the wheels.

When using the extractor:—

(1) Turn screw anti-clockwise to permit the punch end to clear the chain rivet.

(2) Open the jaws by pressing down the lever (see below).

(3) Pass jaws over chain and release the lever. Jaws should rest on a chain roller free of chain link plates (see below).

(4) Turn screw clockwise until punch contacts and pushes out rivet end through chain outer link plate. Unscrew punch, withdraw extractor and repeat complete operation on the adjacent rivet in the same chain outer link plate. The outer plate is then free and the two rivets can be withdrawn from opposite sides with the opposite plate in position. Do not use the removed part again.

When the alterations are finished the chain should be lubricated as shown in Section A12.

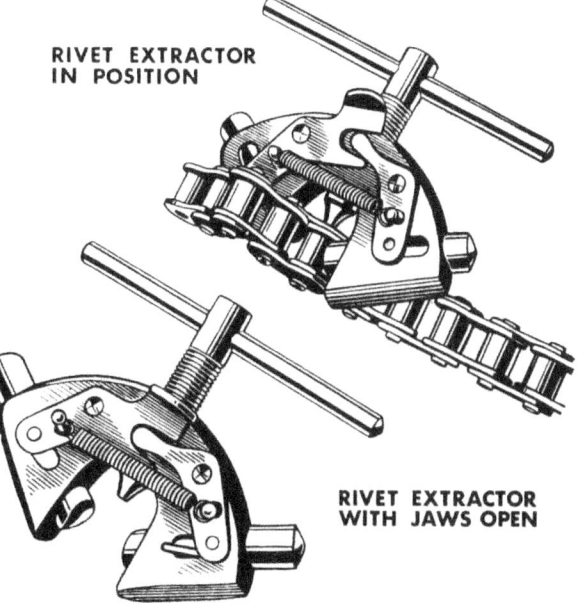

Fig. C11. Chain link rivet extractor

SECTION D

FIVE SPEED GEARBOX

DESCRIPTION	Section
SEQUENCE OF GEARCHANGING...	D1
REMOVING AND REPLACING THE OUTER COVER ASSEMBLY	D2
DISMANTLING AND REASSEMBLING THE KICKSTART MECHANISM	D3
DISMANTLING AND REASSEMBLING THE GEARCHANGE MECHANISM	D4
INSPECTING THE GEARCHANGE AND KICKSTART COMPONENTS	D5
RENEWING KICKSTART AND GEARCHANGE SPINDLE BUSHES	D6
CLUTCH OPERATING MECHANISM	D7
DISMANTLING THE GEARBOX	D8
INSPECTION OF THE GEARBOX COMPONENTS	D9
RENEWING MAINSHAFT AND LAYSHAFT BEARINGS	D10
REASSEMBLING THE GEARBOX	D11
CHANGING THE GEARBOX SPROCKET	D12

D GEARBOX

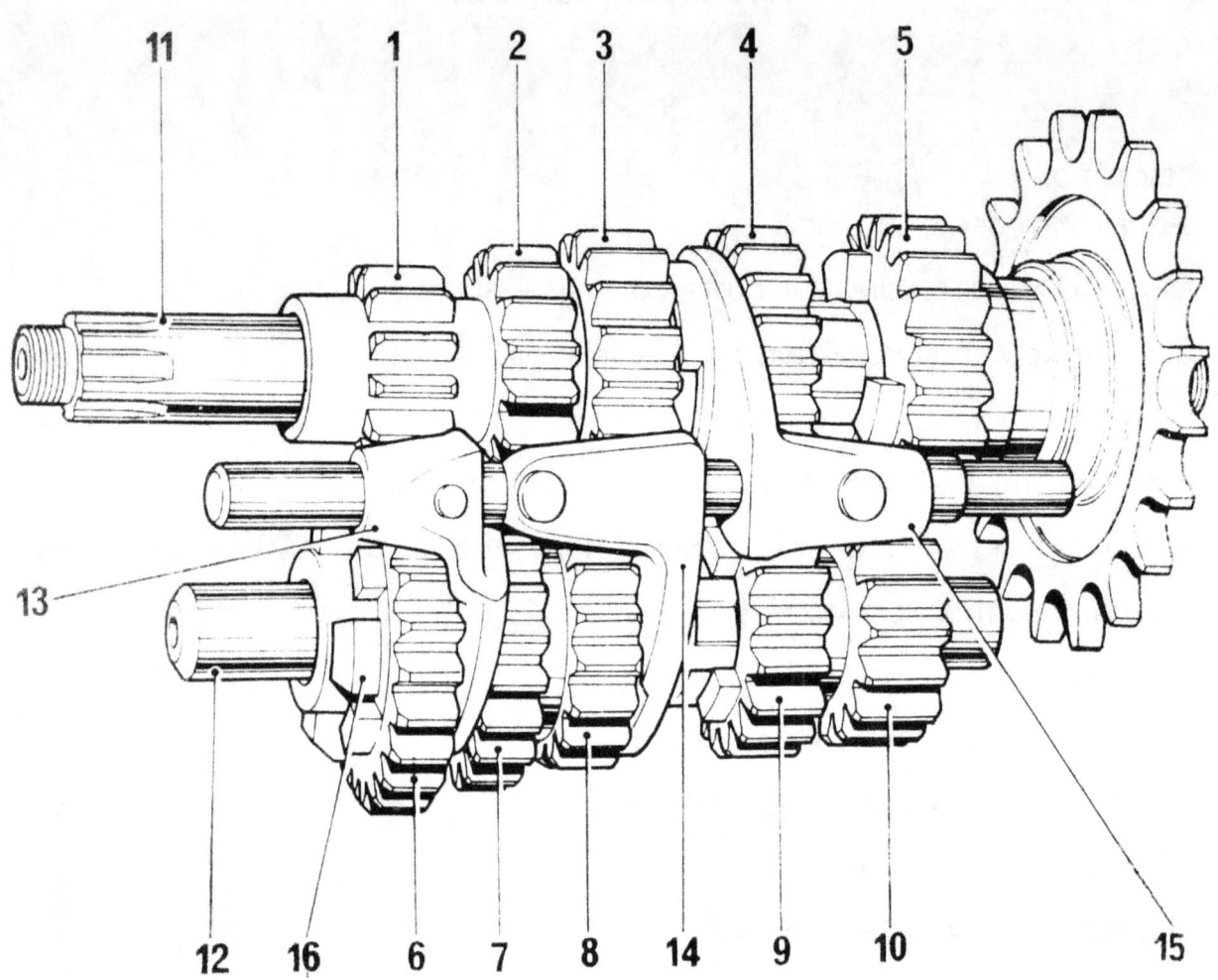

1. Low gear
2. Second gear
3. Third gear
4. Fourth gear
5. Fifth gear
6. Low gear
7. Second gear
8. Third gear
9. Fourth gear
10. Fifth gear
11. Mainshaft
12. Layshaft
13. First gear layshaft selector fork
14. Third gear layshaft selector fork
15. Mainshaft selector fork
16. Layshaft engaging dog

Fig. D1. Plan of Gear Components

SECTION D1

SEQUENCE OF GEARCHANGING

The gearbox is operated by the pedal on the left-hand side of the machine, the pedal being splined to the gear change spindle. (Prior to engine no. HN62501 the gearbox is operated from the right-hand side). Two chamfered plungers with springs fit into the housing in such a way that as the gear pedal is moved up and down the plungers locate in the teeth at the outboard end of the quadrant. The quadrant is pivoted in the centre and the inboard end if formed to mate with the captive pinion of the camplate. See Fig. D2.

Figs. D3(i) to D3(vi) illustrate the camplate with its leaf spring and the three engaging pins of the selector forks which can be seen in the camplate track. The three sliding pinions are moved along the mainshaft and layshaft by the selector forks. The neutral positions of the camplate and gears are shown in Fig. D3(ii).

When the pedal is depressed to engage low gear (first) the camplate is turned anti-clockwise moving the layshaft selector fork to mesh the sliding first gear with the engaging dog on the end of the layshaft. (The engaging dog is illustrated in Fig. D1.)

As second gear is selected by lifting the pedal, the second layshaft selector fork brings the sliding third gear into mesh with the layshaft second gear, while the previous selector fork disengages first gear from the engaging dog.

Movement of the gear lever in the same direction will select third gear by moving the mainshaft sliding gear into mesh with the mainshaft third gear. At the same time the second layshaft selector disengages second gear.

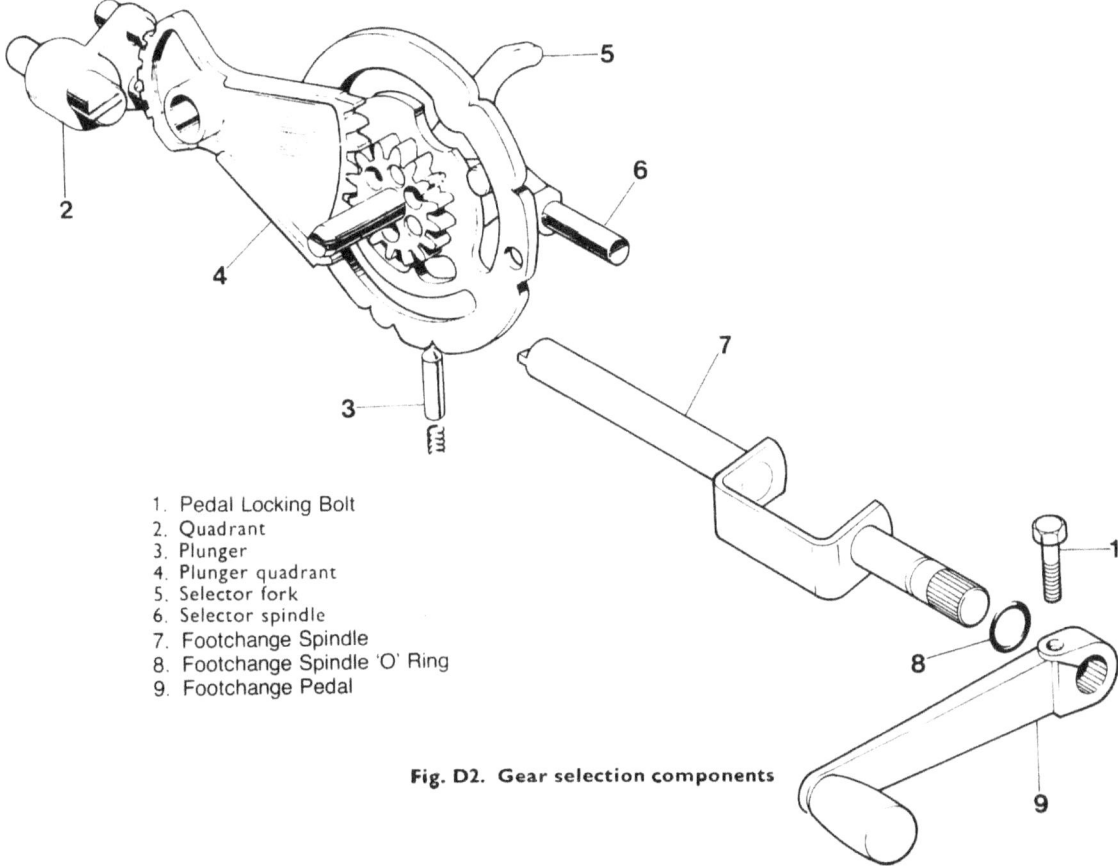

1. Pedal Locking Bolt
2. Quadrant
3. Plunger
4. Plunger quadrant
5. Selector fork
6. Selector spindle
7. Footchange Spindle
8. Footchange Spindle 'O' Ring
9. Footchange Pedal

Fig. D2. Gear selection components

GEARBOX

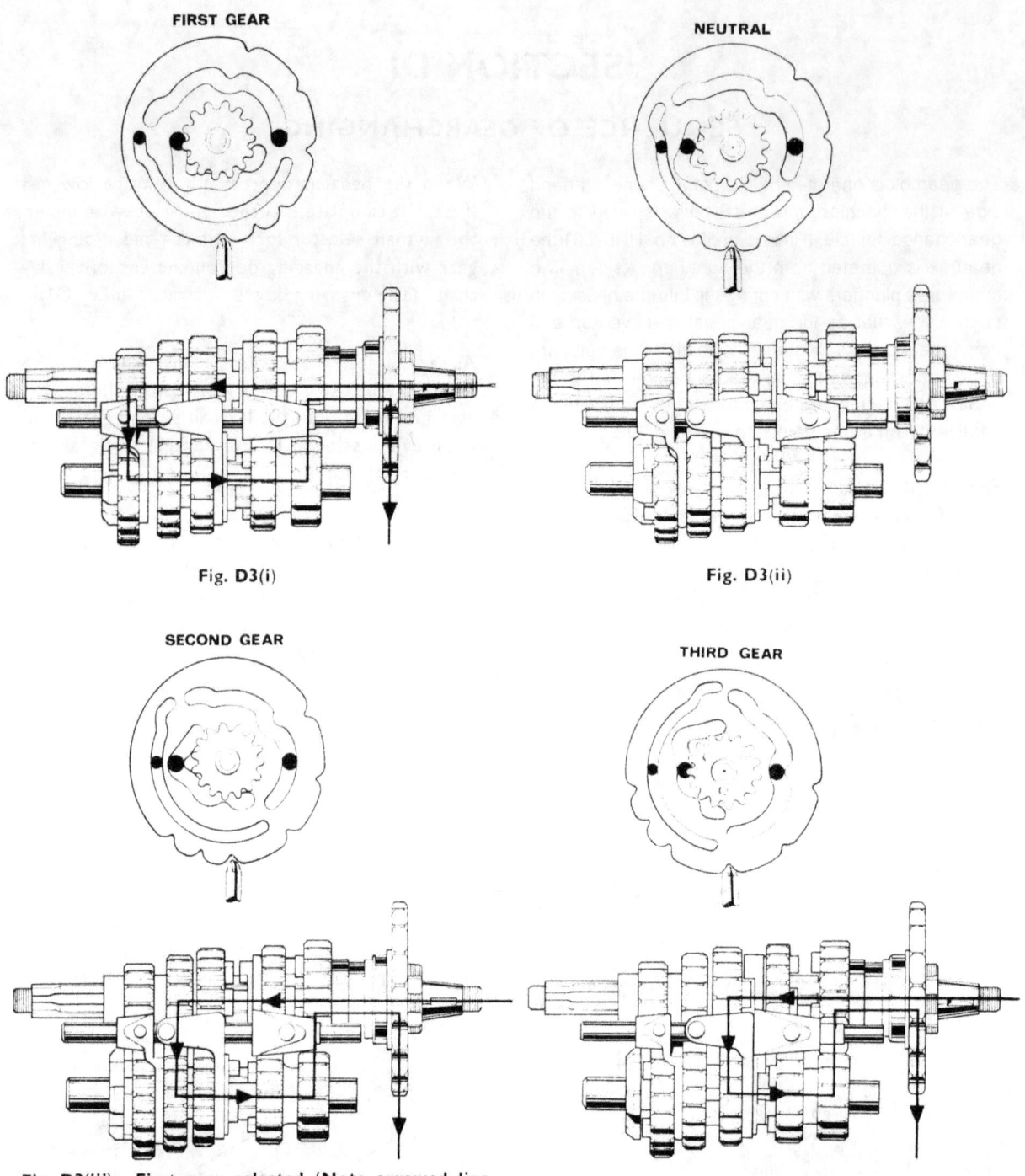

Fig. D3(i)

Fig. D3(ii)

Fig. D3(iii). First gear selected (Note arrowed line showing power being transmitted through the gear cluster)

Fig. D3(iv)

Further movement of the gear lever will select fourth gear by moving the sliding layshaft third gear into mesh with the layshaft fourth gear while the mainshaft fourth gear is moved into a neutral position.

Finally, fifth gear is obtained by a final movement of the lever in the same direction. The mainshaft selector fork will bring the mainshaft sliding gear (fourth gear) into mesh with the mainshaft fifth gear. At the same time the second layshaft sliding gear (third gear) is moved into a neutral position.

It should be noted that throughout the range of gear pedal movements the gear pedal spindle and plunger housing return to the original position ready for the next selection.

GEARBOX

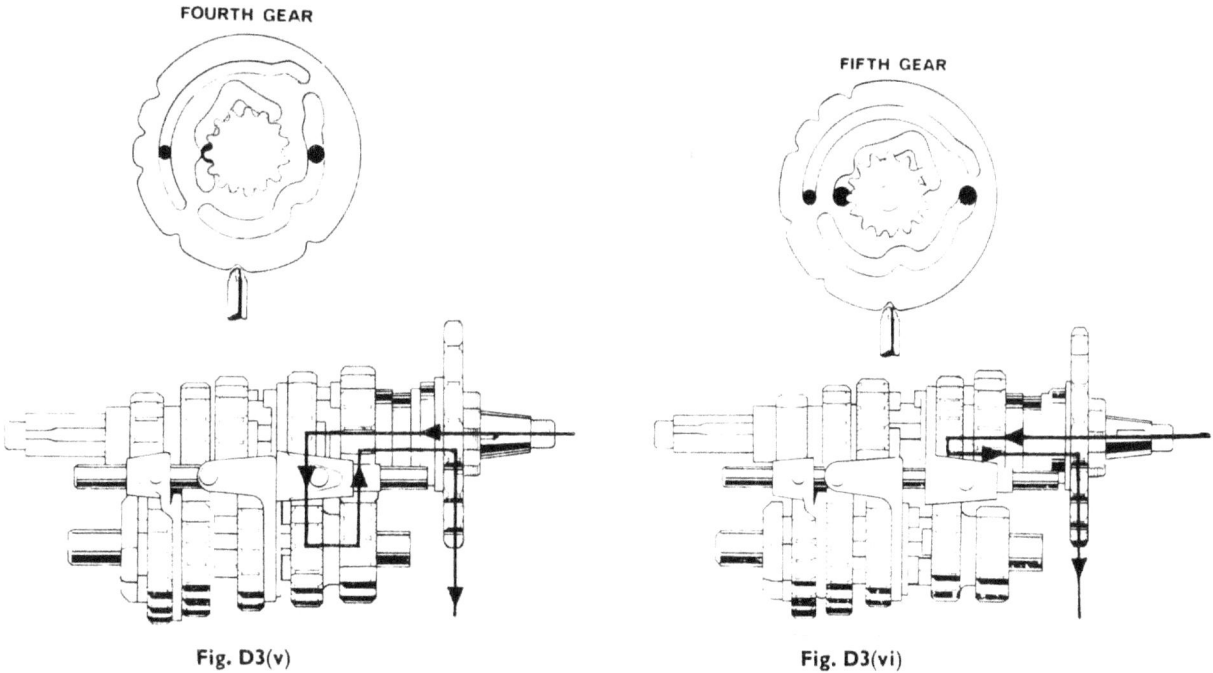

Fig. D3(v)   Fig. D3(vi)

SECTION D2
REMOVING AND REPLACING THE GEARBOX OUTER COVER ASSEMBLY

Remove the right hand exhaust system. See section B13.

Remove the right footrest by detaching the fixing nut from behind the rear engine plate.

Slacken off the clutch cable adjustment and slip out the cable nipple at the handlebar control. Slide the rubber cover up away from the abutment for the cable at the gearbox end and unscrew the abutment.

Remove the large slotted plug from the gearbox outer cover and access will be gained to the clutch operating arm. It is only necessary then to release the cable nipple from the arm with the finger.

Place a drip tray underneath the gearbox and unscrew the gearbox filler plug and drain plug.

Engage 5th (top) gear. This will allow several otherwise difficult nuts to be unscrewed by subsequently applying the rear brake when required.

Unscrew the top and bottom hexagonal nut and the recess screws from the periphery of the gearbox cover. Depress the kickstart lever slightly and tap the cover until it is free.

1. Clutch cable nipple
2. Drain plug
3. Level plug

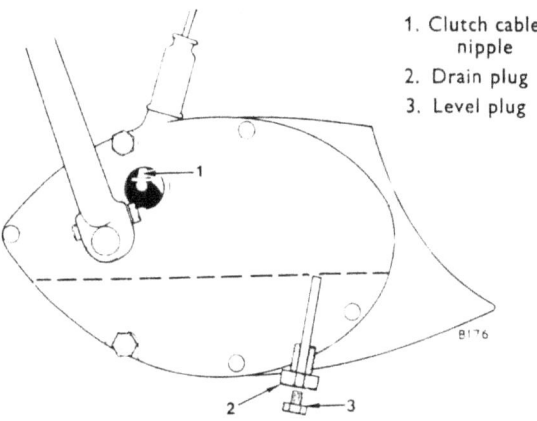

Fig. D4. Showing gearbox oil level and oil drain plugs

When the cover is removed, the gear-change mechanism, kickstart mechanism and clutch operating mechanism will be accessible. The gearchange shaft should be carefully turned, to control the release of the plungers and springs from the gearchange quadrant.

GEARBOX

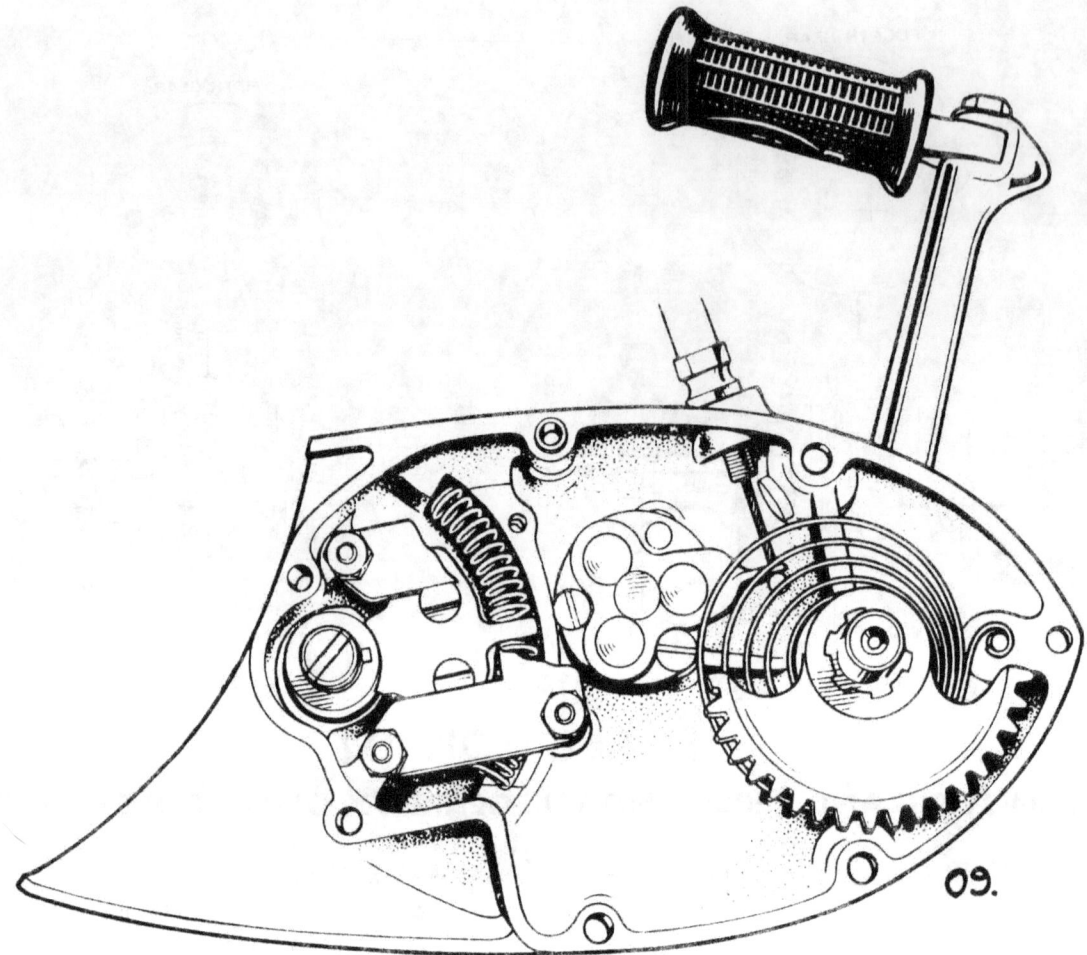

Fig. D5. Gearbox outer cover, showing gearchange mechanism, clutch operating mechanism and kickstart quadrant

Prior to refitting the outer cover ensure that the junction surface is clean and free from any deposits of old jointing compound, then thoroughly clean it in paraffin (kerosene). Apply a fresh coat of jointing compound to the junction surface and ensure that the two location dowels are in position.

Turn the kickstart pedal until it is halfway down its operational stroke and offer the cover to the gearbox. Check that the kickstart pedal returns to its normal fully-returned position. Reassembly then continues as a reversal of the above instructions. Finally, refill the gearbox to the correct level with the recommended grade of oil (see Section A1).

SECTION D3

DISMANTLING AND REASSEMBLING THE KICKSTART MECHANISM

Slacken the kickstarter crank cotter pin nut about two or three turns and release the cotter pin from its locking taper by using a hammer and a soft metal drift. Slide the pedal off the shaft and withdraw the quadrant and spring assembly. Apply the rear brake, bend back the tab on the lock washer and unscrew the kickstart ratchet pinion securing nut from the gearbox mainshaft. Withdraw the pinion, ratchet, spring and sleeve, then thoroughly clean all parts in paraffin (kerosene) and inspect them for wear etc., as shown in Section D5.

If the kickstarter quadrant is to be renewed the spindle should be driven out using a hammer or press and the gear quadrant pressed onto the spindle so that the kickstart crank location flat is positioned correctly relative to the quadrant (see Fig. D6).

GEARBOX

Fig. D6. Kickstart quadrant and spring. Arrow indicates correct spring location

To reassemble the mechanism, first refit the thin walled steel sleeve, spring, pinion and ratchet to the gearbox mainshaft and assemble the tab washer, then screw on the retaining nut to the torque figure given in "General Data". **Do not overtighten the retaining nut as this may result in failure of the thin walled inner steel sleeve.**

Fit the return spring to the kickstart quadrant as shown in Fig. D6. Offer the spindle into the kickstart bush and locate the return spring onto the anchor peg at the rear of the cover. Fit the oil seal over the spindle and assemble the kickstart crank, locking it into position with the cotter pin from the rear. Refit the outer cover as shown in Section D2. Do not forget to refit the oil seal. Refill the gearbox with the correct grade of lubricant (Section A1).

SECTION D4

DISMANTLING AND REASSEMBLING THE GEARCHANGE MECHANISM

Prior to engine no. HN62501 slacken off the gear change pedal locking bolt and withdraw the pedal from the splined shaft. A little leverage between the pedal and the cover may be necessary. For this, choose a suitable tool to avoid damage to the cover.

Remove the four nuts and locking washers securing the guide plate. Withdraw the guide plate, plunger quadrant and curved return springs. Thoroughly clean the parts in paraffin (kerosene) and inspect them for wear etc., as shown in Section D5.

To reassemble the mechanism, offer it to the outer cover bush then refit the two quadrant return springs and ensure that they locate correctly over the step in the cover.

Refit the retainer plate, not forgetting the locking washers which fit one under each of the four nuts. Finally, refit the springs and plungers, taking care that they are not suddenly ejected from their seats during assembly.

SECTION D5

INSPECTING THE GEARCHANGE AND KICKSTART COMPONENTS

GEARCHANGE:

(1) Inspect the gearchange plungers for wear and ensure that they are a clearance fit in the quadrant. Check the plunger springs by comparing their lengths with the figures given in "General Data".

(2) Examine the plunger guide plate for wear and grooving on the taper guide surfaces. Renew the plate if grooving has occurred.

(3) Inspect the footchange return springs for fatigue and if they show signs of corrosion due to condensation, they should be renewed.

(4) Examine the gearchange quadrant bush for wear and possible ovality by inserting the quadrant into the bush and feeling the amount of play.

GEARBOX

(5) Check the tips of the plungers and the teeth of the camplate operating quadrant for chipping and wear. To remove the camplate quadrant, first remove the inner cover as shown in Section D8, then remove the two split pins and withdraw the spindle.

KICKSTART:

(1) Examine the kickstart quadrant for chipped or broken teeth or looseness on the spindle and the kickstart return spring for fatigue cracks and signs of wear, particularly at the centre where it engages on the splines of the spindle.

(2) Examine the kickstart spindle bush for wear. If the required measuring instruments are not available, use the spindle as a gauge and feel the amount of play.

(3) Examine the kickstart ratchet mechanism for wear, giving particular attention to the ratchet teeth ensuring that they have not become chipped or rounded. Check that the thin walled steel bush is a clearance fit in the kickstart pinion and that the spring is not badly worn.

(4) Finally, check that the kickstart stop peg is firmly pressed into the inner cover and is not distorted.

SECTION D6
RENEWING KICKSTART AND GEARCHANGE BUSHES

If it is found necessary to renew the kickstart spindle bush this should be done by completely stripping the outer cover of its assembly parts and heating it to 100°C., then driving the bush out using a suitable shouldered drift. Press in the new bush while the cover is still hot.

The gearchange spindle and plunger assembly are supported in four cast iron bushes. One in the gearbox outer cover, one in the inner cover, one in the L.H. crankcase and one in the primary cover.

Remove the outer cover, see Sections D2 and D4. Using a suitable tap (e.g. ¾in. dia. U.N.C.) cut a thread in the bush to a depth of ½in. (12mm.) heat the cover to 100°C, then insert a suitable bolt. Grip the bolt firmly in a vice then drive the cover away using a hide mallet. A suitably shouldered drift is required to drive in the new bush, which should be done whilst the cover is still hot.

Remove the inner cover see Section D7. Heat the cover to 100°C and remove the bush using a suitable drift. Press in the new bush whilst the cover is still hot.

Remove the primary cover, see Section C3 and remove and replace the bush as above.

The L.H. crankcase bush is not prone to wear even after considerable mileage. However, if necessary, remove the L.H. crankcase half, see Section B34 and using a suitable tap (e.g. ¹³/₁₆ in. dia. × UNC) cut a thread in the bush to a depth of ¾in. (18mm.). Insert a suitable bolt and remove the bush. Drift in the new bush whilst the cover is still hot.

For early models with a right hand footchange adopt a similar procedure for the gearbox outer and inner bushes.

SECTION D7
CLUTCH OPERATING MECHANISM

The clutch operating mechanism, which is situated in the gearbox outer cover, consists of two spring loaded plates held apart by three balls, which are seated in conical indentations in the plates.

Wear in this mechanism is negligible, even after excessive mileage has been covered, so long as the gearbox oil level is maintained at the recommended level. The mechanism is removed as a unit by unscrewing two slotted screws and is then easily dismantled. The parts are arranged as shown in Fig. D7, which should be referred to when reassembling the mechanism.

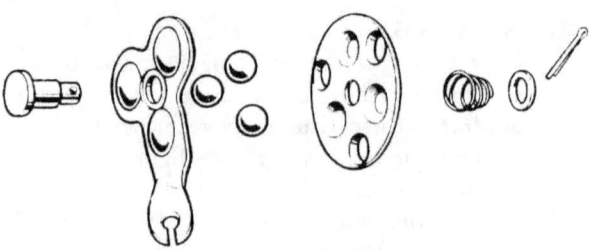

Fig. D7. Exploded view of clutch operating mechanism

SECTION D8

DISMANTLING THE GEARBOX

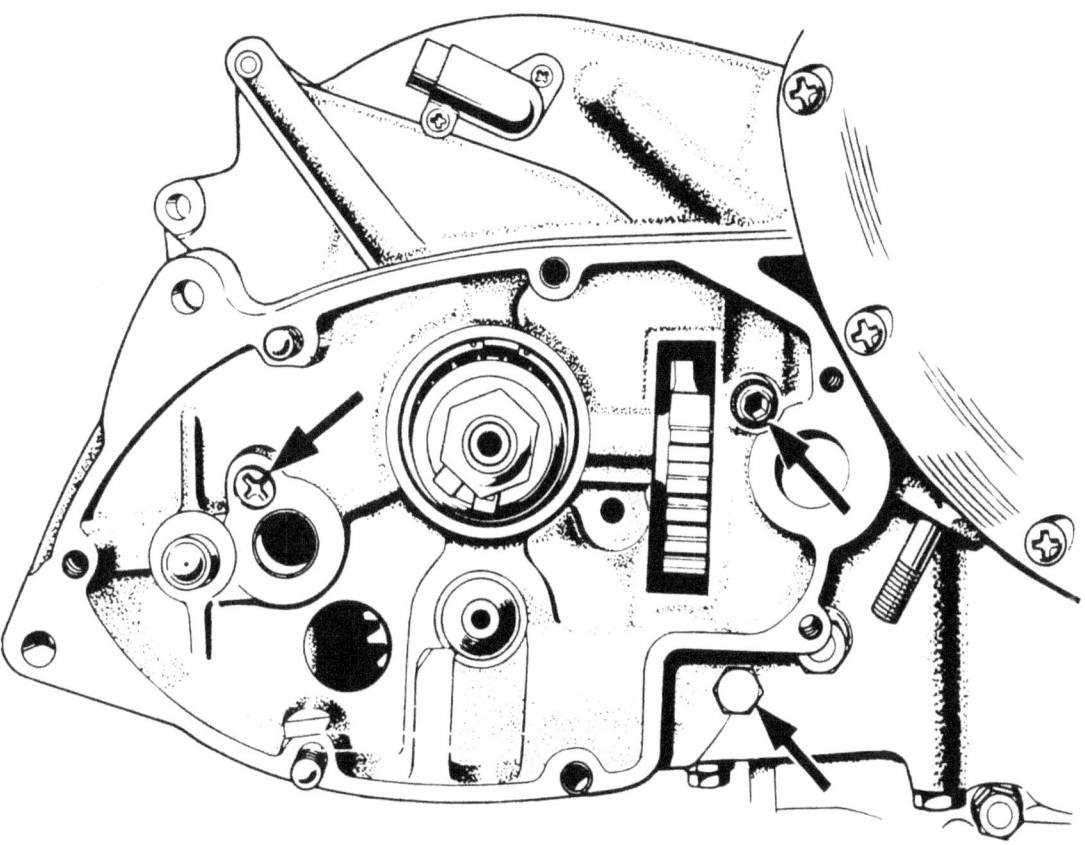

Fig. D8. Gearbox inner cover retaining screws

Remove the gearbox outer cover as shown in Section D2, leaving the gearbox with 5th (top) gear selected.

Remove the two short bolts, two long bolts and a centre nut which serves to retain the rear right engine mounting plate, then withdraw the plate.

Bend back the tags on the lock washer and unscrew the kickstart pinion ratchet retainer nut from the end of the gearbox mainshaft. This should be easily achieved with 5th (top) gear selected and the rear brake applied.

Remove the outer primary cover and dismantle the transmission as shown in Section C, not forgetting, finally to remove the key from the gearbox mainshaft.

The gearbox inner cover is retained by a socket screw, a Phillips recessed screw and a hexagonal bolt (See Fig. D8). When these are removed the cover can be released by tapping it outwards with a hide mallet.

Withdraw the engaging dog from the layshaft. See Fig. D9, then remove the circlip from the end of the layshaft with a pair of circlip pliers. Pull the selector rod out and then remove the layshaft first gear with its selector fork. Withdraw the second gear from the layshaft and then remove the mainshaft complete with first, second and third gears in position. Remove the mainshaft fourth and layshaft third gears with their selector forks and then withdraw the layshaft with the fifth and fourth gears in position. Detach the two brass thrust washers which locate over the needle roller bearings. Before removal of the camplate, the mainshaft high gear will have to be detached from the gearbox sprocket and withdrawn from the crankcase. This can be done by removing the circular plate from the primary inner cover at the rear of the clutch, tapping back the bent-over portion of the locking plate and unscrewing the large hexagonal gearbox

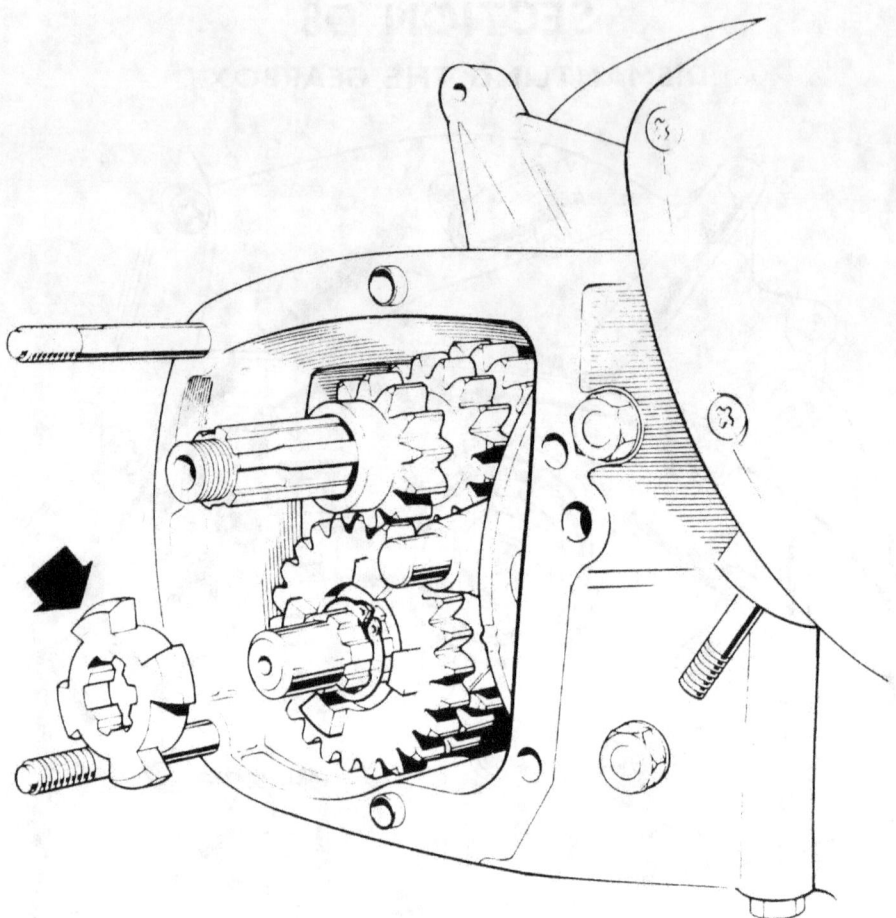

Fig. D9. Showing removal of engaging dog

sprocket nut (1·875″ across the flats and remove the 'O' ring. To facilitate removal of the nut, Workshop Tool number 61-6125 is available. When the nut has been removed, tap the high gear into the gearbox using a hide mallet or a soft metal drift. It is now possible to remove the camplate from its housing in the crankcase. To remove the gearbox sprocket, disconnet the rear chain and remove it from around the sprocket which can now be easily withdrawn through the aperture.

chain and remove it from around the sprocket which can now be easily withdrawn through the aperture.

The oil is prevented from leaving the gearbox through the main bearing by an oil seal which runs on a ground boss on the gearbox sprocket. Check the oil seal for cracking and wear (see Section D10 for bearing and oil seal removal details).

SECTION D9

INSPECTION OF THE GEARBOX COMPONENTS

Thoroughly clean all parts in paraffin (kerosene) and check them for wear and fatigue, as follows:—

(1) Inspect the gearbox housing and inner cover for signs of cracking and damage to the joint faces. Check that the location dowels are in position correctly in the gearbox and inner cover (2 dowels each). In preparation for re-assembly, clean the junction surfaces of the gearbox, inner cover and outer cover of any old deposits of jointing compound.

(2) Examine both the mainshaft and layshaft for signs of fatigue, damaged threads and badly worn splines. Check the extent of wear to the bearing diameters of both shafts by comparing them with the figures given in "General Data". Examine the shafts carefully for signs of seizure.

GEARBOX

Excessive friction resistance and seizure will be indicated by local colouring on the shaft.

(3) Check the layshaft needle roller bearing by inserting the layshaft and feeling the amount of play.

(4) Inspect the gearbox mainshaft bearings for roughness due to pitting or indentation of the ball/roller tracks. Note that the high gear bearing operates directly in a roller bearing pressed into the right hand side crankcase half. If wear is apparent at the high gear bearings (check general data for high gear spigot dimensions), it will be necessary to replace the roller bearing *and* the high gear. Under no circumstances should the bearing or the high gear be replaced independently.
Check the inner cover bearing by feeling the amount of side play of the centre track. It should not be possible to detect any movement by hand if the bearing is in good condition. The mainshaft should be a push fit into the inner cover bearing.

(5) Examine the gears thoroughly, for chipped, fractured or worn teeth. Check the internal splines, dogs and bushes. Make sure that the splines are free on their respective shafts with no tendency to bind, and the bushes in the mainshaft third gear, layshaft second gear and layshaft first gear are not loose or excessively worn. Again, reference should be made to the dimensions given in "General Data".

(6) Check that the selector fork rod is not grooved and that it is a good fit in the gearbox casing and the inner cover. Inspect the selector fork running faces for wear. This will only have occurred if the gearbox is being continually used with a badly worn mainshaft bearing.

(7) The gear selector camplate should be inspected for signs of wear in the selector tracks. Excessive wear will occur if the mainshaft main bearing has worn badly. Check the fit of the camplate spindle in its housing. Examine the camplate gear wheel for excessive wear. Difficulty will be encountered in gear selection, causing subsequent damage to the gears, if this gear is badly worn.

(8) Inspect the mainshaft high gear needle roller bearings for roughness or fracture. Check the mainshaft diameter with the "General Data" and check for surface pitting or damage due to scoring.

SECTION D10

RENEWING MAINSHAFT AND LAYSHAFT BEARINGS

MAINSHAFT

The mainshaft bearings are a press fit into their respective housings and are retained by spring circlips to prevent sideways movement due to end thrust. To remove the right bearing, first lever out the circlip, then heat the cover to approximately 100°C and drive out the bearing using a suitably shouldered drift. The new bearing should be pressed or drifted in whilst the cover is still hot using a suitable tubular drift onto the outer race (2½in. (62mm.) outside diameter × 6in. (150mm.) long). Do not forget to refit the circlip.

To remove the high gear bearing on the left of the machine, first lever out the large oil seal (which must be renewed), then remove the retainer circlip. Carefully heat the casing locally to approximately 100°C., then drive out the bearing from the inside by means of a suitably shouldered drift. Whilst the casing is still hot, drive in the new bearing, using a suitable tubular drift onto the outer race, then refit the circlip and press in the new oil seal.

MAINSHAFT HIGH GEAR BEARINGS

Two caged needle bearings are fitted into each end of the high gear and they can be both pressed out together using a drift of the dimensions shown in Fig. D10.

D GEARBOX

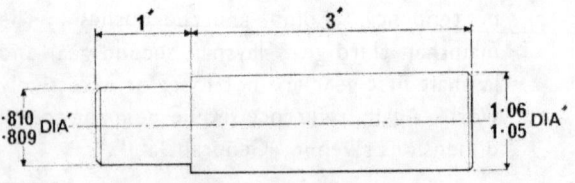

Fig. D 10. Drift dimensions

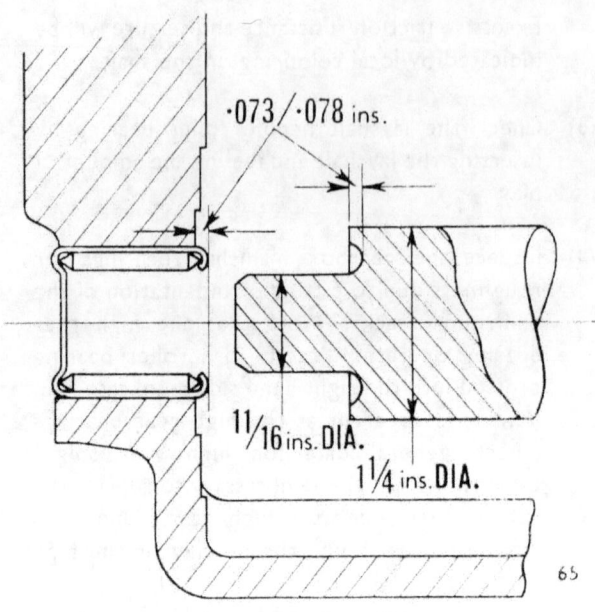

Fig. D12. Sketch of needle roller and drift

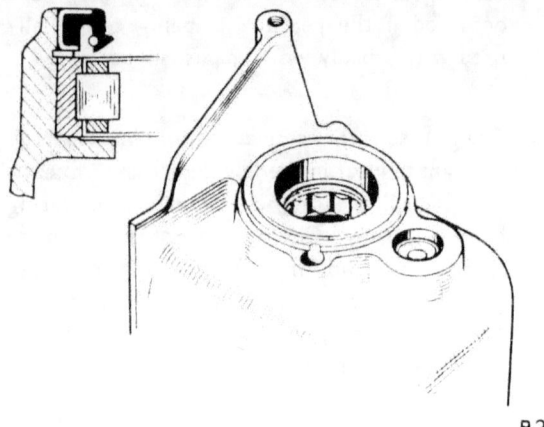

Fig. D11. Section through gearbox mainshaft oil seal

LAYSHAFT

The right needle roller bearing should be removed by heating the cover to approximately 100°C, then pressing or drifting out the bearing using a tool similar to that shown in Fig. D12.

The new bearing should be pressed in, plain end first, whilst the cover is still hot, from the inside of the cover, until ·073/·078in. (1·85/1·98mm.) of the bearing protrudes above the cover face (see Fig. D12)

The left needle roller bearing is of the closed-end type and is accessible from the left, through the sprocket cover plate aperture. The casing should be heated to approximately 100°C and the bearing driven through into the gearbox using a soft metal drift, taking care not to damage the bore into which the bearing fits. The new bearing must be carefully pressed in whilst the casing is hot, until ·073/·078in. (1·85/1·98mm.) protrudes above the spot face surface inside the gearbox. Do not use excessive force or the needle roller outer case may become damaged, resulting in the rollers seizing, or breaking up.

Finally, the outer portion of the bore into which the bearing fits, should be sealed with a suitable proprietary sealant.

SECTION D11

REASSEMBLING THE GEARBOX

Lubricate the camplate spindle and offer it into the spindle housing within the gearbox.

Drive the new oil seal up to the main bearing with the lip and spring towards the bearing. Insert the high gear into the bearing. Lubricate the ground tapered boss of the sprocket with oil and slide it onto the high gear. Fit a new 'O' ring and screw on the securing nut finger tight.

Re-mesh the rear chain with the sprockets and replace the connecting link. Apply the rear brake and tighten the sprocket securing nut using service tool 61-6125 to the torque figure given in "General Data".

GEARBOX

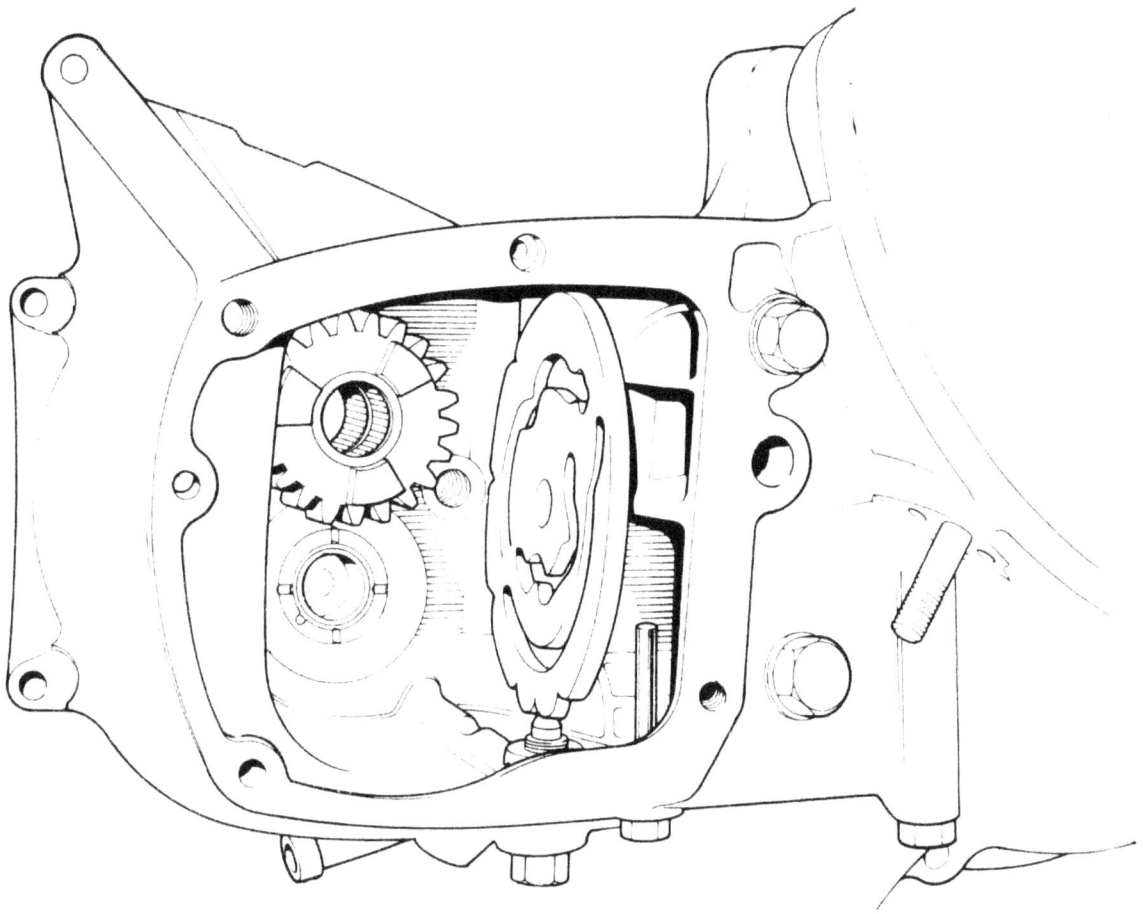

Fig. D13. Reassembling the gearbox. Arrow indicates camplate in the neutral position.

Locate the bronze thrust washer over the inner needle roller bearing. The thrust washer can be held in position by smearing its rear surface with grease. Note that the grooved surface of the thrust washer is towards the layshaft. (See Fig. D13).

Set the camplate in the neutral gear position (See Fig. D13). Lubricate the needle roller bearings in the high gear (use oil recommended in Section A2) and layshaft bearing. Place the mainshaft fourth gear with its respective selector fork onto the mainshaft. See Fig. D1. This selector fork has a large engaging pin and no cuttaway on the housing. Assemble the shaft into the high gear using a heavy grease to retain the selector fork on the gear and in the camplate track. Replace the layshaft assembly with fifth and fourth gears into the gearbox and engage with the mainshaft fifth and fourth gears (note that with the gearbox in the neutral position none of the sliding dogs will be engaged).

Replace the layshaft third gear with its respective selector fork (See Fig. D1). This selector fork has a large engaging pin and a cuttaway on the selector housing. Then replace the mainshaft third gear and engage with the layshaft third. Replace the layshaft second gear after first lubricating the bush with oil. Replace the combined first and second gear onto the mainshaft. Replace the layshaft bottom gear with is selector fork (this selector fork has a small diameter engaging pin and a cuttaway to match the previous selector fork. See Fig. D1. Replace the selector rod. Fit the circlip onto the end of the layshaft and the engaging dog up against the circlip. Turn the camplate towards the inner cover from the top thereby placing the gearbox into the first gear position (note engaging dog on layshaft will be in mesh with the dogs on the layshaft first gear).

Check the camplate operating quadrant is moving freely in the inner cover and position the bronze layshaft thrust washer over the needle roller bearing in the inner cover. Again, use grease to hold the thrust washer in position during assembly.

D GEARBOX

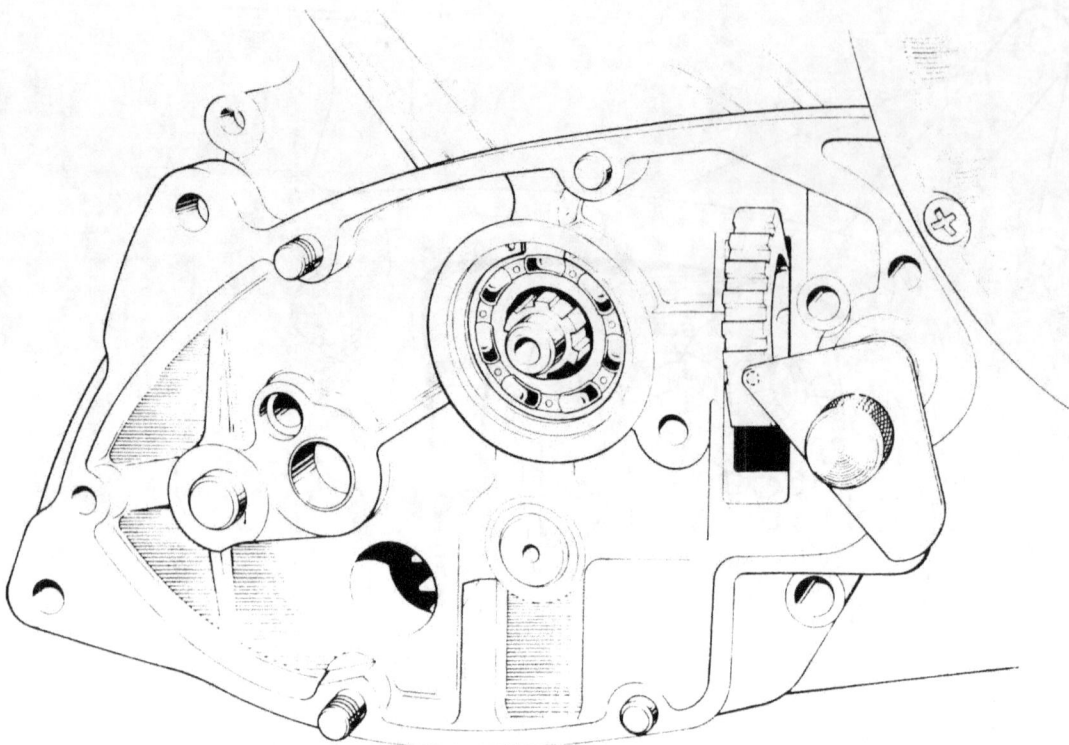

Fig. D14. Refitting the gearbox inner cover using tool 61-7011

Using a pressure oil can, lubricate all the moving parts in the gearbox, then apply a fresh coat of jointing compound to the gearbox junction surface.

Ensure that the two location dowels are in position and offer the inner cover assembly to the gearbox. When the cover is approximately ¼in. (6mm.) away from the gearbox junction face, position the camplate quadrant as detailed in Fig. D14 and position service tool 61-7011 as shown. If this tool is not available line up the top edge of the second tooth on the quadrant with the centre line passing through the footchange spindle housing.

Screw in the socket screw, recessed screw and the bolt, then temporarily assemble the outer cover and gearchange lever and check that the gearchanging sequence is correct by simultaneously operating the gearchange pedal and turning the rear wheel. In the event of any problem of selection it must be assumed that the quadrant teeth are not engaged accurately with the camplate pinion. To rectify this, remove the inner cover again and check that the camplate has been set as shown in Fig. D14. Offer up the inner cover and repeat as previous.

When correct gearchanging is established, re-assemble the kickstart pinion and ratchet, replace the tab washer and screw on the securing nut to the torque figure given in "General Data". To facilitate this, the rear brake should be applied with fifth gear selected.

Refit the gearbox outer cover as shown in section D2 then reassemble the transmission, referring to section A1 for the correct grades of lubricant for the primry chaincase and gearbox. See "General Data" for the correct quantities.

SECTION D12
CHANGING THE GEARBOX SPROCKET

To gain access to the gearbox sprocket, first remove the left footrest, exhaust pipe and the gearchange pedal and then remove the outer primary cover as shown in Section C3.

Remove the pressure plate, clutch plates and withdraw the shock absorber unit, clutch sprocket and footchange shaft as shown in Section C9. Remove the key from the gearbox mainshaft and unscrew the six

GEARBOX

screws which serve to retain the circular cover.

Apply the rear brake, then unscrew the gearbox sprocket securing nut using service tool number 61-6125. The rear chain may now be disconnected and the gearbox sprocket withdrawn through the aperture.

before fitting the new sprocket check that the gearbox oil seal is in good condition and that the rear chain is not excessively worn. Check the extension as shown in Section A12. If the old chain is to be retained for further use it should be thoroughly cleaned in paraffin (kerosene) and lubricated. Fit a new locking plate and new 'O' ring then slide the sprocket over the gearbox mainshaft and high gear. When the sprocket is located on the splines screw on the securing nut finger tight, then re-connect the chain. With the rear brake applied tighten the nut until it is as tight as possible and tap over the lockplate.

When replacing the circular cover plate, use a new paper gasket. Reassembly then continues as a reversal of the above instructions.

SECTION E

FRAME AND ATTACHMENT DETAILS

	Section
REMOVING AND REFITTING THE FUEL TANK	E1
REMOVING SIDE PANELS AND FILTER HOUSING	E2
REMOVING PROP STAND	E3
REMOVING THE CENTRE STAND	E4
REMOVING REAR BRAKE PEDAL	E5
REMOVING AND SERVICING THE REAR BRAKE PEDAL SPINDLE	E6
REMOVING TWINSEAT	E7
CHAINGUARD REMOVAL	E8
CONTROL CABLE REPLACEMENT	E9
REMOVING COIL PLATE	E10
REMOVING REAR LIGHT UNIT	E11
REMOVING HORN	E12
REMOVING REAR STOP SWITCH	E13
REMOVING AND REPLACING THE BATTERY CARRIER ASSEMBLY	E14
REMOVING AND REPLACING THE FLASHER UNIT	E15
REMOVING AND REPLACING THE MUDGUARDS	E16
ADJUSTING THE REAR SUSPENSION	E17
REMOVING AND REFITTING THE REAR SUSPENSION UNITS	E18
STRIPPING AND REASSEMBLING THE SUSPENSION UNITS	E19
REMOVING AND REFITTING THE SWINGING FORK	E20
RENEWING THE SWINGING FORK BUSHES	E21
FRAME ALIGNMENT	E22
REPAIRS	E23
PAINTWORK REFINISHING	E24
FITTING REPLACEMENT SEAT COVERS	E25

FRAME

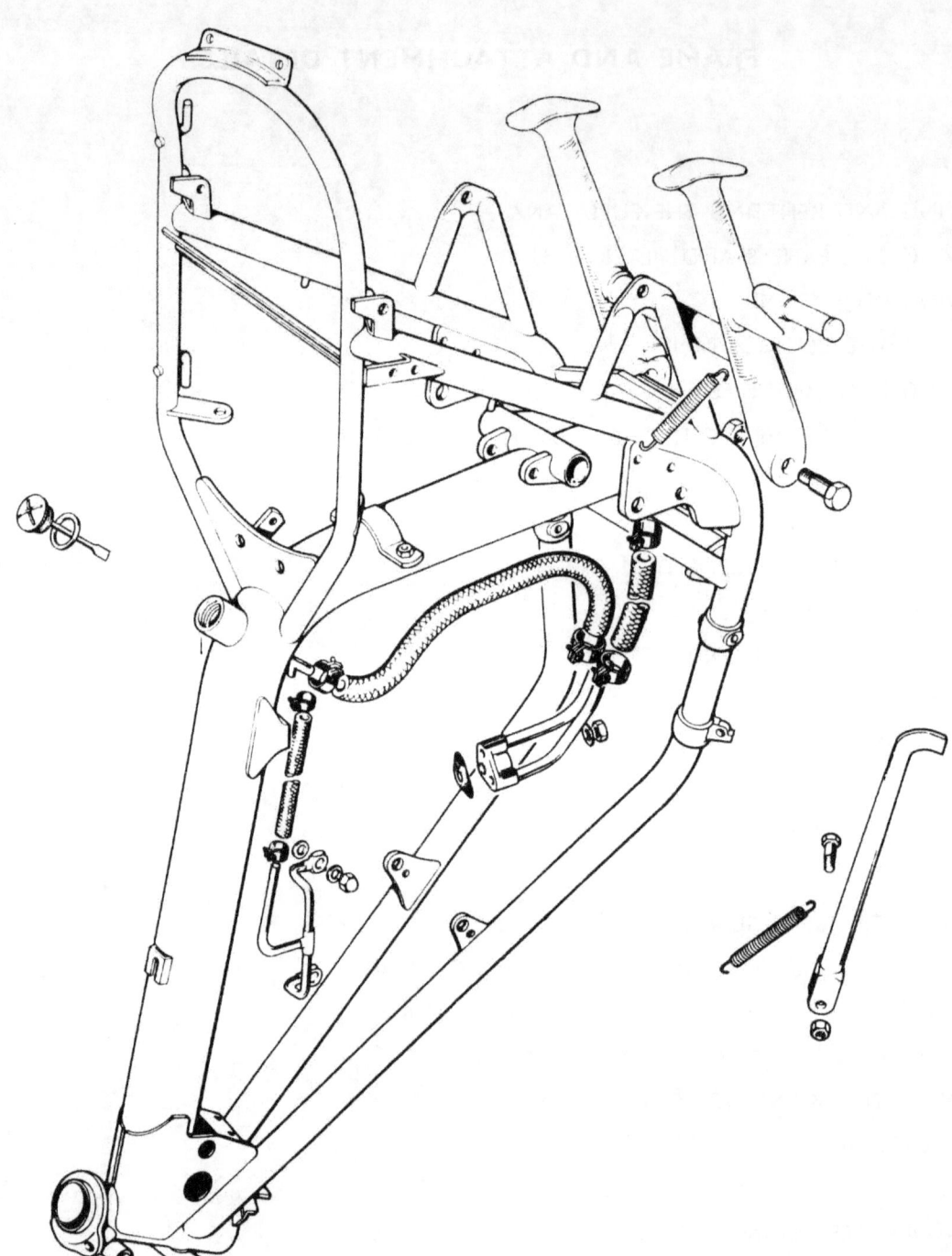

Fig. E1. General arrangement of frame assembly

SECTION E1

REMOVING AND REPLACING THE FUEL TANK

Ensure that the fuel taps are in the "OFF" position and disconnect the feed pipes. Remove the rubber grommet from the centre of the fuel tank and unscrew the sleeve nut revealed below.

The tank can now be pulled away from the frame. Note assembly of rubber sleeve and washers securing the tank. See Fig. E2.

Drain the tank and unscrew the fuel tap assemblies and clean the mesh filters at the intervals stated in "Routine Maintenance".

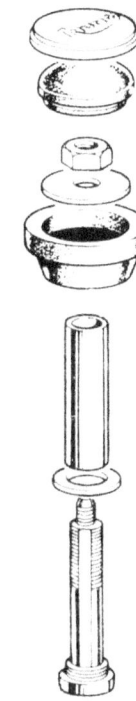

Fig. E2. Fuel tank mounting

SECTION E2

REMOVING SIDE PANELS AND FILTER HOUSING

Remove the outer trim panels by disconnecting the two retaining springs
Detach filter cover by removing the single bolt situated in the centre. Loosen the two bolts and nuts contained inside the housing that retain the side panel. The holes in the panel are slotted; hence the panel can be pulled away from the frame. The rearmost end of the panel is secured to the frame by rubber bushes integral with the panel and pushed onto spigots welded to the frame.

To remove the filter housing remove two securing bolts retaining the housing to the frame and the two 4BA bolts and nuts that secure the two halves of the housing. These are contained in the well at the foremost part of the housing.

FRAME

SECTION E3
REMOVING THE PROP STAND

The prop stand leg is secured to a lug on the frame by means of a bolt and locking nut. Remove the bolt, pull the bolt away from the lug and disconnect the return spring.

When reassembling, attach the spring to the frame and leg, then push the leg onto the lug and fit the bolt.

SECTION E4
REMOVING THE CENTRE STAND

The centre stand is secured to the frame by two bolts passing through welded brackets. Remove the bolts when the stand is in the raised position (i.e. when the return spring is slackest).

When reassembling, bolt the stand to frame and while holding the stand in the raised position stretch the return spring with the aid of a "pozidrive" headed screwdriver (or similar) and attach the spring into position.

SECTION E5
REMOVING REAR BRAKE PEDAL

Remove the locknut and washer then withdraw the brake pedal. When replacing the pedal tighten the securing nut.
Prior to frame no. HN62501 unscrew the brake rod adjustment screw at the rear brake operating lever and remove. Remove the pedal securing bolt and locknut and withdraw the pedal and rod from the machine.
When the pedal has been replaced refer to Section F for the correct adjustment procedure.

SECTION E6
REMOVING AND SERVICING THE REAR BRAKE PEDAL SPINDLE

Detach the rear brake stoplight switch by removing the two cross-head screws.
Remove the inner spindle retaining nut and washer. Using a suitable drift break the taper fit of the trunnion lever on the spindle and then withdraw the spindle and pedal from the R.H. side.
Remove the brake pedal return spring and the distance piece.
NOTE: The recess in the distance piece faces the R.H. side.
Check the brake pedal spindle and the sleeve nut for damage, scoring or excessive play. If necessary replace the spindle and/or sleeve nut.

Liberally grease spindle prior to reassembly.
Replace the sleeve nut and tighten to torque shown in GD and insert pedal spindle complete with brake pedal
Replace the distance piece with the recess located in the protruding sleeve nut. Locate the brake pedal return spring on the frame see Fig. E4.
Reconnect the lever to the spindle and refit the nut and washer finger tight ONLY.
Make up a simple hook with wire or string and connect the spring to the lever. See Fig. E5.
Tighten the nut and washer securely.

FRAME E

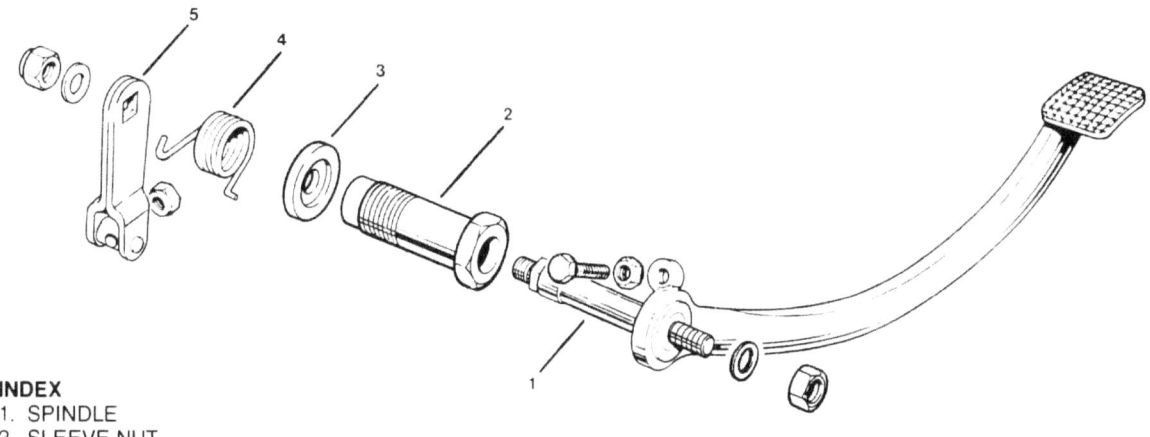

INDEX
1. SPINDLE
2. SLEEVE NUT
3. DISTANCE PIECE
4. BRAKE PEDAL RETURN SPRING
5. TRUNNION LEVER

Fig. E3. Rear brake pedal spindle assembly – exploded

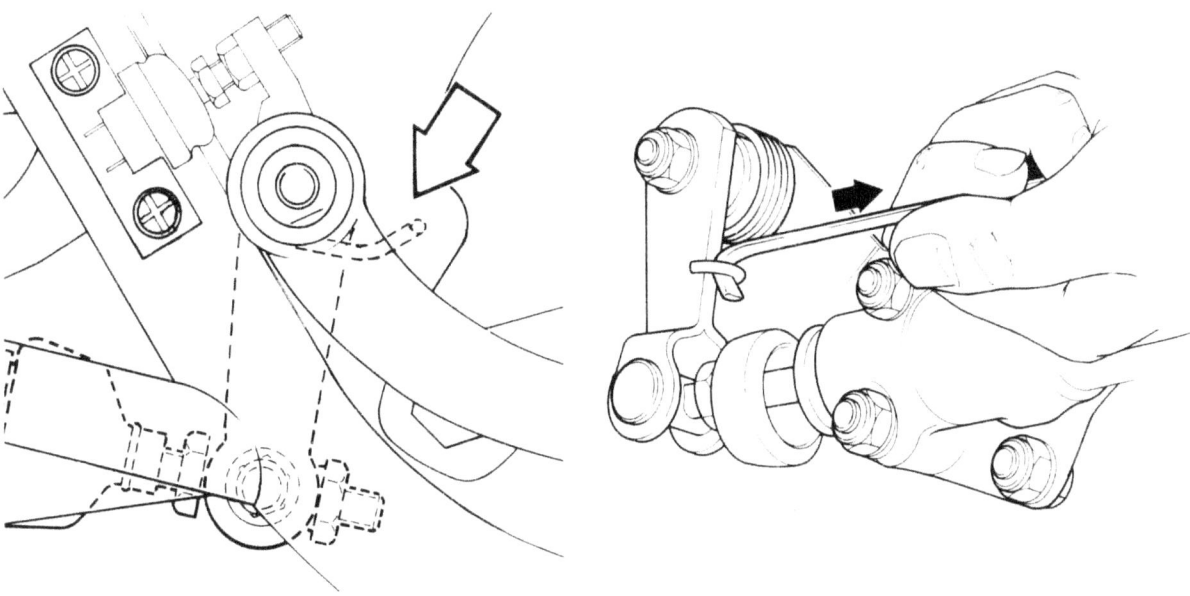

Fig. E4. Brake pedal return spring – frame location

Fig. E5. Refitting the brake pedal return spring
(Shown with rear wheel removed)

E5

E
FRAME

Refit the brake lever and the nut and washer.

NOTE: Do not operate the rear brake while the rear wheel is still removed.

Check the rear brake pedal adjustment. See section F1.

Replace the brake light stop switch assembly. If necessary adjust the movable stop on the brake pedal such that the rear brake light is illuminated (ignition 'ON') when the rear brake is operated.

SECTION E7

REMOVING TWINSEAT

Detach check strap from the underside of the seat by removing the small "pozidrive" screw.

Then remove the two attachment bolts at the front seat hinge and slide the seat away towards the rear of the machine.

SECTION E8

CHAINGUARD REMOVAL

Remove the fixing bolt at the front of the chainguard and loosen the left side lower suspension unit bolt.

The chainguard mounting is slotted at the suspension unit bolt fixing and the chainguard can now be lifted clear and withdrawn from the rear of the machine.

SECTION E9
CONTROL CABLE REPLACEMENT

Clutch Cable
Slacken off the clutch cable adjustment and slip out the cable nipple at the handlebar control. Slide the rubber cover away from the abutment at the gearbox end and unscrew the abutment. Remove the large slotted plug from the gearbox outer cover and access will be gained to the clutch operating arm. It is then only necessary to release the cable nipple from the arm with the finger. Replacement is the reversal of the above instruction. Note that there is a grease nipple incorporated in the outer casing and this should be employed regularly to ensure maximum lubrication of the cable.

Throttle Cable(s)
To remove the throttle cable(s) first of all remove the fuel tank. See Section E1. Remove the top cap(s) from the carburetter(s). It will be found easier to disconnect the cable from the throttle slide if the twist grip is removed from the handlebar and the cable(s) disconnected.

Then pull back the return spring in the throttle slide and remove the needle and needle clip. With the spring still retracted push the cable through the slide and when the nipple is clear pull it across the figure of eight slot and withdraw the cable. Note that early U.K. and General Export T140's have a 'two into one' throttle cable arrangement incorporating a junction box. The cables can be detached from the junction box by unscrewing the two halves of the casing and releasing the nipples.

When reassembling the box grease the internals liberally.

Note: When reassembling the throttle slides into the carburetter do not apply any form of lubricant to the bearing surface; this will undoubtedly cause the slide to stick. Simply remove any surface deposits on the slide with a very fine carborundum paper and then wash with gasoline (petrol).
When the cables have been replaced readjust them as detailed in Section B12.

Air Control Cables – TRV & T140V models only
Remove the top caps of the carburetter(s) as for the throttle cables. To disconnect the air valve, push the valve guide tube and spring along with the air cable until the cable nipple protrudes sufficiently out of its counterbore to be pushed out of its slot. The cable, spring and guide can now be pulled clear of the valve. Disconnect the cable from the control lever by unscrewing the centre fixing nut, removing the lever arm and detaching the nipple.

The air cables incorporate a two into one junction box similar to the junction box for the throttle cables on T140 models. The body of the junction box can be dismantled by unscrewing each half and then disconnecting the nipples therein. When replacing new cables ensure that the junction box is well lubricated with grease.

SECTION E10
REMOVING AND REPLACING THE COIL PLATE

The pressed steel plate holding the two ignition coils, rectifier and condensers is situated beneath the twin-seat. Disconnect all the wiring from the components at the respective terminals. The front of the plate is attached to the rear battery carrier fixing bolts. Remove the two retaining nuts and then detach the two remaining nuts and bolts which attach the rear of the plate to the mudguard. Remove the fixing bolt and detach the rear brake hydraulic reservoir. Take care not to spill any brake fluid. The plate assembly can then be lifted clear of the machine.

Replacment is the reverse of the above instructions. Refer to the wiring diagram for the correct re-wiring procedure. (See Section H19).

E | FRAME

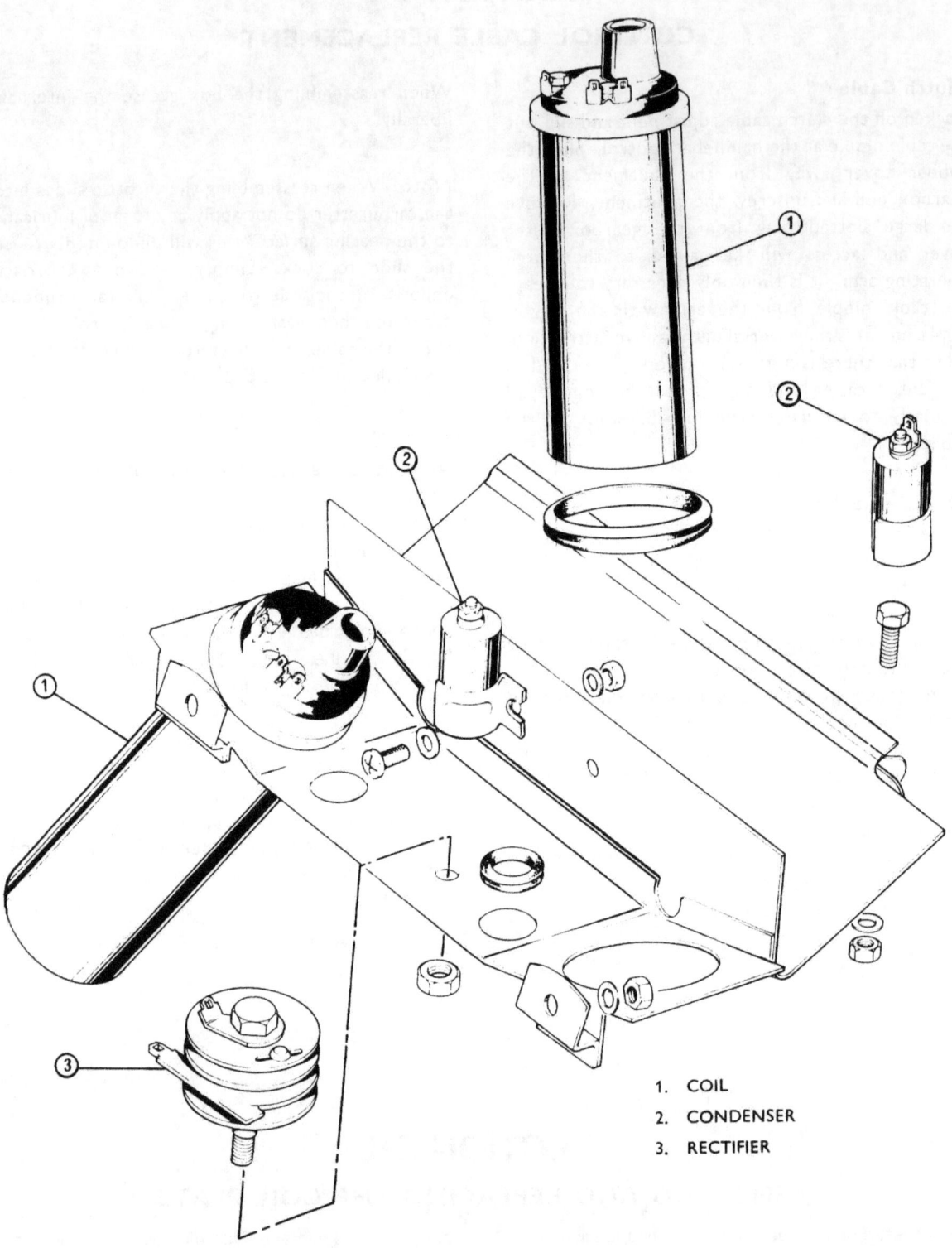

1. COIL
2. CONDENSER
3. RECTIFIER

Fig. E6. Coil plate mountings

FRAME

SECTION E11
REMOVING AND REPLACING REAR LIGHT UNIT

Three bolts attach the unit to the mudguard and these are accessible from underneath the mudguard blade. As the unit is removed disconnect the snap connectors from beneath the housing.
See Section H11 for the dismantling procedure of the tail light.

SECTION E12
REMOVING THE HORN

The horn can be removed from the frame without detaching the fuel tank, but if difficulty is encountered remove the fuel tank as detailed in section E1.

Two nuts and bolts secure the horn to a bracket below and behind the head lug.

SECTION E13
REMOVING REAR STOP SWITCH

Two pozidrive screws secure the stop switch assembly to the rear frame member.

Release these screws and detach the return spring. Disconnect the electrical connections.

SECTION E14
REMOVING AND REPLACING THE BATTERY CARRIER

Using a screwdriver of suitable length remove the three slotted constant diameter bolts that sit in the rubber retaining bushes that secure the carrier to the frame. The mountings towards the rear of the machine have captive nuts attached to the coil plate. The front mounting point has a locking nut on the right side and earth connecting wire underneath. It will now be possible to lift the battery carrier vertically clear of the machine. Replacement is the reversal of the above. Ensure that the earth connection is clean and tight. Replace the battery and note route of breather pipe.

SECTION 15
REMOVING AND REPLACING THE FLASHER UNIT

The flasher unit is contained behind the left side panel. See Section E2 for removing panel. The unit is attached to a damping spring which is in turn bolted to a bracket on the frame. Detach both lucar connectors and release the unit from the spring or remove the assembly of spring and flasher unit. See Fig. E7 for correct mounted position.

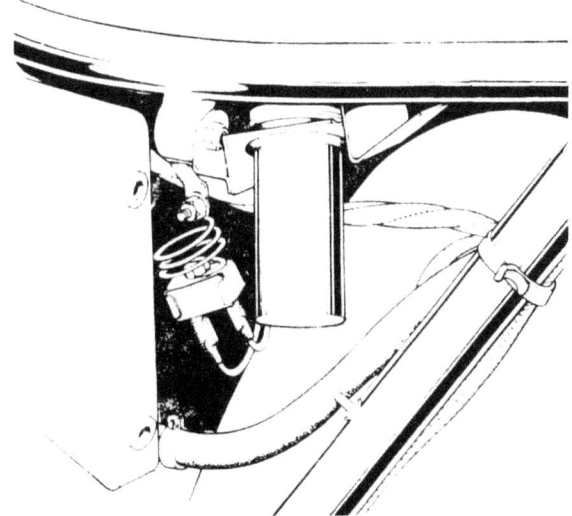

Fig. E7. Showing position of flasher unit

SECTION E16

REMOVING AND REPLACING THE MUDGUARDS

Rear Mudguard

First disconnect the three snap connectors found under the seat, two leading to the flashers and the other leading to the rear brake light. Pull bach the narness retaining clips found on the inside rim of the muguard. (Withdraw green flasher wires through the appropriate grommets.)

Detach the rear light unit by removing the three attachment bolts from underneath the mudguard blade, two of which act as bracket holders for the number plate. Lift the light away from the mudguard and withdraw the wires through the grommet Detach the two nuts and bolts at the front mounting bracket. Remove the two nuts and bolts at the top of the mudguard. Note that the twinseat check strap is attached to one of these bolts. Remove the two nuts and bolts at the rear frame loop and those connecting the grab rail to the mudguard.

Put the motorcycle on its side and withdraw mudguard.

Front Mudguard

To remove the front mudguard detach the four bolts securing the mudguard stay to the fork legs, two found at the fork leg bottom and the others on the mudguard boss found higher up the fork leg.

SECTION E17

ADJUSTING THE REAR SUSPENSION

The movement is controlled by Girling combined coil spring and hydraulic or gas damper units. The hydraulic or gas damping mechanism is completely sealed but the static loading of the spring is adjustable.

A three position cam ring is concealed beneath a sleeve with a castellated adjuster ring. The notch location is not visible but rotation in the direction shown increases the load and vice versa.

Ajusting spanner 60-2184 is needed for this adjustment. Both units must be adjusted equally and a quick visual check can be made on the adjusted positions by comaprison from the rear of the machine.

The standard lowest position is for solo riding, the second position is for heavier solo riders or when luggage is carried on the rear of the machine and the third or highest position is for use when a pillion passenger is being carried.

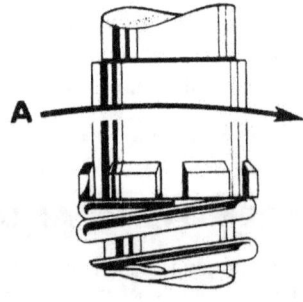

Fig. 8A. Adjusting the rear suspension unit
Note the arrow showing direction of rotation to increase the spring rating.

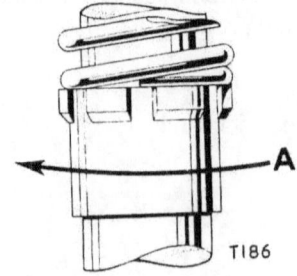

Fig. 8B. Adjusting the rear suspension unit
Prior to frame no. BX05107

FRAME　　E

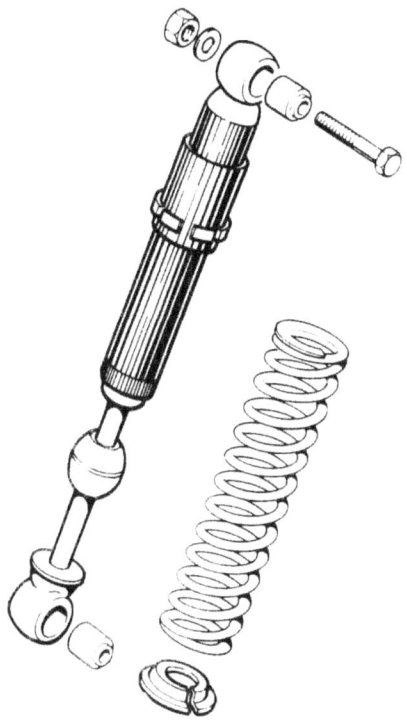

Fig. 9A. Exploded view of the rear suspension unit

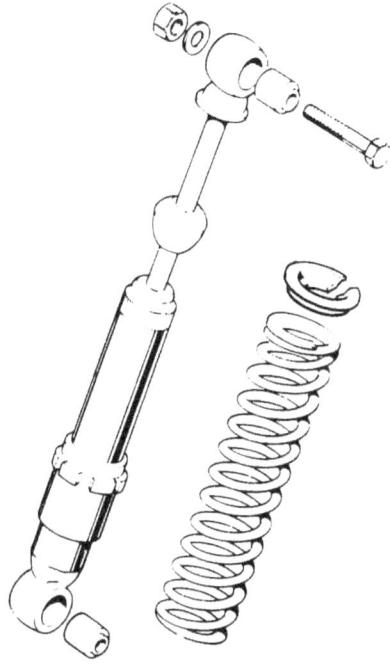

Fig. 9B. Exploded view of the rear suspension unit
Prior to frame no. BX05107

SECTION E18

REMOVING AND REFITTING THE REAR SUSPENSION UNITS

Lift the twinseat by releasing the catch on the right side.

Remove the top two suspension unit bolts. Then remove the lower fixing bolts. Note that the left side fixing bolt secures the rear portion of the chainguard. When replacing the units notice that the top fixing bolts also secure the grab rail.

NOTE: If a unit is inadvertently fitted the wrong way up irrepairable damage will be cause to the damping mechanism within the unit.

WARNING
Models prior to frame no. BX05107 were produced with oil hydraulic rear suspension damper units and must not be mixed with the later gas filled type, nor should they be fitted incorrectly. The gas filled type must be fitted with the castellated load adjusting ring at the TOP of the unit and the oil hydraulic unit with the adjuster ring at the BOTTOM of the unit.

If in doubt the units can be identified as follows:

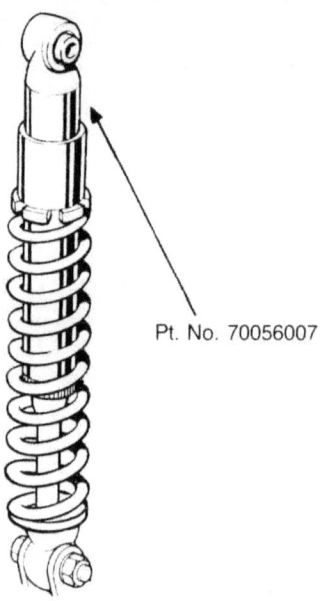

Fig. 10A. Gas filled suspension unit fitted after frame no. BX05107

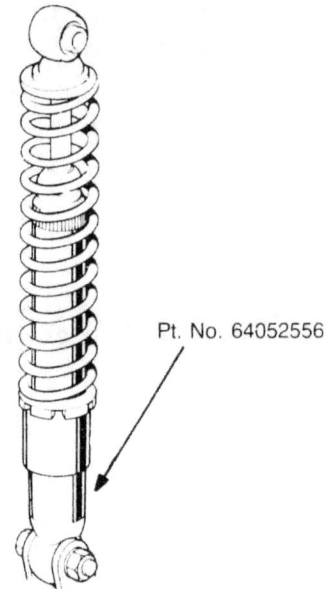

Fig. 10B. Oil hydraulic suspension unit fitted prior to frame no. BX05107

SECTION E19

STRIPPING AND REASSEMBLING THE SUSPENSION UNITS

The suspensions unit consists of a sealed hydraulic/gas damper unit, and outer coiled spring. The static loading on the spring is adjustable and should be set according to the type of conditions under which the machine is to be used (see Section E17).

To dismantle the suspension unit and remove the spring, it is required to compress the spring whilst the retaining collar (two semi-circular spring retainer plate – prior to frame no. BX05107) is removed. To do this first turn the cam until it is in the "LIGHT-LOAD" position, then compress the spring using suitable spring clamps. Remove the spring retainer and withdraw the spring.

The damper unit should be checked for bending of the plunger rod and damping action. Check the bonded pivot bushes for wear and ensure that the sleeve is not loose in the rubber bush.

The bushes can be easily renewed by driving out the old one and pressing in the new one using a smear of soapy water to assist assembly. Under no circumstances should the plunger rod be lubricated.

Note.—For information concerning suspension units or spare parts, the local Girling agent should be consulted.

Reassembly is a reversal of dismantling. Check that the cam is in the light load position before compressing the spring.

SECTION E20

REMOVING AND REFITTING THE SWINGING FORK

Remove the rear wheel. See Section F. Slacken the lower left side suspension unit fixing bolt and remove the front securing bolt. Withdraw the chainguard from the machine. Remove the rear suspension units. See Section E18.

Unscrew the swinging arm spindle nut from the right side and withdraw the spindle from the left side. The swinging arm can now be pulled away from the frame. Note the four rubber dust covers on the pivot housing. Remove the sleeve spindles from the pivot ends and thoroughly wash all parts in kerosene (paraffin). Inspect the bore of the bushes and the diameter of the sleeve spindles for excessive wear. Check the dimensions with the sizes given in "GENERAL DATA". If the working clearance is excessive the bushes will require renewing. See Section E21.

The parts should be reassembled in the order shown in Fig. E11 with a sufficient supply of grease as recommended in Section A1. Assemble the spindle sleeves into their housings and offer the swinging arm up to the frame with the rubber dust covers in position. Refit end thrust washers and replace the spindle. The spindle should be tightened sufficiently until the fork will move upwards and downwards with a little effort.

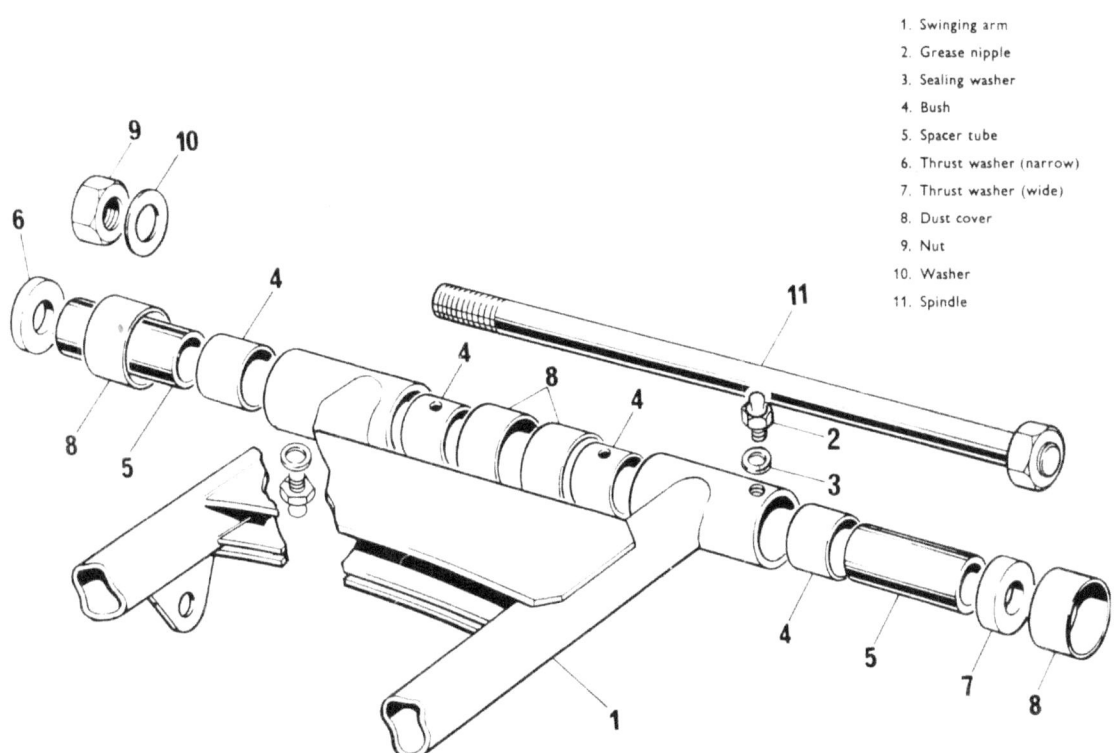

1. Swinging arm
2. Grease nipple
3. Sealing washer
4. Bush
5. Spacer tube
6. Thrust washer (narrow)
7. Thrust washer (wide)
8. Dust cover
9. Nut
10. Washer
11. Spindle

Fig. E11. Swinging arm components

SECTION E21

RENEWING THE SWINGING FORK BUSHES

The bushes can be removed from their respective housings using service tool 61-6117. Assemble the tool into the housing as shown in Fig. E12 (bottom) and by turning the bolt nut it will be possible to extract the bushes into the spacer tube. Reassemble new bushes as shown in Fig. E12 (top). Press in one bush at a time from each end of the housing using a little grease to assist assembly.

The new bushes are of the steel backed pre-sized type and when pressed in will give the correct diametral working clearance.

Alternatively the bushes can be removed using a mild steel shouldered drift of suitable dimensions (i.e. 1 in. dia. and $1\frac{1}{8}$ in. dia.). It will be possible to drift one bush through the housing thereby knocking out the second bush at the same time.

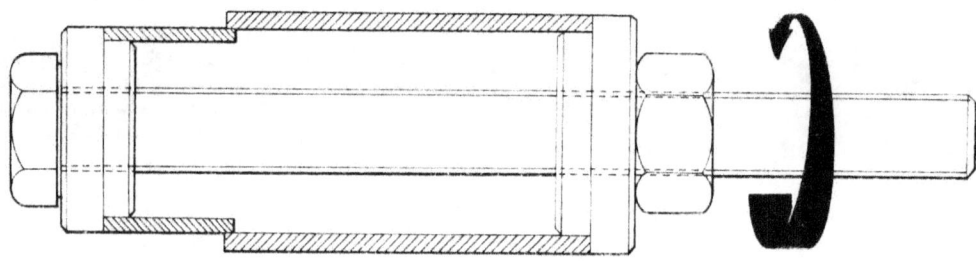

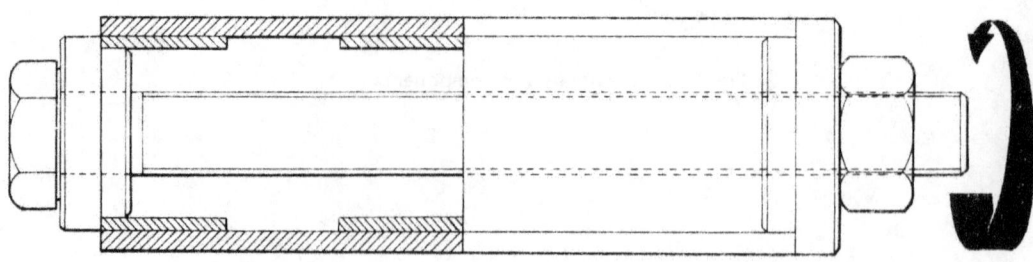

Fig. E12. Removing and replacing the swinging arm bushes using Service Tool 61-6117
(Bottom view shows removal of bush)

SECTION E22
FRAME ALIGNMENT

If the machine has been damaged in an accident the frame must be checked for breakage or fracture at all the welded seams. Due to the design of the frame providing an extremely rigid structure, it is highly unlikely that the frame will bend or twist to any degree without fracture occurring. Under no circumstances should any attempt be made to re-align or reshape the frame as this will cause high stress concentration which can only result in further fracture taking place.

Fracture is likely to occur at the head lug gussets, (particularly in the case of a head-on collision). The frame must be completely stripped down and the steering head races removed. Note the areas at the webs joining the head lug to the main frame tube and at the lower bearing housing in the head lug itself.

See Figs. E13 and E14. Also carefully check the front down tubes for any deforming or splitting. If necessary remove all the paint from the suspected area and check again.

In cases of side collision etc. if the damage is not immediately apparent a simple check can be made by attempting to place spindles or bolts of suitable length and diameter through the swinging arm pivots and engine mounting positions. Mis-alignment will be apparent if the spindle or bolt fouls its exit hole.

Note Fig. E15 for the critical dimensions of the frame. If possible check these if any doubt is revealed.

FRAME

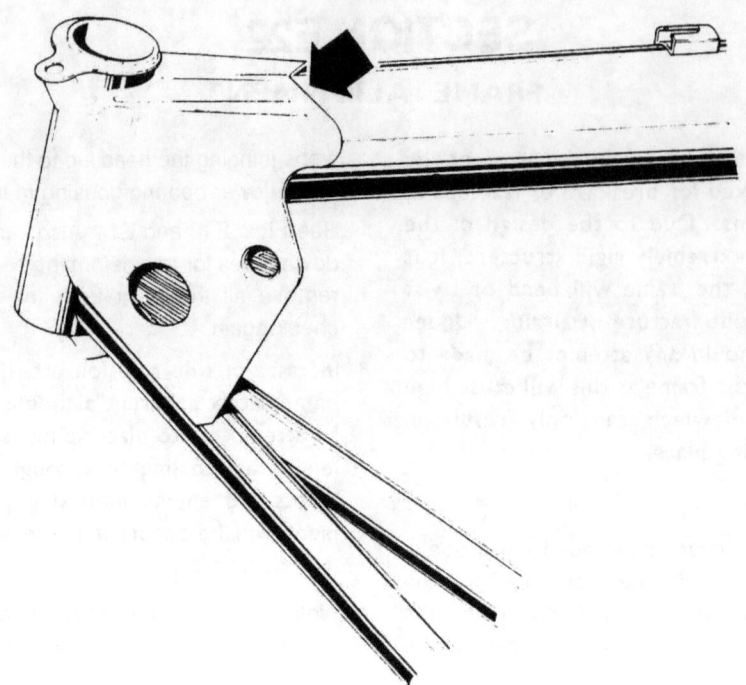

Fig. E13. Fracture at rear of head lug

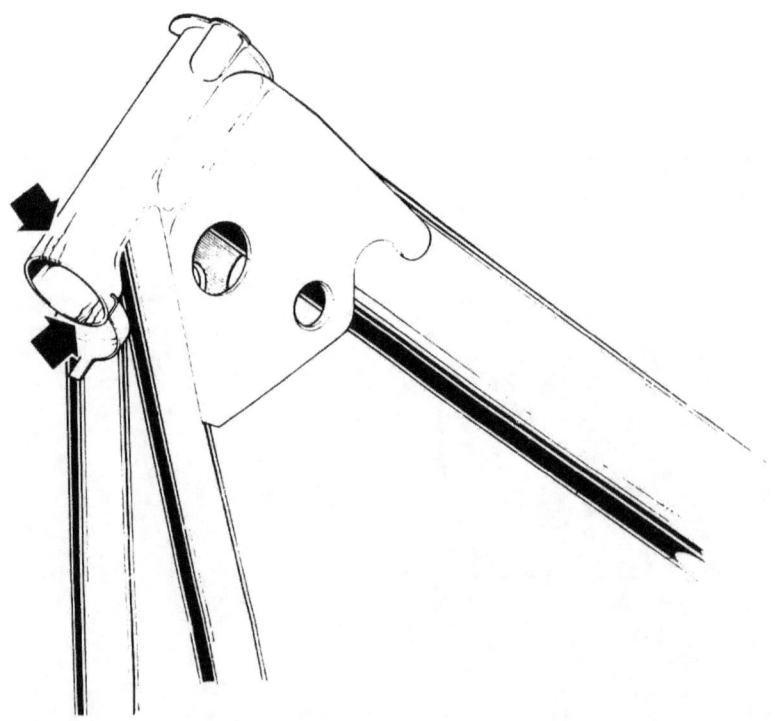

Fig. E14. Fracture at bottom bearing housing

FRAME

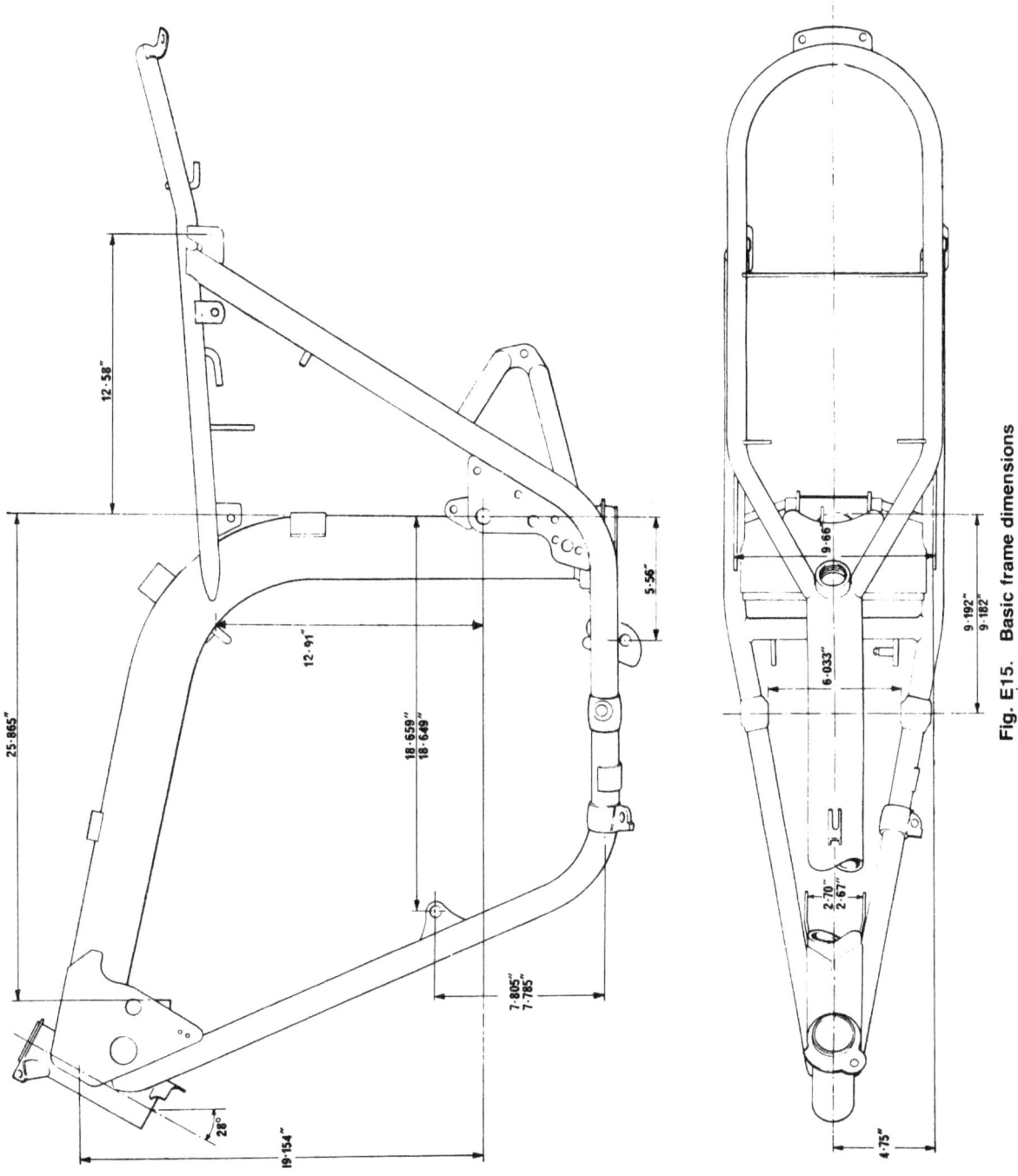

Fig. E15. Basic frame dimensions

FRAME

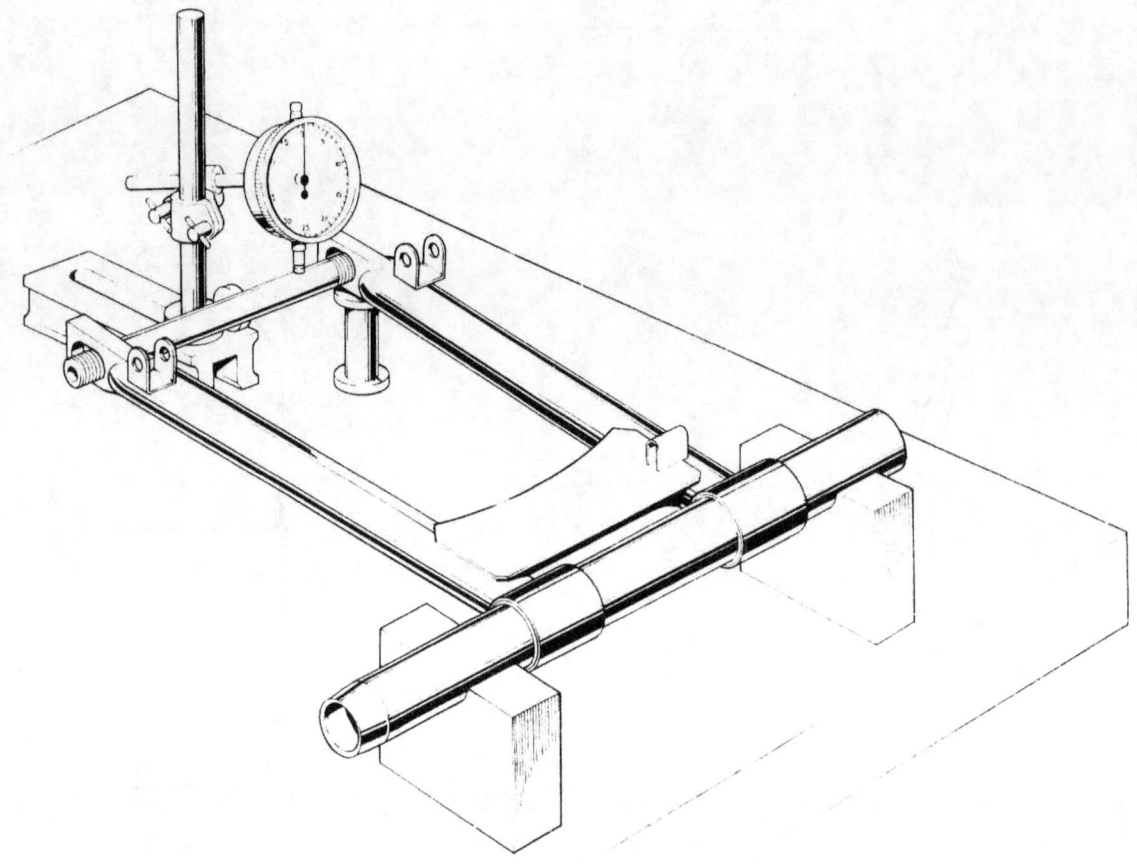

Fig. E16. Checking the swinging fork

SWINGING FORK

It is required to check that the centre line of the pivot spindle is in the same plane as the centre line of the rear spindle. To do this, first place a tube or bar of suitable diameter into the swinging fork bearing bushes, then mount the swinging fork on two "V" blocks, one either side, and clamp it lightly to the edge of the checking table. Fit the rear wheel spindle into the fork end slots or, alternatively, use a straight bar of similar diameter, then support a fork end so that the swinging fork is approximately horizontal. Height readings should then be taken at both ends of the wheel spindle to establish any mis-alignment. (Fig. E16).

Next, check that the distance between the fork ends is as given in "General Data"

It is now necessary to lever the fork ends in the correcting direction until the wheel spindle can be inserted and found to be parallel with the pivot bush centre line. To do this, a bar of 4 ft. length and suitable diameter is required. It is now that great care is required. Insert the bar at the end of the swinging fork adjacent to the suspension unit mounting brackets so that it is over the "high" fork leg and under the "low" fork leg. Exert gentle pressure at the end of the bar then insert the spindle and re-check the alignment. Repeat this procedure using increased loads until the spindle height readings shows that the swinging arm is now mis-aligned in the opposite sense. A small leverage now applied from the other side will bring the wheel back to parallel.

Note: Apply the leverage bar as near as possible to the suspension unit brackets, otherwise the tubes may become damaged. DO NOT USE THE FORK ENDS.

SECTION E23
PAINTWORK REFINISHING

PAINT STRIPPING

Except in cases where a "touch-up" is to be attempted, it is strongly recommended that the old finish is completely stripped and the refinish is carried out from the bare metal. A suitable paint stripper can be obtained from most paint stores and accessory dealers.

The stripper should be applied with a brush and allowed approximately 10 minutes to react. A suitable scraper should be used to remove the old finish, then the surface cleaned with water using a piece of wire wool. Ensure that all traces of paint stripper are removed. If possible, blow out crevices with compressed air.

It is advisable to strip a small area at a time to avoid the stripper drying and also to enable easier neutralizing of the stripper.

Finally, the surface should be rubbed with a grade 270 or 280 emery cloth to give a satisfactory finish then washed off with white spirits or a suitable cleaner solvent.

PRIMING

A thin coat of cellulose primer must be sprayed onto the surface prior to application of an undercoat or stopper. Undercoat and stopper will not adhere satisfactorily to bare metal. It is advisable to thin the primer by adding 1 part cellulose thinners to 1 part primer. Ensure that the primer is dry before advancing further.

APPLYING STOPPER

Imperfections and slight dents in the surface may be filled with stopper, but rubbing down with "wet and dry" should not be attempted until the undercoat or surfacer has been applied.

Apply the stopper with a glazing knife in thin layers, allowing approximately 20 minutes for drying between each layer. After the last layer, allow the stopper about 6 hours (or over-night if possible) to dry. Heavy layers or insufficient drying time will result in risk of surface cracking.

UNDERCOAT (SURFACER)

Most cellulose undercoats also called surfacers, will suffice for a base for TRIUMPH finishes. About two or three coats are required and should be sprayed on in a thinned condition using 1 part cellulose thinners to 1 part undercoat. Allow approximately 20 minutes between each coat.

If stopper has been applied the final layer of undercoat should be sprayed on after smoothing the surface with "wet and dry" abrasive as shown below.

WET AND DRY SANDING

After application of the undercoat, the surface should be rubbed down with 270 or 280 grade abrasive paper used wet. An ideal method is to have a rubber block around which to wrap the emery paper. However, this is only recommendable for flat surfaces; where rapid change of sections occur, a thin felt pad is more useful.

The abrasive paper should be allowed to soak in cold water for at least 15 minutes before use. A useful tip is to smear the abrasive surface of the paper with soap prior to rubbing down. This will prevent clogging and should at least treble the useful life of the paper if it is washed thoroughly after each rub-down.

When the surface is smooth enough, wash it thoroughly with water and dry off with a clean sponge.

If smoother surface than this is required it can be given another layer of undercoat and then the rubbing down procedure repeated using 320 or 400 grade of paper depending upon conditions

FINISHING

Before spraying on the finishing coats the surface must be quite smooth, dry and clean. It is important that conditions are right when finish spraying is to be carried out otherwise complications may occur. Best conditions for outdoor spraying are those on a dry sunny day without wind. Moisture in the atmosphere is detrimental to paint spraying.

FRAME

The first coat should be thinned in the ratio of 50% cellulose thinners to 50% lacquer. Subsequent coats should have a higher proportion of thinners as shown below.

	Cellulose Thinners	Lacquer
1st Coat	50%	50%
2nd Coat	60%	40%
3rd Coat	70%	30%
4th Coat	80%	20%

Between each coat the surface may be flatted by hand with 320 or 400 abrasive paper as required.

Allow at least 10 minutes between each coat and after the final coat leave overnight or 24 hours if possible. For most purposes the 2nd coat of finishing is more than adequate.

POLISHING

The final colour coat must be completely dry before cutting and polishing. Using a clean rag rub down with brass polish or fine cutting paste and burnish to a high gloss using a clean mop before applying a suitable wax polish for protection and shine.

Note.—TRIUMPH supply only the finishing lacquers. These are available in aerosol sprays only.

SECTION E24
FITTING REPLACEMENT SEAT COVERS

'Quiltop' twinseats have a cover retained by sprags which are part of the seat pan.

When fitting a replacement seat cover it is **very important** to first soak the complete cover assembly in hot water in order to soften the plastic so that it can easily be stretched into place. After soaking the cover in hot water, wring out the excess water and you will find that the cover can very easily be stretched into place to give a neat fit without any wrinkles. This job is very difficult if you do not follow this suggested method.

Ideally the seat should be allowed to dry out in a warm place before being put back into service.

SECTION F

BRAKES WHEELS AND TYRES

DESCRIPTION	Section
BRAKE ADJUSTMENTS	F1
BRAKE FLUID LEVEL	F2
BRAKE PAD AND LINING	F3
BLEEDING THE HYDRAULIC SYSTEM	F4
FLUSHING THE HYDRAULIC SYSTEM	F5
HYDRAULIC BRAKE HOSES—REMOVAL AND REPLACEMENT	F6
REAR BRAKE MASTER CYLINDER AND RESERVOIR	F7
FRONT BRAKE AND MASTER CYLINDER	F8
STRIPPING AND REASSEMBLING THE FRONT AND REAR BRAKE CALIPERS	F9
BRAKE DISCS	F10
REMOVING AND REFITTING THE FRONT WHEEL	F11
REMOVING AND REFITTING THE FRONT WHEEL BEARINGS	F12
REMOVING AND REPLACING THE REAR WHEEL	F13
REMOVING AND REPLACING THE REAR WHEEL BEARINGS	F14
STRIPPING AND REASSEMBLING THE REAR BRAKE (PRIOR TO FRAME No. HN62501)	F15
REAR WHEEL REMOVAL AND REPLACEMENT (PRIOR TO FRAME No. HN62501)	F16
REMOVING AND REPLACING REAR WHEEL BEARINGS (PRIOR TO FRAME No. HN62501)	F17
REAR BRAKE ADJUSTMENT	F18
RENEWING BRAKE LININGS	F19
WHEEL BUILDING	F20
WHEEL BALANCING	F21
WHEEL ALIGNMENT	F22
REMOVING AND REFITTING TYRES	F23
SECURITY BOLTS	F24
TYRE MAINTENANCE	F25
TYRE PRESSURES	F26
REAR CHAIN ADJUSTMENT	F27
BRAKING PERFORMANCE DATA	F28
FAULT FINDING—FRONT AND REAR HYDRAULIC DISC BRAKES	F29

BRAKES, WHEELS AND TYRES

DESCRIPTION

All machines are fitted with a Lockheed hydraulic disc brake on the front and rear wheels. (Early models are fitted with a rear drum brake). The disc brake assembly consists of a high quality cast iron disc (hard chrome plate) attached to the wheel hubs and a cast iron brake caliper attached to the left fork leg or the rear swinging fork. The brake caliper houses two co-axially aligned pistons (Fig. F1) and a pair of brake pads the latter being retained by two split pins.

The pistons and their bores are protected by dust seals fitted in the open ends of the bores. (See Fig. F1). Application of the brake lever generates hydraulic pressure within the system and brake caliper causing the pistons (Fig. F1) to apply equal and opposite pressure on the brake pads (Fig. F1) which in turn move into contact with the rotating brake disc. The operation of the master cylinder and hydraulic flow is detailed in Section F7.

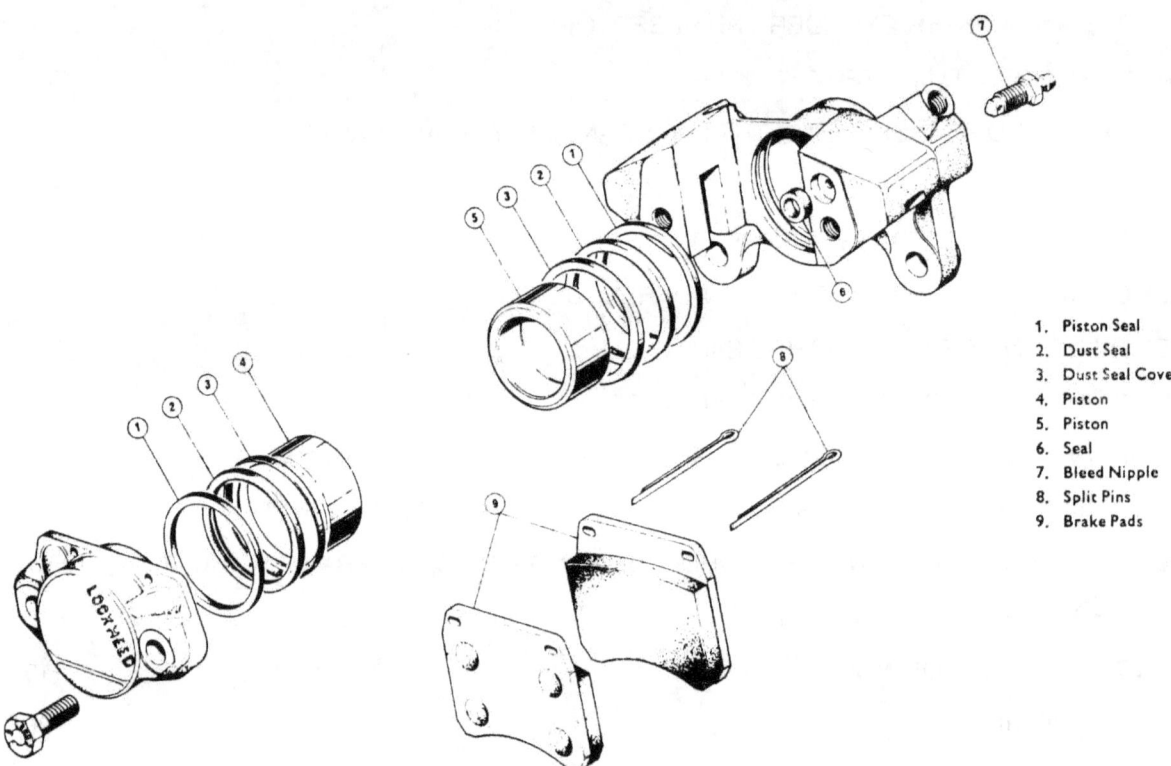

1. Piston Seal
2. Dust Seal
3. Dust Seal Cover
4. Piston
5. Piston
6. Seal
7. Bleed Nipple
8. Split Pins
9. Brake Pads

Fig. F1. Front and rear brake caliper—exploded

BRAKES, WHEELS AND TYRES F

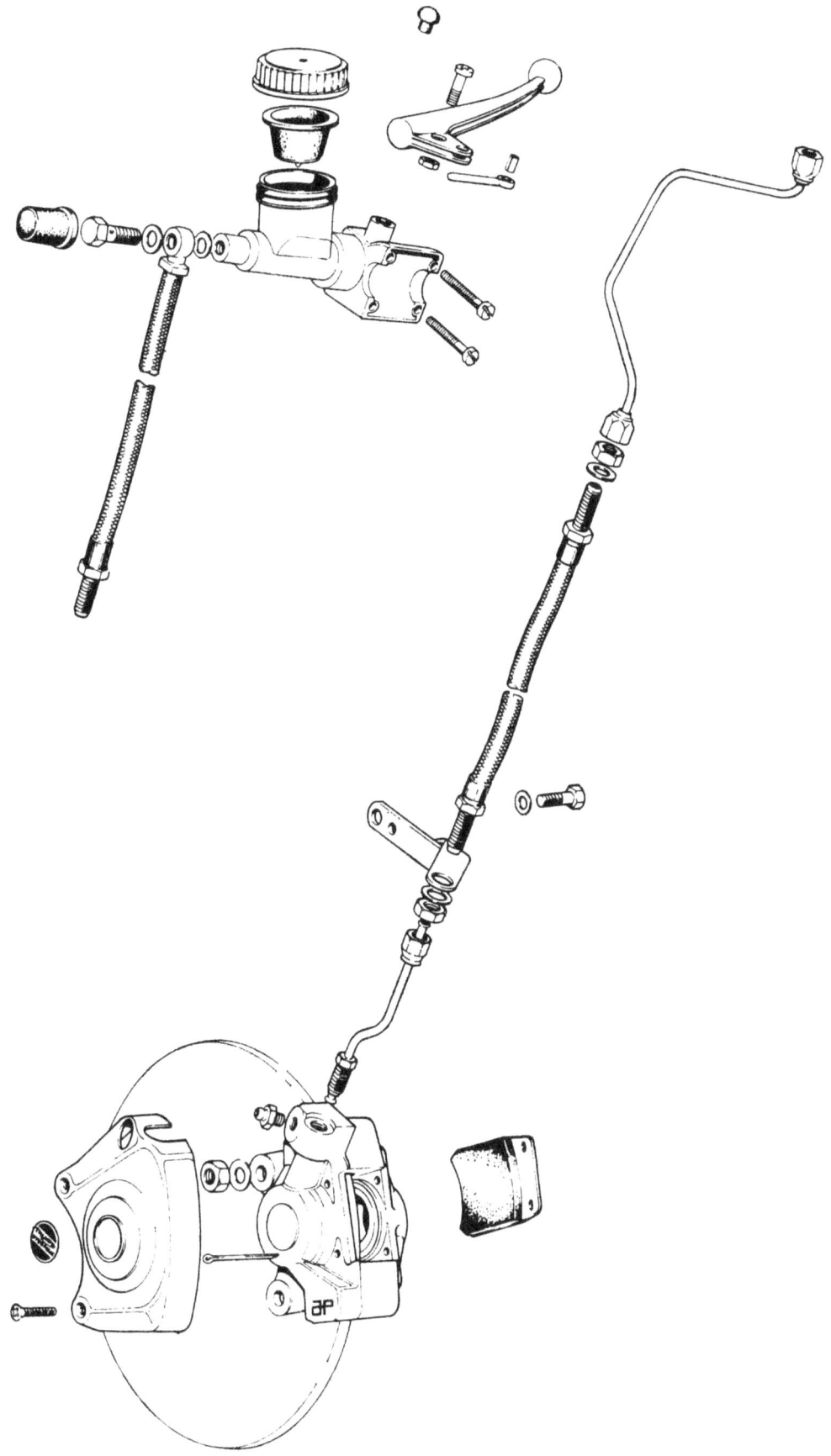

Fig. F2. Front brake components (U.S.A. model shown)

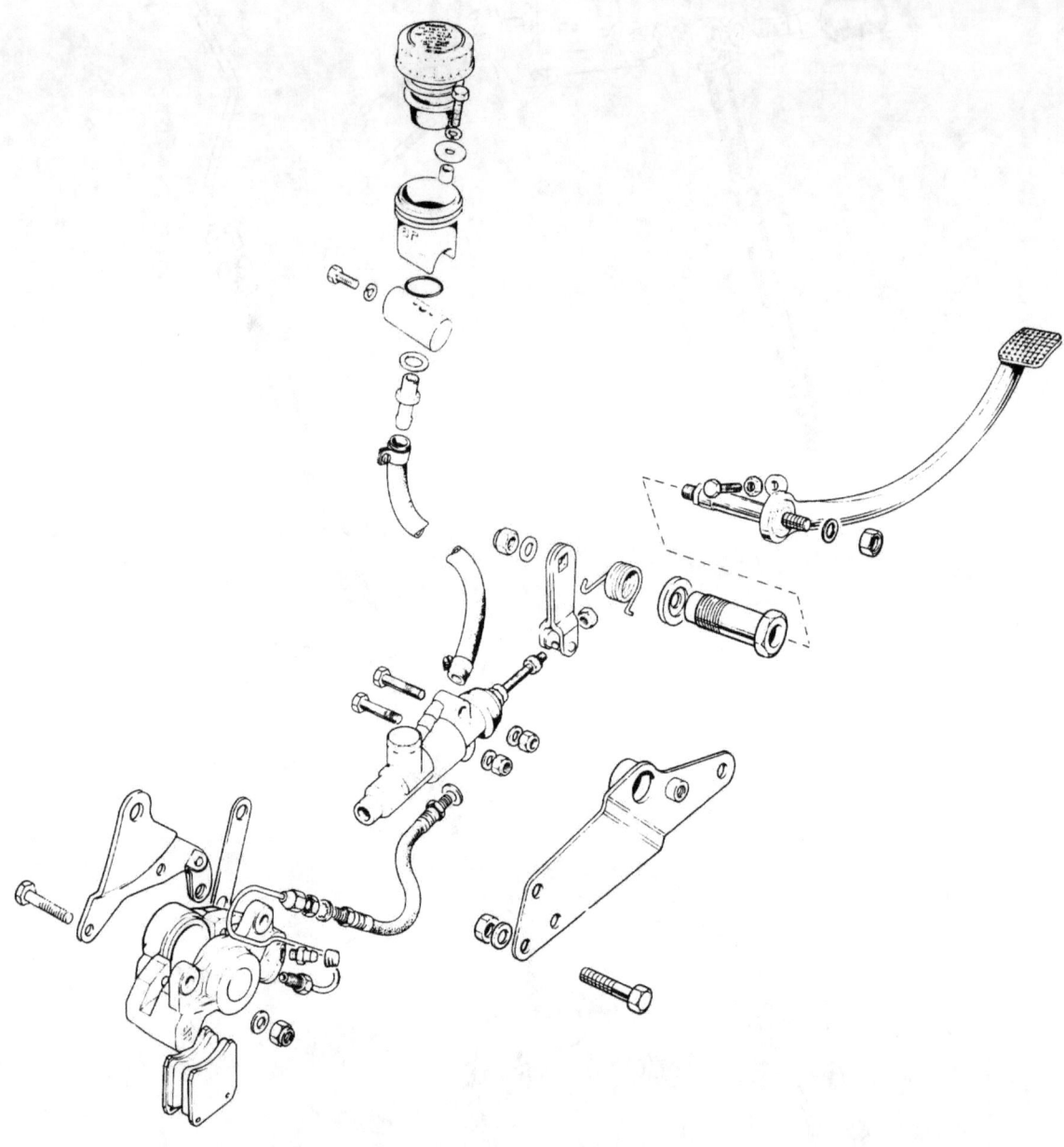

Fig. F3. Rear brake components

SECTION F1

BRAKE ADJUSTMENTS

The brake pads of the disc brake will require no adjustment as the reducing thickness of the friction material is automatically cancelled out by the displacement of hydraulic fluid in the system. However, the rear brake pedal must be positioned to prevent a foul condition against the R.H. footrest and consequently causing the rear brake to bind.

The adjuster nuts (see Fig. F4) should be set to give a MINIMUM clearance of $1/16$ in. (1·58mm.) between the brake pedal and the R.H. footrest. Ensure both the adjuster nuts are tight against the operating lever.

REAR BRAKE ADJUSTMENT— Prior to Frame No. HN62501

Early models are fitted with a rear drum brake fitted with internally expanding fully floating brake shoes. The L.H. rear brake pedal is connected to the brake show operating cam by means of an operating rod which in turn is adjustable.

The brake must be adjusted to give maximum efficiency at all times and for this to be maintained, the shows should be just clear of the drum when the brake is off, and close enough for immediate contact when the brake is applied. The brakes must not be adjusted so closely, however, that they are in continual contact with the drum; excessive heat may be generated, resulting in deterioration of braking efficiency.

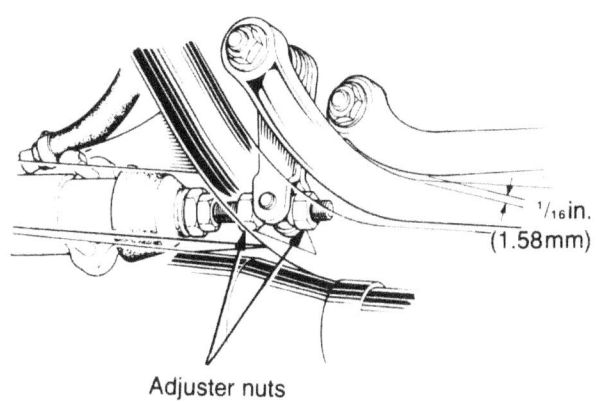

Adjuster nuts

Fig. F4. Rear brake pedal adjustment

The rear brake is adjusted by turning the self-locking sleeve in a clockwise direction (view from the rear of the machine), to shorten the effective length of the brake rod and so open the shoes in the drum.

Note that is maximum efficiency is to be obtained the angle between the brake cable or rod and the operating lever on the brake plate should not exceed 90° when the brake is fully applied.

The rear brake shoes are of the fully-floating type (i.e., they are not pivoted on a fulcrum) and are therefore self-centralizing.

F
BRAKES, WHEELS AND TYRES

SECTION F2

BRAKE FLUID LEVEL

The brake fluid level in the master cylinder reservoir should be as shown in Fig. F5(F). There is a mark running around the inside periphery of the reservoir about ¼ in. (6·35mm.) from the top. The level will drop slightly as the pads wear and when new pads are fitted the fluid will return to the original level provided no leakage has occurred.

It is necessary to 'top-up' the fluid level at the intervals stated in "Routine Maintenace".

Always hold the handebars against full RIGHT lock when 'topping-up' the front brake reservoir. Do not overfill see 'F'.

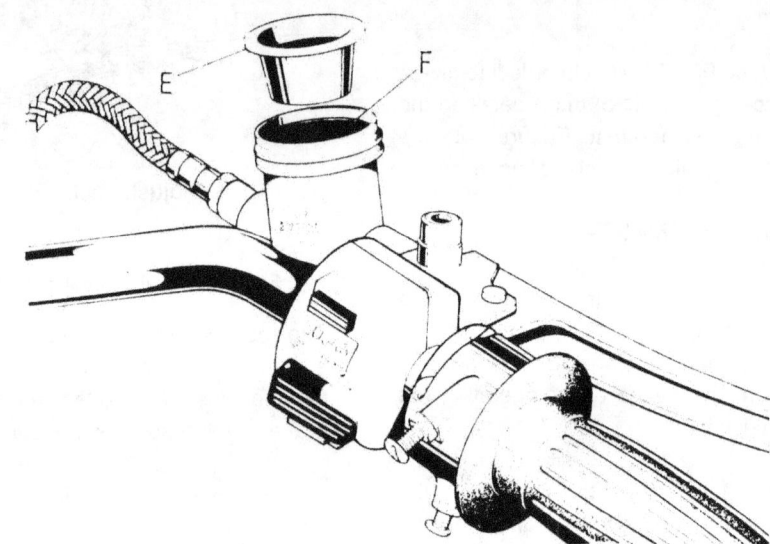

Fig. F5. Showing the front brake reservoir fluid level and cap

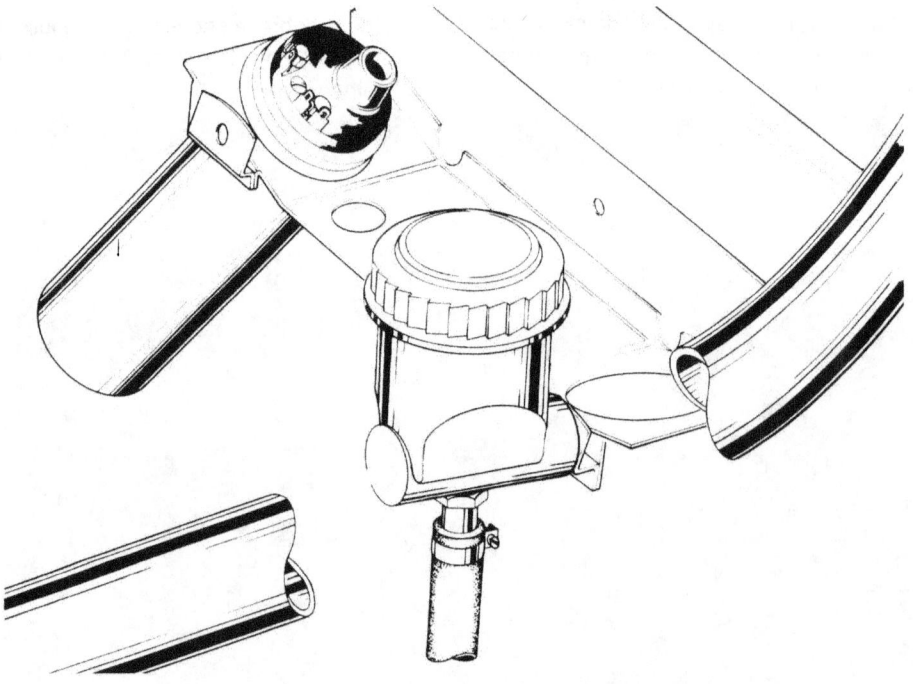

Fig. F6. Rear brake reservoir

F6

SECTION F3

BRAKE PAD LINING—FRONT AND REAR

The brake pads should be examined at regular intervals for wear. The pads will require replacement when the lining thickness reaches a minimum of 1/16 in. (1·6mm.). This can be easily determined by removing the pad from the caliper. Firstly detach the aluminium cover from the caliper (front brake only) by removing the two cross-head screws. Then remove both split pins "B" (See Fig. F7) and pull out both pads "D".

The brake pad friction material is bonded to the pressure plate of the brake pad and therefore can only be renewed by the fitting of complete brake pad assemblies. New split pins are advisable when fitting new or replacing used brake pads.

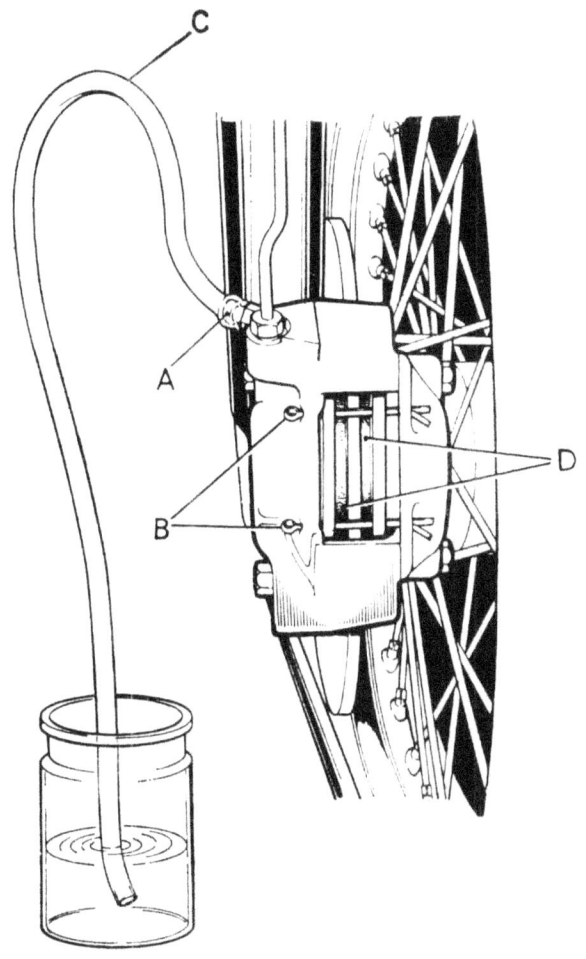

Fig. F7. Showing arrangement for bleeding the front brake

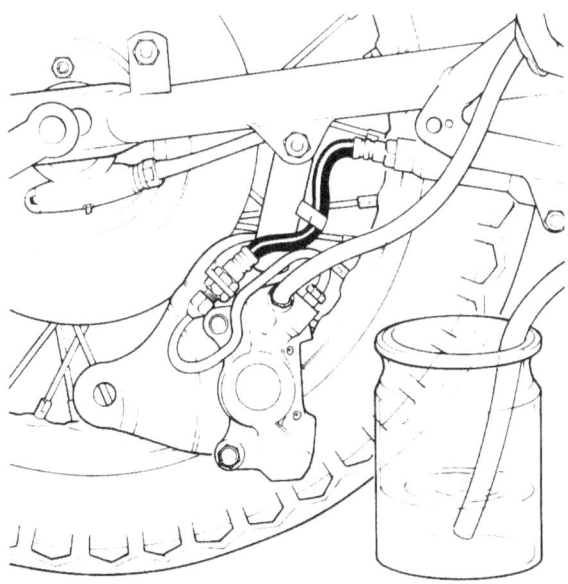

Fig. F8. Showing arrangement for bleeding the rear brake

SECTION F4

"BLEEDING" THE HYDRAULIC SYSTEM—FRONT AND REAR

If at any time it has been found necessary to disconnect a part of the hydraulic system (for repair etc.) it will be necessary to replenish the master cylinder reservoir and "bleed" the system free of trapped air pockets. "Bleeding" (or expelling air from) the hydraulic system is not a routine maintenance operation. Always keep a careful check on the fluid level in the reservoir during "bleeding". It is most important that it is kept at least half full, otherwise air may be drawn into the system necessitating a fresh start.

Fluid drained from the system should not be used again unless it is perfectly clean and free from air bubbles. The fluid should not be used again in any case if it has been in use for some time. To ensure that the fluid is completely free of air bubbles it should be allowed to stand for several hours before use.

Use only the specified type of brake fluid for topping up the reservoir. See General Data.

NOTE: For the rear brake, first partially withdraw the rear wheel spindle, see Section F, out to the L.H. side enabling the brake caliper and mounting bracket to swing down to the position shown in Fig. F9 prior to commencing with the "bleeding" procedure.

Procedure for "bleeding" is as follows (Rear brake is similar):—

Connect a suitable sized rubber "pipe" "C" Fig. F7 to the bleed nipple "A" Fig F7 and suspend the free end of the tube in a glass jar with the open end immersed in at least ½in. (12·7mm.) of brake fluid. Remove the screwed cap from the master cylinder reservoir and take out the rubber diaphram "E" Fig. F5. Now slacken the bleed nipple ½ to ¾ of a turn, (with the bleed pipe still attached).

Ensure that the master cylinder is full of the correct fluid before commencing further. Now pull the front brake lever firmly to the handlebar holding it in that position for a few seconds. Air in the system will now be expelled through the rubber tube and will be observed in the form of bubbles rising in the jar. Release the brake lever and repeat the operation until air bubbles are no longer seen to escape. As a safeguard to prevent any air being drawn back into the system when the lever is released, loop the "bleed" pipe as shown in Fig. 7. This ensures that a "head" of fluid is maintained between the top of the loop and the "bleed" nipple.

When the flow of air bubbles ceases hold the brake lever in the fully "on" position and retighten the bleed nipple (with the "bleed" pipe still connected).

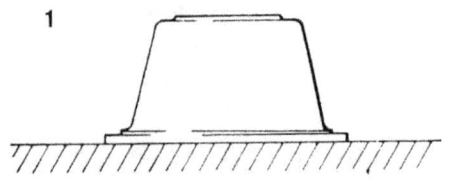

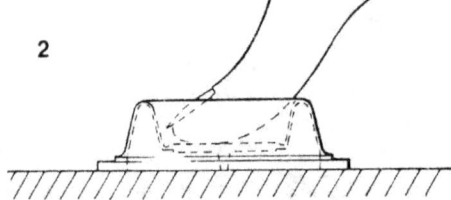

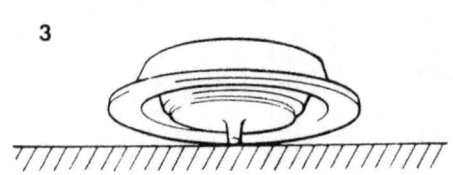

Fig. F9. Folded condition of rubber diaphram

BRAKES, WHEELS AND TYRES

Remember to maintain the level of hydraulic fluid in the master cylinder during the entire operation. The correct level for the fluid is shown in Fig. F5 at "F". This will be the correct level when the brake pads are NEW. When replacing the rubber diaphragm (Fig. F5 "E") it will be easier to replace the cap with the diaphragm in a folded condition. See Fig. F9.

Hold the diaphragm upside down on a flat surface and push the middle section down until it touches the surface it is resting on. It will now remain in that position and the diaphragm can now be replaced into the reservoir and the cap refitted. Do not forget the paper washer that is fitted between the cap and the diaphragm. When fitting the cap make sure it is retightened firmly and make sure that the air vent is unobstructed.

If at any time it has been necessary to replenish the system with hydraulic fluid during the life of one set of brake pads, remember that when new pads are fitted the fluid level spill will arise appreciably in the cylinder and may spill onto the gas tank. Therefore the level will have to be corrected to that shown in Fig. F5. (Hydraulic fluid instantaneously corrodes cellulose paintwork and great care should be exercised when handling this fluid).

SECTION F5

FLUSHING THE HYDRAULIC SYSTEM

If the hydraulic system has been contaminated by foreign matter or other fluids it should be flushed out and refilled with new fluid as described below. The system should be flushed out, in any case, at the interval stated in "Routine Maintenance".

Firstly, pump all the fluid out of the system by opening the bleed screw (connect a pipe to the bleed screw and safely collect in a container) and operating brake lever. Fill the master cylinder reservoir with methylated spirit and pump out through the bleed screw in a manner similar to that described above. Having ensured that all the methylated spirit has passed through the bleed screw replenish the master cylinder reservoir (see Section F2) with the specified grade of Lockheed brake fluid (see "General Data"). "Bleed" the brakes as described in Section F4.

IMPORTANT NOTE: If the system has been contaminated by a mineral oil, all rubber parts including flexible hoses must be replaced.

F BRAKES, WHEELS AND TYRES

SECTION F6

HYDRAULIC BRAKE PIPES AND HOSES—REMOVAL AND REFITMENT

FRONT BRAKE

The hydraulic flow is taken from the master cylinder to the front brake caliper via a rubber pressure hose coupled to a steel brake pipe at the top head lug then to a second hose coupled at the middle lug. The first hose allows for adjustment of the handlebar position. DO NOT adjust the handlebars such that the hose becomes kinked or stretched. The second hose allows for the compression and extension of the front suspension. The position of the hose coupling at the middle lug is important, see Fig. F10.

The brake hoses and pipe should be checked at the intervals stated in "Routine Maintenance" for leakage, chafing or general deterioration. Do not attempt to clear the bore of a flexible hose by probing. If a hose is choked or perished, fit a replacement.

Hoses and pipe may be replced as follows:- Firstly drain the system of its fluid see Section F5. Unscrew the fixing bolt from the end of the master cylinder and detach the union (U.S.A. models only). Note the copper sealing washers at the front and back of the union. These sealing washers must be annealed if they are to be re-used and this is effected by heating the washers to a cherry red colour and plunging them into cold water. (Other export models with low handlebars have a feed hose that screws directly into the master cylinder and this hose should be disconnected at the fork top lug first and then unscrewed from the master cylinder).

Unscrew the union at the top fork lug and disconnect the pipe.

See Fig. F2 for assembly details. Similarly disconnect the remaining pipe and hoses from the middle lug, left fork leg and caliper. Note that the pipe junction at the middle lug is mounted in such a fashion that the rubber hose that hence travels down to the left fork leg is splayed outwards and away from the wheel when the front forks are compressed. See Fig. F10 for detail drawing. **When installing the hose ensure that the coloured stripe travelling the length of the hose is arranged such that it is not twisted. See Fig. F10(A).** To reset the angle as shown simply loosen the bolt clamping nut and alter the position of the bolt accordingly.

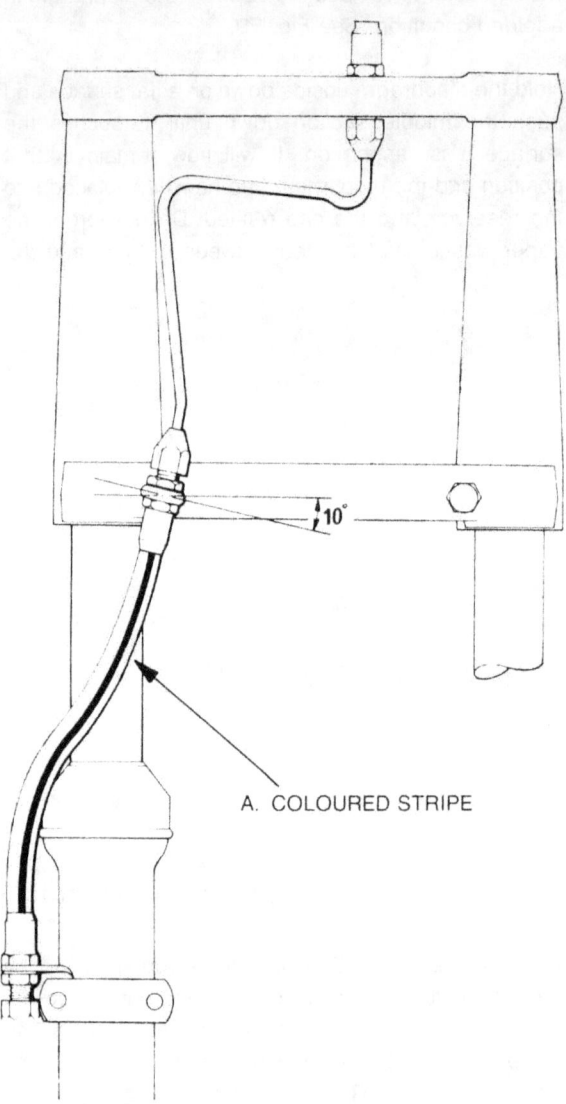

A. COLOURED STRIPE

Fig. F10. Showing front brake pipe installation

Be careful not to overtighten the union nuts as their threads may be easily stripped. After refitting the hoses replenish the system as described in Section F4. Check that no chafing of the hoses or pipes occurs when the handlebars are turned from left lock to right lock and when the front forks are fully compressed.

WHEELS, BRAKES AND TYRES

REAR BRAKE

Brake fluid is contained in a separate reservoir mounted beneath the twinseat. Fluid is supplied to the master cylinder by a rubber hose retained by two hose clips. Hydraulic flow is taken from the master cylinder via a rubber pressure hose to a coupling at the caliper mounting bolt. The final connection is made by a metal pressure pipe to the caliper.

The rubber hose allows for movement of the rear swinging fork.

The brake hose and pressure pipe should be checked at the intervals stated in "Routine Maintenance" for leakage, chafing or general deterioration. Do not attempt to clear the bore of a flexible hose by probing If a hose is choked or perished, fit a replacement.

The hose and pressure pipe may be replaced as follows: Firstly drain the system of its fluid, see Section F5.

Unscrew the union at the rubber hose coupling then unscrew the union out of the caliper and remove the metal pipe.

Remove the locking nut and disconnect the rubber hose from the mounting bracket.

Unscrew and remove the hose assembly and copper washer from the master cylinder.

When refitting the hose tighten the unions such that the hose is in the position shown in Fig. F11. See Fig. F3 for assembly details.

If the copper washer is to be re-used it should be annealed as described in the front brake section.

Be careful not to overtighten the union nuts as their threads may be easily stripped. After refitting the hose replenish and 'bleed' the system as described in Section F4. Check that no chafing of the hose occurs when the rear suspension is compressed or extended. Ensure that the rear metal brake pipe does not foul the caliper casting.

When installing the hose ensure that the coloured stripe travelling the length of the hose is arranged such that it is not twisted. See Fig. F11A.

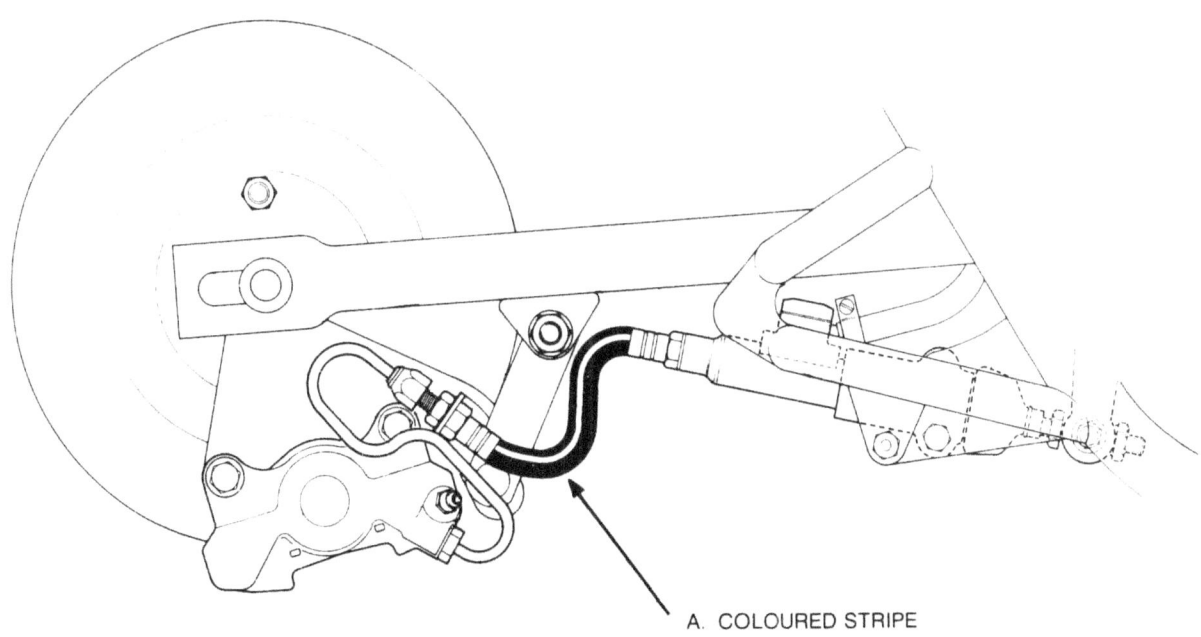

A. COLOURED STRIPE

Fig. F11. Rear brake pipe installation

SECTION F7

REAR BRAKE MASTER CYLINDER AND RESERVOIR

The rear brake master cylinder is a sealed unit and is only serviced as such. The principle of operation is identical to that of the front master cylinder with the exception that the reservoir is mounted remotely beneath the twinseat.

To remove the master cylinder first remove the rear wheel, see Section F13.

Drain the system of its fluid see Section F5.

Disconnect the brake pedal return spring then remove the nut and washer and withdraw the master cylinder operating lever.

Disconnect the reservoir rubber hose from the master cylinder by slackening the clip.

Remove the two nuts and bolts and withdraw the master cylinder from the frame. Unscrew the master cylinder from the rubber hose. Note the copper sealing washer. (If the copper wsher is to be renewed it must be annealed by heating the washer to a cherry red colour and plunging it onto cold water).

Remove the operating lever by removing the adjuster nuts.

Prior to fitting a new master cylinder check the distance between the end of the cast mounting bracket and the face of the pushrod nut, see Fig. F12. This dimension should be 0.35in. to 0.37in. (8·9 to 9·4mm.) and should be adjusted as necessary.

Refitment of the master cylinder is a reversal of the above instructions, but see Section E6 for refitment of the rear brake pedal return spring; Section F for replenishing and bleeding the system with new brake fluid.

Note the nut securing the master cylinder operating lever should be tightened to a torque of 20ft.lbs. (4·8kg.m.).

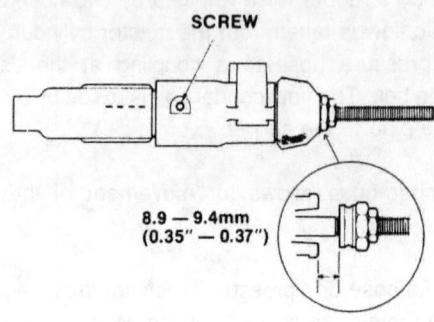

Fig. F12. Push rod adjustment

REAR BRAKE RESERVOIR

To remove the rear brake reservoir first drain the system of its fluid, see Section F5.

Disconnect the rubber hose from the reservoir at the master cylinder.

Lift the twinseat and remove the bolt and washer securing the reservoir assembly to the coil mounting tray.

Remove the reservoir cap, sealing ring and the rubber diaphragm.

Remove the bolt, spring washer, plain washer, distance piece then remove the bowl from the mounting block. Detach the 'O' ring. Refer to Fig. F3.

Reassembly is a reversal of the above instructions, but always fit a new 'O' ring.

Tighten the bowl retaining bolt to a torque of 4 to 5lb.ft. (6 to 7 Nm.).

SECTION F8

FRONT BRAKE MASTER CYLINDER

The master cylinder is mounted in the right hand handlebar electrical switch. It consists of a fluid reservoir bolted to a cylinder body containing a piston, seals and other parts as shown in Fig. F13. With reference to the hydraulic flow diagram (Fig. F14) and the exploded view (Fig. F2) the operation of the cylinder is as follows:— When the front brake lever is pulled on the push rod (1) moves the piston (2) down the bore. The displaced fluid in front of the piston is forced through holes in the check valve (3) lifting the rubber seal clear of the holes to provide an unblocked passage to the wheel cylinders. On releasing the front brake lever the return spring (4) thrust the piston (2) back faster than the fluid is able to return from the wheel cylinders. This creates a partial vacuum in the cylinder which causes fluid to be drawn past the lip of the primary seal (5) from the main reservoir via the main feed port (A) and the small feed holes in the head of the piston (2).

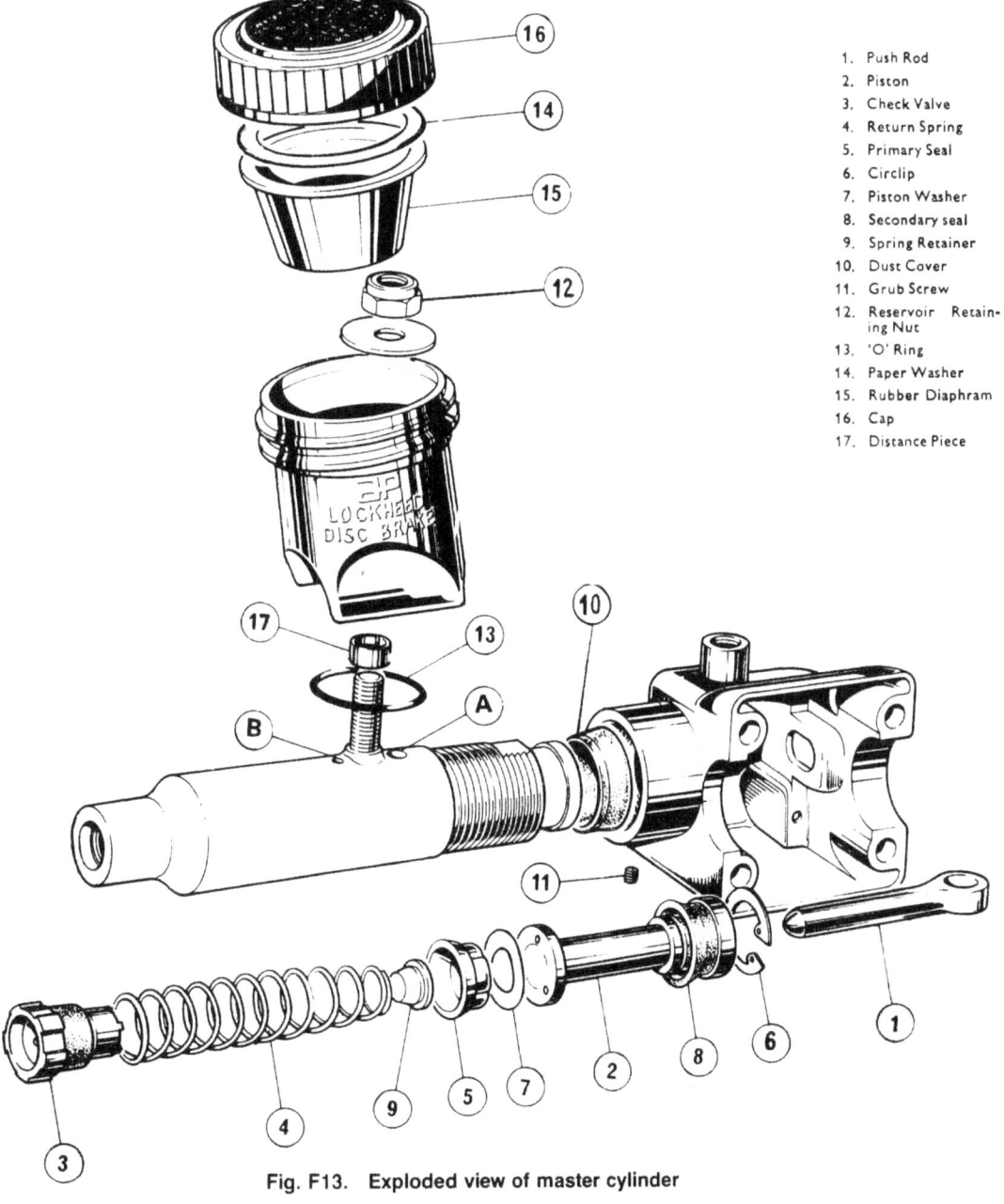

1. Push Rod
2. Piston
3. Check Valve
4. Return Spring
5. Primary Seal
6. Circlip
7. Piston Washer
8. Secondary seal
9. Spring Retainer
10. Dust Cover
11. Grub Screw
12. Reservoir Retaining Nut
13. 'O' Ring
14. Paper Washer
15. Rubber Diaphram
16. Cap
17. Distance Piece

Fig. F13. Exploded view of master cylinder

BRAKES, WHEELS AND TYRES

Meanwhile fluid returning from the wheel cylinder lifts the check valve (3) away from its seat and re-enters the cylinder. When the piston has fully returned a small breather port (B) is uncovered which allows a release of excess fluid to the reservoir and also compensates for contraction and expansion of the fluid due to changes in temperature. The purpose of the check valve (3) is to prevent the re-entry into the master cylinder of fluid pumped into the line during the "bleeding" operation, thus ensuring a fresh charge of fluid at each stroke of the lever.

Removal and dismantling procedure of the cylinder is as follows:— Firstly drain the system of fluid. See Section F5. Remove the rubber hose from the wheel cylinder. Remove the brake lever and push rod by unscrewing the pivot bolt. Unscrew the four retaining screws that retain the right switch console and remove the master cylinder from the handlebar. Detach the reservoir bowl from the cylinder by removing the attachment nut from the inside (See Fig. F13). Note assembly of washer, spacer and 'O' ring. Remove the grub screw that locks the cylinder in position in the switch that locks (See Fig. F13) and then unscrew the cylinder. Detach the rubber boot from the end of the cylinder. Using the push rod (1) depress the piston in the cylinder to relieve the load on the spring and remove the circlip (6). Remove the piston (2) piston washer (7), primary seal (5), return spring (4) and check valve (3). The removal of the primary seal (5) may be simplified by applying gentle air pressure to the pipe connection at the end of the cylinder.

Remove the secondary seal (8) by stretching it over the flange of the piston. Renew all seals and check the bore of the cylinder for deep score marks. If such damage is apparent a new cylinder should be fitted.

It is important that all parts are meticulously cleaned with brake fluid before assembly. Do not use petrol, trichlorethylene or any other similar cleaning agents to wash the parts.

Fit the secondary seal (8) onto the piston (2) so that the lip of the seal faces towards the head (drilled end) of the piston. See Fig. F13. Gently work the seal around the groove with the fingers to ensure that it is properly seated. Fit the spring retainer (9) onto the small end of the spring (4) and the check valve (3) onto the large end. Insert the spring assembly onto the cylinder bore, large end first. Insert the primary seal (5) into the cylinder bore, lip foremost (See Fig. F7), taking care not to damage or turn back the lip. Insert the piston washer (7) into the barrel with the dished side towards the primary seal (5) (See Fig. F.14) followed by the piston, head (drilled end) innermost, see Fig. F12. Push the piston inwards with the end of the push rod and refit the circlip (6). Make sure that the circlip beds evenly in its groove. Refit the boot (10) by stretching it over the barrel. Refit the reservoir bowl, (tighten the securing nut to a torque of 4 to 7 lbs.ft. (6 to 7 Nm.) not forgetting the 'O' ring and test the cylinder by filling the reservoir and pushing the push rod and piston inwards and allowing it to return unassisted. After a few applications fluid should flow from the outlet connection at the cylinder head.

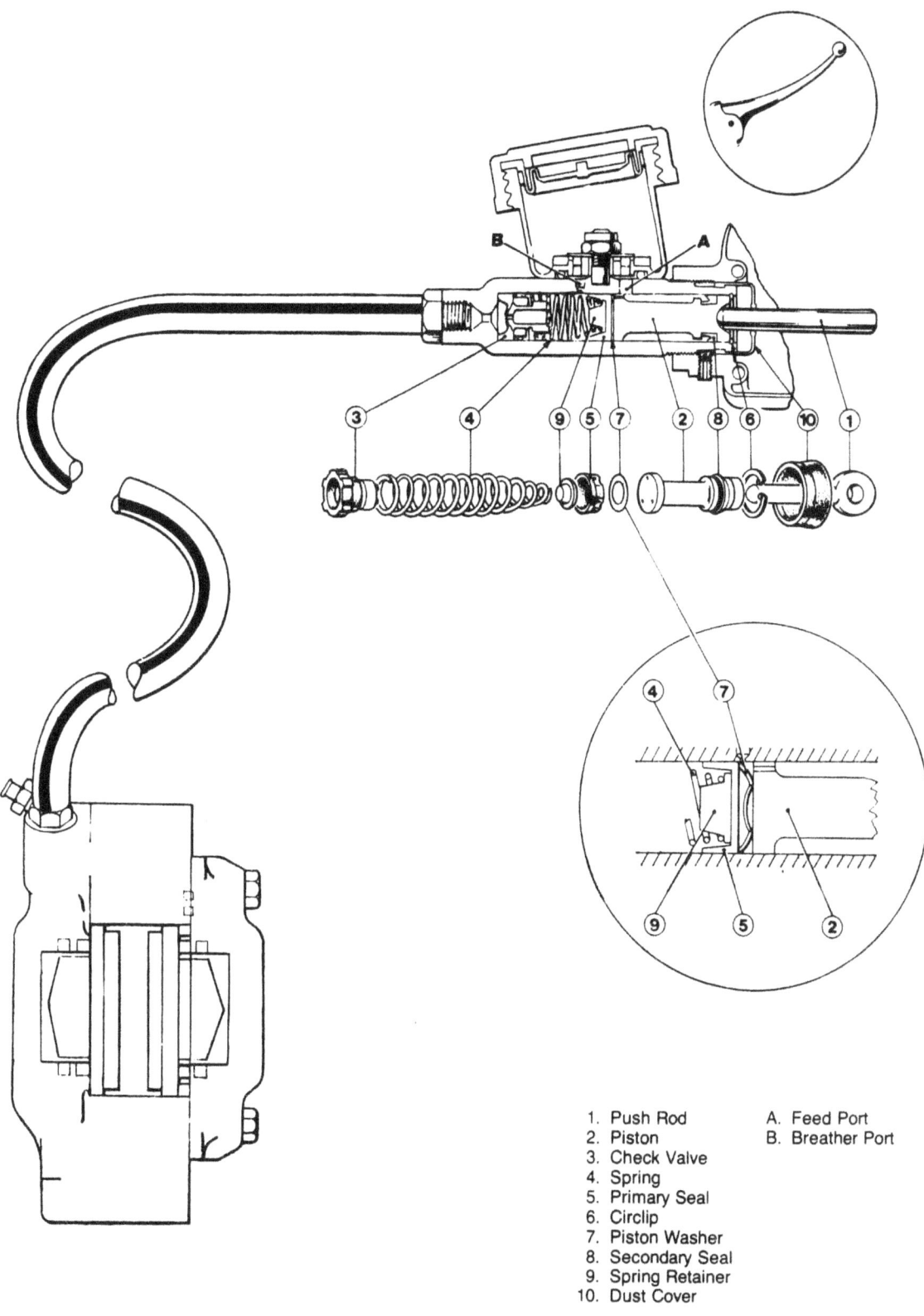

1. Push Rod
2. Piston
3. Check Valve
4. Spring
5. Primary Seal
6. Circlip
7. Piston Washer
8. Secondary Seal
9. Spring Retainer
10. Dust Cover

A. Feed Port
B. Breather Port

Fig. F14. Hydraulic flow diagram—front brake

If necessary refit the return spring. Empty the cylinder of fluid and proceed to re-assemble the cylinder barrel into the switch housing. At this stage the final position of the cylinder barrel in the housing must be determined. Here reference must be made to Fig. F14. It will be observed from Fig. F14 that the lip of the primary seal (5) must be 1/16 of an inch behind the breather port and the reservoir set at an angle of 10° to the vertical. The milled flats on the threaded end of the cylinder are machined relative to the 10° position and the appropriate one must be used when assembly takes place.

The following method can be used to determine the correct linear position of the cylinder barrel.

(1) Remove the reservoir from the cylinder.
(2) Re-assembe the front brake lever and push rod to the switch housing. Tighten the nylon nut to a torque of 5 to 7 lb.ft. (7 to 9 Nm.).
(3) Screw the cylinder barrel into the switch housing whilst holding the brake lever in the closed position until it will screw no further.
(4) Place on finger over the main port (A) Fig. F13 and by blowing through the outlet end of the cylinder it will be observed that no air will escape from the breather port (B) Fig. F13.
(5) Now unscrew the cylinder barrel until air is heard to escape from the breather port (B). At this point the port will have just become uncovered.
(6) Unscrew the barrel one complete turn and set the angle to 10° as shown in Fig. F15. The milled flat on the threaded end of the barrel must be located when the grub screw (Fig. F13) is being re-tightened and will set the angle automatically.

Re-assemble the master cylinder to the handlebar replenish the reservoir with fluid and "bleed" the system as described in Section F4.

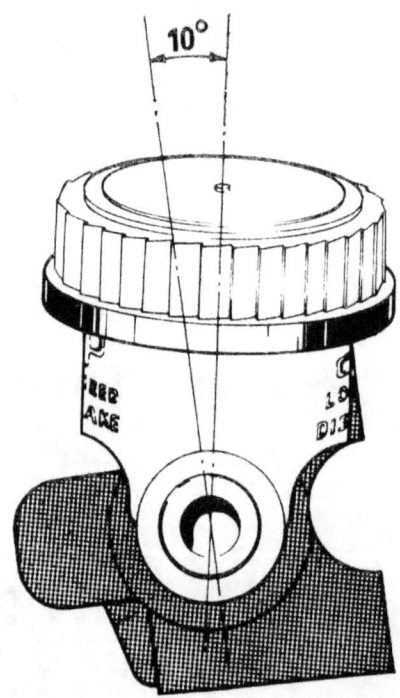

Fig. F15. Showing angle of brake reservoir

BRAKES, WHEELS AND TYRES — F

SECTION F9

STRIPPING AND REASSEMBLING THE FRONT AND REAR BRAKE CALIPERS

FRONT BRAKE

Detach the protection cover from the caliper by removing the two crosshead screws. (See Fig. F1 for exploded view). Drain the system of fluid. See Section F5. Detach the feed pipe from the caliper and remove the two securing nuts at the fork leg and withdraw the caliper from its mounting studs. Remove the two split pins that retain the brake pads and pull them out.

REAR BRAKE

Drain the system of fluid, see Section F5. Remove the R.H. wheel spindle nut and partially withdraw the wheel spindle enabling the caliper and mounting plate to swing down. Remove the caliper to plate securing securing bolts and disconnect the pressure hose from the master cylinder.

NOTE: Take care when handling brake fluid as it is a powerful paint stripper.

Replacment is a reversal of the above but refer to Section F4 for 'bleeding' the system.

No attempt should be made to remove the caliper bridge bolts jointing the two halves of the caliper. There is no necessity to do so and all the servicing can be carried out without splitting the halves, and in addition the bolts are tightened to a critical torque loading.
If in an emergency, the brake caliper has been split and in event of the fluid channel seal being undamaged, the caliper and bridge bolts should be thoroughly cleaned, dried and reassembled and the bridge bolts tightened to a torque loading of 35-40 ft. lbs. (4.8 to 5.5 Kg.m). After reassembling, the brake caliper should be checked for fluid tightness under maximum brake lever pressure.

It should be understood that this procedure will only provide a temporary remedy and the caliper should be returned to the manufacturers for overhaul at the first opportunity. Service the rubber seals as follows:- (read in conjunction with Fig. F1).
A rubber sealing ring (1) is fitted in a groove machined in each pistons bore to seal off the hydraulic fluid. A "U" shaped rubber dust seal (2) having two wiping edges and housed in a metal container (3) is pressed into the open end of the piston bore to prevent the ingress of dust from the brake pads.

The dust seal (2) together with its retainer (3) must be renewed each time they are removed from the piston bore. When the rubber seal (1) is worn or damaged it must be renewed. Before installation the seals should be lubricated with Lockheed disc brake lubricant. The movement of the pistons (4) and (5) within their respective bore extrude the rectangular rubber seal (1) from its groove. On releasing the brake lever the hydraulic pressure collapses and the rubber seal (1) retracts the pistons (4) and (5) a pre-determined amount, thus maintaining a constant clearance between the brake pads and the brake disc when the brakes are not in use.

To remove rubber seals:- Prise out and discard the dust seal (2) and (3) from the open end of each piston bore by inserting a blade of a blunt screwdriver between the seal and retainer. Eject each piston from their bores by applying compressed air to the fluid inlet. Lift out and discard the sealing rings (1) from the grooves in the piston bores by inserting a blunt screwdriver under each ring taking care not to damage the grooves.

Dry the new sealing rings (1) and smear them with Lockheed disc brake lubricant and refit them into the groove of each piston bore so that the large side is nearer the open end of the piston bore. Gently work the sealing rings into their respective grooves with the fingers to ensure correct seating. Dry the pistons and coat with Lockheed disc brake lubricant. Offer up the pistons, closed end first squarely to the bores in the caliper and press the pistons fully home. Dry the dust seals and coat with Lockheed disc brake lubricant.

F BRAKES, WHEELS AND TYRES

Fit a dust seal into a metal retainer and position both squarely into the mouth of one piston bore with the dust seal facing the bore. Press the dust seal into the mouth of the piston bore using a "G" clamp and support plate, until its outer edges are flush with the bore. Repeat with the second dust seal and retainer. Fit new brake pads (See Section F3). Refit the brake caliper. Reconnect the hydraulic feed pipe and "bleed" the system as in Section F4. Refit the protection cover (front brake only).

SECTION F10

BRAKE DISCS

The brake disc will require no maintenance other than when re-newal becomes necessary due to damage or becoming excessively scored. If this occurs the disc must be checked for run-out using a dial test indicator. The maximum reading should not exceed 0.0035 ins. (.089 mm)

To replace the disc, firstly remove the front wheel. See Section F11. Unscrew the four securing nuts and detach the disc. Fit new disc and tighten the nuts diagonally opposite to each other to the torque figure given in General Data.

Replace the wheel into the forks and attach a dial test indicator to the fork leg and check the run-out to the figure previously quoted. If it is outside the limit the disc should be repositioned in an attempt to obtain a more satisfactory combination of machining limits.

Excessive run-out of the brake disc moves the pistons back into the bores and creates excessive lever travel when the brake is applied thus the run-out must be kept to the specified minimum.

BRAKES, WHEELS AND TYRES

SECTION F11

REMOVING AND REFITTING THE FRONT WHEEL

Place the machine on the centre stand or support so that the front wheel is clear of the ground.

Unscrew the eight fork cap nuts and remove both caps and withdraw the front wheel. Do not apply the front brake while the wheel is out of the forks.

To replace the wheel engage the disc between the brake pads in the caliper and replace the fork caps tightening the four nuts of the left hand fork leg before finally tightening the right hand leg. **NOTE: Always tighten the nuts diagonally opposite to each other.**

This will enable the spindle to align correctly with the left fork leg. (See "General Data" for correct torque figures for the cap nuts).

WARNING: Always actuate the front brake PRIOR to moving off with the machine. This will re-charge the hydraulic with fluid in readiness for the first braking application.

SECTION F12

REMOVING AND REFITTING THE FRONT WHEEL BEARINGS

Remove the front wheel (See Section above). Unscrew the wheel spindle fixing nut from the left hand side and then unscrew the retaining ring with service tool 61-3694 (Right hand thread). The left hand bearing can now be removed by driving the wheel spindle through from the right hand side. Withdraw the inner grease retaining disc from the left hand side. To remove the right hand side bearing, spring out the circlip and insert the wheel spindle from the left hand side and drive the bearing out complete with inner and outer grease retaining plates.

NOTE: Early models were fitted with bearings of the non-sealed type. Always fit bearings of the latest sealed type when servicing. The sealed bearings can be easily recognised by the plastic covers fitted to each side of the ball race.

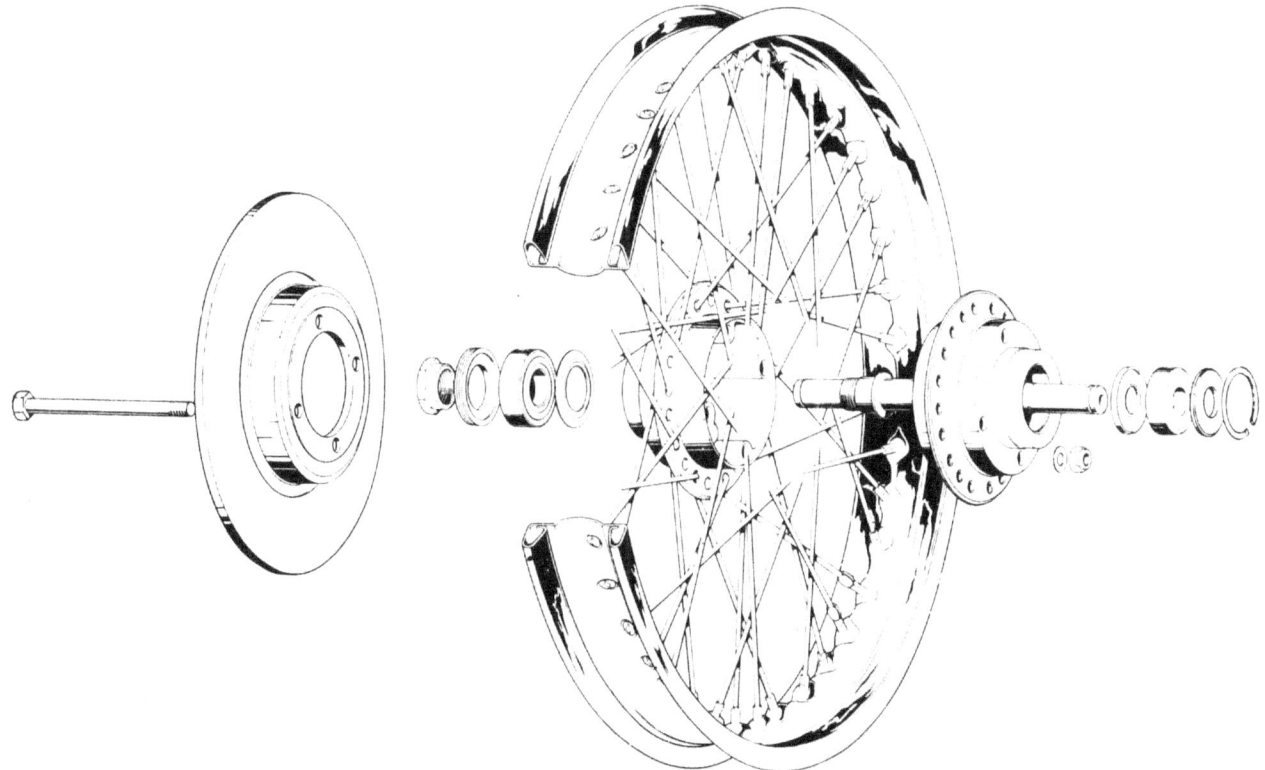

Fig. F16. Exploded view of front wheel bearing arrangement

To refit the bearings first insert the right retainer, bearing and outer dust cap. Refit the spring circlip and insert the shouldered end of the wheel spindle from the left and using it as a drift drive the bearing and grease retainer until they come up to the circlip. Re-insert the spindle the opposite way round and refit the left hand grease retainer disc. Drive the left bearing into position well smeared with grease then screw in the retainer ring (right hand thread) until tight. Using Service Tool No. 61-3694. Tap the spindle from the right to bring the spindle shoulder up against the left bearing. Replace the spindle fixing nut and re-tighten firmly. (Refer to Fig. F16 for layout and identification).

SECTION F13

REMOVING AND FITTING THE REAR WHEEL

Raise the machine on its centre stand then lift the machine an additional 3in. by placing a suitable block underneath the stand. Remove the L.H. muffler by removing the L.H. pillion footrest securing nut and slackening off the muffler to exhaust pipe clamp. Withdraw the muffler. Disconnect the rear chain by removing the split link.

Using a tommy bar to secure the wheel spindle remove the spindle nut. Withdraw the wheel spindle and swing the caliper assembly away from the disc. Carefully allow the wheel to drop then disconnect the speedometer drive cable.

NOTE: Take care not to operate the rear brake lever whilst the caliper is diconnected from the disc.

Take care of the distance piece between the speedometer drive box and the caliper mounting bracket.

Replacement is the reversal of the above instructions but ensure that the closed end of the chain split link faces the direction of travel.

Check the wheel alignment (Section F22) and rear chain adjustment (Section F27).

WARNING: Always actuate the rear brake prior to moving off with the machine. This will re-charge the hydraulic circuit with fluid in readiness for the first braking application.

WHEELS, BRAKES AND TYRES

SECTION F14

REMOVING AND REPLACING THE REAR WHEEL BEARINGS

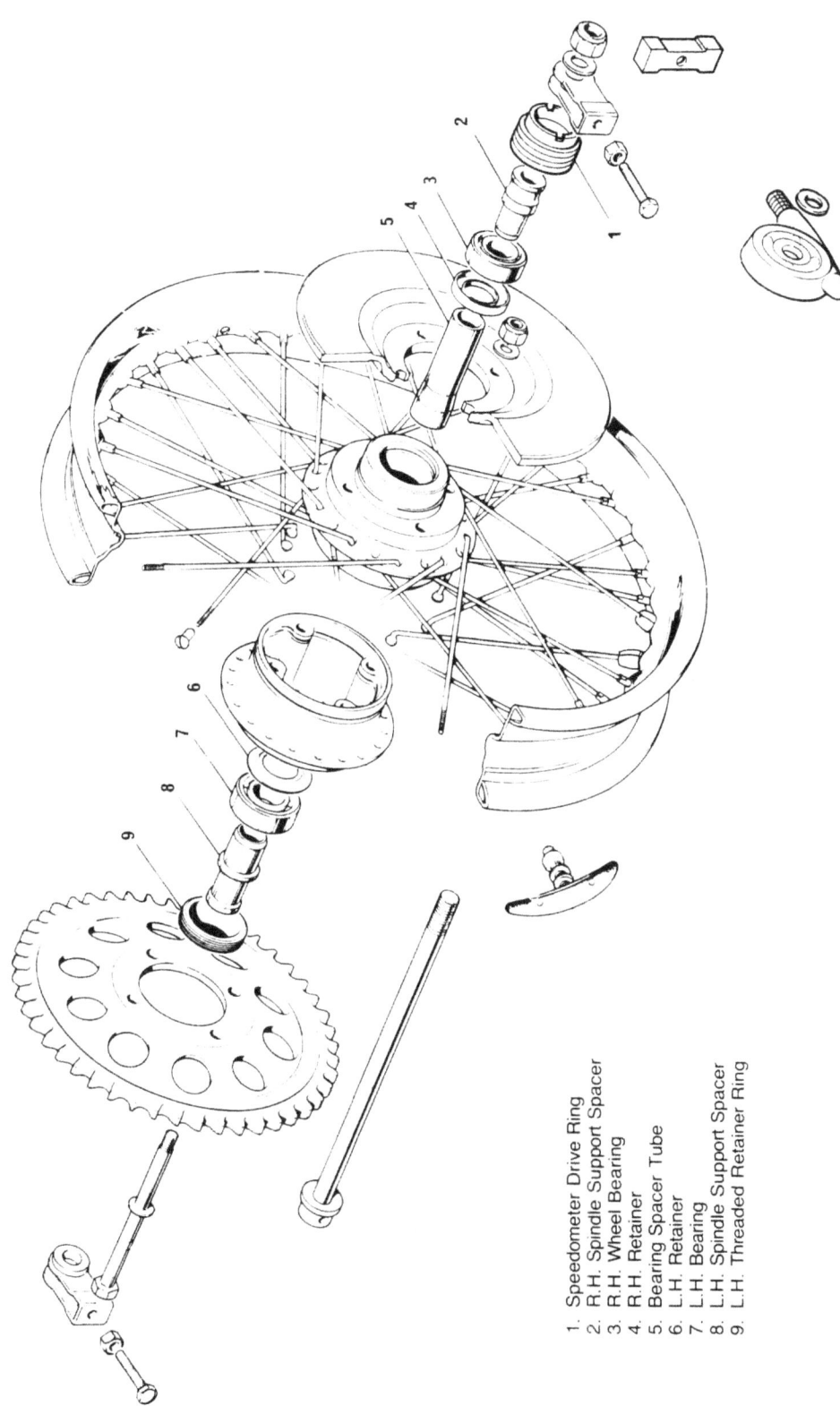

Fig. F17. Rear wheel arrangement

1. Speedometer Drive Ring
2. R.H. Spindle Support Spacer
3. R.H. Wheel Bearing
4. R.H. Retainer
5. Bearing Spacer Tube
6. L.H. Retainer
7. L.H. Bearing
8. L.H. Spindle Support Spacer
9. L.H. Threaded Retainer Ring

F WHEELS, BRAKES AND TYRES

Remove the rear wheel, see Section F13.

Unscrew the speedometer box drive ring (L.H. thread).

Unscrew and remove the L.H. side retainer ring using a punch. (R.H. thread).

Using a long punch drive out the spindle suport spacer from each side.

In most cases the bearing will come out with the spindle support spacers, however, it not then a suitable drift will have to be manufactured (See Fig. F18) and placed into the bearing spacer tube then the bearing (L.H. or R.H.) driven out.

Withdraw the bearing spacer tube.

Remove the bearing retainer cups.

Replacement is a reversal of the above instructions, but refit bearing retainer and assemble the new bearings to the spindle support spacers first then drive the bearing and spacer into the wheel hub. Do not forget to insert the bearing spacer tube prior to assembly.

NOTE: Early models were fitted with bearings of the non-sealed type. Always fit the latest sealed type of bearing when servicing. The sealed bearings can be recognised by the plastic covers fitted to each side of the ball race.

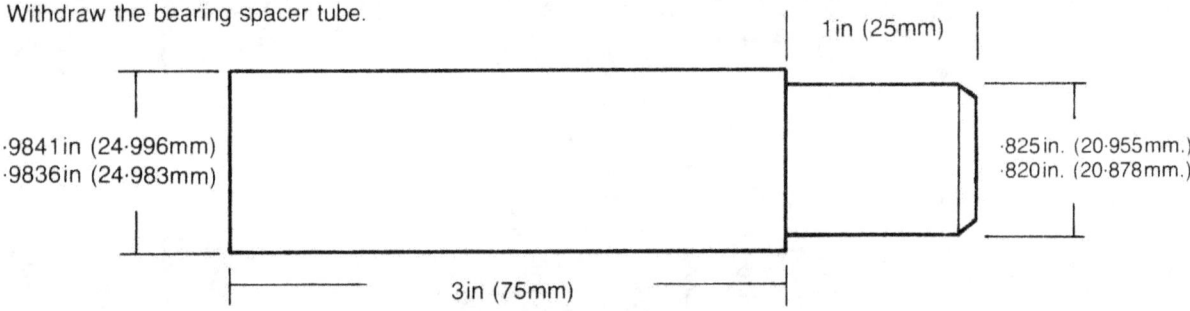

Fig. F18. Rear wheel bearing drift

SECTION F15

STRIPPING AND REASSEMBLING REAR BRAKE
(PRIOR TO FRAME No. HN62501)

Access to the rear brake shoes is gained by removing the rear wheel. (See Section F16). remove the brake shoes by lifting one brake shoe away from the brake plate until the return spring becomes disconnected. (See Fig. F19).

Check the linings for wear. If the lining has worn down to the surface of any of the rivets then the linings must be replaced. Check the surface of the brake drum; if heavy scoring or damage is evident the wheel hubs need replacing.

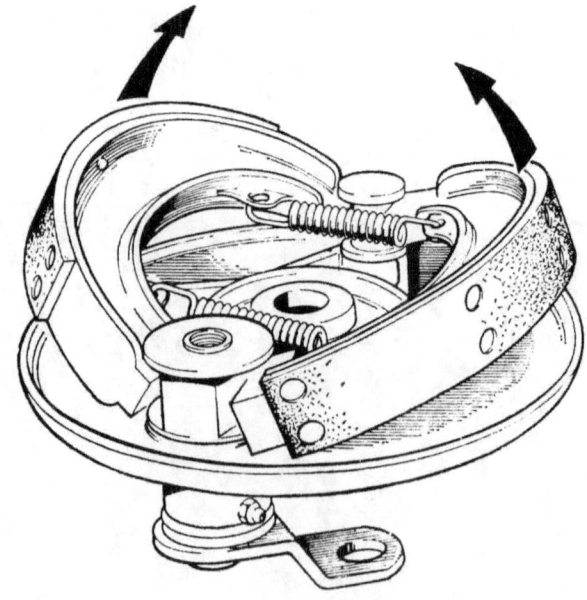

Fig. F19. Removing brake shoes

BRAKES, WHEELS AND TYRES

To reassemble the brake shoes to the brake anchor plate first place the two brake shoes on the bench on their relative positions. Fit the return springs to the retaining hooks, then taking a shoe in each hand (see Fig. F19) and at the same time holding the springs in tension, position the shoes as shown over the cam and fulcrum pin and snap down into position by pressing on the outer edges of the shoes.

Note. When replacing the brake shoes, note that the leading and trailing brake shoes are not interchangeable and ensure that they are in their correct relative positions as shown in Fig. F20.

The rear brake has a fully floating cam and therefore the shoes are automatically self centralising.

Adjustment of the rear brake is achieved by the wing nut on the rear end of the brake operating rod. Turn the nut clockwise to reduce clearance. From the static position before the brake is applied there should be about $\frac{1}{2}$ in. (1·2 cm.) of free movement before the brake starts to operate.

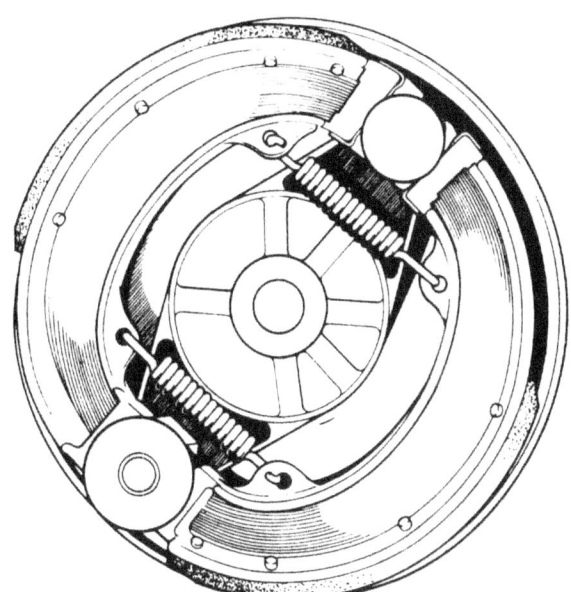

Fig. F20. Position of brake shoes

SECTION F16

REAR WHEEL REMOVAL AND REPLACEMENT
PRIOR TO FRAME No. HN62501

Support the machine on a suitable stand so that the rear wheel is approximately 12 in. clear of the ground. Uncouple the rear chain at its spring link and remove it from the rear wheel sprocket. Leave the chain in position on the gearbox sprocket; this will much simplify replacement.

Disconnect the speedometer drive cable at the drive gearbox at the right side of the rear wheel. Detach the torque arm at the brake plate and remove the bolt and nut from the front fixing. Loosen the bottom left side suspension unit bolt and lift chainguard for clearance. Loosen the wheel spindle nut at the right-hand side and pull the wheel out of the swinging fork and away from the machine. When replacing the wheel check section F22 for front and rear wheel alignment and section F27 for rear chain adjustment.

SECTION F17

REMOVING AND REPLACING REAR WHEEL BEARINGS PRIOR TO FRAME No. HN62501

The hub is fitted with two identical single row ball bearings which are a press fit into the hub.

Remove the speedometer drive ring (left hand thread) from the right side and the bearing retaining ring (right hand thread) from the left side. Use service tool no. 61-3694 to remove bearing retainer. Using a drift (of the dimensions shown in Fig. F21) knock out the spacer tube contained between the bearings taking one bearing with it. This operation can be carried out from either side of the wheel. See Fig. F22.

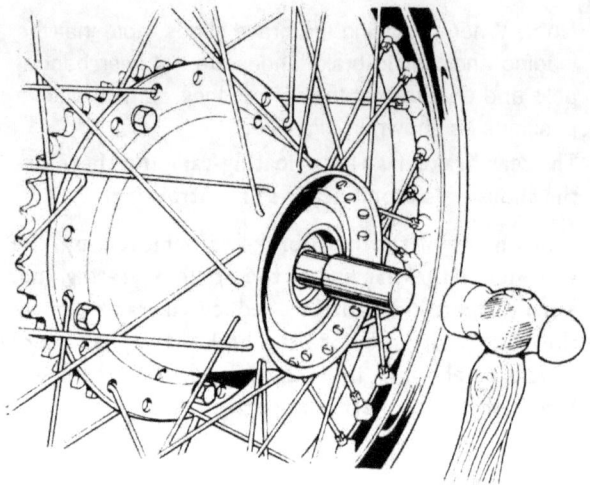

Fig. F22. Drifting the wheel bearings

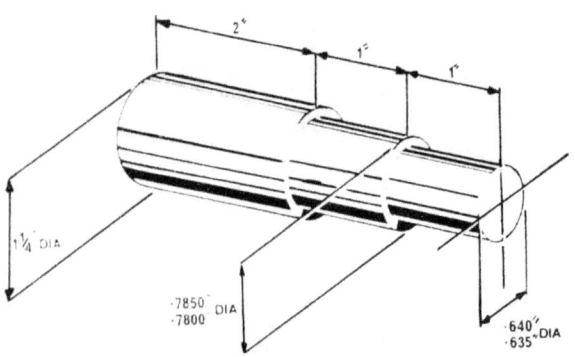

Fig. F21. Wheel bearing drift

The cups behind the bearings should not require attention. But if replacement is necessary knock them out using a drift from inside the hub.

Replace the bearing onto the spacer tube and place the assembly into the hub from the left side. Drift the bearing into the housing and down onto the retainer with a suitable diameter drift. Force must be applied to the outer ring of the bearing and not the inner ring. If possible use a hand press for replacing these bearings.

if a drift of the correct dimensions is not used then the spacer tube will be damaged and have to be replaced.

Replace the retaining ring and tighten using tool No. 61-3694. Replace the remaining bearing from the right side.

The bearing is an interference fit on the spacer tube and should be removed using the same drift as before. The spacer tube and drift can now be used to knock the remaining bearing out of the hub. Remove the bearing from the spacer tube.

NOTE: Early models were fitted with bearings of the non-sealed type. Always fit the latest type of sealed bearing when servicing. The sealed bearings can be easily recognised by the pastic covers fitted to each side of the ball race.

Reassembly of the hub is simply the reverse of the dismantling procedure but, when pressing the bearings in, apply pressure only to the outside ring of the bearing and ensure that the retainer on the left-hand side is quite tight.

BRAKES, WHEELS AND TYRES   F

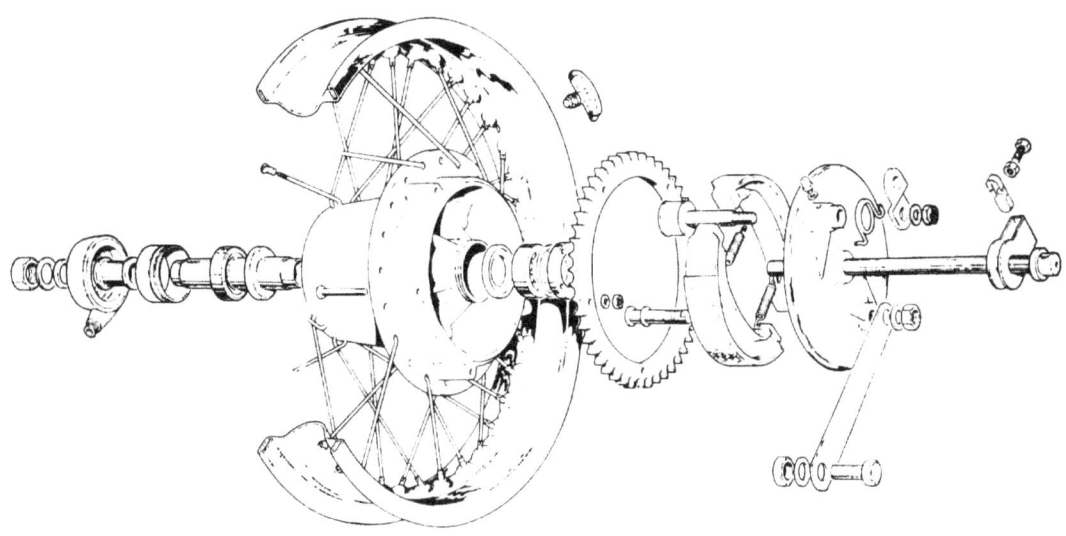

Fig. F23. Exploded view of rear wheel assembly

SECTION F18

REAR BRAKE ADJUSTMENT

The rear brake does not require any adjustment other than setting the clearance between the brake pedal and the R.H. footrest. See Section F1.

For machines prior to frame no. HN62501 fitted with a rear drum brake the following procedure applies:

The brake must be adjusted to give maximum efficiency at all times and for this to be maintained, the shoes should be just clear of the drum when the brake is off, and close enough for immediate contact when the brake is applied. The brakes must not be adjusted so closely, however, that they are in continual contact with the drum; excessive heat may be generated, resulting in deterioration of braking efficiency.

The rear brake is adjusted by turning the self-locking sleeve in a clockwise direction (viewed from the rear of the machine), to shorten the effective length of the brake rod and so open the shoes in the drum.

Note that if maximum efficiency is to be obtained, the angle between the brake cable or rod and the operating lever on the brake plate should not exceed 90° when the brake is fully applied.

The rear brake shoes are of the fully-floating type (i.e., they are not pivoted on a fulcrum) and are therefore self-centralizing.

SECTION F19

RENEWING REAR BRAKE LININGS

Hold the shoe firmly in a vice and, using a good sharp chisel, cut off the peened-over portion of the rivet as shown below.

Drive out the rivets with a suitable pin punch and discard the old lining. Reverse the shoe in the vice and draw-file the face of the shoe to remove any burrs.

Clamp the new lining tightly over the shoes and, using the shoe holes as a jig, drill straight through the lining with a $\frac{5}{32}$ in. diameter drill.

Remove the clamps and, holding the lining carefully in the vice, counterbore or countersink (according to the type of rivet used) each hole to no more than two-thirds the thickness of the lining, i.e., if the lining is $\frac{3}{16}$ in. thick, then the counterbore must not be deeper than $\frac{1}{8}$ in.

Having prepared the linings for riveting, start at the centre and position the lining with one or more rivets.

Place a suitable mandrel in the vice, clamp the linings to the shoes with either small "G" or toolmakers clamps and peen-over the rivets as

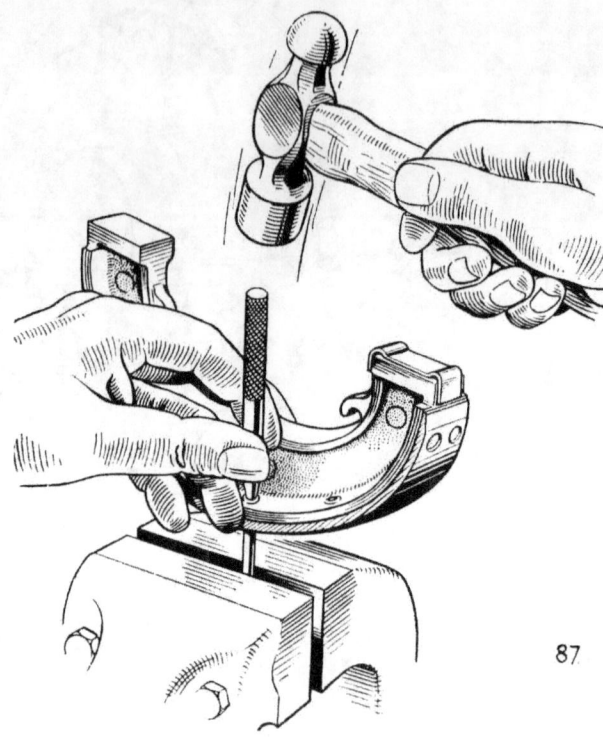

Fig. F25. Punching lining rivets

shown in Fig. F25, working alternatively outwards fom the centre.

The mandrel used in the vice must be flat on the end and the diameter should be no more than that of the rivet head. It will also help to bed the rivet down if a hollow punch is used before peening.

Note. If the clamps are used correctly, that is, next to the rivet being worked on, the linings can be fitted tightly to the shoe.

If the linings are fitted incorrectly, a gap will occur between the lining and the shoe, resulting in inefficient and "spongy" braking.

When the riveting is completed, file a good chamfer at each end of the lining to approximately half its depth and lightly draw-file the face of the lining to remove any fraze caused by the drilling.

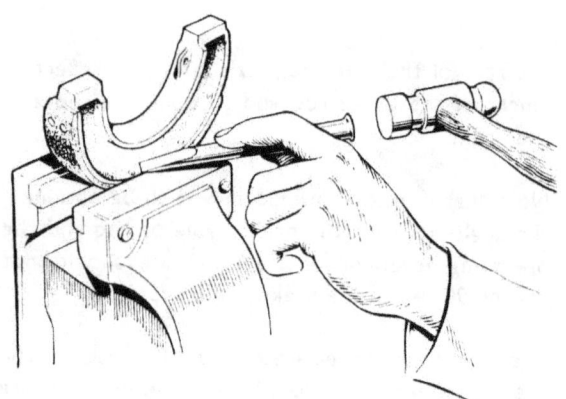

Fig. F24. Chiselling off brake rivets

BRAKES, WHEELS AND TYRES

SECTION F20
WHEEL BUILDING

This is a job which is best left to the specialist as it is essential that the wheel is laced correctly and that when truing, the spokes are correctly tensioned.

It is however, possible for the less experienced to avoid trouble by periodically examining the wheels. As spokes and nipples bed down the tension will be lost and unless this is corrected the spokes will chafe and ultimately break.

Periodically test the tension either by "ringing", that is striking with a metal tool or by placing the fingers and thumb of one hand over two spokes at a time and pressing them together.

If tension has been lost there will be no ringing tone and the spokes will move freely across each other. When a spoke needs tensioning, the nipple through the rim must be screwed further on to the spoke but at the same time, the truth of the wheel must be checked and it may be necessary to ease the tension at another part of the wheel in order to maintain its truth.

It will therefore be obvious that spoke replacement, spoke tensioning or wheel truing are not operations to be treated lightly.

Careful examination of the wheel will show that for every spoke there is another pulling in the opposite direction and that the adjacent spoke goes to the opposite side of the hub.

Increasing the tension tends to pull the rim so, to counteract this, it is sometimes necessary to increase the tension on the spoke or spokes either side to maintain the truth of the wheel.

With a little care and patience it is possible for the unskilled to at least re-tension the spokes but, turn each nipple only a little at a time as, once the spoke is under tension only a fraction of a turn is sometimes sufficient to throw the rim badly out of truth.

SECTION F21
WHEEL BALANCING

When a wheel is out of balance it means that there is more weight in one part than in another. This is very often due to variation in the tyre and at moderate speeds will not be noticed but at high speeds it can be very serious, particularly if the front wheel is affected.

Wheel balancing can be achieved by fitting standard one ounce and half ounce weights which are readily available, as required. All front wheels are balanced complete with tyre and tube before leaving the factory and if for any reason the tyre is removed it should be replaced with the white balancing "spot" level with the valve. If a new tyre is fitted, existing weights should be removed and the wheel re-balanced, adding weights as necessary until it will remain in any position at rear. Make sure that the brake is not binding while the balancing operation is being carried out.

For normal road use it is not found necessary for the rear wheel to be balanced in this way.

SECTION F22
FRONT AND REAR WHEEL ALIGNMENT

When the rear wheel has been fitted into the frame it should be aligned correctly by using two straight edges or "battens" about 7 feet long. With the machine off the stand the battens should be placed alongside the wheel, one either side of the machine and each about four inches from the ground. When both are touching the rear tyre on both sides of the wheel the front wheel should be mid way between and parallel to both battens. Turn the front wheel slightly until this can be seen. Any necessary adjustments must be made by first slackening the rear wheel spindle nut, then turning the spindle adjuster nuts as required ensuring that the rear chain adjustment is maintained. Refer to Fig. F26 for illustration of correct alignment. Note that the arrows indicate the adjustment required.

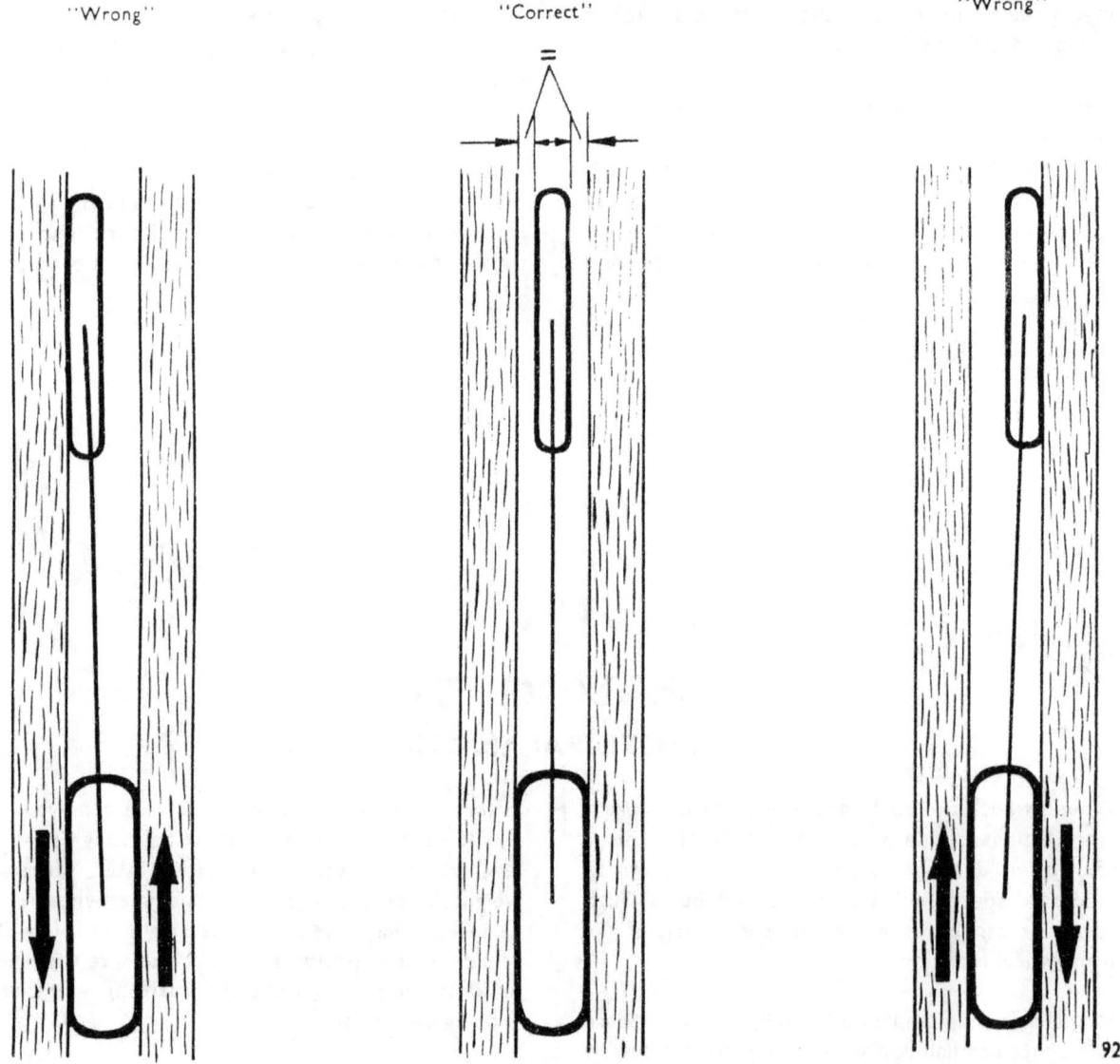

Fig. F26. Aligning the front and rear wheels

SECTION F23

REMOVING AND REFITTING TYRES

To remove the tyre first remove the valve cap and valve core, using the valve cap itself to unscrew the core. Unscrew the knurled valve securing nut and then place all parts where they will be free from dirt and grit. It is recommended that the cover beads are lubricated with a little soapy water before attempting to remove the tyre. The tyre lever should be dipped in this solution before each application. First, insert a lever at the valve position and whilst carefully pulling on this lever, press the tyre bead into the well of the rim diametrally opposite the valve position (see Fig. F27). Insert a

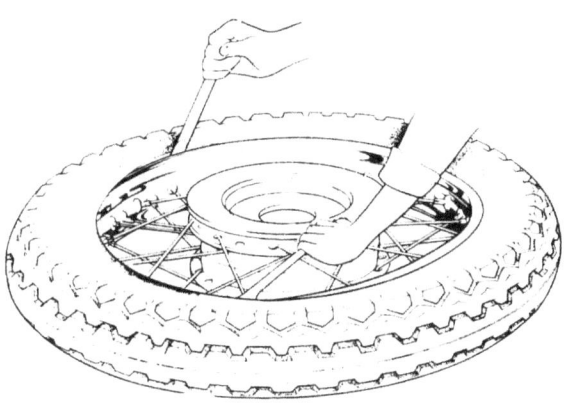

Fig. F28. Removing the first bead of the tyre, using two tyre levers

Fig. F27. Removing the first bead of the tyre—Lever inserted close to valve whilst bead is pressed into well on opposite side of wheel

second lever close to the first and prise the bead over the rim flange. Remove the first lever and reinsert a little further round the rim from the second lever. Continue round the bead in steps of two to three inches until the bead is completely away from the rim. Push the valve out of the rim and then withdraw the inner tube. To completely remove the tyre first stand the wheel upright and then insert a lever between the remaining bead and the rim. The tyre should be easily removed from the rim as shown in Fig. F28.

REFITTING THE TYRE

First place the rubber rim band into the well of the rim and make sure that the rough side of the rubber band is fitted against the rim and that the band is central in the well. Replace the valve core and inflate the inner tube sufficiently to round it out without stretch, dust it with french chalk and insert it into the cover with the valve located at the white "balancing spot" leaving it protruding outside the beads for about four inches either side of the valve. At this stage it is advisable to lubricate the beads and levers with soapy water (see Fig. F29).

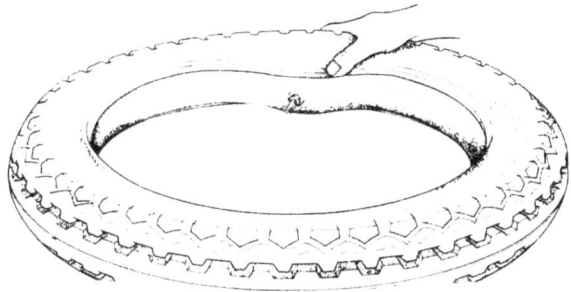

Fig. F29. Cover and tube assembled read for refitting to the wheel

Squeeze the beads together at the valve position to prevent the tube from slipping back inside the tyre and offer the cover to the rim, as shown in Fig. F30, at the same time threading the valve through the valve holes in the rim band and rim. Allow the first bead to go into the well of the rim and the other bead to lie above the level of the rim flange.

F WHEELS, BRAKES AND TYRES

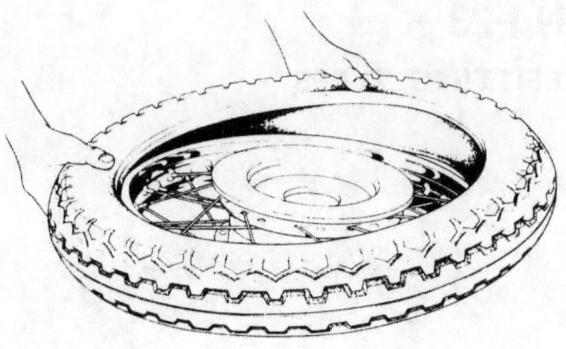

Fig. F30. Refitting the tyre to the wheel. Note valve engaged in rim hole

Press the second bead into the well of the rim diametrally opposite the valve. Insert a lever as close as possible to the point where the bead passes over the flange and lever the bead into the flange, at the same time pressing the fitted part of the bead into the well of the rim. Repeat until the bead is completely over the flange, finishing at the valve position (see Fig. F32).

Working from the valve, press the first bead over the rim flange by hand, moving forward in small steps and making sure that the part of the bead already dealt with, lies in the well of the rim. If necessary use a tyre lever for the last few inches, as shown in Fig. F31. During this operation continually check that the inner tube is not trapped by the cover bead.

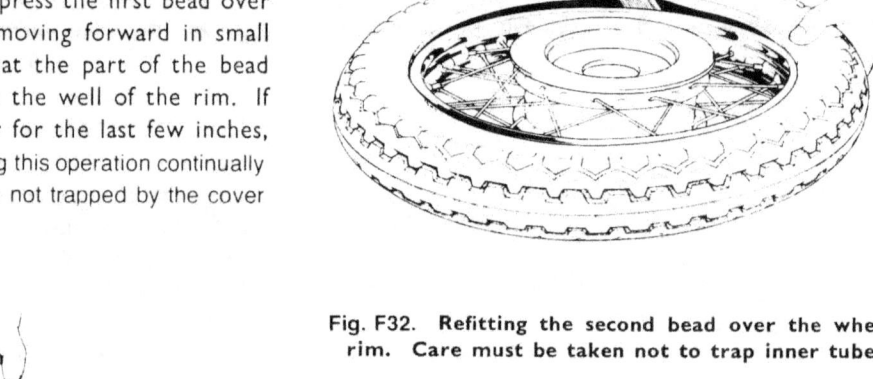

Fig. F32. Refitting the second bead over the wheel rim. Care must be taken not to trap inner tube

Fig. F31. Levering the first bead onto the rim

Push the valve inwards to ensure that the tube near the valve is not trapped under the bead. Pull the valve back and inflate the tyre. Check that the fitting line on the cover is concentric with the top of the rim flange and that the valve protrudes squarely through the valve hole. Fit the knurled rim nut and valve cap. The tyre pressure should then be set to the figure given in General Data.

SECTION F24
SECURITY BOLTS

Security bolts are fitted to the rear wheel to prevent the tyre "creeping" on the rim when it is subjected to excessive acceleration or braking. Such movement would ultimately result in the valve being torn from the inner tube. There are two security bolts fitted to the rear wheel, which are equally spaced either side of the valve and thereby do not affect the balance of the wheel.

Note. The security bolt nuts must not be overtightened, otherwise excessive distortion may occur.

BRAKES, WHEELS AND TYRES

Where a security bolt is fitted the basic procedure for fitting and removing the tyre is the same, but the following instruction should be followed:—

(1) Remove the valve cap and core as described.
(2) Unscrew the security bolt nut and push the bolt inside the cover.
(3) Remove the first bead as described.
(4) Remove the security bolt from the rim.
(5) Remove the inner tube as described.
(6) Remove the second bead and tyre.

For refitting the tyre and inner tube:—
(1) Fit the rim band.

(2) Fit the first bead to the rim without the inner tube inside.
(3) Assemble the security bolt into the rim, putting the nut onto the first few threads (see Fig. F34).
(4) Partly inflate the inner tube and fit it into the the tyre.
(5) Fit the second bead but keep the security bolt pressed well into the tyre, as shown in Fig. F33, and ensure that the inner tube does not become trapped at the edges.
(6) Fit the valve stem nut and inflate the tyre.
(7) Bounce the wheel several times at the point where the security bolt is fitted and then tighten the security bolt nut.

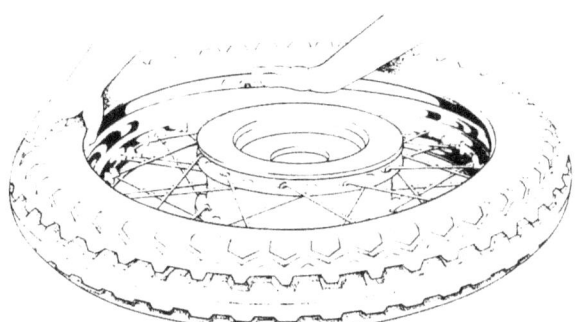

Fig. F33. Placing the security bolt in position

Fig. F34. Refitting the second bead with the security bolt in position

SECTION F25

TYRE MAINTENANCE

To obtain optimum tyre mileage and to eliminate irregular wear on the tyres it is essential that the recommendations governing tyre pressures and general maintenance are followed. The following points are laid out with this in mind.

(1) Maintain the correct inflation pressure as shown in "General Data". Use a pressure gauge frequently. It is advisable to check and restore tyre pressures at least once per week. Pressures should always be checked when tyres are cold and not when they have reached normal running temperatures.

(2) When a pillion passenger or additional load is carried, the rear tyre pressure should be increased appropriately to cater for the extra load.

(3) Unnecessary rapid acceleration and fierce braking should always be avoided. This treatment invariably results in rapid tyre wear.

(4) Regular checks should be made for flints, nails, small stones etc, which should be removed from the tread or they may ultimately penetrate and damage the casing and puncture the tube.

(5) Tyres and spokes should be kept free of oil, grease and paraffin. Regular cleaning should be carried out with a cloth and a little petrol (gasoline).

(6) If tyres develop irregular wear, this may be corrected by reversing the tyre to reverse its direction of rotation.

F
BRAKES, WHEELS AND TYRES

Before inflating, check that the fitting line on the tyre wall just above the bead on each side is concentric with the rim.

If necessary bounce the wheel to help seat the tyre but, see that there is adequate pressure to prevent damaging the tyre or tube and only use moderate force. If the tyre will not seat, it is better to release the pressure, apply soap solution to lubricate and re-inflate.

Inflate to the required pressure and check fitting lines again. Inflation should not be too rapid, particularly at the commencement, to allow the beads to seat correctly on the rim.

See that the valve protrudes squarely through the valve hole before screwing down the knurled nut and finally, replace the dust cap.

SECTION F26
TYRE PRESSURES

The recommended inflation pressure as shown in "General Data", are based on a riders weight of 140lb. If the riders' weight exceeds 140lb. the tyre pressure should be increased as follows:—

Front Tyre
Add 1lb. per square inch for every 28lb. in excess of 140lb.

Rear Tyre
Add 1lb. per square inch for every 14lb. in excess of 140lb.

SECTION F27
REAR CHAIN ADJUSTMENT

REAR CHAIN
The adjustment of the rear chain is controlled by draw bolts fitted to each end of the rear wheel spindle. The correct adjustment for the rear chain is ¾in. free movement with the machine on its wheels and the chain at its tightest point or 1¾in. with the machine on the stand and the chain at its slackest point. If the adjustment of the chain is outside these limits it should be corrected by loosening the wheel spindle nuts (and the brake torque stay nut on the anchor plate prior to frame no. HN62501) and then adjusting the draw bolts an equal number of turns. Always apply the brake pedal to centralise the brake plate and keep it applied while you tighten the spindle nut. Recheck the chain adjustment. If the wheel alignment was correct originally the adjustment of the nuts by an equal number of turns should preserve that alignment but if you are doubtful whether the rear wheel is in line then you should use a straight edge or piece of string alongside the rear wheel; making allowance for the difference in section between the rear tyre and the front tyre and then tighten or loosen the draw bolt adjuster on the right side so that the rear wheel lines up with the front wheel. If the rear wheel is not in line the road holding of the machine will be adversely affected and the effect on the rear chain and rear wheel sprocket will cause rapid wear. When the adjustment is satisfactory check the tightness of the wheel spindle nut, adjuster draw bolts (and brake torque stay nuts. Finally check the adjuster of the brake operating rod. Prior to frame no. HN62501). There is no automatic oil feed to the rear chain which should be lubricated manually with an oil gun weekly.

WARNING: For machines with a rear disc brake always actuate the rear brake prior to moving off with the machine. This will re-charge the hydraulic circuit with fluid in readiness for the first braking application.

BRAKES, WHEELS AND TYRES   **F**

SECTION F28
BRAKING PERFORMANCE DATA

The following information is in accordance with the requirements of the U.S. Federal Highway Administration, Department of Transportation

This figure indicates braking performance that can be met or exceeded by the vehicles to which it applies, without locking the wheels, under different conditions of loading.

The information presented represents results obtainable by skilled drivers under controlled road and vehicle conditions, and the information may not be correct under other conditions.

Description of vehicles to which this table applies:—
TRIUMPH T140V BONNEVILLE 750

A. Fully Operational Service Brake

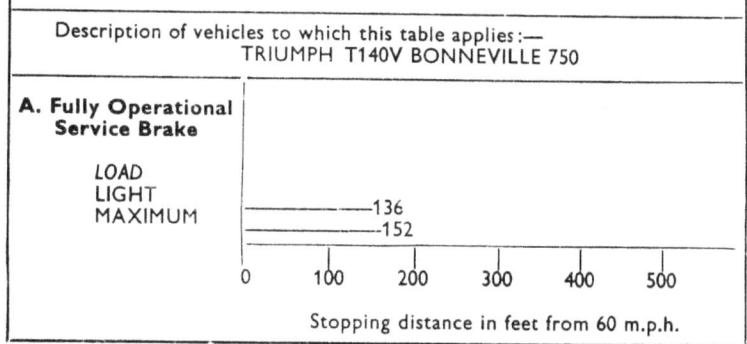

Stopping distance in feet from 60 m.p.h.

This figure indicates passing times and distances that can be met or exceeded by the vehicles to which it applies, in the situations diagrammed below.

The low-speed pass assumes an initial speed of 20 m.p.h. and a limiting speed of 35 m.p.h. The high-speed pass assumes an initial speed of 50 m.p.h. and a limiting speed of 80 m.p.h.

Notice:—The information presented represents results obtainable by skilled drivers under controlled road and vehicle conditions, and the information may not be correct under other conditions.

Description of vehicles to which this table applies:—
AS ABOVE

Summary Table

LOW-SPEED PASS 373 feet; 7.9 seconds
HIGH-SPEED PASS 932 feet; 9.3 seconds

LOW-SPEED
INITIAL SPEED:

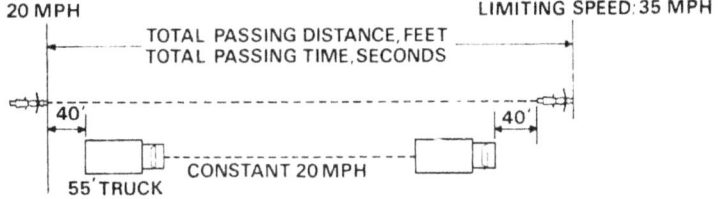

HIGH-SPEED
INITIAL SPEED:

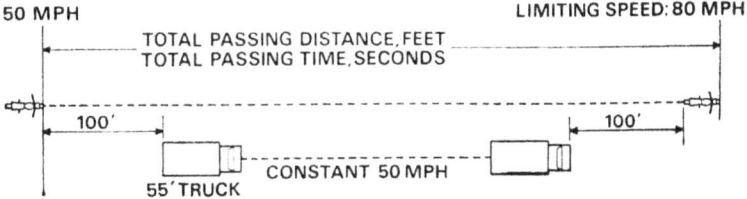

The following information is in accordance with the requirements of the U.S. Federal Highway Administration, Department of Transportation.

This figure indicates braking performance that can be met or exceeded by the vehicles to which it applies, without locking the wheels, under different conditions of loading.

The information presented represents results obtainable by skilled drivers under controlled road and vehicle conditions, and the information may not be correct under other conditions.

Description of vehicles to which this table applies:—
TRIUMPH TR7V TIGER 750

A. Fully Operational Service Brake

LOAD
LIGHT
MAXIMUM

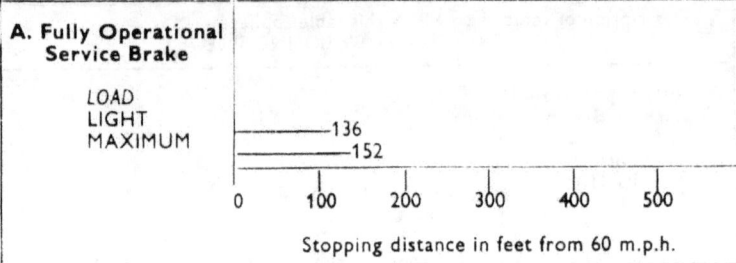

Stopping distance in feet from 60 m.p.h.

This figure indicates passing times and distances that can be met or exceeded by the vehicles to which it applies, in the situations diagrammed below.

The low-speed pass assumes an initial speed of 20 m.p.h. and a limiting speed of 35 m.p.h. The high-speed pass assumes an initial speed of 50 m.p.h. and a limiting speed of 80 m.p.h.

Notice:—The information presented represents results obtainable by skilled drivers under controlled road and vehicle conditions, and the information may not be correct under other conditions.

Description of vehicles to which this table applies:—
AS ABOVE

Summary Table

LOW-SPEED PASS 375 feet; 8.0 seconds
HIGH-SPEED PASS 940 feet; 9.4 seconds

LOW-SPEED
INITIAL SPEED:
20 MPH   LIMITING SPEED: 35 MPH

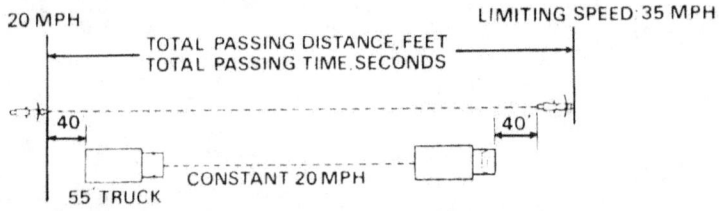

HIGH-SPEED
INITIAL SPEED
50 MPH   LIMITING SPEED: 80 MPH

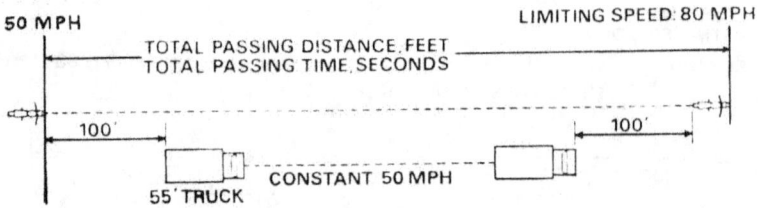

SECTION F29

FAULT FINDING—FRONT AND REAR HYDRAULIC DISC BRAKES

PROBLEM	POSSIBLE CAUSE	ACTION
Excess travel of the front brake lever rear brake pedal or 'spongy' feel when applying either brake.	(a) Air trapped in the hydraulic system (b) Incorrect positioning of master cylinder (c) Fluid leak past the main seal in the master cylinder.	Bleed the system, see Section F4 Reset positon, see Section F7 & F8 Examine the seals, see Section F7 F8.
Fluid level falls in either the front or rear brake fluid reservoirs	(a) Friction pads wearing normally. (b) Brake fluid leaking	Top up the fluid, see Section F2. Check all the hoses, pipes and unions without applying the brakes and look for evidence of leaks. Repeat check with the brakes held on under pressure. If necessary tighten any unions or replace/service any components, see Section F.
Brakes drag with subsequent overheating of disc resulting in brake 'fade'.	(a) Reservoir filler cap has a blocked (b) Incorrect positioning of the cylinder (c) The friction pads binding in their recess or the caliper piston is sticking. (d) The brake fluid is contaminated with fuel, paraffin or oil.	Clean and insect the filler cap vent hole. Clear the hole if necessary. Reset positon, see Section F7 & F8 Remove the friction pads and clean out their recesses. Clean the exposed surface of the pistons with clean brake fluid. If a piston is found to be seized then a new caliper assembly must be fitted. If any high spots are found on the friction pad backing plates remove them with a file. If contamination is suspected, first check by smelling the fluid in the reservoirs. If necessary dismantle the front brake master cylinder and check to see if the seals are considerably swollen. If so all rubber components must be replaced, see Section F8. If the rear system is suspected the master cylinder must be replaced as a unit. Before fitting any new parts flush the system, see Section F5.

WHEELS, BRAKES AND TYRES

PROBLEM	POSSIBLE CAUSE	ACTION
Inefficient braking	(a) New friction pads, but are not "bedded-in".	Frequent use of brake will cure complaint.
	(b) Friction pads glazed on the brake disc has oxidised.	Remove the friction pads and remove any glazed areas with a fine abrasive. Inspect the contact area of the disc, any minor imperfections can be removed with a fine carborundum paper but if in doubt replace the disc.
	(c) Friction pads contaminated by oil, grease or brake fluid.	Replace the friction pads
Friction pads wear rapidly	(a) Friction pads fitted are the incorrect grade.	Replace pads with the correct type.
	(b) Brake disc has a scored contact area.	Minor imperfection may be removed with a fine grade carborundum paper, but otherwise replace the disc.
	(c) Partly or completely seized caliper piston.	If the piston is found to be seized the the whole caliper assembly must be replaced.
Squealing brakes	(a) Friction pads vibrate at a high frequency.	Remove the friction pads and lubricate the metal backing plate with high melting point copper based grease such as 'COPASLIP'. DO NOT allow the grease to contact the friction pad material.
	(b) Loose caliper mounting bolts.	Confirm and rectify by tightening the bolts.

SECTION G

TELESCOPIC FORKS

INDEX

	Section
DESCRIPTION	—
STEERING HEAD ADJUSTMENT	G1
RENEWING HEAD RACES	G2
STRIPPING AND REASSEMBLING THE FORK LEGS	G3
FORK ALIGNMENT	G4
HYDRAULIC DAMPING	G5

TELESCOPIC FORKS

DESCRIPTION

The front fork is of the telescopic type using high grade steel tube stanchions. They are ground to a micro finish and hard chromium plated over their entire length.

The alloy bottom members are precision bored and provide the bearing for the stanchion. Internal main springs are fitted and locate on the damper tube.

An oil seal is contained in the top lip of each bottom member and is protected by a rubber dust cover.

Oil is contained in each bottom member and serves the dual purpose of damping and lubrication. Oil is added by removal of the fork cap nuts and drained at the plugs provided.

Damping of the fork action is achieved by the use of a damper valve in conjunction with a series of bleed holes in a fixed valve.

SECTION G1

STEERING HEAD ADJUSTMENT

It is most important that the steering head bearings are always correctly adjusted.

Place a strong support underneath the engine so that the front wheel is raised clear of the ground then, standing in front of the wheel, attempt to push the lower fork legs backwards and forwards. Should any play be detected, the steering head must be adjusted.

If possible, ask a friend to place the fingers of one hand lightly round the head lug, whilst the forks are being pulled back and forth. Any play will be felt quite easily by the fingers.

It should be possible to turn the forks from side to side quite smoothly and without any "lumpy" movement. If the movement is "lumpy", the rollers are indented into the races or broken. In either case the complete bearing should be renewed.

To adjust the steering head assembly, slacken the clamp nut B, Fig. G1 and the top yoke adjuster nut A then tighten down the adjuster nut until adjustment is correct. There should be no play evident in the races but great care must be taken not to overtighten, or the balls will become indented into the races, making steering extremely difficult and dangerous.

Having carried out the adjustment, tighten the clamp nuts and the top yoke pinch bolt securely. Re-check the adjustment.

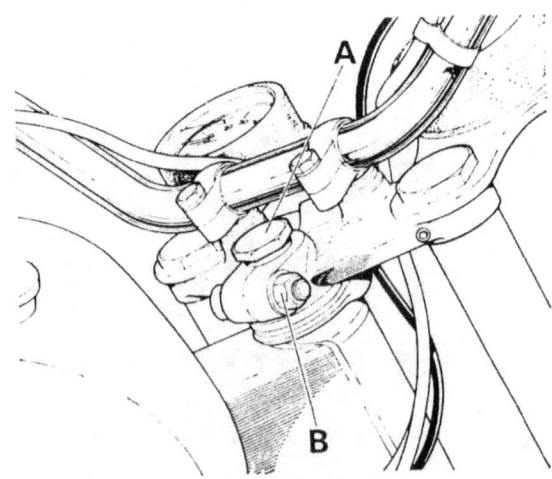

Fig. G1. Steering head adjustment

TELESCOPIC FORKS

SECTION G2
RENEWING HEAD RACES

Place a strong support underneath the engine so that the front wheel is raised clear of the ground. Remove the front wheel (see Section F11). Remove the front mudguard (see Section E16).

The steering head can be dismantled without stripping the forks. First, disconnect the hydraulic brake pipe from the top and middle lug. See section F6. Remove the headlamp. See section H10. Detach the handle bar complete by unscrewing the two self locking nuts which secure the two eye bolts in the top lug. See fig. G2. Remove fork cap nuts. Place the speedometer and tachometer to one side after first disconnecting the drive cables and illuminating lights.

Slacken the top lug pinch bolt (A) fig. G1 and remove adjuster and middle nut (B). Loosen both the top lug stanchion pinch bolts with an allen key. Slide fork leg and stanchion from the lugs.

Using a raw-hide mallet strike the undersides of the top lug alternately to release it from the stanchions. Place the yoke to one side and withdraw the steering stem out of the head lug. The taper roller bearings can now be removed from the stem and the top lug for cleaning and inspection. Check for pitting and fracture of the roller surface. The bearing must be replaced if any of these faults are in evidence.

The steering head outer races have a very long serviceable life and should not need replacement for a very considerable mileage. If however their replacement is deemed necessary the races can be removed using a suitable drift from inside the head lug. Replacement of the new race is effected by using service tool 61-6121. Do not forget to refit the bearing abutment rings behind the outer races. Reassembly is the reverse of the above procedure. Grease the bearings prior to replacement, see Section A1 for correct grade. Note that head of both the top lug and stanchion must be flush leaving the head of the inner retaining plug standing proud. Care must be taken to ensure that the headlamp shrouds are located correctly in the prespective recesses in the top plug. Note that when refitting the plastic dust cover ensure that it sits square to allow the adjuster nut, Fig. G1 (A) to locate on the bearing. Readjust the steering head bearing as in Section G1. Reassemble the hydraulic system as described in Section F6.

SECTION G3
STRIPPING AND REASSEMBLING THE FORK LEGS

Before-commencing work on the forks it is advisable to have the following service tools and replacemenst available:

(a) Oil seal for fork leg (2)

(b) Oil seal for damper valve (2)

(c) Service tool (61-6113)

Remove small drain plug at the bottom of each fork adjacent to the wheel spindle and drain out the oil by pumping the forks up and down. Support the machine on a box with the front wheel clear of the ground. Remove front wheel as described in Section F11. Remove front mudguard as described in Section E16.

Detach the handlebar complete by unscrewing the two self locking nuts which secure the two eye bolts in the top lug. Remove fork cap nuts. Place the speedometer and tachometer to one side after first disconnecting the drive cable and illuminating lights.

Disconnect the hydraulic brake pipe at middle lug and fork leg to stanchion. (See Section F6.) Remove caliper and place carefully to one side. Unscrew the two allen pinch bolts at the back of the top head lug. Remove alluminium cap screws with suitably sized allen key.

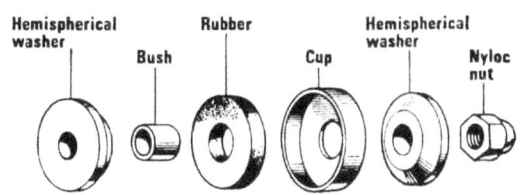

Fig. G2. Handlebar mountings

TELESCOPIC FORKS

Remove the stanchion top nuts then remove the internal fork springs. Using service tool 61-6113 placed down into the stanchion; hold the valve assembly while the retaining allen screw is being unscrewed at the base of the fork leg.

At this stage it will be possible to remove the fork leg by sliding it from the stanchion. Remove the stanchions by slackening the pinch bolts on the bottom yoke and withdrawing the stanchions. When refitting tighten the pinch bolts to 18/20 lbs /ft.

The dust cover on the fork leg can easily be prised off by hand.

The damper valve assembly is retained in the bottom of the stanchion by an aluminium nut which should be carefully removed with a ring spanner or similar.

The valve assembly consists of a fixed bleed valve which has its own oil seal, a clapper valve, a spring support nut and a rebound spring. It should not be necessary to strip this assembly unless the fixed bleed valve has contracted damage in any way.

The oil seal on the bleed valve can easily be replaced by hand. If using a screwdriver to prise the seal away from the valve be careful not to damage the bearing surface as the material is a soft alloy. (Refer to Fig. G3 for details of the assembly).

Care must be taken not to lose the sealing washer contained in the bottom of the fork leg. The base of the valve stem rests on this seal and the allen screw is replaced from the outside of the leg. Refer to the exploded drawing on page G6 for assembly details.

Remove the retainer cap and pull out the oil seal from the top of the fork leg.

Early models were fitted with an interference fit seal which can be removed with a tool of the design shown in Fig. G4. This tool can be simply manufactured from a strip of mild steel material approx. 12in. long × 1in. wide and 1/8in. depth. The design is such that the tool does not come into direct contact with the aluminium fork leg thereby causing unreparable damage. As an alternate a long tyre lever carefully used will be found adequate. **Note.** When using either of these tools make several attempts to remove the seal by working around the periphery of the fork leg, otherwise the tool will rip through the lip of the seal.

NOTE: Always use the latest push fit seal and retainer caps when servicing seals on early models.

Place the stanchion into the fork leg and place a small polythene bag over the top lip of the stanchion. Push the oil seal over the stanchion and down into position on the fork leg. It is important that the polythene is used because the lip of stanchion has a sharp edge that may easily scratch or damage the precision edge of the seal. Even a scratch that may not be readily visible to the eye will cause leakage at the seal.

Push a new seal into position then fit the retainer and tap home.

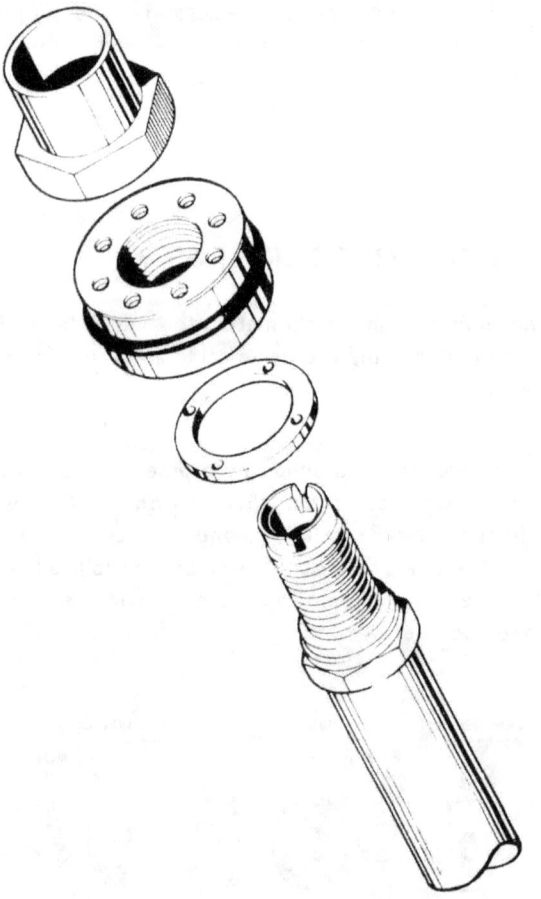

Fig. G3. Damper valve assembly

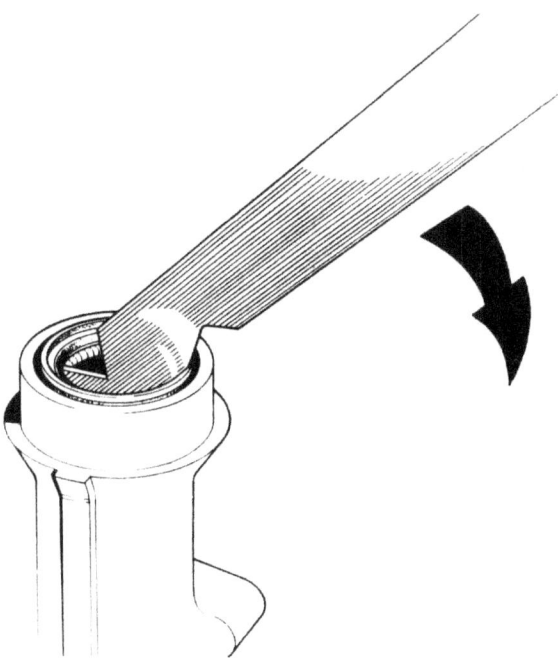

Fig. G4. Removing oil seal

Check all components for cleanliness and wash in fuel if necessary. Examine the bore of the stanchion and clean with a cloth pushed into the bore.

Reassembly of the fork leg is a reversal of the dismantling procedure. Replace the valve into the bottom of the stanchion. Apply some red loctite to the aluminium retaining nut and tighten to a torque of 25 ft./lbs.

Check that the small "Dowty" sealing washer is located in the well in the base of the fork leg. (If this washer shows signs of damage or wear it must be replaced).

Push the rubber dust cover onto it's location groove on the fork leg and then replace the leg on the stanchion.

As the leg is refitted onto the stanchion the stem of the damper valve assembly must be located on top of the "Dowty" sealing washer. If difficulty is encountered during this operation, service tool 61-6113 which is used to retain the valve assembly while it is being removed may be used to navigate the damper valve onto its location.

The allen screw can then be replaced into the bottom of the fork leg and tightened as described above.

Replace fork leg and stanchion by sliding it up through the rubber stop, middle lug, headlamp bracket and top lug until the top of the stanchion and the surface of the top lug lie exactly flush. Retighten top lug and middle lug pinch bolts to a torque setting of 20 ft/lbs.

Replace the fork springs and refill the fork legs with the correct quantity of oil. See Section A15.

Coat the threads of the stanchion top nuts with "well seal" jointing compound and refit, tightening to a torque of 15ft./lbs. Replace fork cap nuts and tighten them both to a torque of 30ft./lbs. Reconnect the speedometer drive cable and illuminating lights.

Refit the caliper on fork leg and reassemble the hydraulic brake system as described in Section F6 and F4. Replace the handlebars (see Section G3).

Replace the front mudguard. Refit the front wheel (see Section F11).

G

TELESCOPIC FORKS

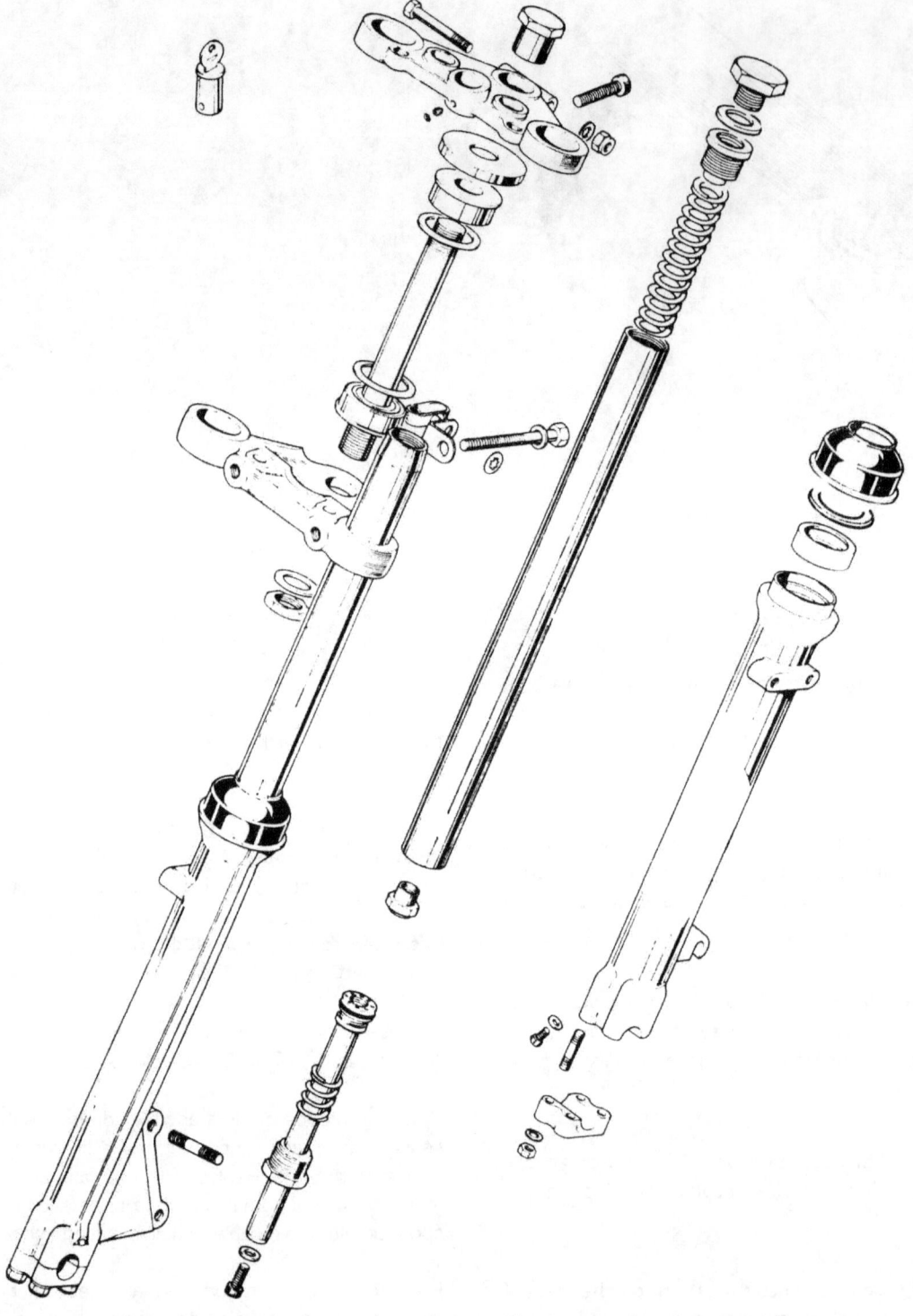

Fig. G5. Fork assembly details

SECTION G4

FORK ALIGNMENT

After replacing the fork legs, mudguard and wheel, it may be found that the fork is incorrectly aligned.

To rectify this, the fork wheel spindle cap nuts must first be screwed up tight on the right-hand leg and the spindle cap on the left-hand leg slackened off. Also loosen the top caps and the pinch bolts in both the bottom and top yokes. The forks should now be pumped up and down several times to line them up and then tightened up from bottom to top, that is, wheel spindle, bottom yoke pinch bolts, top caps and finally, the steering stem pinch bolt in the top yoke.

If, after this treatment, the forks still do not function satisfactorily then either the fork stanchions are bent or one of the yokes is twisted.

The stanchions can only be accurately checked for straightness with special equipment such as a surface plate. Special gauges are also required to check the yokes. It is possible, however, to make a reasonable check of the stanchions by rolling them on a surface plate or flat surface such as a piece of plate glass, but it is not a simple operation to straighten a bent tube, and a new part may be necessary.

Check the stanchions for truth by rolling them slowly on a flat checking table. A bent stanchion may be realigned if the bow does not exceed $\frac{5}{32}$ in. maximum. To realign the stanchion, a hand press is required. Place the stanchion on two swage "V" blocks at either end and apply pressure to the raised portion of the stanchion. By means of alternately pressing in this way and checking the stanchion on a flat table the amount of bow can be reduced until it is finally removed.

Having checked the stanchions for straightness and reset as necessary, the top and bottom yokes can now be checked. First, assemble the two stanchions into the bottom yoke so that a straight edge across the lower ends is touching all four edges of the tubes, then tighten the pinch bolts. Now view them from the side; the two stanchions should be quite parallel. Alternatively, the lower 12 in. of the stanchions can be placed on a surface plate, when there should be no rocking.

To reset, hold one stanchion in a vice (using soft clamps) and reposition the other stanchion, using a longer and larger diameter tube to obtain sufficient leverage. Having checked the stanchions this way, check the gap between them on the ground portion.

The next step is to place the top yoke in position over the stanchions, when the steering stem should be quite central.

The final step is to check if the tubes are parallel when assembled into the top yoke only. In this case the bottom yoke can be fitted loosely on the tubes, acting as a pilot only.

Though it is permissible to rectify slight errors in alignment by resetting, it is much safer to replace the part affected especially when there is excessive misalignment. Works reconditioned units are available to owners in the United Kingdom through the dealer network.

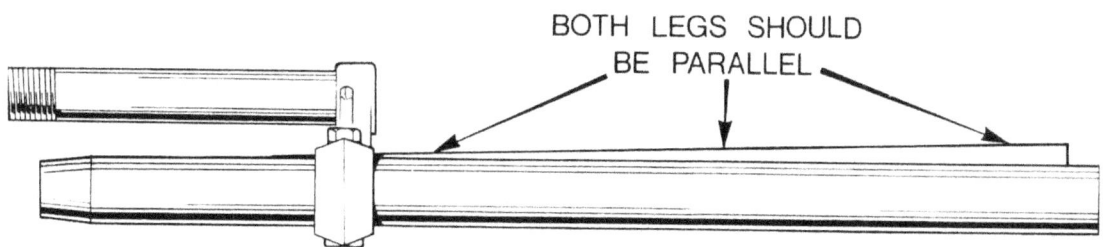

Fig. G6. Fork leg alignment

SECTION G5
HYDRAULIC DAMPING

Note the valve assembly which is retained in the bottom of the fork leg. Bleed holes are contained in the valve stem and in a sub-assembly at the top of the stem. This particular valve operates in conjunction with a damper valve which acts as a restrictor.

Oil is contained in the bottom member the level of which is always above the valve assembly. On compression the oil is forced through bleed holes in the valve stem. As the travel increases the bleed holes are progressively sealed off by a plastic sleeve and the damping increases until finally the stanchion is trapped on a cushion of oil which acts as the final bump stop. During this operation a vacuum is created in the space formed between the bottom of the stanchion and the damper valve, hence oil is transferred into this compartment through the eight bleed holes in the valve.

On expansion the oil in this newly formed compartment is compressed, the damper valve closes and the oil is bled through four small holes in the damper valve itself and then progressively through the holes in the valve stem. While this operation is being executed, oil is transferred back into the bottom member in readiness for the next compression.

SECTION H

ELECTRICAL SYSTEM

INTRODUCTION

BATTERY INSPECTION AND MAINTENANCE ... H1
    DESCRIPTION
    (a) ROUTINE MAINTENANCE
    (b) MAXIMUM PERMISSABLE ELECTROLYTE TEMPERATURES DURING CHARGING

COIL IGNITION SYSTEM ... H2
    DESCRIPTION
    (a) CHECKING THE LOW TENSION CIRCUIT FOR CONTINUITY
    (b) FAULT FINDING IN THE LOW TENSION CIRCUIT
    (c) IGNITION COILS
    (d) CONTACT BREAKER
    (e) CHECKING THE HIGH TENSION CIRCUIT

SPARKING PLUGS ... H3

CHARGING SYSTEM ... H4
    DESCRIPTION
    (a) CHECKING THE D.C. OUTPUT AT THE RECTIFIER
    (b) CHECKING THE ALTERNATOR OUTPUT
    (c) RECTIFIER MAINTENANCE AND TESTING
    (d) CHECKING THE CHARGING CIRCUIT FOR CONTINUITY
    (e) CONSTRUCTING A 1 OHM LOAD RESISTOR

ZENER DIODE CHARGE CONTROL AND TEST PROCEDURE ... H5

ZENER DIODE LOCATION ... H6

ALTERNATOR AND STATOR DETAILS (Specifications and Output Figures): ... H7

ELECTRIC HORN ... H8

HEADLAMP ... H9
    DESCRIPTION
    BEAM ADJUSTMENTS

HEADLAMP REMOVING AND REFITTING ... H10

TAIL AND STOPLAMP UNIT ... H11

FUSES ... H12

IGNITION SWITCH ... H13

IGNITION CUT-OUT BUTTON ... H14

WARNING LAMPS ... H15

STOP LAMP SWITCHES ... H16

OIL PRESSURE SWITCH ... H17

CAPACITOR IGNITION ... H18
    IDENTIFICATION OF CAPACITOR TERMINALS
    STORAGE LIFE
    TESTING
    SERVICE NOTES
    WIRING

WIRING DIAGRAMS ... H19

ELECTRICAL SYSTEM

INTRODUCTION

The electrical system is supplied from an alternating current generator contained in the primary chaincase and driven from the crankshaft. The single charge rate generator output is then converted into direct current by a silicon diode rectifier. The direct current is supplied to a 12 volt 8 ampere/hour battery with a Zener diode in circuit to regulate the battery current.

The current is then supplied to the ignition system which is controlled by a double contact breaker driven direct from the exhaust camshaft. The contact breaker feeds two ignition coils, one for each cylinder, and the two capacitors are mounted separately in a waterproof pack. The battery supplies current for the headlamp, tail lamp and instruments and warning lamps.

The routine maintenance needed by the various components is set out in the following sections. All electrical components and connections including the earthing points to the frame of the machine must be clean and tight.

No emergency start facility is provided since there is however sufficient voltage to start the machine when a discharged battery is in circit.

A single 12 volt 8 amp/hr battery is used.

SECTION H1
BATTERY INSPECTION AND MAINTENANCE

The battery containers are moulded in translucent polystyrene through which the acid level can be seen. The battery top is so designed that when the cover is in position, the special anti-spill filler plugs are sealed in a common venting chamber. Gas from the filler plugs leaves this chamber through a vent pipe union at the side of the top. The vent at the other side of the top is sealed off. Polythene tubing is attached to the vent pipe union to lead corrosive fumes away from parts of the machine which may otherwise suffer damage.

To prepare a dry-charged battery for service, first discard the vent hole sealing tape and then pour into each cell pure dilute sulphuric acid of appropriate specific gravity to THE COLOURED LINE. (See table (a)). Allow the battery to stand for at least one hour for the electrolyte to settle down, thereafter maintain the acid level at the coloured line by adding distilled water.

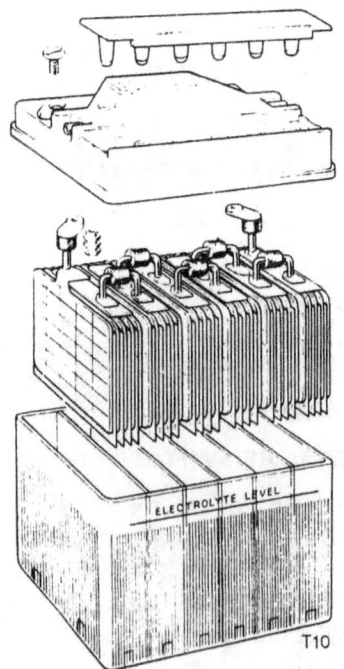

Fig. H1. Exploded view of battery

ELECTRICAL SYSTEM

H1. PART A. ROUTINE MAINTENANCE

Every week examine the level of the electrolyte in each cell. Lift the battery out of the carrier so that the coloured filling line can be seen. Add distilled water until the electrolyte level reaches this line.

Note.—On no account should batteries be topped up to the separator guard but only to the coloured line.

With this type of battery, the acid can only be reached by a miniature hydrometer, which would indicate the state of charge.

Great care should be taken when carrying out these operations not to spill any acid or allow a naked flame near the electrolyte. The mixture of oxygen and hydrogen given off by a battery on charge, and to a lesser extent when standing idle, can be dangerously explosive.

The readings obtained from the battery electrolyte should be compared with those given in table (a).

SPECIFIC GRAVITY OF ELECTROLYTE FOR FILLING THE BATTERY

U.K. and Climates normally below 90°F (32·2°C)		Tropical Climates over 90°F (32·2°C)	
Filling	Fully charged	Filling	Fully charged
1·260	1·280/1·300	1·210	1·220/1·240

Every 1,000 miles (1,500 k.m.) or monthly, or more regularly in hot climates the battery should be cleaned as follows. Remove the battery cover and clean the battery top. Examine the terminals: if they are corroded scrape them clean and smear them with a film of petroleum jelly, such as vaseline. Remove the vent plugs and check that the vent holes are clear and that the rubber washer fitted under each plug is in good condition. Note that current batteries have the plugs en bloc and no washers are used on this type.

H1. PART B. MAXIMUM PERMISSABLE ELECTROLYTE TEMPERATURE DURING CHARGE

Climates normally Below 80°F (27°C)	Climates between 80–100°F (27–38°C)	Climates frequently above 100°F (38°C)
100°F (38°C)	110°F (43°C)	120°F (49°C)

Notes.
The specific gravity of the electrolyte varies with the temperature. For convenience in comparing specific gravities, they are always corrected to 60°F., which is adopted as a reference temperature. The method of correction is as follows:

For every 5°F. below 60°F. deduct ·020 from the observed reading to obtain the true specific gravity at 60°F. For every 5°F. above 60°F., add ·020 to the observed reading to obtain the true specific gravity at 60°F.

The temperature must be indicated by a thermometer having its bulb actually immersed in the electrolyte and not the ambient temperature. To take a temperature reading tilt the battery sideways and then insert into the electrolyte.

ELECTRICAL SYSTEM

SECTION H2
COIL IGNITION SYSTEM

DESCRIPTION

The coil ignition system comprises two ignition coils and a contact breaker fitted in the timing cover and driven by the exhaust camshaft. The ignition coils are mounted behind the gearbox on a pressed steel mounting plate. Apart from cleaning the coils, in between the terminals and checking the low tension and high tension connections, the coils will not require any other attention. Testing the ignition coils is amply covered in H2 Part C below whilst testing the contact breaker is described in H2 Part D. The 10CA type of contact breaker is used. The condensers are mounted underneath the twin-seat on the electrical platform.

The best method of approach to a faulty ignition system, is that of first checking the low tension circuit for continuity as shown in H2 Part A, and then following the procedure laid out in H2 Part B to locate the fault(s).

Failure to locate a fault in the low tension circuit indicates that the high tension circuit or sparking plugs are faulty, and the procedure detailed in H2 Part E must be followed. Before commencing any of the following tests, however, the contact breaker and sparking plugs must be cleaned and adjusted to eliminate this possible source of fault.

H2 PART A. CHECKING THE LOW TENSION CIRCUIT FOR CONTINUITY

To check whether there is a fault in the low-tension circuit and to locate its position, the following tests should be carried out:—

First inspect the in-line fuse in the battery earth cable (brown/blue lead) and replace if suspect.

Check also the cut-out switch; this can be done by disconnecting the white, and white/yellow lead from the left handlebar switch and connecting them together. This will complete the ignition circuit by by-passing the cut-out switch.

H2 PART B. FAULT FINDING IN THE LOW TENSION CIRCUIT

To trace a fault in the low tension wiring, turn the ignition switch to "IGN" position and then crank the engine until both sets of contacts are opened, or alternatively, place a piece of insulating material between both sets of contacts whilst the following test is carried out.

With the aid of a D.C. voltmeter and 2 test-prods (voltmeter 0–15 volts for 12 volt electrical systems), make a point to point check along the low tension circuit starting at the battery and working right through to the ignition coils, stage by stage, in the following manner, referring to the relevant wiring diagram in Section H14.

Note.—It will be necessary to disconnect the Zener Diode before the test is carried out. To do this remove the brown/blue lead from the Diode centre terminal. (See Section H5 for Diode location).

(1) First, establish that the battery is earthed correctly by connecting the volt meter across the battery negative terminal and the machine frame earth. No voltage reading indicates that the red earthing lead is faulty (or the fuse blown, where fitted). Also, a low reading would indicate a poor battery earth connection. Check also the fuse in the main negative lead.

(2) Connect the voltmeter between the left ignition coil (−Ve) terminal and earth and then the right ignition coil (−Ve) terminal and earth. No voltage reading indicates a breakdown between the battery and the coil (−Ve) terminal, or that the switch connections are faulty.

(3) Connect the voltmeter between ignition switch input terminal and earth. No reading indicates that the brown and blue lead has faulty connections. Check for voltage at the brown/blue lead connections at rectifier, and lighting switch terminals No's 2 and 3.

ELECTRICAL SYSTEM

(4) Connect the voltmeter across ignition switch output terminal and earth. No reading indicates that the ignition switch is faulty and should be replaced. Battery voltage reading at this point but not at the ignition coil (−Ve) terminals indicates that the white lead has become "open circuit" or become disconnected.

(5) Disconnect the black/white, and black/yellow leads from the (+Ve) terminals of each ignition coil. Connect the voltmeter across the (+Ve) terminal of the left coil and earth and then the (+Ve) terminal of the right coil and earth. No reading on the voltmeter in either case indicates that the coil primary winding is faulty and a replacement ignition-coil should be fitted.

(6) With both sets of contacts open reconnect the ignition coil leads and then connect the voltmeter across both sets of contacts in turn. No reading in either case indicates that there is a faulty connection or the internal insulation has broken down in one of the condensers (capacitors).

If a capacitor is suspected then a substitution should be made and a re-test carried out.

(7) Finally, reconnect the Zener Diode brown/blue lead and then connect the voltmeter between the Zener Diode centre terminal and earth. The voltmeter should read battery volts. If it does not the Zener Diode is faulty and a substitution should be made. Refer to Section H5 for the correct procedure for testing a Zener Diode on the machine. Ignition coil check procedure is given in Section H2, Part C.

H2 PART C. IGNITION COILS

The ignition coils consist of primary and secondary windings wound concentrically about a laminated soft iron core, the secondary winding being next to the core. The primary winding usually consists of some 300 turns of enamel covered wire and the secondary some 17,000–26,000 turns of much finer wire—also enamel covered. Each layer is paper insulated from the next in both primary and secondary windings.

To test the ignition coils on the machine, first ensure that the low tension circuit is in order as described in H2 Part A above then disconnect the high tension leads from the left and right sparking plugs.

Turn the ignition switch to the on position and crank the engine until the contacts (those with the black/yellow lead from the ignition coil) for the right cylinder are closed. Flick the contact breaker lever open a number of times whilst the high tension lead from the right ignition coil is held about $\frac{3}{16}$ in. away from the cylinder head. If the ignition coil is in good condition a strong spark should be obtained. If no spark occurs this indicates the ignition coil to be faulty.

Repeat this test for the left high tension lead and coil by cranking the engine until the contacts with the black/white lead from the remaining ignition coil are closed.

Before a fault can be attributed to an ignition coil it must be ascertained that the high tension cables are not cracked or showing signs of deterioration, as this may often be the cause of mis-firing etc. It should also be checked that the ignition points are actually making good electrical contact when closed and that the moving contact is insulated from earth (ground) when open. See Test H2 Part B. It is advisable to remove the ignition coils and test them by the method described below.

BENCH TESTING AN IGNITION COIL

Connect the ignition coil into the circuit shown in Fig. H3 and set the adjustable gap to 9 mm. for 17M12 types (12 volt). With the contact breaker running at 100 r.p.m. and the coil in good condition, not more than 5% missing should occur at the spark gap over a period of 15 seconds. The primary winding can be checked for short-circuit coils by connecting an ohmeter across the low tension terminals. The reading obtained should be within the figures quoted hereafter (at 20°C).

ELECTRICAL SYSTEM

Coil	Primary Resistance	
	Min.	Max.
17M12	3·0 ohms.	3·4 ohms.

reduction in capacity, indicated by excessive arcing when in use, and overheating of the contact faces, a check should be made by substitution.

Particular attention is called to the periodic lubrication procedure for the contact breaker which is given in Section A. When lubricating the parts ensure that no oil or grease gets onto the contacts.

If it is felt that the contacts require surface grinding then the complete contact breaker unit should be removed as described in Section B26 and the moving contacts disconnected by unscrewing the nut which secures the low tension lead, removing the lead and nylon bush. The spring and contact point can be removed from the pivot spindle.

Repeat this procedure for the other contact point.

Grinding is best achieved by using a fine carborundum stone or very fine emery cloth, afterwards wiping away any trace of dirt or metal dust with a clean petrol (gasoline) moistened cloth. The contact faces should be slightly domed to ensure point contact. There is no need to remove the pitting from the fixed contact.

When reassembling, the nylon bush is fitted through the low tension connection tab, and through the spring location eye.

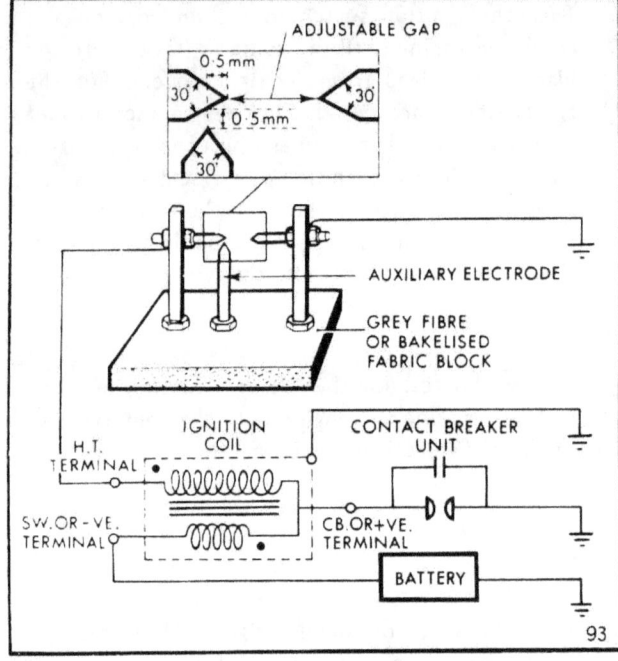

Fig. H2. Ignition coil test rig

H2 PART D. CONTACT BREAKER

Faults occurring at the contact breaker are in the main due to, incorrect adjustment of the contacts or the efficiency being impaired by piling, pitting or oxidation of the contacts due to oil etc. Therefore, always ensure that the points are clean and that the gap is adjusted to the correct working clearance as described in Section B26.

To test for a faulty condenser, first turn the ignition switch to the on position and then take voltage readings across each set of contacts in turn with the contacts open. No reading indicates that the condenser internal insulation has broken down. Should the fault be due to a condenser having a

H2 PART E. CHECKING THE HIGH TENSION CIRCUIT

If ignition failure or mis-firing occurs, and the fault is not in the low tension circuit, then check the ignition coils as described in Part C. If the coils prove satisfactory, ensure that the high tension cables are not the cause of the fault.

If a good spark is available at the high tension cable, then the sparking plug suppressor cap or the sparking plug itself may be the cause of the fault. Clean the sparking plug and adjust the electrodes to the required setting as described in Section H3 and then re-test the engine for running performance. If the fault recurs then it is likely the suppressor caps are faulty and these should be renewed.

SECTION H3
SPARKING PLUGS

It is recommended that the sparking plugs be inspected, cleaned and tested every 3,000 miles (4,800 km.) and new ones fitted every 12,000 miles (20,000 km.).

To remove the sparking plugs a box spanner ($\frac{13}{16}$ in. (19·5 mm.) across flats) should be used and if any difficulty is encountered a small amount of penetrating oil (see lubrication chart Section A1) should be placed at the base of the sparking plug and time allowed for penetration. When removing the sparking plugs identify each plug with the cylinder from which it was removed so that any faults revealed on examination can be traced back to the cylinder concerned.

Due to certain features of engine design the sparking plugs will probably show slightly differing deposits and colouring characteristics. For this purpose it is recommended that any adjustments to carburation etc., which may be carried out to gain the required colour characteristics should always be referred to the left cylinder.

Examine both plugs for signs of oil fouling. This will be indicated by a wet, shiny, black deposit on the central insulator. This is caused by excessive oil in the combustion chamber during combustion and indicates that the piston rings or cylinder bores are worn.

Next examine the plugs for signs of petrol (gasoline) fouling. This is indicated by a dry, sooty, black deposit which is usually caused by over-rich carburation, although ignition system defects such as a discharged battery, faulty contact breaker, coil or capacitor defects, or a broken or worn out cable may be additional causes. To rectify this type of fault the above mentioned items should be checked with special attention given to carburation system. Again, the left plug should be used as the indicator. The right plug will almost always have a darker characteristic.

Over-heating of the sparking plug electrodes is indicated by severely eroded electrodes and a white, burned or blistered insulator. This type of fault is usually caused by weak carburation, although plugs which have been operating whilst not being screwed down sufficiently can easily become over-heated due to heat that is normally dissipated through to the cylinder head not having an adequate conducting path. Over-heating is normally symptomised by pre-ignition, short plug life, and "pinking" which can ultimately result in piston crown failure. Unecessary damage can result from over-tightening the plugs and to achieve a good seal between the plug and cylinder head a torque wrench should be used to tighten the plugs to the figure quoted in "General Data".

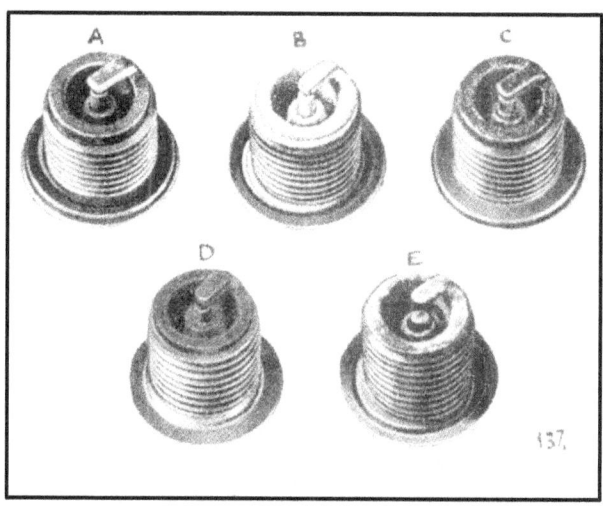

Fig. H3. Sparking plug diagnosis

A plug of the correct grade will bear a light flaky deposit on the outer rim and earth electrode, and these and the base of the insulator will be light chocolate brown in colour. A correct choice of plug is marked A. B shows a plug which appears bleached, with a deposit like cigarette ash; this is too 'hot-running' for the performance of the engine and a cooler-running type should be substituted. A plug which has been running too 'cold' and has not reached the self-cleaning temperature is shown at C. This has oil on the base of the insulator and electrodes, and should be replaced by a plug that will burn off deposits and remove the possibility of a short-circuit. The plug marked D is heavily sooted, indicating that the mixture has been too rich, and a further carburation check should be made. At illustration E is seen a plug which is completely worn out and badly in need of replacement.

To clean the plugs it is preferable to make use of a properly designed proprietary plug cleaner. The maker's instructions for using the cleaner should be followed carefully.

H ELECTRICAL SYSTEM

When the plugs have been carefully cleaned, examine the central insulators for cracking and the centre electrode for excessive wear. In such cases the plugs have completed their useful life and new ones should be fitted.

Finally, before re-fitting the sparking plugs the electrodes should be adjusted to the correct gap setting of ·020 in. (·5 mm.). Before refitting sparking plugs the threads should be cleaned by means of a wire brush and a minute amount of graphite grease smeared onto the threads. This will prevent any possibility of thread seizure occurring.

If the ignition timing and carburation settings are correct and the plugs have been correctly fitted, but over-heating still occurs then it is possible that carburation is being adversely affected by an air leak between the carburetter, manifold and the cylinder head. This possibility must be checked thoroughly before taking any further action. When it is certain that none of the above mentioned faults are the cause of over-heating then the plug type and grade should be considered.

Normally the type of plugs quoted in "General Data" are satisfactory for general use of the machine, but in special isolated cases, conditions may demand a plug of a different heat range. Advice is readily available to solve these problems from the plug manufacturer who should be consulted.

Note.—If the machine is of the type fitted with an air filter or cleaner and this has been removed it will affect the carburation of the machine and hence may adversely affect the grade of sparking plugs fitted.

SECTION H4
CHARGING SYSTEM

DESCRIPTION

The charging current is supplied by the alternator, but due to the characteristics of alternating current the battery cannot be charged direct from the alternator. To convert the alternating current to direct current a full wave bridge rectifier is connected into the circuit. The alternator gives full output, all the alternator coils being permanently connected across the rectifier. For this reason the alternator has only 2 output leads.

Excessive charge is absorbed by the Zener Diode which is connected across the battery. Always ensure that the ignition switch is in the "OFF" position whilst the machine is not in use, to prevent overheating of the ignition coils, and discharging the battery.

To locate a fault in the charging circuit, first test the alternator as described in H4 Part B. If the alternator is satisfactory, the fault must lie in the charging circuit, hence the rectifier must be checked as given in Section H4 Part C and then the wiring and connections as shown in Section H4 Part D.

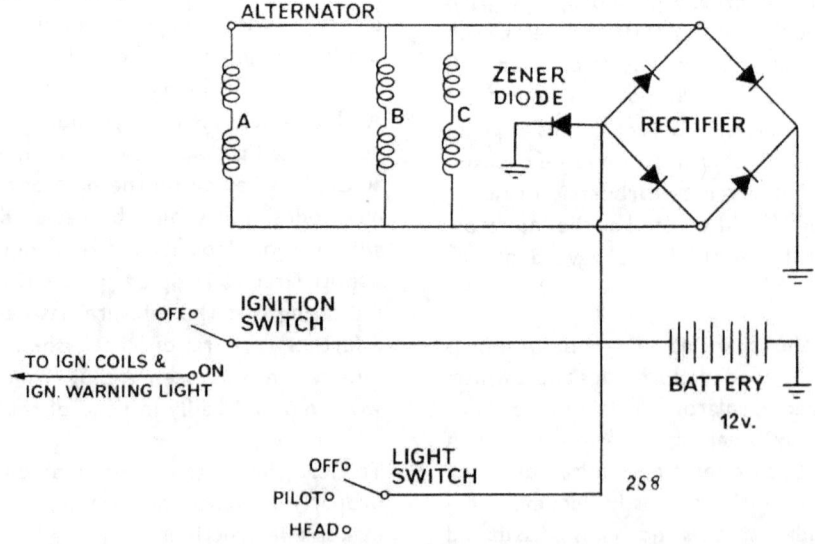

Fig. H4. Schematic diagram of 12 volt charging circuit

ELECTRICAL SYSTEM

H4 PART A. CHECKING THE D.C. OUTPUT AT THE RECTIFIER

For this test the battery must be in good condition and a good state of charge, therefore before conducting the test ensure that the battery is up to the required standard, or alternatively fit a good replacement battery.

Disconnect the brown/blue centre lead at the rectifier, connect D.C. ammeter (0–15 amp.) in series between the main brown/blue lead and the centre terminal, then start the engine and run it at approximately 3,000 r.p.m. (equivalent to 45 m.p.h. in top gear).

Note.—Ensure that the ammeter is well insulated from the surrounding earth points otherwise a short circuit may occur.

A single charge rate is used and irrespective of switch positions the minimum D.C. output from the rectifier at 3,000 r.p.m. should be no less than 9·5 amperes.

H4 PART B. CHECKING THE ALTERNATOR OUTPUT

Disconnect the alternator output cables underneath the engine.

Connect an A.C voltmeter (0–15 volts) with 1 ohm load resistor in parallel with each of the alternator leads in turn as shown in the table Fig. H20, and run the engine at 3,000 r.p.m. (equivalent to 45 m.p.h. in top gear) and observe the voltmeter readings. A suitable 1 ohm load resistor can be made from a piece of nichrome wire as shown in Section H7 Part E.

From the results obtained, the following deductions can be made:—

(i) If the readings are all equal to or higher than 9 volts then the alternator is satisfactory.

(ii) A low reading on any group of coils indicates either that the leads concerned are chafed or damaged due to rubbing on the chains or that some turns of the coils are short circuited.

(iii) Low readings for all parts of the test indicates either that the green/white lead has become chafed or damaged due to rubbing on the chain(s) or that the rotor has become partially demagnetised. If the latter case applies, check that this has not been caused by a faulty rectifier or that the battery is of incorrect polarity, and only then fit a new rotor.

(iv) A zero reading for any group of coils indicates that a coil has become disconnected, is open circuit, or is earthed.

(v) A reading obtained between any one lead and earth indicates that coil windings or connections have become earthed.

If any of the above mentioned faults occur, always check the stator leads for possible chain damage before attempting repairs or renewing the stator.

It is beyond the scope of this manual to give instruction for the repair of faulty stator windings.

H4 PART C. RECTIFIER MAINTENANCE AND TESTING

The silicon bridge rectifier requires no maintenance beyond checking that the connections are clean and tight, and that the nut securing the rectifier to the frame is tight. It should always be kept clean and dry to ensure good cooling, and spilt oil washed off immediately with hot water.

Note.—The nuts clamping the rectifier plates together must not be disturbed or slackened in any way.

When tightening the rectifier securing nut, hold the spanners as shown in Fig. H5, for if the plates are twisted, the internal connections will be broken. Note that the circles marked on the fixing bolt and nut indicate that the thread form is ¼ in. U.N.F.

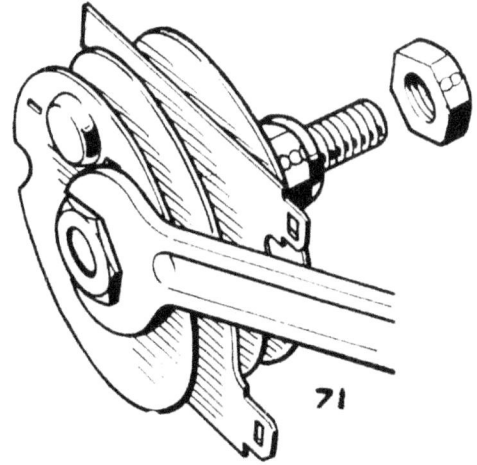

Fig. H5. Refitting the rectifier

ELECTRICAL SYSTEM

TESTING THE RECTIFIER

For test purposes disregard the end earth (ground) terminal

To test the rectifier, first disconnect the brown/blue lead from the rectifier centre terminal and insulate the end of the lead to prevent any possibility of a short circuit occurring, and then connect a D.C. voltmeter (with 1 ohm load resistor in parallel) between the rectifier centre terminal and earth.

Note. Voltmeter positive terminal to frame earth (ground) and negative terminal to centre terminal on rectifier.

Turn the ignition switch to the 'ignition only' position and start the engine.

With the engine running at approximately 3,000 r.p.m. (approximately 45 m.p.h. in top gear) observe the voltmeter readings. The reading obtained should be at least 7·5V minimum.

(i) If the reading is equal to or slightly greater than that quoted, then the rectifier elements in the forward direction are satisfactory.

(ii) If the reading is excessively higher than the figures given, then check the rectifier earthing bolt connection.

(iii) If the reading is lower than the figures quoted or zero readings are obtained, then the rectifier or the charging circuit wiring is faulty and the rectifier should be disconnected and bench tested so that the fault can be located.

Note that all of the above conclusions assume that the alternator A.C. output figures were satisfactory. Any fault at the alternator will, of course, reflect on the rectifier test results. Similarly any fault in the charging circuit wiring may indicate that the rectifier is faulty. The best method of locating a fault is to disconnect the rectifier and bench-test it as shown below:

BENCH TESTING THE RECTIFIER

For this test the rectifier should be disconnected and removed. Before removing the rectifier, disconnect the leads from the battery terminals to avoid the possibility of a short circuit occurring.

Using a 12 volt battery and 1 ohm load resistor, connect the D.C. voltmeter in the V2 position, as shown in Fig. H6. Note the battery voltage (should be 12V) and then connect the voltmeter in V1 position whilst the following tests are conducted.

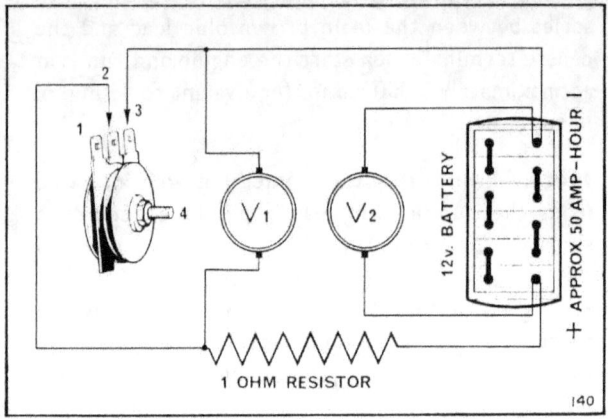

Fig. H6. Bench testing the rectifier

A voltmeter in position V1 will measure the volt drop across the rectifier plate. In position V2 it will measure the supply voltage to check that it is the recommended 12 volts on load.

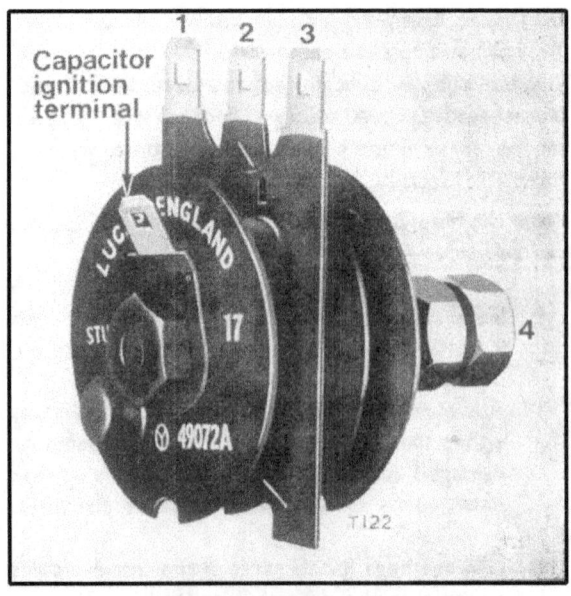

Fig. H7. Rectifier—showing terminal connections for bench tests 1 and 2

ELECTRICAL SYSTEM

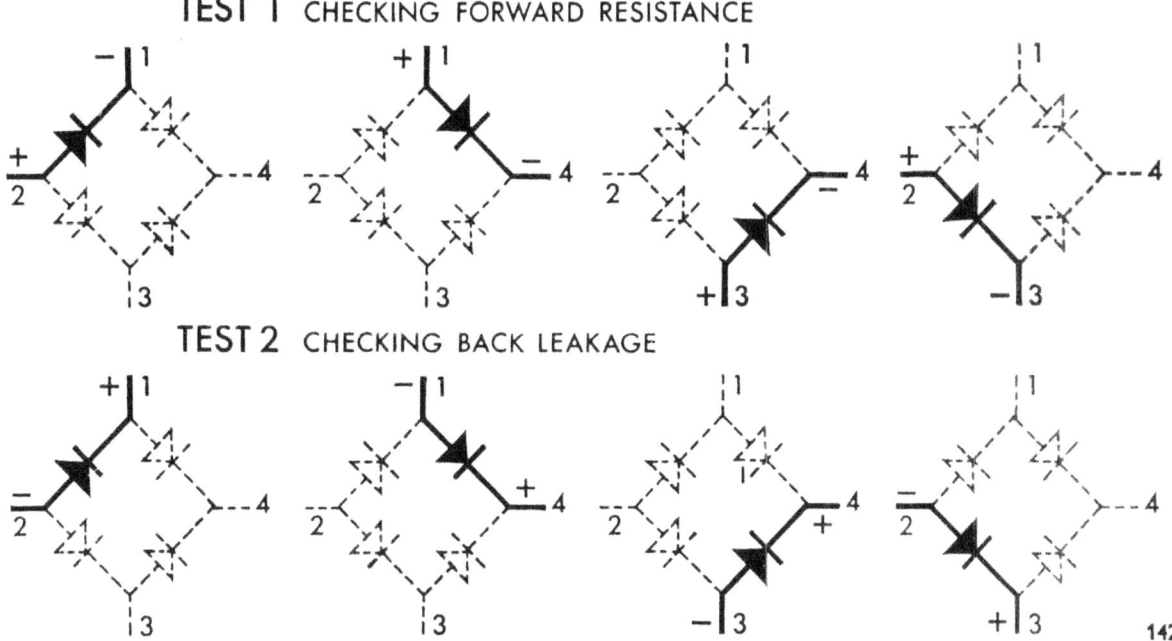

Fig. H8. Rectifier test sequence for checking forward resistance and back leakage

Test 1. With the test leads, make the following connections but keep the testing time as short as possible to avoid overheating the rectifier cell: (a) 1 and 2, (b) 1 and 4, (c) 3 and 4, (d) 3 and 2. Each reading should not be greater than 2·5 volts with the battery polarity as shown.

Test 2. Reverse the leads or battery polarity and repeat Test 1. The readings obtained should not be more than 1·5 volts below battery voltage (V_2) (i.e. 10·5 volts minimum.)

If the readings obtained are not within the figures given, then the rectifier internal connections are shorting or aged and the rectifier should be renewed.

H4 PART D. CHECKING THE CHARGING CIRCUIT FOR CONTINUITY

All six alternator coils are connected in parallel so that the full alternator output is available irrespective of the lighting switch position. This also makes an emergency start system unnecessary and it is therefore possible to use a simplified wiring circuit.

First check that there is voltage at the battery and that it is correctly connected into the circuit +ve earth (ground). Ensure that the fuse has not blown.

(i) First, check that there is voltage at the rectifier centre terminal by connecting a D.C. voltmeter, with 1 ohm load resistor in parallel, between the rectifier centre terminal (not the end terminal and earth (remember (+ve) positive earth (ground)). The voltmeter should read battery volts. If it does not, disconnect the alternator leads at the snap connectors under the engine unit.

(a) Fit a jumper lead across the brown/blue and green/yellow connections at the rectifier, and check the voltage at the snap connector. This test will indicate whether the harness alternator lead is open circuit.

(b) Repeat this test at the rectifier for the white/green lead.

H4 PART E. CONSTRUCTING A ONE-OHM LOAD RESISTOR

The resistor used in the following tests must be accurate and constructed so that it will not overheat otherwise the correct values of current or voltage will not be obtained.

H11

ELECTRICAL SYSTEM

A suitable resistor can be made from 4 yards (3¾ metres) of 18 S.W.G. (·048 in. (i.e. 1·2 m.m.) dia.) NICHROME wire by bending it into two equal parts and calibrating it as follows:—

(1) Fix a heavy gauge flexible lead to the folded end of the wire and connect this lead to the positive terminal of a 6 volt battery.

(2) Connect a D.C. voltmeter (0–10V) across the battery terminals and an ammeter (0–10 amp) between the battery negative terminal and the free ends of the wire resistance, using a crocodile clip to make the connection.

(3) Move the clip along the wires, making contact with both wires until the ammeter reading is numerically equal to the number of volts indicated on the voltmeter. The resistance is then 1 ohm. Cut the wire at this point, twist the two ends together and wind the wire on an asbestos former approximately 2 inches (5 cm.) dia. so that each turn does not contact the one next to it.

SECTION H5

ZENER DIODE CHARGE CONTROL

DESCRIPTION

The Zener Diode output regulating system uses all the coils of the 6-coil alternator connected permanently across the rectifier, provides automatic control for the charging current. The Diode may be connected through the ignition switch or direct to the centre terminal of the rectifier.

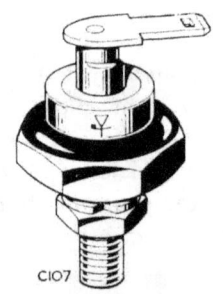

Fig H9. Zener Diode

Assuming the battery is in a low state of charge its terminal voltage (the same voltage is across the Diode) will also be low, therefore the maximum charging current will flow into the battery from the alternator. At first none of the current is by-passed by the Diode because of it being non-conducting due to the low battery terminal volts. However, as the battery is quickly restored to a full state of charge, the system voltage rises until at 13·5 volts the Zener Diode is partially conducting, thereby providing an alternative path for a small part of the charging current. Small increases in battery voltage result in large increases in Zener conductivity until, at approximately 15 volts about 5 amperes of the alternator output is by-passing the battery. The battery will continue to receive only a portion of the alternator output as long as the system voltage is relatively high.

Depression of the system voltage, due to the use of headlamp or other lighting equipment, causes the Zener Diode current to decrease and the balance to be diverted and consumed by the component in use.

If the electrical loading is sufficient to cause the system voltage to fall to 14 volts, the Zener Diode will revert to a high resistance state of non-conductivity and the full generated output will go to meet the demands of the battery.

MAINTENANCE

The Zener Diode is mounted in the right side air cleaner body. The aluminium construction of this lug acts as a heat sink for excess current. Providing the Diode and the heat sink are kept clean, and provided with an adequate airflow, to

ELECTRICAL SYSTEM

ensure maximum efficiency, and provided a firm flat "metal to metal" contact is mantained between the base of the Diode and the surface of the heat sink, to ensure adequate heat flow, no maintenance will be necessary.

ZENER DIODE— CHARGING REGULATOR

TEST PROCEDURE

(Procedure for Testing on the Machine)

The test procedure given below can be used when it is required to check the performance of the Zener Diode type ZD715 whilst it is in position on the machine. It is essential that the battery is in a fully charged state otherwise the tests below will not be accurate. If in doubt, substitute a battery that is fully charged.

Good quality moving coil meters should be used when testing. The voltmeter should have a scale 0–18, and the ammeter 0–5 amps min. The test procedure is as follows:—

(A) Disconnect the cable from the Zener Diode and connect ammeter (in series) between the Diode Lucar terminal and cable previously disconnected. The ammeter red or positive lead must connect to the Diode Lucar terminal.

(B) Connect voltmeter across Zener Diode and heat sink. The red or positive lead must connect to the heat sink which is earthed to the frame of the machine by its fixing bolts and a separate earth lead. The black lead connects to the Zener Lucar terminal.

(C) Start the engine, ensure that all lights are off, and gradually increase engine speed while at the same time observing both meters:—

(i) the series connected ammeter must indicate zero amps, up to 12·75 volts, which will be indicated on the shunt connected voltmeter as engine speed is slowly increased.

(ii) increase engine speed still further, until Zener current indicated on ammeter is 2·0 amp. At this value the Zener voltage should be within 13·5 volts to 15·3 volts.

TEST CONCLUSIONS:—

If the ammeter in test (i) registers any current at all before the voltmeter indicates 13·0 volts, then a replacement Zener Diode must be fitted.

If test (i) is satisfactory but in test (ii) a higher voltage than that stated is registered on the voltmeter, before the ammeter indicates 2·0 amp, then a replacement Zener Diode must be fitted.

ELECTRICAL SYSTEM

SECTION H6
ZENER DIODE LOCATION

The Zener Diode is mounted in the wall of the right hand side half of the air cleaner body. The aluminium construction of the air cleaner body serves as a heatsink and dissipates excess charge current in the form of heat. (See Section H5).

To remove the diode, first remove the R.H. air cleaner outer cover, see Section B6.

When refitting, the diode nut must be tightened with extreme care to a maximum torque of 22/28 lb. in. Also great care must be taken to ensure that any foreign matter does not become trapped between the bottom face of the diode and the wall of the cleaner body.

Any such particle would cause an air gap thereby reducing the heat conductivity between the diode and the body causing overheating of the diode insulation and resulting in damage.

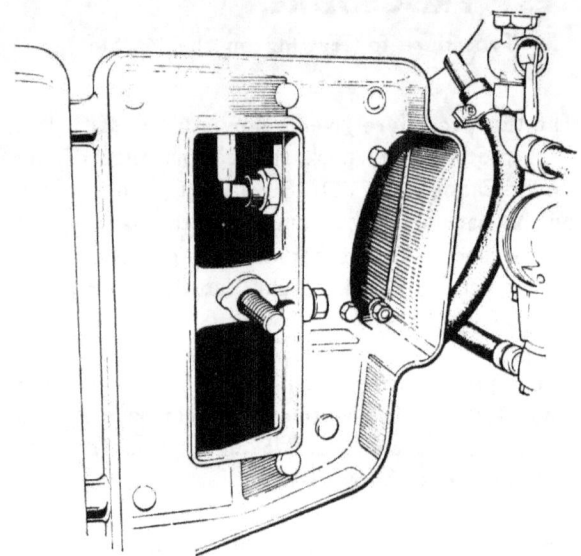

Fig. H10. Location of Zener Diode

SECTION H7
ALTERNATOR AND STATOR DETAILS

MODELS	System voltage	Ignition type	Alternator type	Stator No.
T140V TR7V	12 V.	Coil	RM.21	47205

Fig. H11. Alternator—type and stator details

SECTION H8

ELECTRIC HORN

DESCRIPTION

The horn is of a high frequency single note type and is operated by direct current from the battery. The method of operation is that of a magnetically operated armature, which impacts on the cone face, and causes the tone disc of the horn to vibrate. The magnetic circuit is made self interrupting by contacts which can be adjusted externally.

If the horn fails to work, check the horn connection wiring. Check the battery for state of charge. A low supply voltage at the horn will adversely effect horn performance. If the above checks are made and the fault is not remedied, then adjust the horn as follows.

HORN ADJUSTMENT

When adjusting and testing the horn, do not depress the horn push for more than a fraction of a second or the circuit wiring may be overloaded.

A small hexagon head adjustment screw situated near the terminals is provided to take up wear in the internal moving parts of the horn. To adjust, turn this screw anticlockwise until the horn just fails to sound, and then turn it back (clockwise) about one quarter to half a turn.

SECTION H9

HEADLAMP

DESCRIPTION

The headlamp is of the sealed beam unit type and access is gained to the bulb and bulb holder by withdrawing the rim and beam unit assembly. To do so, slacken the screw at the top of the headlamp and prise off the rim and beam unit assembly.

The bulb can be removed by first pressing the cylindrical cap inwards and turning it anticlockwise. The cap can then be withdrawn and the bulb is free to be removed.

When fitting a new bulb, note that it locates by means of a cutaway and projection arrangement. also note that the cap can only be replaced one way, the tabs being staggered to prevent incorrect reassembly. Check the replacement bulb voltage and wattage specification and type before fitting. Focusing with this type of beam unit is unnecessary and there is no provision for such.

BEAM ADJUSTMENTS

The beam must in all cases be adjusted as specified by local lighting regulations. In the United Kingdom the Transport Lighting Regulations reads as follows:—

A lighting system must be arranged so that it can give a light which is incapable of dazzling any person standing on the same horizontal plane as the vehicle at a greater distance than twenty five feet from the lamp, whose eye level is not less than three feet—six inches above that plane.

The headlamp must therefore be set so that the main beam is directed straight ahead and parallel with the road when the motorcycle is fully loaded.

To achieve this, place the machine on a level road pointing towards a wall at a distance of 25 feet away, with a rider and passenger, on the machine, slacken the two pivot bolts at either side of the headlamp and tilt the headlamp until the beam is focused at approximately two feet six inches from the base of the wall. Do not forget that the headlamp should be on "full beam" lighting during this operation.

ELECTRICAL SYSTEM

SECTION H10

REMOVING AND REFITTING THE HEADLAMP

Disconnect the leads from the battery terminals then slacken the light unit securing screws at the top of the headlamp. Prise the rim of the light unit free.

Disconnect the two red earth wires from their copper holders, one on the main bulb retaining cap and the other from the bottom of the inside shell. Remove all connectng wires from the six snap connectors and those positioned on the light switch.

Remove the three warning lights from the shell, and the pilot light from the light unit. Withdraw the harness from the headlamp through the appropriate grommets after bending back the harness retaining clips.

Reassembly is the reversal of the above procedure, but reference should be made to the wiring diagram. See section H19. Finally set the headlamp main beam. As described in Section H9.

SECTION H11

TAIL AND STOP LAMP UNIT

Access to the bulbs in the tail and stop lamp unit is achieved by unscrewing the two slotted screws which secure the lens. The bulb is of the double-filament offset pin type and when a replacement is carried out, ensure that the bulb is fitted correctly.

Check that the two supply leads are connected correctly and check the earth (ground) lead to the bulb holder is in satisfactory condition.
When refitting the lens, do not overtighten the fixing screws or the lens may fracture as a result.

SECTION H12

FUSES

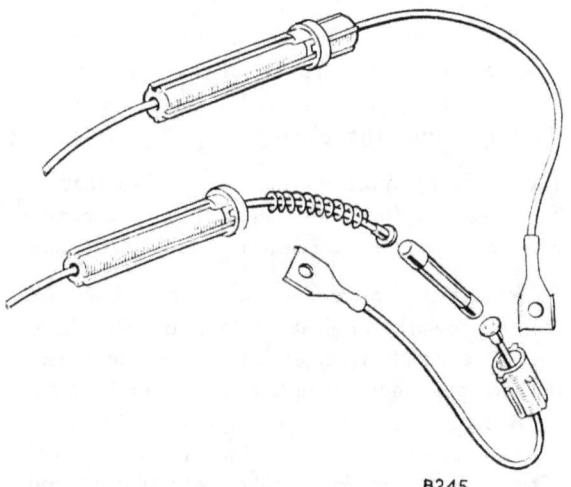

The fuse is to be found on the brown/blue live lead from the battery negative terminal. It is housed in a quickly detachable shell and is of 35 amp fuse rating.

Before following any fault location procedure always check that the fuse is not the source of the fault. A new fuse-cartridge should be fitted if there is any doubt about the old one.

Fig. H12. Exploded view of fuseholder assembly

ELECTRICAL SYSTEM

SECTION HH13

IGNITION SWITCH

All models are fitted with an ignition switch incorporating a "barrel" type lock. These locks use individual "Yale" type keys and render the ignition circuit inoperative when the switch is turned off and the key removed. It is advisable for the owner to note the number stamped on the key to ensure a correct replacement in the event of the key being lost.

Three Lucar connectors are incorporated in the switch and these should be checked from time to time to ensure good electrical contact.

The ignition switch is positioned on the left side headlamp bracket. To detach first remove the rubber cover and the lucar connectors at the back of the switch and then the large retaining nut.

The battery leads should be removed before attempting to remove the switch to avoid a short circuit.

The lock is retained in the body of the switch by a spring loaded plunger. This can be depressed with a pointed instrument through a small hole in the side of the switch body and the lock assembly withdrawn after the lock and switch together have been detached from the machine.

SECTION H14

FLASHER LAMPS

Access to the bulb in the flasher lamp unit can be obtained by unscrewing the two Phillips head screws. To remove the bulb, depress inwards and turn anti-clockwise. When replacing the bulb make sure it is securely fitted.

REMOVING AND REFITTING FRONT FLASHER LAMPS

Remove the headlamp rim and light unit. See section H10. Disconnect the green wires at the snap connectors. Remove the flasher lamp by loosening the locking nut and turning the lamp unit anti-clockwise.

Finally pull the green wire through the flasher stalk and grommet. When refitting check the general data for locking nut torque.

REMOVING AND REFITTING REAR FLASHER LAMPS

Disconnect the battery terminals and green wires at the snap connectors, found under the seat and repeat as in the removal of front flasher unit.

ELECTRICAL SYSTEM

SECTION H15
WARNING LAMPS

Warning lamps are fitted into the headlamp shell on all models. The green light indicates high beam. The orange warning light serves the flasher lamps and becomes illuminated in conjunction with the flasher lamps when they are operational. The red warning light is connected into the ignition circuit and also to an electrically controlled oil pressure switch situated at the timing cover. This results in the warning light operating as soon as the ignition is turned on with the engine stopped but extinguishes as oil pressure develops beyond a predetermined minimum critical pressure when the motor is running.

SECTION H16
STOP LAMP SWITCHES

A rear stop light switch is fitted to both front and rear braking systems and operate independantly.

The rear brake switch is fitted to the frame behind the rear brake pedal and is controlled by adjusting the short bolt and locknut mounted at the pedal pivot. Adjustment should be such that the rear brake light becomes illuminated immediately the brake is applied. Other than checking the terminals for cleanliness and security the unit will require no further maintainance.

The front brake stop switch is contained in the right hand handle-bar switch housing and is actuated by a push rod situated in the brake lever. The push rod length is adjusted by means of a small screw found in the hollow of the lever.

To make the adjustment slacken the screw with the lever in the closed position until the rear stop light becomes illuminated. Now screw in the adjuster until the rear light is extinguished. The rear stop light should now operate as soon as the front brake is applied. The internal electrical connections are all soldered and will require no maintainance.

SECTION H17
OIL PRESSURE SWITCH

The oil pressure switch is a sealed unit fitted into the front of the timing cover on all models.

The oil switch is designed to operate at 3-5lb./in.^{2} (0·2 to 0·35kg./cm.^{2}) pressure at which stage the oil warning light will be extinguished. There is no simple method of checking the function of the switch except by substitution.

SECTION H18
CAPACITOR IGNITION (MODEL 2MC)

The Lucas motor cycle capacitor system has been developed to enable machines to be run with or without a battery. The rider therefore has the choice of running with normal battery operation or running without battery if desired (e.g. competing in trials or other competitive events) and for emergency operation in case of battery failure.

Machines can readily be started without the battery and run as normal with full use of standard lighting. When stationary, however, parking lights will not work unless the battery is connected. The capacitor system also has the advantage of being less critical with regard to alternator timing.

The system utilises the standard 12-volt battery-coil ignition equipment with the Zener diode charging regulator mounted on an efficient heat sink, plus a spring mounted high capacity electrolytic capacitor (Model 2MC), of a special shock-resistant type.

The energy pulses from the alternator are stored by the capacitor to ensure that sufficient current flows through the ignition coil at the moment of contact opening, thus producing an adequate spark for starting. When running, the capacitor also helps to reduce the d.c. voltage ripple.

Also with this system alternator timing is less critical. Provided the centres of the rotor and stator poles are roughly in line in the fully retarded position (i.e. as normal battery) emergency start condition which is 30° past magnetic neutral) satisfactory starting will be obtained. Furthermore any auto-advance angle and speed characteristics may be used and perfect running ignition performance achieved.

IDENTIFICATION OF CAPACITOR TERMINALS

The 2MC capacitor is an electroclytic (polarised) type and care must be taken to see that the correct wiring connections are made when fitting. Spare Lucar connectors are supplied to assist in connecting up. Looking at the terminal end of the unit it will be seen that there are two sizes of Lucar connector. The small $\frac{3}{16}$ in. Lucar is the *positive* (earth) terminal the rivet of which is marked with a spot of red paint. The double $\frac{1}{4}$ in. Lucar forms the *negative* terminal.

The illustration on the previous page shows the spring and capacitor. The capacitor should be positioned with its terminals pointing downwards. When fitting the spring to the capacitor, insert the capacitor at the widest end of the spring and push it down until the small coil locates in the groove on the capacitor body.

STORAGE LIFE OF MODEL 2MC CAPACITOR

The life of the 2MC is very much affected by storage in high temperatures. The higher the temperature the shorter its shelf life. At normal temperature i.e. 20°C. (68°F.) it will have a shelf life of about 18 months. At 40°C. (86°F.) about 9 to 12 months. Therefore, storing in a cool place will maintain their efficiency.

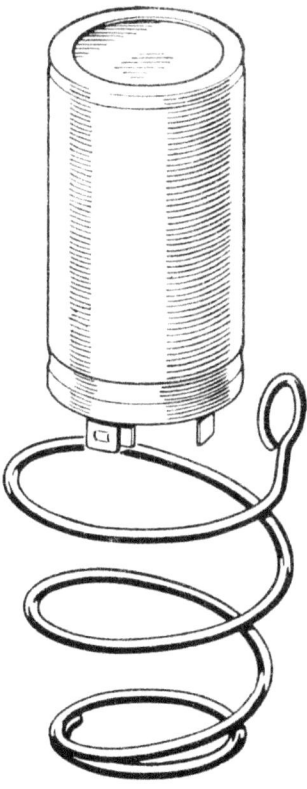

Fig. H13. Capacitor and spring

H ELECTRICAL SYSTEM

TESTING

The efficiency of a stored capacitor can be determined fairly accurately with the aid of a voltmeter (scale 0-12 volts) connected to the terminals of a charged capacitor and the steady reading on the meter noted. The procedure is as follows:—

(a) Connect the capacitor to a 12-volt supply and leave connected for 5 seconds. Observe carefully the polarity of connections, otherwise the capacitor may be ruined.

(b) Disconnect the supply leads and allow the charged capacitor(s) to stand for at least 5 *minutes*.

(c) Connect the voltmeter leads to the capacitor and note the steady reading. This should not be less than 9·0 volts for a serviceable unit. If it is less, the capacitor is leaking and must be replaced.

If a voltmeter is not available a rough check can be made by following the procedures in (a) and (b) and using a single strand of copper wire instead of the voltmeter to short-circuit the capacitor terminals. A good spark will be obtained from a serviceable capacitor at the instant the terminals are shorted together.

WIRING AND INSTALLATION

The capacitor is fitted into the spring and should be mounted with its terminals downwards. The capacitor negative terminal *and* Zener diode must be connected to the rectifier centre (d.c.) terminal (brown/white), and the positive terminal must be connected to the centre bolt earthing terminal.

The mounting spring should be attached to any convenient point under the twin seat.

SERVICE NOTES

Before running a 2MC equipped machine with the battery disconnected it is essential that the *battery negative lead be insulated* to prevent it from reconnecting and shorting to earth (frame of machine). This can be done by removing the fuse from its holder and replacing it with a length of $\frac{1}{4}$ in. dia. dowel rod or other insulating medium.

A faulty capacitor may not be apparent when used with a battery system. To prevent any inconvenience arising, periodically check that the capacitor is serviceable by disconnecting the battery to see if the machine will start and run in the normal manner, with full lighting also available.

Do not run the machine with the Zener Diode disconnected as the 2MC capacitor will be damaged due to excessive voltage.

A capacitor kit is available under part number C.P.210.

ELECTRICAL SYSTEM

SECTION H19
WIRING DIAGRAM

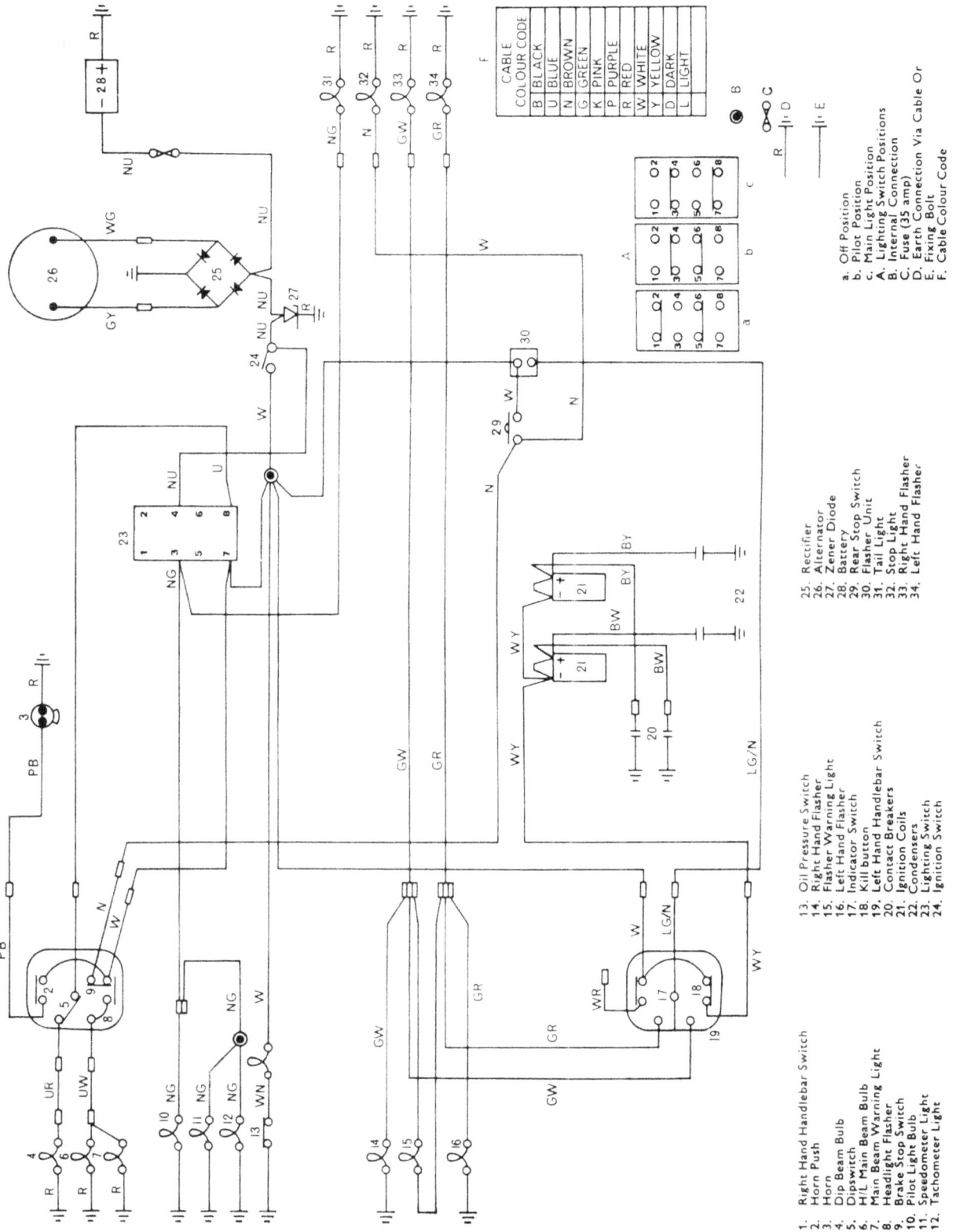

Fig. H14. Wiring diagram

H ELECTRICAL SYSTEM

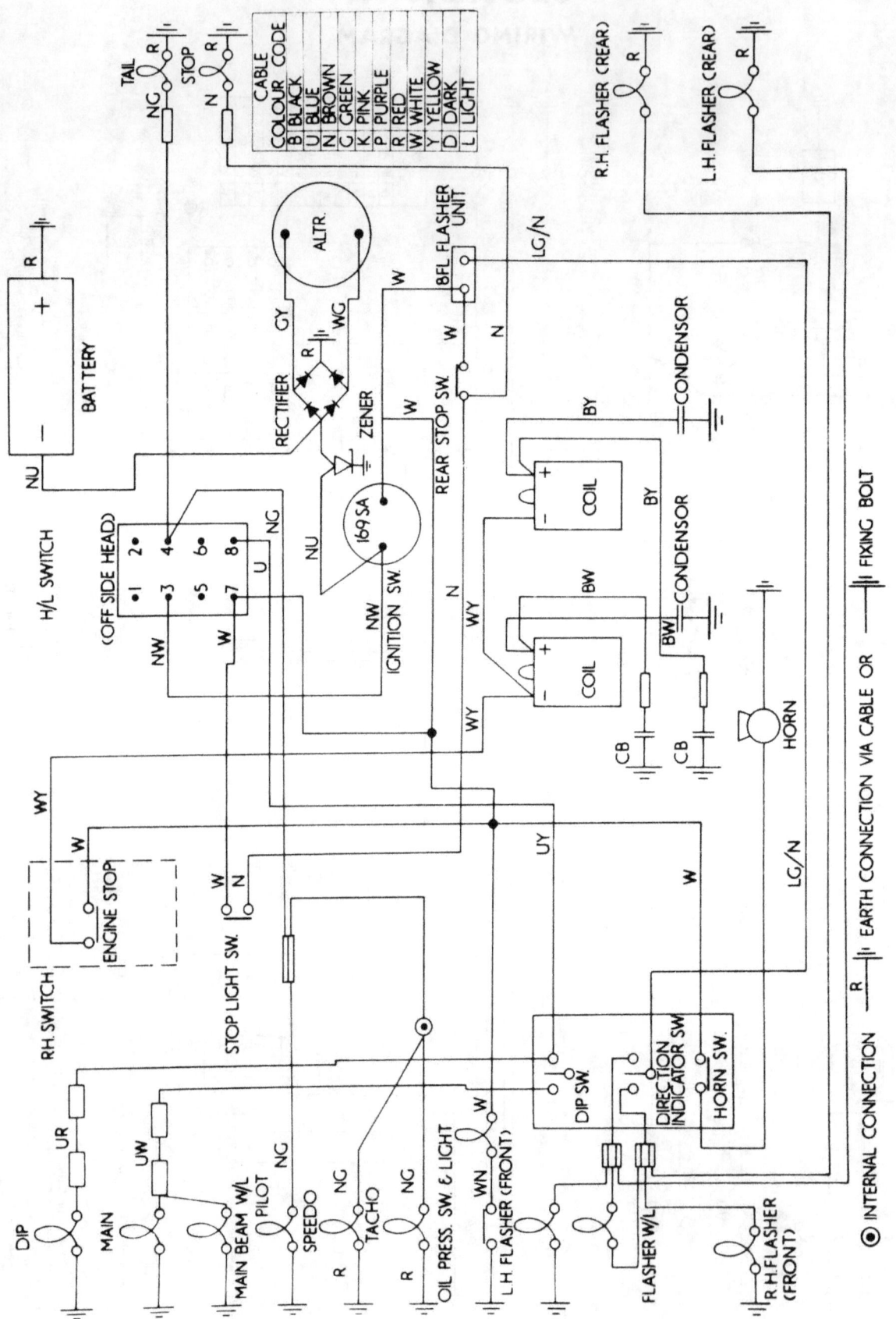

H22

1979 T140E
Ignition System
Charging System
Description
&
Troubleshooting Guide

Published 12/79
Part No. 99-7140

TRIUMPH MOTORCYCLES
1979 Electrical Specification

Major changes from 1978 to 1979 are a new design alternator (Model RM24) and the introduction of electronic ignition. Other changes include restyling of the switchgear and headlight and the repositioning of the warning lights and ignition/light switch, which are now mounted between the speedometer and tachometer.

The charging system comprises the alternator (rotor and stator), a plate-type rectifier pack and a voltage control zener diode. These components and a circuit diagram are illustrated in FIGS. 1 & 2.

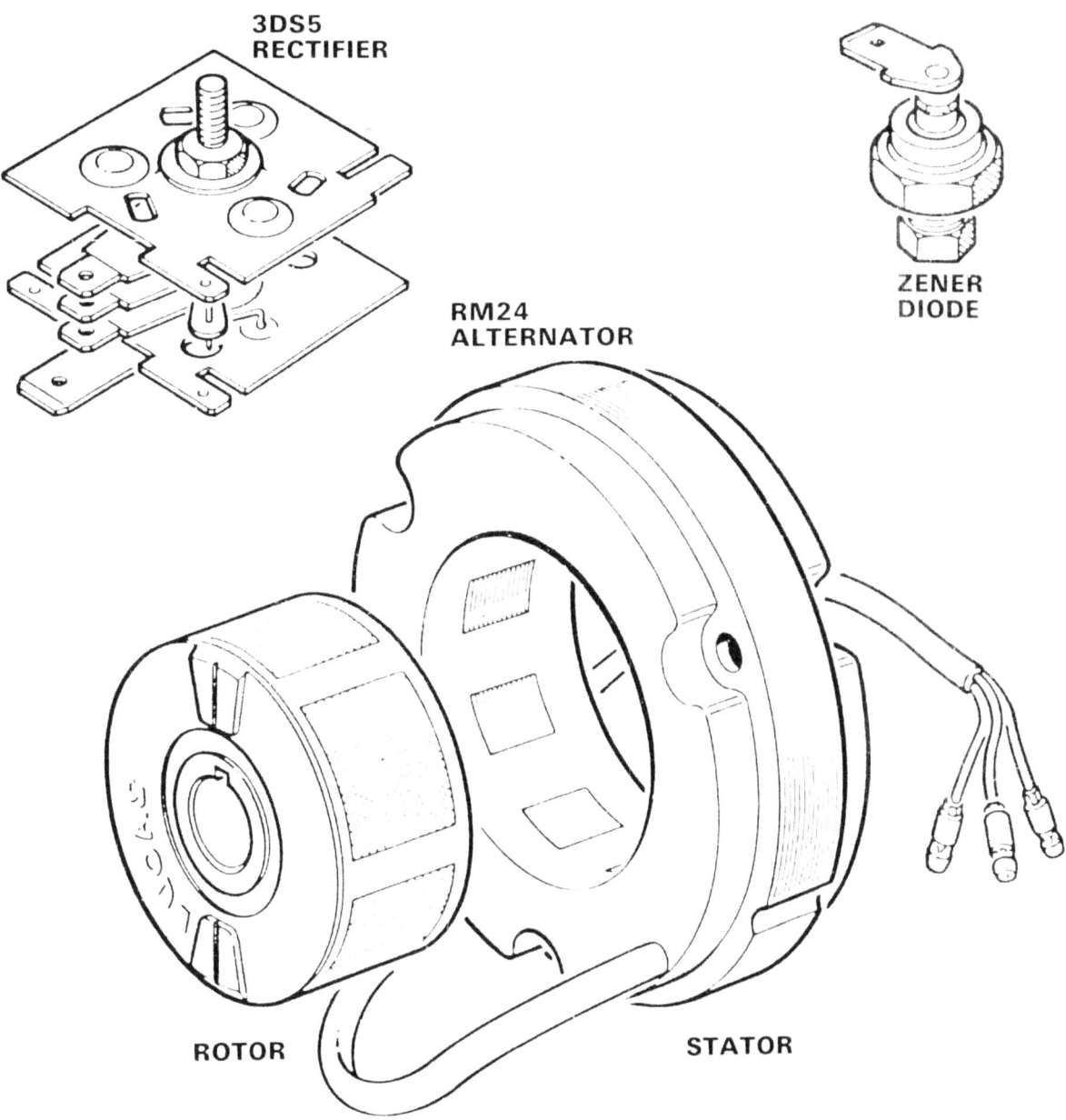

FIG. 1. CHARGING SYSTEM COMPONENTS

Further information may be obtained from:
Technical Service Department   Customer Information Section.
Lucas Electrical Limited Parts & Service Division. Great Hampton Street Birmingham B18 6AU.

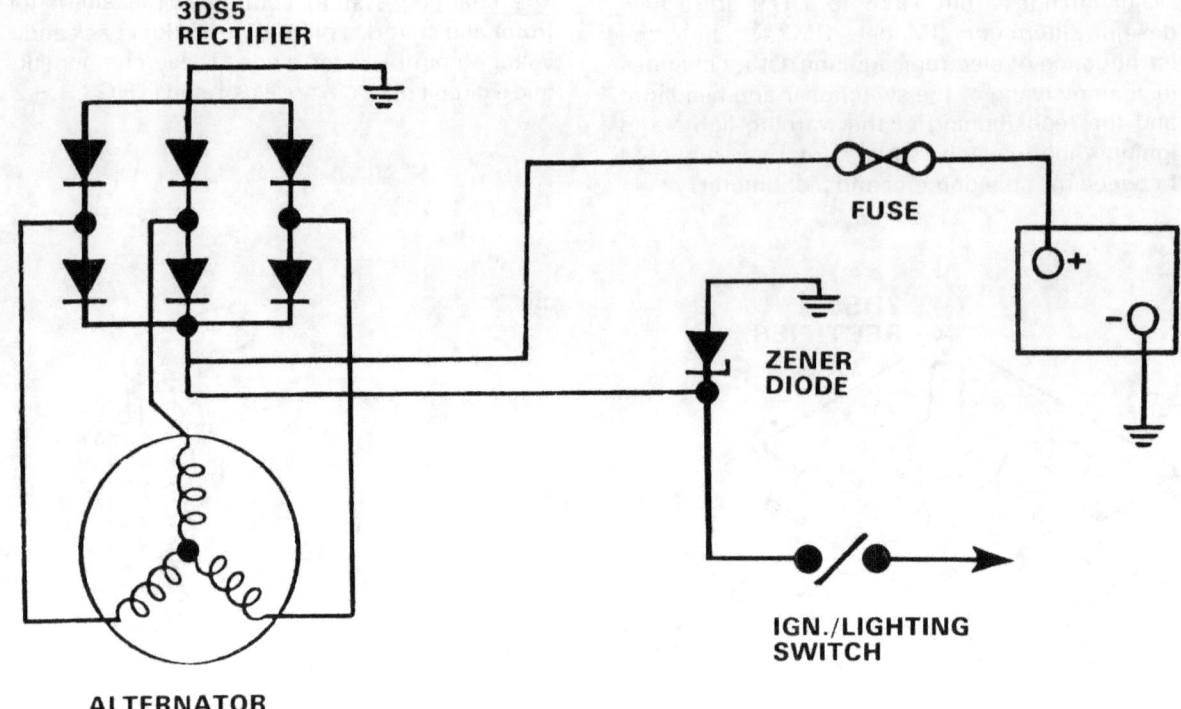

FIG. 2. CHARGING CIRCUIT

The ignition system comprises an electronic amplifier unit, a pick-up assembly, a reluctor and two (twin) ignition coils. These components and a circuit diagram are illustrated in FIGS. 3 & 4.

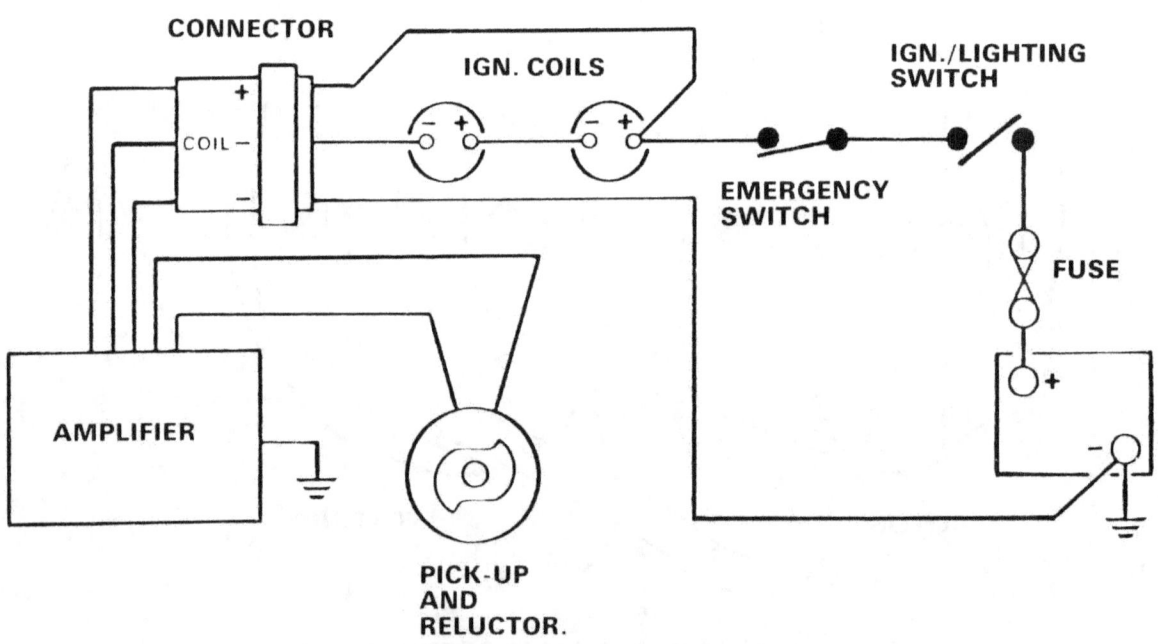

FIG. 3. IGNITION CIRCUIT

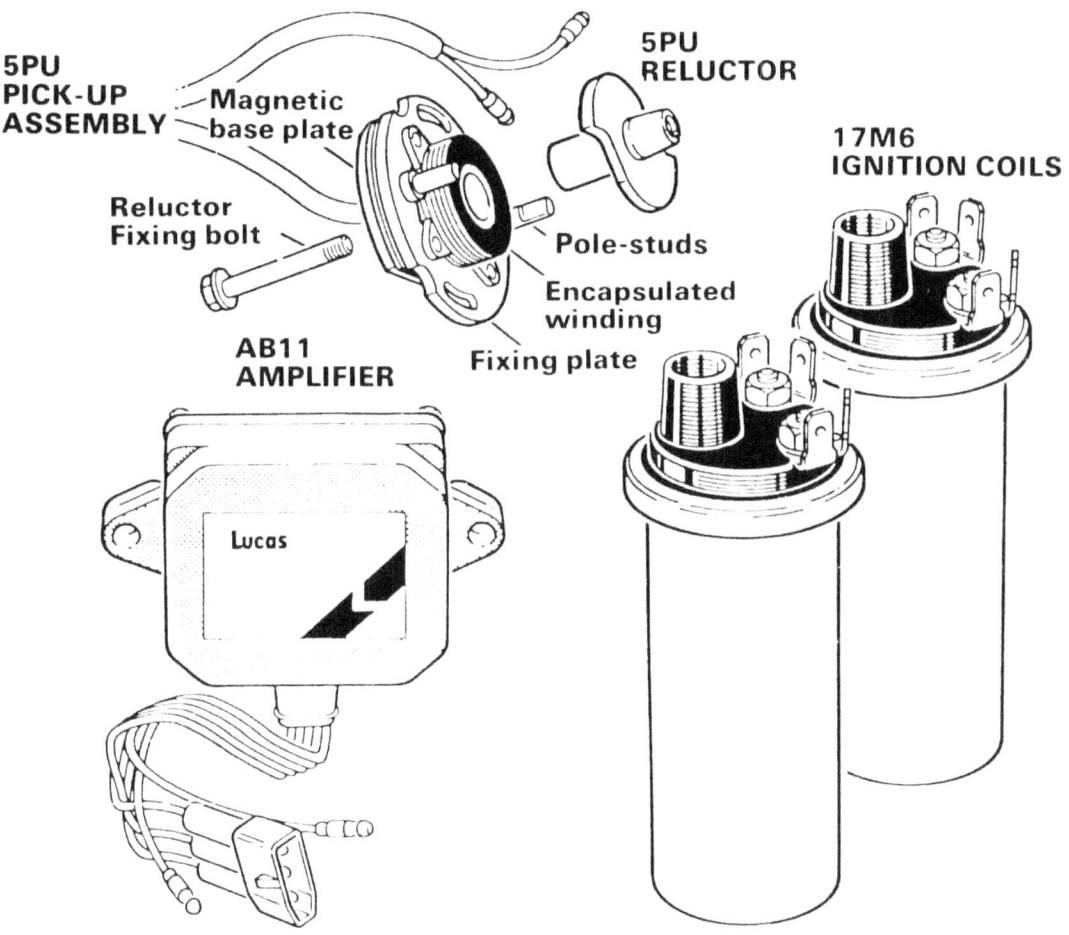

FIG. 4. IGNITION SYSTEM COMPONENTS

1 CHARGING SYSTEM TECHNICAL DATA

The alternator produces 3 phase AC, rectified to DC by a 3DS5 rectifier and voltage controlled by a zener diode.

Alternator RM24

Rotor	Permanent magnet
Stator	3-phase AC
AC output (Measured between any two stator leads)	4·5V (min.) at 1000 rev/min 6·5V (min.) at 5000 rev/min
DC output (Measured between rectifier large terminal and earth)	11A (max.) at 5000 rev/min
Stator resistance (Measured between any two stator leads)	0·80 - 0·95 ohm
Stator insulation leads and laminations).	100 megohms (min.) at 5000V

Rectifier 3DS5

Six diode plate-type rectifier............................. Surge and polarity conscious. The DC circuits must not be disconnected while the engine is running.

Zener diode voltage regulator

Standard negative earth type
Regulating voltage... 14·7 - 15·8V

2. IGNITION SYSTEM TECHNICAL DATA

The two 6V ignition coils are connected in series to provide simultaneous HT sparking. The engine still fires in the correct sequence with the spurious sparks having no effect.

The primary circuit of the ignition coils is electronically switched by the remotely mounted amplifier unit which is triggered by pulses from the pick-up and reluctor working in conjunction with each other.

17M6 Ignition coil
Primary winding resistance: 1·7 - 1·9 ohms.

AB11 Amplifier
A remotely mounted electronic switching system contained in a cast aluminum box.

5PU Pick-up
A rivetted assembly comprising encapsulated winding, a fixing plate with pole-studs, and a permanent magnet sandwiched between the fixing plate and a base plate. The assembly is a stationary component mounted in the engine crankcase, around the reluctor. Two fixing screws tighten on slots in the fixing plate, the slots providing adjustments for static ignition timing.

5PU Reluctor
A specially shaped steel timing device, mounted on the end of the camshaft. Its position relative to the camshaft is determined by a keyway. Fixing is by means of a hexagon-headed bolt.

Working Principles
When the ignition is switched ON, the amplifier unit is conductive and current flows through the primary windings of the two series-connected ignition coils and through the amplifer unit to earth.

A permanent magnetic field surrounds the pick-up base plate, the encapsulated winding and the pole-studs. When the engine is cranked the arms of the rotating reluctor approach these poles, causing the field strength to change which produces a pulse in the pick-up winding. This pulse is transmitted to the amplifier unit, causing it to switch off and break the primary circuit of the ignition coils. The HT spark is then produced in the conventional manner.

Operating Characteristics

(i) **Electronic advance curve**
The advance curve is automatically determined by the amplifier unit.

ENGINE REV/MIN	DEGREES ADVANCE
100	0
500	9
1000	19
2000	30
3000	36
3500	38
5000	40

(ii) **Voltage operating range**
Limits: 8 - 16V. Within this voltage range:

(a) A maximum timing tolerance of 1·5 is permissible at 2000 reluctor rev/min.

(b) Consistent sparking, without missing, must occur at reluctor speed range of 90 - 4000 rev/min.

3. CHARGING SYSTEM FAULT DIAGNOSIS AND TESTING

NOTE 1
If the battery is incapable of starting the engine, it must be recharged or a slave battery utilized for testing purposes. (Observe polarity. Reverse connections will damage the rectifier.)

NOTE 2
Test requirements: centre zero 25A moving-coil ammeter
AC Voltmeter
DC Voltmeter
1 ohm (100W) load resistor.

Flat or Discharged Battery
SUSPECT: The battery, the alternator and rectifier, and the voltage control zener diode (proceed to TEST 1).

Overcharged Battery
SUSPECT: Voltage control zener diode (proceed TEST 1).

TEST 1: Alternator Charging Current.

Connect ammeter in series with the battery positive cable. It is convenient to do this at the battery feed side of the main fuse, in which case connect BLACK lead to cable and RED lead to fuse.

Run the engine at approximately 2000 rev/min and switch the headlamp to main beam. The ammeter should show a small amount of charge, indicating the alternator is exceeding the maximum continuous electrical load.

If the test is satisfactory, stop engine, restore original connections and proceed directly to TEST 5.

If the test is unsatisfactory, proceed to TEST 2.

TEST 2. Alternator AC Output.

Disconnect the three snap connectors between alternator and rectifier. Connect AC voltmeter, with a 1 ohm (100W) load resistor across its terminals, for three tests as shown in FIG. 5. Run the engine at approximately 2000 rev/min for each test.

The voltmeter should show 5V minimum for all three tests, in which case the alternator AC output is satisfactory. Stop engine, restore original connections and proceed to TEST 3

If zero or a low voltage is obtained in two tests, the alternator stator is faulty.

If zero or a low voltage is obtained in all three tests, either the alternator stator is faulty or the rotor is demagnetized. Determine whether the stator can be eliminated by checking the resistance and insulation of its windings.

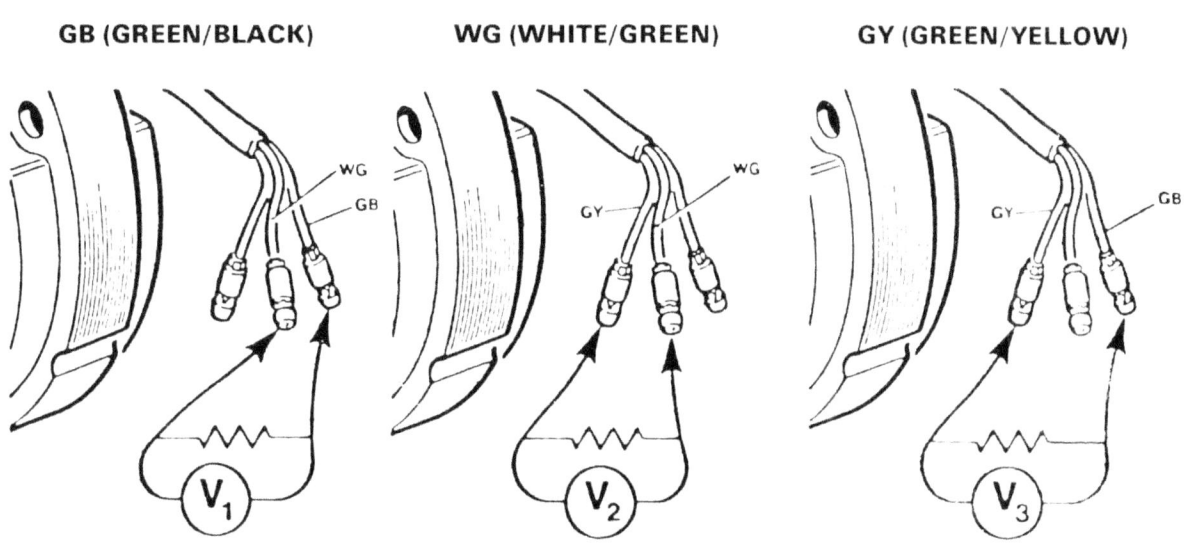

FIG. 5. ALTERNATOR AC OUTPUT TEST

TEST 3: Alternator AC Continuity

Remove the ignition amplifier housing, for access to the rectifier.

Disconnect the three alternator connections to the rectifier (See FIG. 6.) and repeat TEST 2 at the ends of the disconnected rectifier leads. The test result should be the same as TEST 2, in which case stop the engine, restore original connections and proceed to TEST 4.

Test unsatisfactory, check snap connectors and leads to rectifier.

TEST 4: Rectifier DC Output

Disconnect the large (DC output) terminal of the rectifier. Connect DC voltmeter with a 1 ohm (100W) load resistor across its terminals, as shown in FIG. 7. Run the engine at approximately 2000 rev/min.

The voltmeter should show 9V min., in which case stop engine, restore original connections and refit the ignition amplifier housing and proceed to TEST 5.

If zero or a low voltage is obtained, the rectifer is faulty.

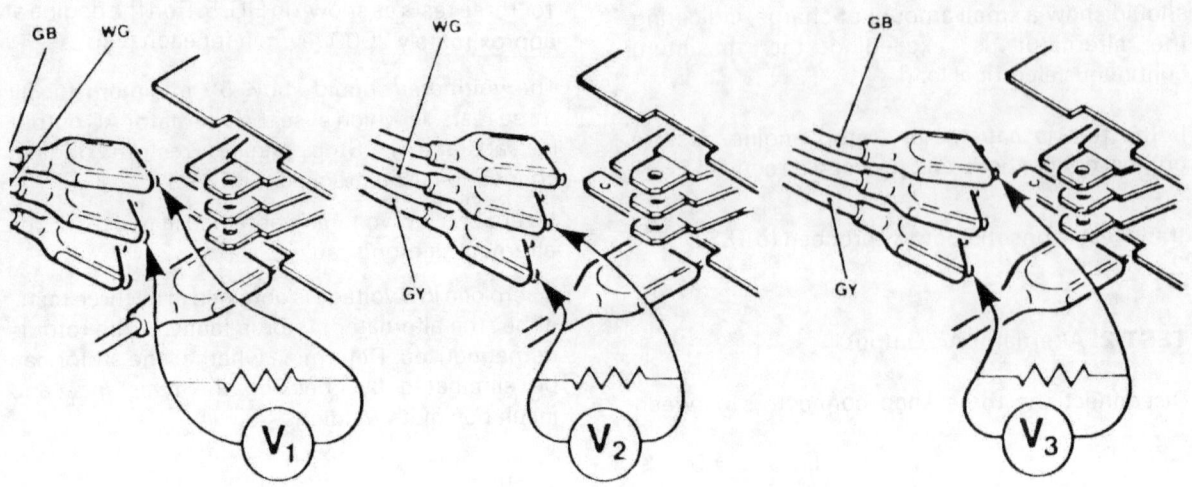

Fig. 6. ALTERNATOR AC CONTINUITY TEST

TEST 5: Zener Diode Voltage Regulator

Disconnect zener diode. Connect ammeter and DC voltmeter as shown in FIG.8.

Note: The load resistor connected across the voltmeter and DC voltmeter as shown in FIG.8.

Start and run engine at increasing speed until ammeter shows 2A, then observe voltmeter reading.

The voltmeter should show 13·5 - 15·3V, in which case the charging system is now proved satisfactory. Stop the engine, restore original connections and fit new battery.

If voltage is outside the limits, replace zener diode.

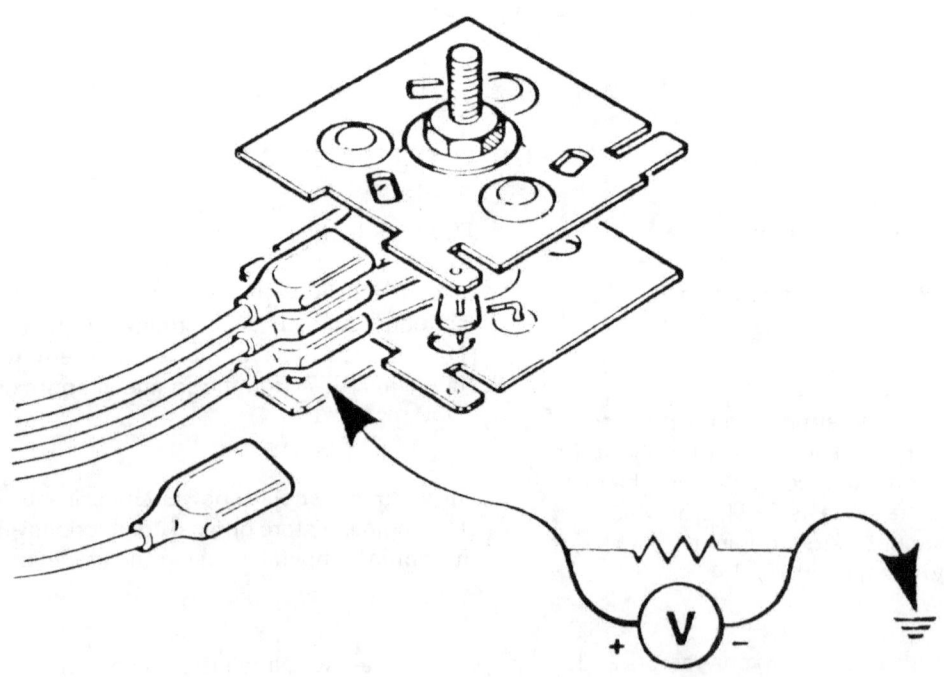

FIG. 7. RECTIFIER DC OUTPUT TEST

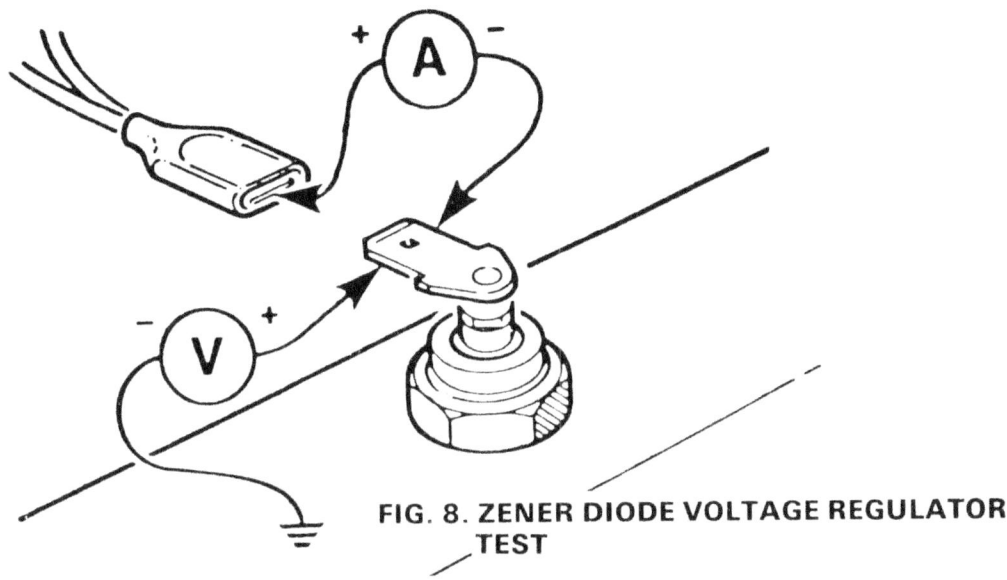

FIG. 8. ZENER DIODE VOLTAGE REGULATOR TEST

4. IGNITION SYSTEM FAULT DIAGNOSIS AND TESTING

NOTE: Test requirements: DC voltmeter
Ohmmeter

Engine Fails to Start
Suspect: Discharged battery or no spark at one or both spark plugs.
Check battery and if satisfactory proceed to TEST 1.

Engine Runs on One Cylinder Only
Suspect: Spark plug, HT lead, or ignition coil. Proceed to TEST 1, then if necessary TEST 2.

Engine Misfires or Runs Erratic
Suspect: Spark plugs, HT leads, ignition timing, ignition coil, electronic amplifier and associated pick-up.

Clean spark plugs and check gaps. Check timing. Finally, prove all items by substitution.

TEST 1: HT Spark at Plugs.

Remove spark plugs and lay them on engine, HT leads connected and spark gaps visible. Switch on ignition, crank engine and check for regular sparking at both plugs.

If the test is satisfactory, check ignition timing. If this is also satisfactory, then the ignition system is not the cause of the engine failing to start.

If sparking occurs at one plug only, interchange the two plugs and repeat the test. If fault is now transferred from one HT lead to the other, replace the non-sparking plug. If fault is not transferred, either the HT lead or ignition coil associated with the non-sparking plug is faulty (proceed to TEST 2). Leave spark plugs removed from engine.

If there is no sparking at both plugs, check primary circuit of ignition coils (proceed directly to TEST 3).

TEST 2: HT Spark at Ignition Coils

Remove HT leads from one of the ignition coils and fit substitute lead. Position free end of lead 6mm or ¼" from a good earth point (e.g. coil fixing bracket). Switch on ignition, crank engine and check for regular sparking at end of lead. Repeat test with other coil.

Sparking from both coils, replace faulty HT lead (Reference TEST 1).

Sparking from one coil only, replace non-sparking coil.

No sparking from either coil, check primary circuit of ignition coils (proceed to TEST 3). Leave spark plugs removed from engine.

TEST 3: Ignition Coil Primary Circuit

With reference to FIG. 9, disconnect the WB (WHITE/BLACK) lead from ignition coil No. 2, switch on the ignition and connect DC voltmeter in four tests A, B, C, & D as shown.

Voltmeter should show battery voltage (12V) for each test, in which case leave ignition switched on and voltmeter connected as for Test D and proceed directly to (v).

(i) No voltage in Test A: Ascertain reason for lack of supply voltage between coil, ignition switch and battery.

(ii) No voltage in Test B: Coil primary winding open-circuit. Replace coil.

(iii) No voltage in Test C: Coil-to-coil WP (WHITE/PINK) lead open-circuit.

(iv) No voltage in Test D: Coil primary winding open-circuit. Replace coil.

(v) Reconnect WB (WHITE/BLACK) lead to coil No. 2 Voltmeter needle should now show zero volts, indicating the coil primary circuit is satisfactory. Proceed to TEST 4, leaving ignition switched on and volt-meter connected as for Test 3D.

If voltmeter still shows battery voltage, the coil primary circuit is not being connected to earth by the function of the amplifier, which is now suspect.

Before replacing the amplifier, check the wiring.

(i) Disconnect the amplifier at the 3-pin molded connector assembly.

(ii) Identify main harness side of the connector assembly.

(iii) Connect voltmeter in three tests A, B, and C as shown in FIG.

Voltmeter should show battery voltage for each test. If the test is satisfactory, amplifier is faulty. If zero voltage is shown in any test, rectify open circuit lead(s) or connection(s).

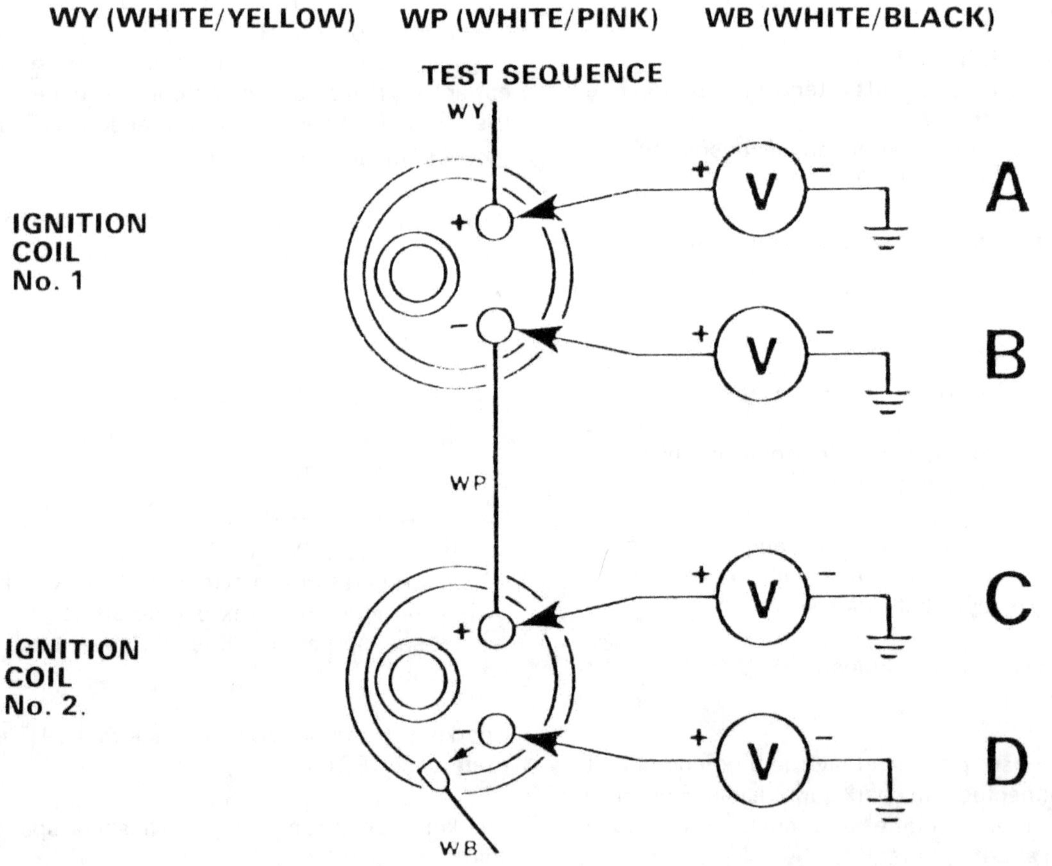

Fig. 9. IGNITION COIL PRIMARY CIRCUIT TEST

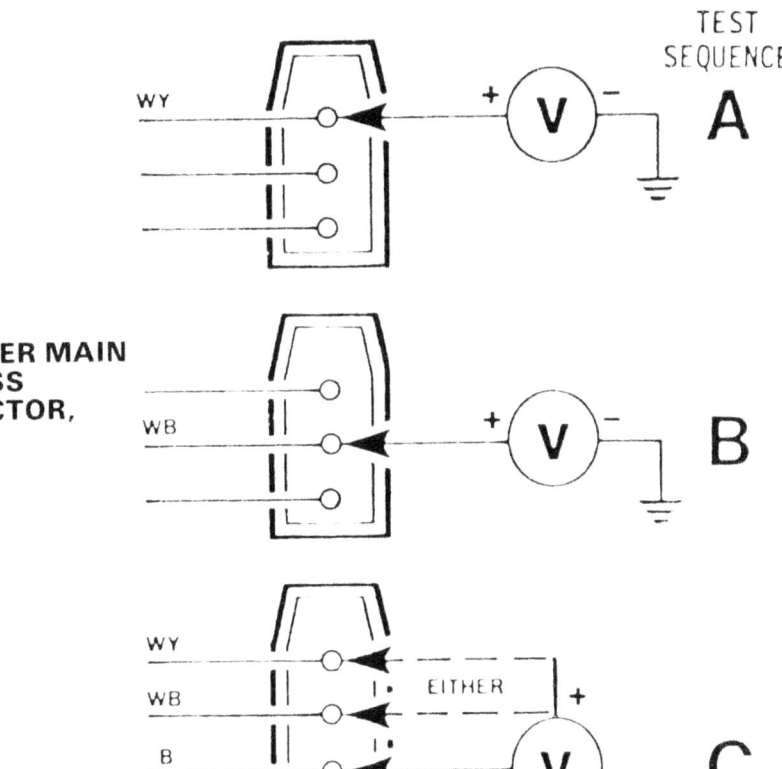

FIG. 10. AMPLIFIER MAIN HARNESS CONNECTOR, wiring tests

TEST 4: Amplifier Switching
Voltmeter connected as in Test 3D, crank engine. The voltmeter needle should now oscillate between zero volts and battery voltage (12V), confirming the coil primary circuit is being switched on and off by the amplifier unit. The ignition system is therefore satisfactory.

If the voltmeter needle remains at zero volts while the engine is cranked, the amplifier unit and its associated pick-up are both suspect. Check whether the pick-up can be eliminated, TEST 5.

TEST 5: Pick-up Winding Resistance Continuity

Disconnect the WHITE/ORANGE and WHITE/PURPLE leads at the amplifier unit. Identify the two leads connected to the pick-up and check the resistance and continuity of the pick-up winding by connecting an ohmmeter between the two leads. Ohmmeter should shown 650 - 750 ohms.

If the test is satisfactory, replace the amplifier.

If the test is unsatisfactory, replace the pick-up.

NOTE: The pick-up fixing screws also determine the rotary position in which the pick-up is fixed relative to ignition timing. The screws locate in slots which provide adjustment for ignition timing when the pick-up is fitted. Before disturbing the fixing screws of the original pick-up, choose a datum point on the pick-up (e.g. a shoulder of the magnetic base plate) and scribe a mark on the engine as a timing reference otherwise when fitting the new pick-up the timing will need to be reset and this will necessitate the use of a strobe light.

TEST 6: Ignition Timing
A strobe light is necessary. Remove plug cover on opposite side of engine from pick-up, to expose timing mark on alternator rotor. Refer to motorcycle manufacturer's instructions for ignition timing data and procedure.

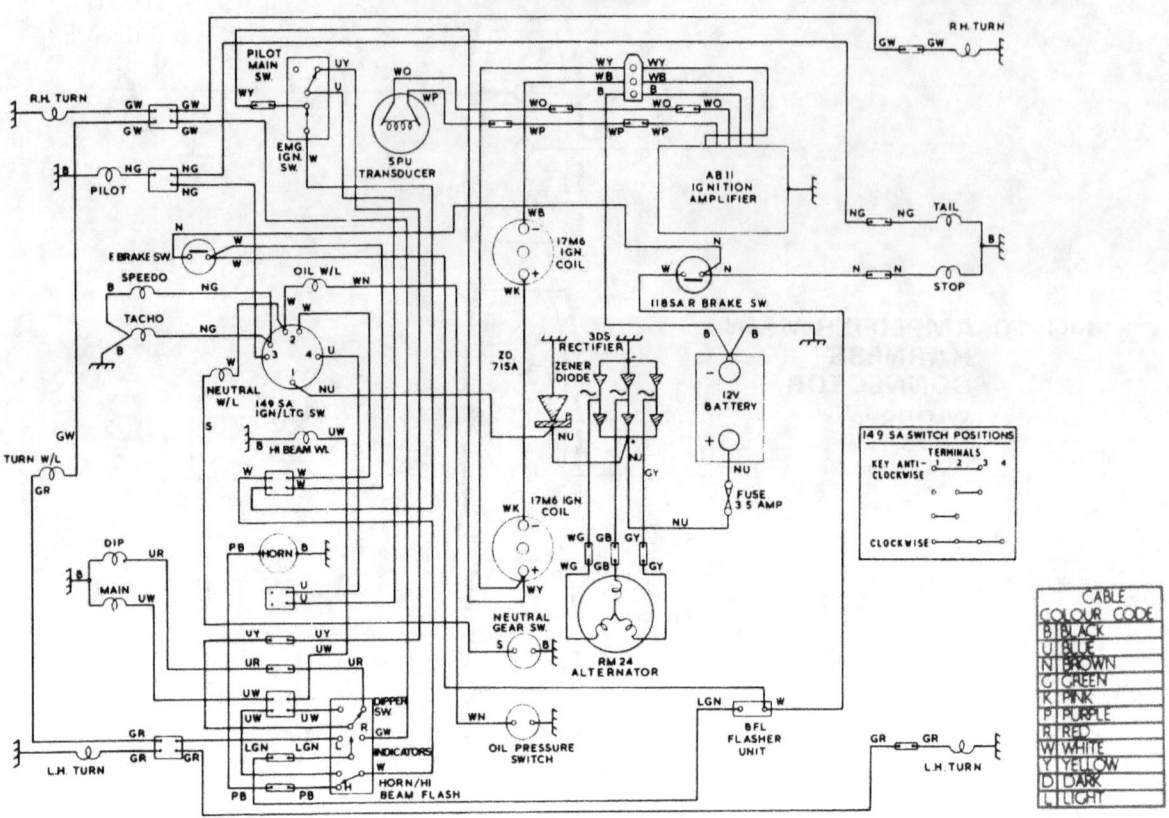

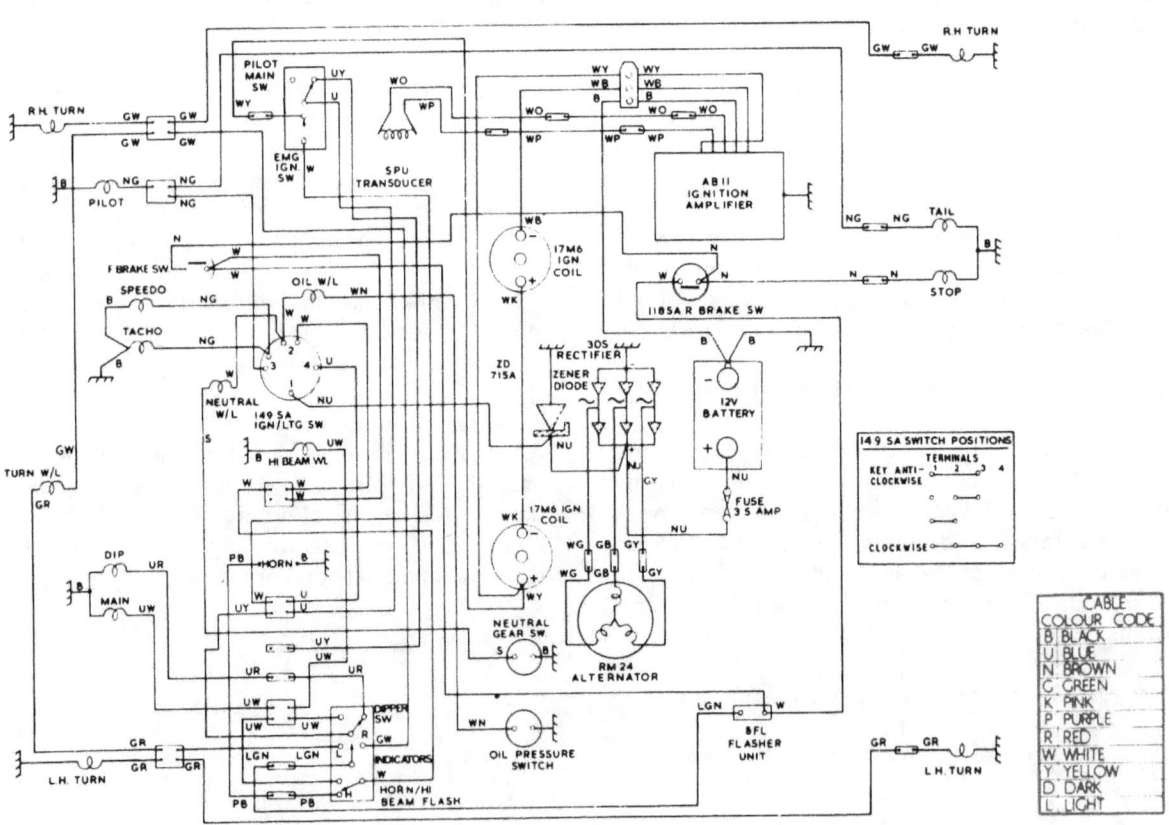

Lights on with ignition (California - Canada)

SECTION J

WORKSHOP SERVICE TOOLS

INTRODUCTION

This section of the Workshop Manual illustrates pictorially the workshop service tools that are available for carrying out the major dismantling and re-assembly operations on the UNIT CONSTRUCTION 750 c.c. Triumph Motorcycle.

The section is divided into sub-sections relating to the main section headings in this manual, illustrating those tools mentioned and used in the appropriate section text.

	Section
ENGINE...	J1
TRANSMISSION	J2
GEARBOX	J3
WHEELS	J4
FRONT FORKS	J5

SECTION J1
ENGINE

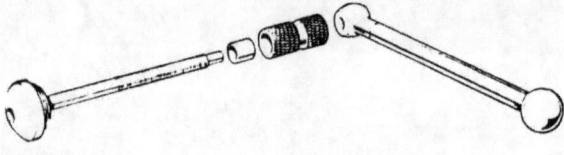

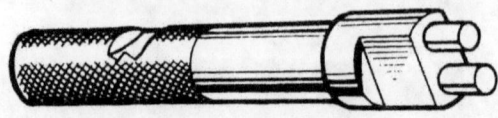

61-6008. Tappet guide block punch

26/8

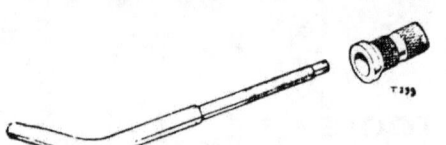

61-6063. Valve guide removal and replacement tool

61-7010. Sleeve nut adaptor tool—cylinder head

61-7019. Oil seal compressor for replacing the rocker spindle

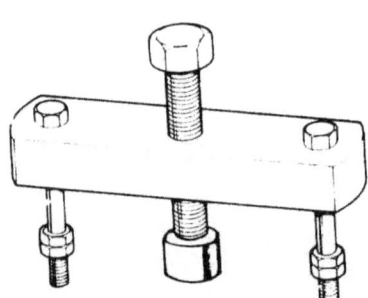

61-6132. Camwheel extractor.

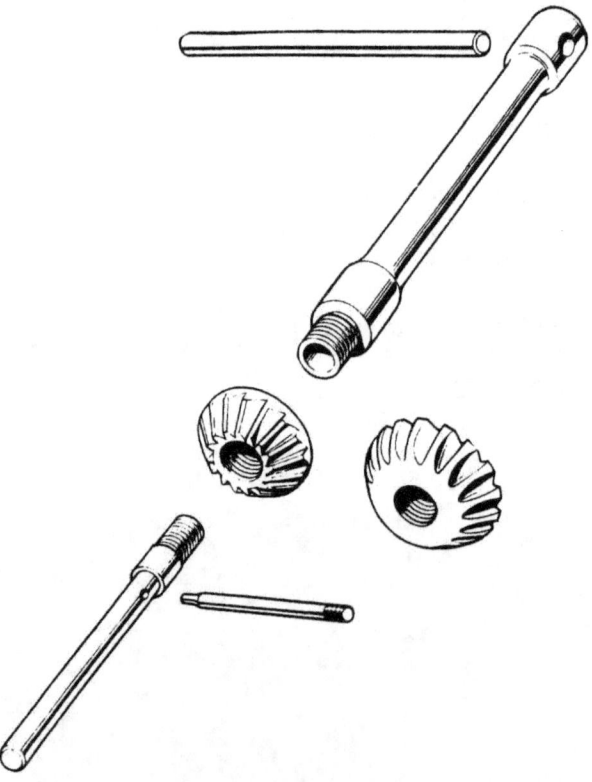

61-7025 Valve seat cutter (inlet)
61-7026 Valve seat cutter (exhaust)
61-7027 Blending cutter (inlet)
61-7028 Blending cutter (exhaust)
61-7029 Arbor, pilot and tommy bars

SERVICE TOOLS   J

ENGINE (CONTINUED) J1

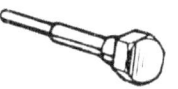

26/3

61-7023. Contact breaker cam extractor

26/4

61-7013. Pilot for contact breaker oil seal when replacing timing cover

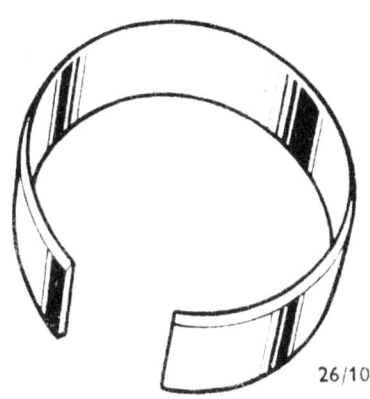

26/10

61-6135. Piston ring collar (75mm)

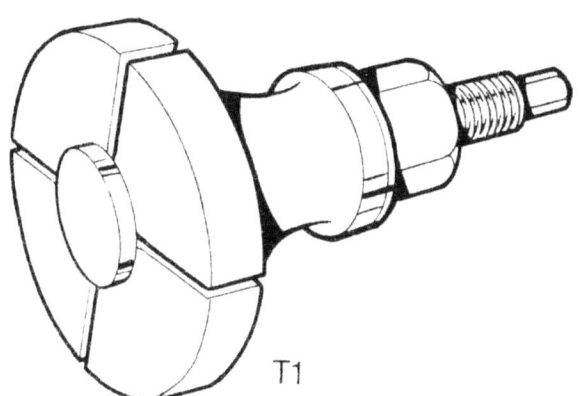

T1

61-7017. Roller bearing outer race removal tool

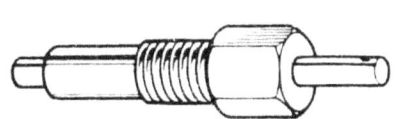

61-7022. Flywheel locating body and plunger

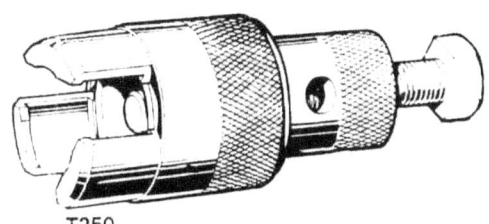

T250

61-6019. Crankshaft pinion extractor

J3

SECTION J2
TRANSMISSION

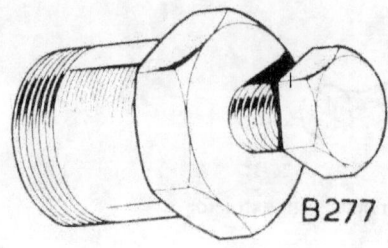

61-7014. Clutch hub extractor

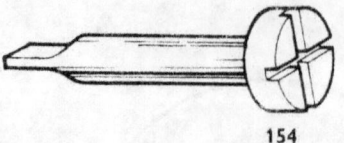

61-7012. Chain tensioner adjuster plug

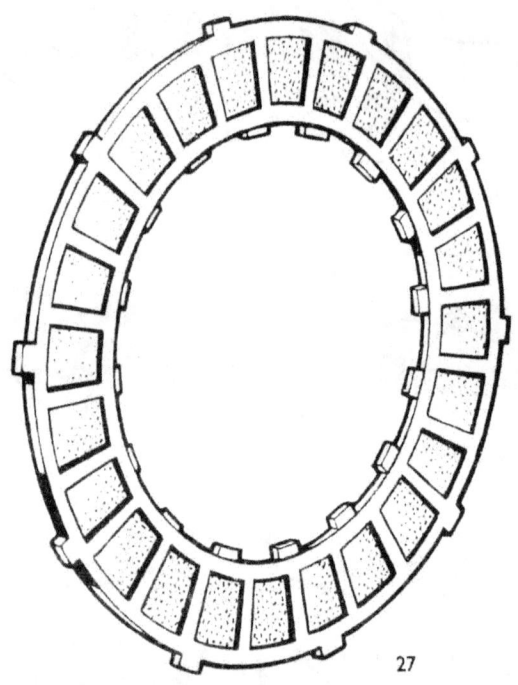

61-3768. Clutch locking plate

SECTION J3
GEARBOX

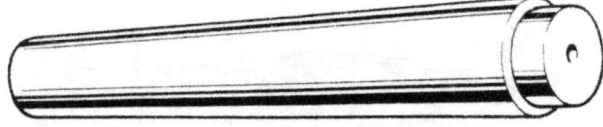

61-6026. Gearbox main bearing shouldered punch

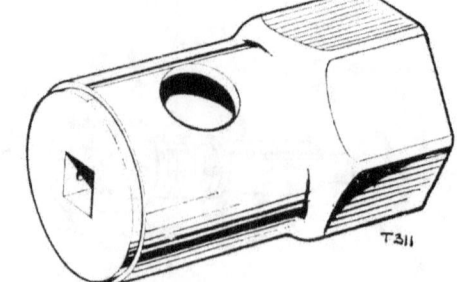

61-6125 Gearbox nut spanner

SERVICE TOOLS J

GEARBOX (CONTINUED)

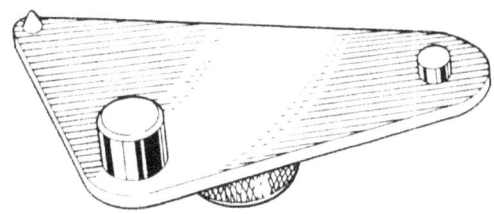

61-7011. Gear box assembly tool—quadrant locator

SECTION J4
WHEELS

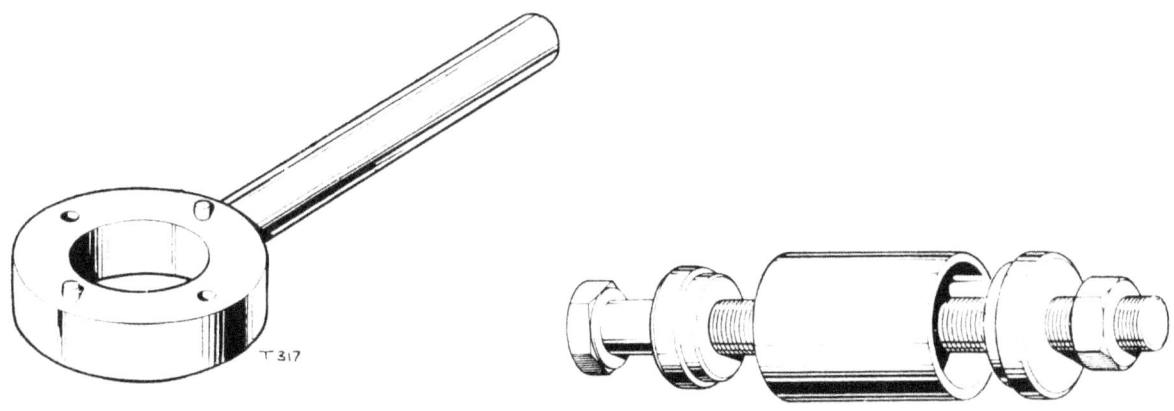

61-3694. Front wheel bearing locking ring spanner

Swinging arm bush remover and replacer No. 61-6117

SECTION J5
FRONT FORKS

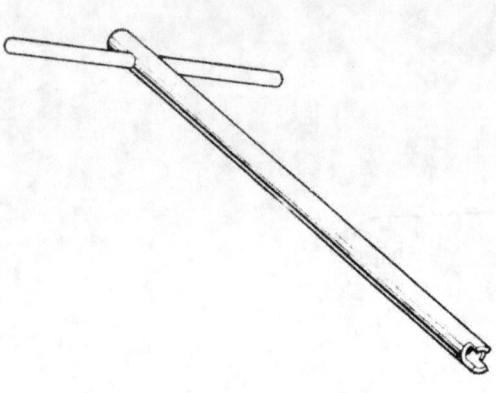

Fork damper valve removal tool No. 61-6113

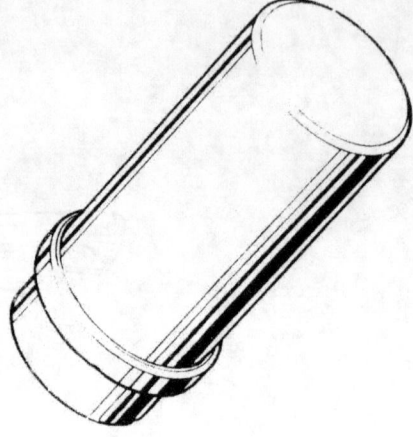

Head race bearing drift 61-6121

CONVERSION TABLES

INCHES TO MILLIMETRES—UNITS

Inches	0	10	20	30	40
0		254·0	508·0	762·0	1016·0
1	25·4	279·4	533·4	787·4	1041·4
2	50·8	304·8	558·8	812·8	1066·8
3	76·2	330·2	584·2	838·2	1092·2
4	101·6	355·6	609·6	863·6	1117·6
5	127·0	381·0	635·0	889·0	1143·0
6	152·4	406·4	660·4	914·4	1168·4
7	177·8	431·8	685·8	939·8	1193·8
8	203·2	457·2	711·2	965·2	1219·2
9	228·6	482·6	736·6	990·6	1244·6

One Inch—25·399978 millimetres
One Metre—39·370113 inches
One Mile—1·6093 kilos
One Kilo—·62138 miles

DECIMALS TO MILLIMETRES—FRACTIONS

1/1000		1/100		1/10	
inches	mm.	inches	mm.	inches	mm.
·001	·0254	·01	·254	·1	2·54
·002	·0508	·02	·508	·2	5·08
·003	·0762	·03	·726	·3	7·62
·004	·1016	·04	1·016	·4	10·16
·005	·1270	·05	1·270	·5	12·70
·006	·1524	·06	1·524	·6	15·24
·007	·1778	·07	1·778	·7	17·79
·008	·2032	·08	2·032	·8	20·32
·009	·2286	·09	2·286	·9	22·86

CONVERSION TABLES

FRACTIONS TO DECIMALS AND MILLIMETRES

Fractions			Decimals	mm.
		1/64	·015625	·3969
	1/32		·03125	·7937
		3/64	·046875	1·1906
1/16			·0625	1·5875
		5/64	·078125	1·9844
	3/32		·09375	2·3812
		7/64	·109375	2·7781
1/8			·125	3·1750
		9/64	·140625	3·5719
	5/32		·15625	3·9687
		11/64	·171875	4·3656
3/16			·1875	4·7625
		13/64	·203125	5·1594
	7/32		·21875	5·5562
		15/64	·234375	5·9531
1/4			·25	6·3500
		17/64	·265625	6·7469
	9/32		·28125	7·1437
		19/64	·296875	7·5406
5/16			·3125	7·9375
		21/64	·328125	8·3344
	11/32		·34375	8·7312
		23/64	·359375	9·1281
3/8			·375	9·5250
		25/64	·390625	9·9219
	13/32		·40625	10·3187
		27/64	·421875	10·7156
7/16			·4375	11·1125
		29/64	·453125	11·5094
	15/32		·46875	11·9062
		31/64	·484375	12·3031
1/2			·5	12·7000

Fractions			Decimals	mm.
		33/64	·515625	13·0969
	17/32		·53125	13·4937
		35/64	·546675	13·8906
9/16			·5625	14·2875
		37/64	·578125	14·6844
	19/32		·59375	15·0812
		39/64	·609375	15·4781
5/8			·625	15·8750
		41/64	·640625	16·2719
	21/32		·65685	16·6687
		43/64	·671875	17·0656
11/16			·6875	17·4625
		45/64	·703125	17·8594
	23/32		·71875	18·2562
		47/64	·734375	18·6531
3/4			·75	19·0500
		49/64	·765625	19·4469
	25/32		·78125	19·8437
		51/64	·796875	20·2406
13/16			·8125	20·6375
		53/64	·828125	21·0344
	27/32		·84375	21·4312
		55/64	·859375	21·8281
7/8			·875	22·2250
		57/64	·890625	22·6219
	29/32		·90625	23·0187
		59/64	·921875	23·4156
15/16			·9375	23·8125
		61/64	·953125	24·2094
	31/32		·96875	24·6062
		63/64	·984375	25·0031
1				25·4000

MILLIMETRES TO INCHES—UNITS

mm.	0	10	20	30	40
0		·39370	·78740	1·18110	1·57480
1	·03937	·43307	·82677	1·22047	1·61417
2	·07874	·47244	·86614	1·25984	1·65354
3	·11811	·51181	·90551	1·29921	1·69291
4	·15748	·55118	·94488	1·33858	1·73228
5	·19685	·59055	·98425	1·37795	1·77165
6	·23622	·62992	1·02362	1·41732	1·81103
7	·27559	·66929	1·06299	1·45669	1·85040
8	·31496	·70866	1·10236	1·49606	1·88977
9	·35433	·74803	1·14173	1·53543	1·92914

mm.	50	60	70	80	90
0	1·96851	2·36221	2·75591	3·14961	3·54331
1	2·00788	2·40158	2·79528	3·18891	3·58268
2	2·04725	2·44095	2·83465	3·22835	3·62205
3	2·08662	2·48032	2·87402	3·26772	3·66142
4	2·12599	2·51969	2·91339	3·30709	3·70079
5	2·16536	2·55906	2·95276	3·34646	3·74016
6	2·20473	2·59843	2·99213	3·38583	3·77953
7	2·24410	2·63780	3·03150	3·42520	3·81890
8	2·28347	2·67717	3·07087	3·46457	3·85827
9	2·32284	2·71654	3·11024	3·50394	3·89764

MILLIMETRES TO INCHES—FRACTIONS

1/1000	
mm.	inches
0·001	·000039
0·002	·000079
0·003	·000118
0·004	·000157
0·005	·000197
0·006	·000236
0·007	·000276
0·008	·000315
0·009	·000354

1/100	
mm.	inches
0·01	·00039
0·02	·00079
0·03	·00118
0·04	·00157
0·05	·00197
0·06	·00236
0·07	·00276
0·08	·00315
0·09	·00354

1/10	
mm.	inches
0·1	·00394
0·2	·00787
0·3	·01181
0·4	·01575
0·5	·01969
0·6	·02362
0·7	·02756
0·8	·03150
0·9	·03543

CONVERSION TABLES

DRILL SIZES

Letter	Size	Letter	Size
A	·234	N	·302
B	·238	O	·316
C	·242	P	·323
D	·246	Q	·332
E	·250	R	·339
F	·257	S	·348
G	·261	T	·358
H	·266	U	·368
I	·272	V	·377
J	·277	W	·386
K	·281	X	·397
L	·290	Y	·404
M	·295	Z	·413

Number	Size	Number	Size	Number	Size	Number	Size
1	·2280	14	·1820	27	·1440	40	·0980
2	·2210	15	·1800	28	·1405	41	·0960
3	·2130	16	·1770	29	·1360	42	·0935
4	·2090	17	·1730	30	·1285	43	·0890
5	·2055	18	·1695	31	·1200	44	·0860
6	·2040	19	·1660	32	·1160	45	·0820
7	·2010	20	·1610	33	·1130	46	·0810
8	·1990	21	·1590	34	·1110	47	·0785
9	·1960	22	·1570	35	·1100	48	·0760
10	·1935	23	·1540	36	·1065	49	·0730
11	·1910	24	·1520	37	·1040	50	·0700
12	·1890	25	·1495	38	·1015	51	·0670
13	·1850	26	·1470	39	·0995	52	·0635

WIRE GAUGES

No. of Gauge	Imperial Standard Wire Gauge		Brown and Sharpe's American Wire Gauge	
	Inches	Millimetres	Inches	Millimetres
0000	·400	10·160	·460	11·684
000	·372	9·448	·410	10·404
00	·348	8·839	·365	9·265
0	·324	8·299	·325	8·251
1	·300	7·620	·289	7·348
2	·276	7·010	·258	6·543
3	·252	6·400	·229	5·827
4	·232	5·892	·204	5·189
5	·212	5·384	·182	4·621
6	·192	4·676	·162	4·115
7	·176	4·470	·144	3·664
8	·160	4·064	·128	3·263
9	·144	3·657	·114	2·906
10	·128	3·251	·102	2·588
11	·116	2·946	·091	2·304
12	·104	2·641	·081	2·052
13	·092	2·336	·072	1·827
14	·080	2·032	·064	1·627
15	·072	1·828	·057	1·449
16	·064	1·625	·051	1·290
17	·056	1·422	·045	1·149
18	·048	1·219	·040	1·009
19	·040	1·016	·035	·911
20	·036	·914	·032	·811
21	·032	·812	·028	·722
22	·028	·711	·025	·643
23	·024	·609	·023	·573
24	·022	·558	·020	·511
25	·020	·508	·018	·454
26	·018	·457	·016	·404
27	·0164	·416	·014	·360
28	·0148	·375	·012	·321
29	·0136	·345	·011	·285
30	·0124	·314	·010	·254

FOOT POUNDS TO KILOGRAMETRES

	0	1	2	3	4	5	6	7	8	9	
—		0.138	0.227	0.415	0.553	0.691	0.830	0.968	1.106	1.244	—
10	1.383	1.521	1.659	1.797	1.936	2.074	2.212	2.350	2.489	2.627	10
20	2.765	2.903	3.042	3.180	3.318	3.456	3.595	3.733	3.871	4.009	20
30	4.148	4.286	4.424	4.562	4.701	4.839	4.977	5.116	5.254	5.392	30
40	5.530	5.668	5.807	5.945	6.083	6.221	6.360	6.498	6.636	6.774	40
50	6.913	7.051	7.189	7.328	7.466	7.604	7.742	7.881	8.019	8.157	50
60	8.295	8.434	3.572	8.710	8.848	8.987	9.125	9.263	9.401	9.540	60
70	9.678	9.816	9.954	10.093	10.231	10.369	10.507	10.646	10.784	10.922	70
80	11.060	11.199	11.337	11.475	11.613	11.752	11.890	12.028	12.166	12.305	80
90	12.443	12.581	12.719	12.858	12.996	13.134	13.272	13.411	13.549	13.687	90

MILES TO KILOMETRES

	0	1	2	3	4	5	6	7	8	9	
—		1.609	3.219	4.828	6.437	8.047	9.656	11.265	12.875	14.484	—
10	16.093	17.703	19.312	20.922	22.531	24.140	25.750	27.359	28.968	30.578	10
20	32.187	33.796	35.406	37.015	38.624	40.234	41.843	43.452	45.062	46.671	20
30	48.280	49.890	51.499	53.108	54.718	56.327	57.936	59.546	61.155	62.765	30
40	64.374	65.983	67.593	69.202	70.811	72.421	74.030	75.639	77.249	78.858	40
50	80.467	82.077	83.686	85.295	86.905	88.514	90.123	91.733	93.342	94.951	50
60	96.561	98.170	99.780	101.389	102.998	104.608	106.217	107.826	109.436	111.045	60
70	112.654	114.264	115.873	117.482	119.092	120.701	122.310	123.920	125.529	127.138	70
80	128.748	130.357	131.967	133.576	135.185	136.795	138.404	140.013	141.623	143.232	80
90	144.841	146.451	148.060	149.669	151.279	152.888	154.497	156.107	157.716	159.325	90

POUNDS TO KILOGRAMS

	0	1	2	3	4	5	6	7	8	9	
—		0.454	0.907	1.361	1.814	2.268	2.722	3.175	3.629	4.082	—
10	4.536	4.990	5.443	5.987	6.350	6.804	7.257	7.711	8.165	8.618	10
20	9.072	9.525	9.079	10.433	10.886	11.340	11.793	12.247	12.701	13.154	20
30	13.608	14.061	14.515	14.968	15.422	15.876	16.329	16.783	17.237	17.690	30
40	18.144	18.597	19.051	19.504	19.953	20.412	20.865	21.319	21.772	22.226	40
50	22.680	23.133	23.587	24.040	24.494	24.948	25.401	25.855	26.308	26.762	50
60	27.216	27.669	28.123	28.576	29.030	29.484	29.937	30.391	30.844	31.298	60
70	31.751	32.205	32.659	33.112	33.566	34.019	34.473	34.927	35.380	35.834	70
80	36.287	36.741	37.195	37.648	38.102	38.855	39.009	39.463	39.916	40.370	80
90	40.823	41.277	41.731	42.184	42.638	43.091	43.545	43.998	44.452	44.906	90

MILES PER GALLON (IMPERIAL) TO LITRES PER 100 KILOMETRES

10	28.25	15	18.83	20	14.12	25	11.30	30	9.42	35	8.07	40	7.06	50	5.65	60	4.71	70	4.04
10½	26.90	15½	18.22	20½	13.78	25½	11.08	30½	9.26	35½	7.96	41	6.89	51	5.54	61	4.63	71	3.98
11	25.68	16	17.66	21	13.45	26	10.87	31	9.11	36	7.85	42	6.73	52	5.43	62	4.55	72	3.92
11½	24.56	16½	17.12	21½	13.14	26½	10.66	31½	8.97	36½	7.74	43	6.57	53	5.33	63	4.48	73	3.87
12	23.54	17	16.61	22	12.84	27	10.46	32	8.83	37	7.63	44	6.42	54	5.23	64	4.41	74	3.82
12½	22.60	17½	16.14	22½	12.55	27½	10.27	32½	8.69	37½	7.53	45	6.28	55	5.13	65	4.35	75	3.77
13	21.73	18	15.69	23	12.28	28	10.09	33	8.56	38	7.43	46	6.14	56	5.04	66	4.28	76	3.72
13½	20.92	18½	15.27	23½	12.02	28½	9.91	33½	8.43	38½	7.34	47	6.01	57	4.96	67	4.22	77	3.67
14	20.18	19	14.87	24	11.77	29	9.74	34	8.31	39	7.24	48	5.89	58	4.87	68	4.16	78	3.62
14½	19.48	19½	14.49	24½	11.53	29½	9.58	34½	8.19	39½	7.15	49	5.77	59	4.79	69	4.10	79	3.57

CONVERSION TABLES

PINTS TO LITRES

	0	1	2	3	4	5	6	7	8
—	—	·568	1·136	1·705	2·273	2·841	3·841	3·978	4·546
¼	·142	·710	1·279	1·846	2·415	2·983	3·552	4·120	4·688
½	·284	·852	1·420	1·989	2·557	3·125	3·125	4·262	4·830
¾	·426	·994	1·563	2·131	2·699	3·267	3·836	4·404	4·972

GALLONS (IMPERIAL) TO LITRES

	0	1	2	3	4	5	6	7	8	9	
—		4·546	9·092	13·638	18·184	22·730	27·276	31·822	36·368	40·914	—
10	45·460	50·005	54·551	59·097	63·643	63·189	72·735	77·281	81·827	86·373	10
20	90·919	95·465	100·011	104·557	109·103	113·649	118·195	122·741	127·287	131·833	20
30	136·379	140·924	145·470	150·016	154·562	159·108	163·645	168·200	172·746	177·292	30
40	181·838	186·384	190·930	195·476	200·022	204·568	209·114	213·660	218·206	222·752	40
50	227·298	231·843	236·389	240·935	245·481	250·027	254·473	259·119	263·605	268·211	50
60	272·757	277·303	281·849	286·395	290·941	295·487	300·033	304·579	309·125	313·671	60
70	318·217	322·762	327·308	331·854	336·400	340·946	245·492	350·038	354·584	359·130	70
80	363·676	368·222	372·768	377·314	381·860	386·406	390·952	395·498	400·044	404·590	80
90	409·136	413·681	418·227	422·773	427·319	431·865	436·411	440·957	445·503	450·049	90

POUNDS PER SQUARE INCH TO KILOGRAMS PER SQUARE CENTIMETRE

	0	1	2	3	4	5	6	7	8	9	
—		0·070	0·141	0·211	0·281	0·352	0·422	0·492	0·562	0·633	—
10	0·703	0·773	0·844	0·914	0·984	1·055	1·125	1·195	1·266	1·336	10
20	1·406	1·476	1·547	1·617	1·687	1·758	1·828	1·898	1·969	2·039	20
30	2·109	2·179	2·250	2·320	2·390	2·461	2·531	2·601	2·672	2·742	30
40	2·812	2·883	2·953	3·023	3·093	3·164	3·234	3·304	3·375	3·445	40
50	3·515	3·586	3·656	3·726	3·797	3·867	3·937	4·007	4·078	4·148	50
60	4·218	4·289	4·359	4·429	4·500	4·570	4·640	4·711	4·781	4·851	60
70	4·921	4·992	5·062	5·132	5·203	5·273	5·343	5·414	5·484	5·554	70
80	5·624	5·695	5·765	5·835	5·906	5·976	6·046	6·117	6·187	6·257	80
90	6·328	6·398	6·468	6·538	6·609	6·679	6·749	6·820	6·890	6·960	90

U.N.E.F. SCREW THREADS

Dia.	No. of thds.	Core dia.	Tap drill	Dia.	No. of thds.	Core dia.	Tap drill
1/4 in.	32	·2162 in.	5·60 mm.	1 in.	20	·9459 in.	61/64 in.
5/16 in.	32	·2787 in.	7·20 mm.	1-1/16 in.	18	1·0024 in.	1·010 in.
3/8 in.	32	·3412 in.	11/32 ins	1-1/8 in.	18	1·0649 in.	1·072 ins.
7/16 in.	28	·3988 in.	10·20 mm.	1-3/16 in.	18	1·1274 in.	1·135 in.
1/2 in.	28	·4613 in.	11·80 mm.	1-1/4 in.	18	1·1899 in.	1·196 in.
9/16 in.	24	·5174 in.	13·30 mm.	1-5/16 in.	18	1·2524 in.	32·00 mm.
5/8 in.	24	·5799 in.	14·75 mm.	1-3/8 in.	18	1·3149 in.	33·50 mm.
11/16 in.	24	·6424 in.	·6480 in.	1-7/16 in.	18	1·3774 in.	1·385 ins.
3/4 in.	20	·6959 in.	45/64 in.	1-1/2 in.	18	1·4399 in.	1·447 in.
13/16 in.	20	·7584 in.	49/64 in.	1-9/16 in.	18	1·4948 in.	1-1/2 in.
7/8 in.	20	·8209 in.	53/64 in.	1-5/8 in.	18	1·5649 in.	1·572 in.
15/16 in.	20	·8834 in.	57/64 in.	1-11/16 in.	18	1·6274 in.	41·50 mm.

B.A. SCREW THREADS

No.	Dia. of bolt	Thds. per inch	Dia. tap drill	Core dia.
0	·2362	25·4	·1960	·1890
1	·2087	28·2	·1770	·1661
2	·1850	31·4	·1520	·1468
3	·1614	34·8	·1360	·1269
4	·1417	38·5	·1160	·1106
5	·1260	43·0	·1040	·0981
6	·1102	47·9	·0935	·0852
7	·0984	52·9	·0810	·0738
8	·0866	59·1	·0730	·0663
9	·0748	65·1	·0635	·0564
10	·0669	72·6	·0550	·0504
11	·0591	81·9	·0465	·0445
12	·0511	90·9	·0400	·0378
13	·0472	102·0	·0360	·0352
14	·0394	109·9	·0292	·0280
15	·0354	120·5	·0260	·0250
16	·0311	133·3	·0225	·0220

CONVERSION TABLES

B.S.W. SCREW THREADS

Dia. of bolt (inch)	Threads per inch	Dia. tap drill (inch)	Core dia.
1/4	20	·1968	·1860
5/16	18	1/4	·2412
3/8	16	5/16	·2950
7/16	14	23/64	·3460
1/2	12	13/32	·3933
9/16	12	15/32	·4558
5/8	11	17/32	·5086
11/16	11	37/64	·5711
3/4	10	41/64	·6219
13/16	10	45/64	·6844
7/8	9	3/4	·7327
15/16	9	13/16	·7952
1	8	55/64	·8399

B.S.F. SCREW THREADS

Dia. of bolt (inch)	Threads per inch	Dia. tap drill (inch)	Core dia.
7/32	28	·1770	·1731
1/4	26	·2055	·2007
9/32	26	·238	·2320
5/16	22	·261	·2543
3/8	20	·316	·3110
7/16	13	3/8	·3664
1/2	16	27/64	·4200
9/16	16	·492	·4825
5/8	14	35/64	·5335
11/16	14	39/64	·5960
3/4	12	21/32	·6433
13/16	12	23/32	·7058
7/8	11	25/32	·7586
1	10	57/64	·8719
1-1/8	9	1	·9827
1-1/4	9	1-1/8	1·1077
1-3/8	8	1-15/64	1·2149
1-1/2	8	1·358	1·3399
1-5/8	8	1-31/64	1·4649

U.N.C. SCREW THREADS

Dia.	No. of thds.	Core dia.	Tap drill
1/4 in.	20	·1959 in.	5·20 mm.
5/16 in.	18	·2524 in.	6·60 mm.
3/8 in.	16	·3073 in.	8·00 mm.
7/16 in.	14	·3602 in.	9·40 mm.
1/2 in.	13	·4167 in.	10·80 mm.
9/16 in.	12	·4723 in.	12·20 mm.
5/8 in.	11	·5266 in.	13·50 mm.
3/4 in.	10	·6417 in.	16·50 mm.
7/8 in.	9	·7547 in.	49/64 in.
1 in.	8	·8647 in.	22·25 mm.
1-1/8 in.	7	·9704 in.	63/64 in.
1-1/4 in.	7	1·0954 in.	1-7/64 in.
1-3/8 in.	6	1·1946 in.	1-13/64 in.
1-1/2 in.	6	1·3196 in.	1-21/64 in.
1-3/4 in.	5	1·5335 in.	1-35/64 in.
2 in.	4-1/2	1·7594 in.	1-25/32 in.

U.N.F. SCREW THREADS

Dia.	No. of thds.	Core dia.	Tap drill
1/4 in.	28	·2113 in.	5·50 mm.
5/16 in.	24	·2674 in.	6·90 mm.
3/8 in.	24	·3299 in.	8·50 mm.
7/16 in.	20	·3834 in.	9·90 mm.
1/2 in.	20	·4459 in.	11·50 mm.
9/16 in.	18	·5024 in.	12·90 mm.
5/8 in.	18	·5649 in.	14·50 mm.
3/4 in.	16	·6823 in.	11/16 in.
7/8 in.	14	·7977 in.	0·804 in.
1 in.	12	·9098 in.	23·25 mm.
1-1/8 in.	12	1·0348 in.	26·50 mm.
1-1/4 in.	12	1·1598 in.	29·50 mm.
1-3/8 in.	12	1·2848 in.	1·290 in.
1-1/2 in.	12	1·4098 in.	36·00 mm.

VELOCEPRESS MANUALS – MOTORCYCLE BY MAKE

AJS 1932-1948 SINGLES & TWINS 250cc THRU 1000cc (BOOK OF)
AJS 1945-1960 SINGLES 350cc & 500cc MODELS 16 & 18 (BOOK OF)
AJS 1955-1965 SINGLES 350cc & 500cc (BOOK OF)
AJS 1957-1966 FACTORY WSM - ALL SINGLES & TWINS
ARIEL UP TO 1932 (BOOK OF)
ARIEL 1932-1939 PREWAR MODELS (BOOK OF)
ARIEL 1933-1951 (WORKSHOP MANUAL)
ARIEL 1939-1960 4 STROKE SINGLES (BOOK OF)
ARIEL 1958-1964 LEADER & ARROW FACTORY WSM & PARTS LIST
ARIEL 1958-1964 LEADER & ARROW (BOOK OF)
BMW R26 R27 (1956-1967) FACTORY WORKSHOP MANUAL
BMW R50 R50S R60 R69S (1955-1969) FACTORY WORKSHOP MANUAL
BRIDGESTONE 90 SERIES FACTORY WSM & PARTS CATALOGUE
BRIDGESTONE 175 SERIES FACTORY WSM & PARTS CATALOGUE
BRIDGESTONE 350 SERIES FACTORY WSM & PARTS CATALOGUES
BSA SERVICE SHEETS MASTER CATALOGUE ALL MODELS 1945-1967
BSA BANTAM D1 TO D7 1948-1966 FACTORY SERVICE SHEETS MANUAL
BSA BANTAM ALL MODELS FROM 1948 ONWARDS (BOOK OF)
BSA BANTAM D14 FACTORY SERVICE MANUAL
BSA DANDY FACTORY WORKSHOP MANUAL (COMPILATION)
BSA SINGLES & V-TWINS UP TO 1926 inc. 1927 SUPPLEMENT (BOOK OF)
BSA SINGLES & V-TWINS UP TO 1930 (BOOK OF)
BSA SINGLES & V-TWINS UP TO 1935 (BOOK OF)
BSA SINGLES & V-TWINS 1936-1939 (BOOK OF)
BSA C10, C11 & C12 1945-1958 FACTORY SERVICE SHEETS MANUAL
BSA OHV & SV SINGLES 250-600cc 1945-1959 (BOOK OF)
BSA C15 & B40 1958-1967 FACTORY SERVICE SHEETS MANUAL
BSA OHV & SV SINGLES 250cc (ONLY) 1954-1970 (BOOK OF)
BSA B31, B32, B33 & B34 1945-60 FACTORY SERVICE SHEETS MANUAL
BSA OHV SINGLES 350 & 500cc 1955-1967 (BOOK OF)
BSA M20, M21 & M33 1945-1963 FACTORY SERVICE SHEETS MANUAL
BSA TWINS A7 & A10 1948-1962 FACTORY SERVICE SHEETS MANUAL
BSA TWINS A7 & A10 1948-1962 (BOOK OF)
BSA TWINS A50 & A65 1962-1965 FACTORY WORKSHOP MANUAL
BSA TWINS A50 & A65 1962-1969 (SECOND BOOK OF)
DOUGLAS 1929-1939 PREWAR ALL MODELS (BOOK OF)
DOUGLAS 1948-1957 POSTWAR ALL MODELS FACTORY SHOP MANUAL
DUCATI 160cc, 250cc & 350cc OHC MODELS FACTORY SHOP MANUAL
HONDA 50cc ALL MODELS UP TO 1970 INC MONKEY & TRAIL (BOOK OF)
HONDA 90cc ALL MODELS UP TO 1966 (BOOK OF)
HONDA TWINS & SINGLES 50cc THRU 305cc 1960-1966 (BOOK OF)
HONDA TWINS ALL MODELS 125cc THRU 450cc UP TO 1968 (BOOK OF)
HONDA C100 50cc SUPER CUB O.H.C. 1959-1962 FACTORY WSM
HONDA C110 50cc SPORT CUB O.H.C. 1960-1962 FACTORY WSM
HONDA 50-65-70-90cc O.H.C. SINGLES 1959-1983 FACTORY WSM
HONDA 100-125cc SINGLES CB/CD/CL/SL/TL 1970-1984 FACTORY WSM
HONDA 125-150cc TWINS C/CS/CB/CA 1959-1966 FACTORY WSM
HONDA 125-160-175-200cc TWINS 1965-1978 WORKSHOP MANUAL
HONDA 250-305cc TWINS C/CS/CB 1961-1968 FACTORY WSM
HOHDA 250-350cc TWINS CB/CL/SL 1968-1973 FACTORY WSM
HONDA 250-360cc TWINS CB/CL/CJ 1974-1977 FACTORY WSM
HONDA 350F & 400F 4-CYLINDER 1972-1977 FACTORY WSM
HONDA 450cc TWINS CB/CL 1965-1974 K0 TO K7 WORKSHOP MANUAL
HONDA 500cc & 550cc 4-CYL 1971-1978 FACTORY WORKSHOP MANUAL
HONDA 750cc SHOC 4-CYL 1969-1978 K0~K8 WORKSHOP MANUAL
INDIAN PONYBIKE, BOY RACER & PAPOOSE ILL PARTS LIST & SALES LIT
J.A.P. ENGINES 1927-1952 & MOTORCYCLES 1934-1952 (BOOK OF)
MATCHLESS 1931-1939 ALL MODELS 250cc THRU 990cc (BOOK OF)
MATCHLESS 1945-1956 350 & 500cc SINGLES (BOOK OF)
MATCHLESS 1955-1966 350 & 500cc SINGLES (BOOK OF)
MATCHLESS 1957-1966 FACTORY WSM - ALL SINGLES & TWINS
NEW IMPERIAL ALL SV & OHV FROM 1935 ONWARDS (BOOK OF)
NORTON 1932-1939 PREWAR MODELS (BOOK OF)
NORTON 1932-1947 (BOOK OF)
NORTON 1938-1956 (BOOK OF)
NORTON 1945-1963 MODELS 16H, Big4, ES2, 19 & 50 WSM'S & PARTS
NORTON 1955-1963 MODELS 19, 50 & ES2 (BOOK OF)
NORTON 1948-1970 DOMINATOR TWINS FACTORY WSM'S & PARTS
NORTON 1955-1965 DOMINATOR TWINS (BOOK OF)
NORTON 1960-1970 TWIN CYLINDER FACTORY WORKSHOP MANUAL
NORTON 1970-1975 COMMANDO 850 & 750cc FACTORY WSM
NORTON 1975-1978 MK 3 COMMANDO 850 cc FACTORY WSM
PANTHER 1932-1958 LIGHTWEIGHT MODELS 250 & 350cc (BOOK OF)
PANTHER 1938-1966 HEAVYWEIGHT MODELS 600 & 650cc (BOOK OF)
RALEIGH MOTORCYCLES 1919-1933 (BOOK OF)
ROYAL ENFIELD 1934-1946 SINGLES & V TWINS (BOOK OF)
ROYAL ENFIELD 1937-1953 SINGLES & V TWINS (BOOK OF)
ROYAL ENFIELD 1946-1962 SINGLES (BOOK OF)
ROYAL ENFIELD 1948-1963 500cc TWINS FACTORY WORKSHOP MANUAL
ROYAL ENFIELD 1952-1963 700cc TWINS FACTORY WORKSHOP MANUAL
ROYAL ENFIELD 1956-1966 250cc CRUSADER & 350cc NEW BULLET WSM
ROYAL ENFIELD 1958-1966 250cc & 350cc SINGLES (SECOND BOOK OF)
ROYAL ENFIELD 1962-1970 INTERCEPTOR WSM'S & PARTS (Compilation)
RUDGE 1933-1939 (BOOK OF)
SACHS 1968-1975 100cc & 125cc ENGINES WSM & M/CYCLE PARTS LIST
SUNBEAM 1928-1939 (BOOK OF)
SUNBEAM 1946-1957 S7 & S8 (BOOK OF)
SUZUKI 50cc & 80cc UP TO 1966 (BOOK OF)
SUZUKI T10 1963-1967 FACTORY WORKSHOP MANUAL
SUZUKI T20 & T200 1965-1969 FACTORY WORKSHOP MANUAL
SUZUKI TWINS 1962 ONWARDS 125-500cc WORKSHOP MANUAL
TRIUMPH 1935-1949 SINGLES & TWINS (BOOK OF)
TRIUMPH 1937-1961 SINGLES SV & OHV 250cc-600cc + TERRIER & CUB
TRIUMPH 1945-1955 PRE-UNIT 350cc, 500cc & 650cc TWINS WSM No.11
TRIUMPH 1945-1959 TWINS (BOOK OF)
TRIUMPH 1956-1969 TWINS (BOOK OF)
TRIUMPH 1956-1962 PRE-UNIT 500cc & 650cc TWINS WSM No.17
TRIUMPH 1957-1963 UNIT CONSTRUCTION 350-500cc WSM No.4
TRIUMPH 1963-1974 UNIT CONSTRUCTION 350-500cc FACTORY WSM
TRIUMPH 1963-1970 UNIT CONSTRUCTION 650cc FACTORY WSM
TRIUMPH 1968-1974 TRIDENT T150 & T150V FACTORY WSM
TRIUMPH 1971-1973 650cc OIL-IN-FRAME FACTORY WSM
TRIUMPH 1973-1978 750cc BONNEVILLE & TIGER FACTORY WSM
TRIUMPH 1979-1983 750cc T140, TR7 & TR65 FACTORY WSM
VELOCETTE 1925-1970 ALL SINGLES & TWINS (BOOK OF)
VELOCETTE 1933-1952 MOV-MAC-MSS RIGID FRAME FACTORY WSM
VELOCETTE 1946-1971 MSS-VENOM-THRUXTON-VIPER FACTORY WSM
VILLIERS ENGINE UP TO 1959 INC. 3 WHEELERS (BOOK OF)
VILLIERS ENGINE UP TO 1969 (BOOK OF)
VINCENT 1935-1955 (WORKSHOP MANUAL)
YAMAHA 1961-1967 YA5 & YA6 (WORKSHOP MANUAL & ILL PARTS LIST)
YAMAHA 1971-1972 JT1 & JT2 (WORKSHOP MANUAL & ILL PARTS LIST)

VELOCEPRESS TECHNICAL BOOKS – MOTORCYCLE

1930'S BRITISH MOTORCYCLE CARBS & ELEC COMPONENTS (BOOK OF)
1930'S BRITISH MOTORCYCLE ENGINES (OVERHAUL & MAINTENANCE)
1930'S BRITISH MOTORCYCLE GEARBOXES & CLUTCHES (BOOK OF)
CATALOG OF BRITISH MOTORCYCLES (1951 MODELS)
LUCAS ELECTRONICS BRITISH M/CYCLES REPAIR & PARTS (1950-1977)
MOTORCYCLE ENGINEERING (P.E. Irving)
MOTORCYCLE ROAD TESTS 1949-1953 (Motor Cycle Magazine UK)
SPEED AND HOW TO OBTAIN IT (Motor Cycle Magazine UK)
TUNING FOR SPEED (P.E. Irving)
WIPAC (COMBO) MANUAL NUMBER 3 + M/CYCLE & SCOOTER MANUAL

VELOCEPRESS MANUALS – SCOOTERS BY MAKE

BSA SUNBEAM SCOOTER WORKSHOP MANUAL 1959-1965
BSA SUNBEAM SCOOTER 1959-1965 (BOOK OF)
LAMBRETTA 1947-1957 ALL 125 & 150cc MODELS (BOOK OF)
LAMBRETTA 1957-1970 LI & TV MODELS (SECOND BOOK OF)
NSU PRIMA 1956-1964 ALL MODELS (BOOK OF)
TRIUMPH TIGRESS SCOOTER WORKSHOP MANUAL 1959-1965
TRIUMPH TIGRESS SCOOTER (BOOK OF)
VESPA 1951-1961 (BOOK OF)
VESPA 1955-1963 125 & 150cc & GS MODELS (SECOND BOOK OF)
VESPA 1955-1968 GS & SS (BOOK OF)
VESPA 1963-1972 90, 125 & 150cc (THIRD BOOK OF)

VELOCEPRESS MANUALS – MOPEDS & MOTORIZED BICYCLES

CYCLEMOTOR (BOOK OF)
NSU QUICKLY 1953-1963 ALL MODELS (BOOK OF)
PUCH MAXI N & S MAINTENANCE & REPAIR (3 MANUAL COMPILATION)
RALEIGH MOPEDS 1960-1969 (BOOK OF)

VELOCEPRESS MANUALS - THREE WHEELER'S

BOND MINICAR THREE WHEELER 1948-1967 (BOOK OF)
BMW ISETTA FACTORY WORKSHOP MANUAL
BSA THREE WHEELER (BOOK OF)
RELIANT REGAL THREE WHEELER 1952-1973 (BOOK OF)
VINTAGE MORGAN THREE WHEELER (BOOK OF)

VELOCEPRESS MANUALS – AUTOMOBILE BY MAKE

ALFA ROMEO GIULIA WORKSHOP MANUAL 1300 TO 2000cc 1962-1975
ALFA ROMEO GIULIA TECH MANUAL CARBURETED CARS FROM 1962
ALFA ROMEO GIULIA TECH MANUAL FUEL INJECTED CARS FROM 1969
ALFA ROMEO GIULIETTA & GIULIA 750 & 101 SERIES 1955-1965 WSM
AUSTIN-HEALEY SPRITE & MG MIDGET WORKSHOP MANUAL 1958-1971
BMW 600 LIMOUSINE FACTORY WORKSHOP MANUAL
BMW 600 LIMOUSINE OWNERS HAND BOOK & SERVICE MANUAL
BMW 2000 & 2002 1966-1976 WORKSHOP MANUAL
CORVAIR 1960-1969 WORKSHOP MANUAL
CORVETTE V8 1955-1962 WORKSHOP MANUAL
FERRARI HANDBOOK ROAD & RACE CARS (SERVICE/SPECS) 1948-1958
FERRARI 250/GT SERVICE & MAINTENANCE MANUAL 1956-1965
FIAT 500 FACTORY WORKSHOP MANUAL 1957-1973
FIAT 600, 600D & MULTIPLA FACTORY WORKSHOP MANUAL 1955-1969
JAGUAR E-TYPE 3.8 & 4.2 SERIES 1 & 2 WORKSHOP MANUAL
JAGUAR MK 7, 8, 9 & XK120, 140, 150 WORKSHOP MANUAL 1948-1961
METROPOLITAN FACTORY WORKSHOP MANUAL
MGA & MGB OWNERS HANDBOOK & WORKSHOP MANUAL
MG MIDGET TC, TD, TF & TF1500 WORKSHOP MANUAL
PORSCHE 356 1948-1965 WORKSHOP MANUAL
PORSCHE 911 2.0, 2.2, 2.4 LITRE 1964-1973 WORKSHOP MANUAL
PORSCHE 911 2.7, 3.0, 3.2 LITRE 1973-1989 WORKSHOP MANUAL
PORSCHE 912 WORKSHOP MANUAL
PORSCHE 914/4 & 914/6 1.7, 1.8, 2.0 LITRE 1970-1976 WSM
TRIUMPH TR2, TR3, TR4 1953-1965 WORKSHOP MANUAL
VOLKSWAGEN TRANSPORTER, TRUCKS & WAGONS 1950-1979 WSM
VOLVO 1944-1968 ALL MODELS WORKSHOP MANUAL

VELOCEPRESS TECHNICAL BOOKS - AUTOMOBILE

HOW TO BUILD A FIBERGLASS CAR
HOW TO BUILD A RACING CAR
HOW TO RESTORE THE MODEL 'A' FORD
MASERATI OWNER'S HANDBOOK
PERFORMANCE TUNING THE SUNBEAM TIGER
SOUPING THE VOLKSWAGEN
SOLEX CARBURETORS (EMPHASIS ON UK & EU AUTOMOBILES)
SU CARBURETORS (EMPHASIS ON UK AUTOMOBILES)
WEBER CARBURETORS (EMPHASIS ON ALFA & FIAT)

VELOCEPRESS BOOKS & GUIDES - AUTOMOBILE

COMPLETE CATALOG OF JAPANESE MOTOR VEHICLES
FERRARI 308 SERIES BUYER'S AND OWNER'S GUIDE
FERRARI BROCHURES AND SALES LITERATURE 1968-1989
FERRARI SERIAL NUMBERS PART I - ODD NUMBERS TO 21399
FERRARI SERIAL NUMBERS PART II - EVEN NUMBERS TO 1050
HENRY'S FABULOUS MODEL "A" FORD
MASERATI BROCHURES AND SALES LITERATURE

VELOCEPRESS BOOKS – RACING

CARRERA PANAMERICANA - MEXICAN ROAD RACE (BOOK OF)
DIALED IN - THE JAN OPPERMAN STORY
VEDA ORR'S NEW REVISED HOT ROD PICTORIAL

www.VelocePress.com

www.ingramcontent.com/pod-product-compliance
Lightning Source LLC
Chambersburg PA
CBHW080733300426
44114CB00019B/2576